FOREWORD

No English speaking home library is complete without a full set of Libretti of the Gilbert and Sullivan Operas.

To those who are familiar with the operas, there is endless pleasure to be derived from reading Gilbert's brilliant dialogue and lyrics in the seclusion of one's own home. The action of the operas reforms in the mind as the eyes follow the script.

To those who are not so well acquainted with the operas there is a wealth of interest and amusement to be had by simply reading the lines. Gilbert reads almost as well in the home as he appeals to the ear in the theatre. His command of the English language was wonderful. It is said that his practice was to first write a number of pages of dialogue and then condense them into a quarter of that space without losing any of the full meaning. His concise expressions, such as "let the punishment fit the crime" from the Mikado's song, have been a joy to speakers and newspaper writers.

Like the works of Shakespeare his Libretti is "full of quotations". Many Gilbert and Sullivan "fans" pride themselves upon being able to recite from memory some of his lyrics, such as the Chancellor's song in "Iolanthe", and many wagers have been won and lost by those who claim to be word perfect.

This volume, containing the complete libretti of the popular operas of the Gilbert and Sullivan Series should be a useful reference book for amateurs and a source of endless pleasure to the general public.

FREDERICK HOBBS.

TABLE OF CONTENTS

•

Authentic Libretti
of the new
GILBERT AND SULLIVAN LIBRARY

The Gondoliers;

OR,

THE KING OF BARATARIA

BY

Sir W. S. GILBERT

AND

Sir ARTHUR S. SULLIVAN

The Bass Publishers

The Gondoliers;

OR

THE KING OF BARATARIA

THE DUKE OF PLAZA-TORO
(*a Grandee of Spain*)

LUIZ (*his Attendant*)

DON ALHAMBRA DEL BOLERO (*the Grand Inquisitor*)

MARCO PALMIERI
GIUSEPPE PALMIERI
ANTONIO
FRANCESCO
GIORGIO
ANNIBALE
} (*Venetian Gondoliers*)

THE DUCHESS OF PLAZA-TORO
CASILDA (*her Daughter*)

GIANETTA
TESSA
FIAMETTA
VITTORIA
GIULIA
} (*Contadine*)

INEZ (*the King's Foster-mother*)

Chorus of Gondoliers and Contadine, Men-at-Arms
Heralds, and Pages.

ACT. I—THE PIAZZETTA, VENICE.

ACT II.—PAVILION IN THE PALACE OF BARATARIA

(*An interval of three months is supposed to elapse between
Acts I. and II.*)

DATE 1750.

The Gondoliers;

OR

THE KING OF BARATARIA

ACT I.

SCENE—THE PIAZZETTA, VENICE. *The Ducal Palace on the right.*

FIAMETTA, GIULIA, VITTORIA, *and other Contadine discovered, each tying a bouquet of roses.*

CHORUS OF CONSTADINE

List and learn, ye dainty roses,
  Roses white and roses red,
Why we bind you into posies
  Ere your morning bloom has fled.
By a law of maiden's making,
Accents of a heart that's aching,
Even though that heart be breaking,
  Should by maiden be unsaid:
Though they love with love exceeding,
They must seem to be unheeding—
Go ye then and do their pleading,
  Roses white and roses red!

Fiametta.

Two there are for whom, in duty,
  Every maid in Venice sighs—
Two so peerless in their beauty
  That they shame the summer skies.
We have hearts for them, in plenty,
  They have hearts, but all too few,
We, alas, are four and twenty!
  They, alas, are only two!
We alas!

Cho.
Alas!

Fia.
Are four and twenty,
They alas!

Cho.
Alas!

Fia.
Are only two,

Cho.
They, alas, are only two, Alas!
Now ye know, ye dainty roses,
Why we bind you into posies,
  Ere your morning bloom has fled,
  Roses white and roses red!

(During this chorus Antonio, Francesco, Giorgio, and other Gondoliers have entered unobserved by the Girls—at first two, then two more, then four, then half-a-dozen, then the remainder of the Chorus.)

SOLI.

Franc.
Good morrow, pretty maids; for whom prepare ye
These floral tributes extraordinary?

Fia.
For Marco and Giuseppe Palmieri,
The pink and flower of all the Gondolieri.

Giu.
They're coming here, as we have heard but lately.
To choose two brides from us who sit sedately.

Ant.
Do all you maidens love them?

All.
Passionately!

Ant.
These gondoliers are to be envied greatly!

Gior.
But what of us, who one and all adore you?
Have pity on our passion, we implore you!

Fia.
These gentlemen must make their choice before you;

Vit.
In the meantime we tacitly ignore you.

Giu.
When they have chosen two that leaves you plenty—
Two dozen we, and ye are four-and-twenty.

Fia. & Vit.
Till then, enjoy your *dolce far niente*.

Ant.
With pleasure, nobody *contradicente!*

SONG.—*Antonio and Chorus.*

For the merriest fellows are we, tra la,
That ply on the emerald sea, tra la;
  With loving and laughing,
  And quipping and quaffing,
We're happy as happy can be, tra la—
  As happy as happy can be!

With sorrow we've nothing to do, tra la,
And care is a thing to pooh-pooh, tra la;
  And Jealousy yellow,

3

Unfortunate fellow,
We drown in the shimmering blue, tra la—
We drown in the shimmering blue!

Fia. (*looking off*).
See, see, at last they come to make their
    choice—
Let us acclaim them with united voice.
(*Marco and Giuseppe appear in gondola
    at back.*)

Cho. (*Girls*).
Hail, hail! gallant gondolieri, ben' venuti!
Accept our love, our homage, and our duty.
(*Marco and Giuseppe jump ashore—the
    girls salute them.*)

DUET.—*Marco and Giuseppe, with
    Chorus of Girls.*

Mar. and Giu.
Buon' giorno, signorine!
Girls.
    Gondolieri carissimi!
    Siamo contadine!
Mar. & Giu. (*bowing*).
    Servitori umilissimi!
    Per chi questi fiori—
    Questi fiori bellissimi?
Girls.
    Per voi, bei signori
    O eccellentissimi!
[*The girls present their bouquets to Marco and
Giuseppe, who are overwhelmed with them,
and carry them with difficulty.*]
Mar. & Giu. (*their arms full of flowers*).
    O ciel!
Girls.
    Buon' giorno, cavalieri!
Mar. & Giu. (*deprecatingly*).
    Siamo gondolieri.
(*to Fia. & Vit.*)
    Signorina, io t'amo!
Girls (*deprecatingly*).
    Contadine siamo.
Mar. & Giu.
    Signorine!
Girls (*deprecatingly*).
    Contadine!
(*curtseying to Mar. and Giu.*)
    Cavalieri.
Mar. & Giu. (*deprecatingly*).
    Gondolieri!
    Poveri gondolieri!
Cho.
    Buon' giorno, signorine, &c.

DUET.—*Marco and Giuseppe.*

We're called *gondolieri*,
But that's a vagary,
It's quite honorary

The trade that we ply.
For gallantry noted
Since we were short-coated
To beauty devoted.
{Giuseppe } and I
{Are Marco}
When morning is breaking,
Our couches forsaking,
To greet their awaking
    With carols we come.
At summer day's nooning,
When weary lagooning,
Our mandolins tuning,
    We lazily thrum.
When vespers are ringing,
To hope ever clinging,
With songs of our singing
    A vigil we keep,
When daylight is fading,
Enwrapt in night's shading,
With soft serenading
    We sing them to sleep.
We're called *gondolieri*, &c.

RECIT.—*Marco and Giuseppe.*

Mar.
And now to choose our brides!
Giu.
    As all are young and fair,
    And amiable besides,
Both.
    We really do not care
    A preference to declare.
Mar.
    A bias to disclose
    Would be indelicate—
Giu.
    And therefore we propose
    To let impartial Fate
    Select for us a mate!
All.
    Viva!
Girls.
    A bias to disclose
    Would be indelicate—
Men.
    But how do they propose
    To let impartial Fate
    Select for them a mate?
Giu.
    These handkerchiefs upon our eyes be good
        enough to bind,
Mar.
    And take good care that both of us are ab-
        solutely blind;
Both.
    Then turn us round—and we, with all con-
        venient despatch,

4

Will undertake to marry any two of you
we catch!

All.

Viva!
They undertake to marry {us they catch!
any two of {them they catch!

(*The girls prepare to bind their eyes as
directed.*)

Fia. (*to Marco*).

Are you peeping?
Can you see me?

Mar.

Dark I'm keeping,
Dark and dreamy!

(*Marco slyly lifts bandage.*)

Vit. (*to Giuseppe*).

If you're blinded
Truly say so.

Giu.

All right-minded
Players play so! (*slyly lifts bandage.*)

Fia. (*detecting Marco*).

Conduct shady!
They are cheating!
Surly they de-
Serve a beating! (*replaces bandage.*)

Vit. (*detecting Giuseppe*).

This too much is;
Maidens mocking—
Conduct such is
Truly shocking! (*replaces bandage.*)

All.

You can spy, sir!
Shut your eye, sir!
You may use it by-and-bye, sir!
You can see, sir!
Don't tell me, sir!
That will do—now let it be, sir!

Chorus of Girls.

My papa he keeps three horses,
Black, and white, and dapple grey, sir;
Turn three times, then take your courses,
Catch whichever girl you may, sir!

Chorus of Men.

My papa, etc.

*Marco and Giuseppe turn round, as directed,
and try to catch the girls. Business of blind-
man's buff. Eventually Marco catches Gianetta, and Giuseppe catches Tessa. The two
girls try to escape, but in vain. The two
men pass their hands over the girls' faces to
discover their identity.*

Giu. (*guessing*).

I've at length achieved a capture!
This is Tessa! (*removes bandage.*) Rapture,
rapture!

Mar. (*guessing*).

To me, Gianetta, fate has granted! (*removes
bandage*)
Just the very girl I wanted!

Giu. (*politely to Mar.*)

If you'd rather change—

Tessa.

My goodness!
This indeed is simple rudeness.

Mar. (*politely to Giu.*)

I've no preference whatever—

Gia.

Listen to him! Well, I never!

(*Each man kisses each girl.*)

Gia.

Thank you, gallant *gondolieri!*
In a set and formal measure
It is scarcely necessary
To express our pleasure.
Each of us to prove a treasure,
Conjugal and monetary,
Glady will devote our leisure,
Gallant *gondolieri.*
Tra la, la, la, la, la! &c.

Tessa.

Gay and gallant *gondolieri,*
Take us both and hold us tightly,
You have luck extraordinary;
We might have been unsightly!
If we judge your conduct rightly,
'Twas a choice involuntary;
Still we thank you most politely.
Gay and gallant *gondolieri!*
Tra la, la, la, la, la! &c.

Chorus of Girls.

Thank you, gallant *gondolieri,*
In a set and formal measure,
It is scarcely necessary
To express our pleasure.
Each of us to prove a treasure,
Gladly will devote our leisure,
Gay and gallant *gondolieri!*
Tra la, la, la, la, la! &c.

All.

Fate in this has put his finger—
Let us bow to Fate's decree,
Then no longer let us linger,
To the altar hurry we!

(*They all dance off two and two—Gianetta
with Marco, Tessa with Giuseppe.*)

*Flourish. A gondola arrives at the Piazzetta
steps, from which enter the Duke of Plaza-
Toro, the Duchess, their daughter Casilda,
and their attendant Luiz, who carries a drum.
All are dressed in pompous, but old and
faded clothes.*

(Entrance of Duke, Duchess, Casilda and Luiz)

Duke.
From the sunny Spanish shore,
The Duke of Plaza-Tor'—

Duch.
And His Grace's Duchess true—

Cas.
And His Grace's daughter, too—

Luiz.
And His Grace's private drum
To Venetia's shores have come:

All.
And if ever, ever, ever
They get back to Spain,
They will never, never, never
Cross the sea again—

Duke.
Neither that Grandee from the Spanish
shore,
The noble Duke of Plaza Tor'—

Duch.
Nor his Grace's Duchess, staunch and true—

Cas.
You may add, his Grace's daughter, too—

Luiz.
Nor his Grace's own particular drum
To Venetia's shores will come.

All.
If ever, ever, ever
They get back to Spain,
They will never, never, never
Cross the sea again!

Duke.
At last we have arrived at our destination.
This is the Ducal Palace, and it is here that
the Grand Inquisitor resides. As a Castilian
hidalgo of ninety-five quarterings, I regret
that I am unable to pay my state visit on a
horse. As a Castilian hidalgo of that description, I should have preferred to ride through
the streets of Venice; but owing, I presume,
to an unusually wet season, the streets are in
such a condition that equestrian exercise is
impracticable. No matter. Where is our
suite?

Luiz *(coming forward)*.
Your Grace, I am here.

Duch.
Why do you not do yourself the honour to
kneel when you address his Grace?

Duke.
My love, it is so small a matter! *(to Luiz)*
Still, you may as well do it. *(Luiz kneels.)*

Cas.
The young man seems to entertain but an
imperfect appreciation of the respect due
from a menial to a Castilian hidalgo.

Duke.
My child, you are hard upon our suite.

Cas.
Papa, I've no patience with the presumption
of persons in his plebeian position. If he
does not appreciate that position, let him be
whipped until he does.

Duke.
Let us hope the omission was not intended as
a slight. I should be much hurt if I thought
it was. So would he. *(To Luiz.)* Where
are the halberdiers who were to have had the
honour of meeting us here, that our visit to
The Grand Inquisitor might be made in becoming state?

Luiz.
Your Grace, the halberdiers are mercenary
people who stipulated for a trifle on account.

Duke.
How tiresome! Well, let us hope the Grand
Inquisitor is a blind gentleman. And the
band who were to have had the honour of
escorting us? I see no band!

Luiz.
Your Grace, the band are sorbid persons who
required to be paid in advance.

Duch.
That's so like a band!

Duke *(annoyed)*.
Insuperable difficulties meet me at every turn!

Duch.
But surely they know his Grace?

Luiz.
Exactly—they know his Grace.

Duke.
Well, let us hope that the Grand Inquisitor is
a deaf gentleman. A cornet-à-piston would
be something. You do not happen to possess
the accomplishment of tootling like a cornet-
à-piston?

Luiz.
Alas no, your Grace! But I can imitate a
farmyard.

Duke *(doubtfully)*.
I don't see how that would help us. I don't
see how we could bring it in.

Cas.
It would not help us in the least. We are not
a parcel of graziers come to market, dolt!
(Luiz rises.)

Duke.
My love, our suite's feelings! *(To Luiz.)*
Be so good as to ring the bell and inform the
Grand Inquisitor that his Grace the Duke
of Plaza-Toro, Count Matadoro Baron Pica-
doro—

Duch.
And suite—

Duke.
And suite—have arrived at Venice, and seek—

Cas.
Desire—

Duch.
Demand!

Duke.
And demand an audience.

Luiz.
Your Grace has but to command.

Duke (much moved).
I felt sure of it—I felt sure of it! (*Exit Luiz into Ducal Palace.*) And now, my love —(*aside to Duchess*), Shall we tell her? I think so—(*aloud to Casilda.*) And now, my love, prepare for a magnificent surprise. It is my agreeable duty to reveal to you a secret which should make you the happiest young lady in Venice!

Cas.
A secret?

Duch.
A secret which, for State reasons, it has been necessary to preserve for twenty years.

Duke.
When you were a prattling babe of six months old you were married by proxy to no less a personage than the infant son and heir of His Majesty the immeasurably wealthy King of Barataria!

Cas.
Married to the infant son of the King of Barataria? Was I consulted? (*Duke shakes his head.*) Then it was a most unpardonable liberty!

Duke.
Consider his extreme youth and forgive him. Shortly after the ceremony that misguided monarch abandoned the creed of his forefathers, and became a Wesleyan Methodist of the most bigoted and persecuting type. The Grand Inquisitor determined that the innovation should not be perpetuated in Barataria, caused your smiling and unconscious husband to be stolen and conveyed to Venice. A fortnight since the Methodist Monarch and all his Wesleyan Court were killed in an insurrection, and we are here to ascertain the whereabouts of your husband, and to hail you, our daughter, as Her Majesty, the reigning Queen of Barataria! (*Kneels.*)

(*During this speech Luiz re-enters.*)

Duch.
Your Majesty! (*Kneels.*)

Duke.
It is at such moments as these that one feels how necessary it is to travel with a full band.

Cas.
I, the Queen of Barataria! But I've nothing to wear! We are practically penniless!

Duke.
That point has not escaped me. Although I am unhappily in straitened circumstances at present, my social influence is something enormous; and a company, to be called the Duke of Plaza-Toro, Limited, is in course of formation to work me. An influential directorate has been secured, and I shall myself join the Board after allotment.

Cas.
Am I to understand that the Queen of Barataria may be called upon at any time to witness her honoured sire in process of liquidation?

Duch.
The speculation is not exempt from that drawback. If your father should stop, it will, of course, be necessary to wind him up.

Cas.
But it's so undignified—it's so degrading! A Grandee of Spain turned into a public company! Such a thing was never heard of!

Duke.
My child, the Duke of Plaza-Toro does not follow fashions—he leads them. He always leads everybody. When he was in the army he led his regiment. He occasionally led them into action. He invariably led them out of it.

Song.—*Duke of Plaza-Toro.*

In enterprise of martial kind,
　When there was any fighting,
He led his regiment from behind—
　He found it less exciting.
But when away his regiment ran,
　His place was at the fore, O—
　　That celebrated,
　　Cultivated,
　　Underrated,
　　　Nobleman,
　The Duke of Plaza-Toro!

All.
In the first and foremost flight, ha, ha!
You always found that knight, ha, ha!
　　That celebrated,
　　Cultivated,
　　Underrated,
　　　Nobleman,
　The Duke of Plaza-Toro!

When, to evade Destruction's hand,
　To hide they all proceeded,
No soldier in that gallant band
　Hid half as well as he did.
He lay concealed throughout the war,

7

And so preserved his gore, O!
    That unaffected,
    Undetected,
    Well-connected
        Warrior,
The Duke of Plaza-Toro!

All.

In every doughty deed, ha, ha!
He always took the lead, ha, ha!
    That unaffected,
    Undetected,
    Well-connected
        Warrior,
The Duke of Plaza-Toro!

When told that they would all be shot
    Unless they left the service,
That hero hesitated not,
    So marvellous his nerve is.
He sent his resignation in,
    The first of all his corps, O!
    That very knowing,
    Overflowing,
    Easy-going,
        Paladin,
The Duke of Plaza-Toro!

All.

To men of grosser clay, ha, ha!
He always showed the way, ha, ha!
    That very knowing,
    Over-flowing,
    Easy-going,
        Paladin,
The Duke of Plaza-Toro!

(*Exeunt Duke and Duchess into Grand Ducal Palace. As soon as they have disappeared, Luiz and Casilda rush to each other's arms.*)

RECIT. and DUET.—*Casilda and Luiz.*

O rapture, when alone together
    Two loving hearts and those that bear them
May join in temporary tether,
    Though fate apart should rudely tear them.

Cas.

Necessity, Invention's mother,
    Compelled me to a course of feigning—
But, left alone with one another,
    I will atone for my disdaining!
        Ah, well beloved,
        Mine angry frown
        Is but a gown
        That serves to dress
        My gentleness!

Luiz.

        Ah, well beloved,
        Thy cold disdain,
        It gives no pain—
        'Tis mercy, played
        In masquerade!

Both.

        Ah, well beloved, &c.

Cas.

O Luiz, Luiz—what have you said! What have I done! What have I allowed you to do!

Luiz.

Nothing, I trust, that you will ever have reason to repent. (*Offering to embrace her.*)

Cas. (*withdrawing from him.*)

Nay, Luiz, it may not be. I have embraced you for the last time.

Luiz (*amazed*).

Casilda!

Cas.

I have just learnt, to my surprise and indignation, that I was wed in babyhood to the infant son of the King of Barataria!

Luiz.

The son of the King of Barataria? The child who was stolen in infancy by the Inquisition?

Cas.

The same. But, of course, you know his story.

Luiz.

Know his story? Why, I have often told you that my mother was the nurse to whose charge he was entrusted!

Cas.

True. I had forgotten. Well, he has been discovered, and my father has brought me here to claim his hand.

Luiz.

But you will not recognize this marriage? It took place when you were too young to understand its import.

Cas.

Nay, Luiz, respect my principles and cease to torture me with vain entreaties. Henceforth my life is another's.

Luiz.

But stay—the present and the future—*they* are another's; but the past—that at least is is ours, and none can take it from us. As we may revel in naught else, let us revel in that!

Cas.

I don't think I grasp your meaning.

Luiz.

Yet it is logical enough. You say you cease to love me?

Cas. (*demurely*).

I say I *may* not love you.

Luiz.

Ah, but you do not say you *did* not love me?

Cas.

I loved you with a frenzy that words are powerless to express—and that but ten brief minutes since!

8

Luiz.

Exactly. My own—that is, until ten minutes since, my own—my lately loved, my recently adored—tell me that until, say a quarter of an hour ago, I was all in all to thee! (*embracing her.*)

Cas.

I see your idea. It's ingenious, but don't do that. (*releasing herself.*)

Luiz.

There can be no harm in revelling in the past.

Cas.

None whatever, but an embrace cannot be taken to act retrospectively.

Luiz.

Perhaps not!

Cas.

We may recollect an embrace—I recollect many—but we must not repeat them.

Luiz.

Then let us recollect a few!

(*A moment's pause, as they recollect, then both heave a deep sigh.*)

Luiz.

Ah, Casilda, you were to me as the sun is to the earth!

Cas.

A quarter of an hour ago?

Luiz.

About that.

Cas.

And to think that, but for this miserable discovery, you would have been my own for life!

Luiz.

Through life to death—a quarter of an hour ago!

Cas.

How greedily my thirsty ears would have drunk the golden melody of those sweet words a quarter—well, it's now about twenty minutes since. (*Looking at her watch.*)

Luiz.

About that. In such a matter one cannot be too precise.

Cas.

And now our love, so full of life, is but a silent, solemn memory!

Luiz.

Must it be so, Casilda?

Cas.

Luiz, it must be so!

DUET.—*Casilda and Luiz.*

Luiz.

There was a time—
    A time for ever gone—ah, woe is me!

It was no crime
    To love but thee alone—ah, woe is me!
One heart, one life, one soul,
    One aim, one goal—
Each in the other's thrall,
    Each all in all, ah, woe is me!

Both.

Oh, bury, bury—let the grave close o'er
The days that were—that never will be more!
Oh, bury, bury love that all condemn,
And let the whirlwind mourn its requiem!

Cas.

Dead as the last year's leaves—
    As gathered flowers—ah, woe is me!
Dead as the garnered sheaves,
    That love of ours—ah, woe is me!
Born to fade and die
    When hope was high,
Dead and as far away
    As yesterday!—ah, woe is me!

Both.

Oh, bury, bury—yet the grave close o'er, &c.

(*Re-enter from the Ducal Palace the Duke and Duchess, followed by Don Alhambra Bolero, the Grand Inquisitor.*)

Duke.

My child, allow me to present to you His Distinction Don Alhambra Bolero, the Grand Inquisitor of Spain. It was His Distinction who so thoughtfully abstracted your infant husband and brought him to Venice.

Don Al.

So this is the little lady who is so unexpectedly called upon to assume the functions of Royalty! And a very nice little lady, too!

Duke.

Jimp, isn't she?

Don Al.

Distinctly jimp. Allow me. (*offers his hand. She turns away scornfully*). Naughty temper!

Duke.

You must make some allowance. Her Majesty's head is a little turned by her access of dignity.

Don Al.

I could have wished that Her Majesty's access of dignity had turned it in this direction.

Duch.

Unfortunately, if I am not mistaken, there appears to be some little doubt as to His Majesty's whereabouts.

Cas. (*aside*).

A doubt as to his whereabouts? Then we may yet be saved!

Don Al.

A doubt? Oh dear no—no doubt at all! He is here, in Venice, plying the modest but picturesque calling of a gondolier. I can give you his address—I see him every day! In the entire annals of our history there is absolutely no circumstance so entirely free from all manner of doubt of any kind whatever! Listen, and I'll tell you all about it.

Song.—*Don Alhambra (with Duke, Duchess, Casilda and Luiz).*

I stole the Prince, and brought him here,
  And left him gaily prattling
With a highly respectable gondolier,
Who promised the Royal babe to rear,
And teach him the trade of a timoneer
  With his own beloved bratling.

    Both of the babes were strong and stout,
      And, considering all things, clever.
    Of *that* there is no manner of doubt—
    No probable, possible shadow of doubt—
      No possible doubt whatever.

But owing, I'm much disposed to fear,
  To his terrible taste for tippling,
That highly respectable gondolier
Could never declare with a mind sincere
Which of the two was his offspring dear,
  And which the Royal stripling!

    Which was which he could never make
      out
    Despite his best endeavour.
    Of *that* there is no manner of doubt—
    No probable, possible shadow of doubt—
      No possible doubt whatever.

Time sped, and when at the end of a year
  I sought that infant cherished.
That highly respectable gondolier
Was lying a corpse on his humble bier—
I dropped a Grand Inquisitor's tear—
  That gondolier had perished.

    A taste for drink, combined with gout,
      Had doubled him up for ever,
    Of *that* there is no manner of doubt—
    No probable, possible shadow of doubt—
      No possible doubt whatever.

The children followed his old career—
  (This statement can't be parried)
Of a highly respectable gondolier:
Well, one of the two (who will soon be here)—
But *which* of the two it is not quite clear—
  Is the Royal Prince you married!

    Search in and out and round about
      And you'll discover never
    A tale so free from every doubt—
    All probable, possible shadow of doubt—
      All possible doubt whatever!

All.
    A tale so free from every doubt, &c.

Cas.
  Then do you mean to say that I am married to one of two gondoliers, but it is impossible to say which?

Don Al.
  Without any doubt of any kind whatever. But be reassured: the nurse to whom your husband was entrusted is the mother of the musical young man who is such a past-master of that delicately modulated instrument (*indicating the drum*). She can, no doubt, establish the King's identity beyond all question.

Luiz.
  Heavens, how did he know that?

Don Al.
  My young friend, a Grand Inquisitor is always up to date. (*To Cas.*) His mother is at present the wife of a highly respectable and old-established brigand, who carries on an extensive practice in the mountains around Cordova. Accompanied by two of my emissaries, he will set off at once for his mother's address. She will return with them, and if she finds any difficulty in making up her mind, the persuasive influence of the torture chamber will jog her memory.

  Recit.—(*Casilda and Don Alhambra.*)

Cas.
  But, bless my heart, consider my position!
    I am the wife of one, that's very clear;
  But who can tell, except by intuition,
    Which is the Prince, and which the Gondolier!

Don Al.
  Submit to fate without unseemly wrangle:
    Such complications frequently occur—
  Life is one closely complicated tangle:
    Death is the only true unraveller!

      Quintet.

Duke, Duchess, Casilda, Luiz and Grand Inquisitor.

All.
  Try we life-long, we can never
    Straighten out life's tangled skein,
  Why should we, in vain endeavour,
    Guess and guess and guess again?

Luiz.
    Life's a pudding full of plums,

Duchess.
    Care's a canker that benumbs.

All.
    Life's a pudding full of plums,
    Care's a canker that benumbs.
  Wherefore waste our elocution
  On impossible solution?

10

Life's a pleasant institution,
    Let us take it as it comes!

Set aside the dull enigma,
    We shall guess it all too soon;
Failure brings no kind of stigma—
    Dance we to another tune!

All.
        String the lyre and fill the cup,
        Lest on sorrow we should sup.
Hop and skip to fancy's fiddle,
Hands across and down the middle—
Life's perhaps the only riddle
        That we shrink from giving up!

(*Exeunt all into Ducal Palace, except Luiz, who goes off in gondola.*)

(*Enter Gondoliers and Contadine, followed by Marco, Gianetta, Giuseppe, and Tessa.*)

Cho.
    Bridegroom and bride!
        Knot that's insoluble,
        Voices all voluble
    Hail it with pride.

    Bridegroom and bride!
        We in sincerity,
        Wish you prosperity,
    Bridegroom and bride!

SONG.—*Tessa.*

Tessa.
When a merry maiden marries,
Sorrow goes and pleasure tarries;
    Every sound becomes a song,
    All is right, and nothing's wrong!
From to-day and ever after
Let our tears be tears of laughter.
    Every sigh that finds a vent
    Be a sigh of sweet content!
When you marry merry maiden,
Then the air with love is laden;
    Every flower is a rose,
        Every goose becomes a swan,
    Every kind of trouble goes
        Where the last year's snows have gone!

Cho.
    Sunlight takes the place of shade
    When you marry merry maid!

Tessa.
When a merry maiden marries
Sorrow goes and pleasure tarries;
    Every sound becomes a song—
    All is right, and nothing's wrong.
Gnawing Care and aching Sorrow
Get ye gone until to-morrow;
    Jealousies in grim array,
    Ye are things of yesterday!
When you marry merry maiden,
Then the air with joy is laden;
    All the corners of the earth

Ring with music sweetly played,
Worry is melodious mirth,
    Grief is joy in masquerade;

Cho.
    Sullen night is laughing day—
    All the year is merry May!

(*At the end of the song, Don Alhambra enters at back. The Gondoliers and Contadine shrink from him, and gradually go off, much alarmed.*)

Giu.
And now our lives are going to begin in real earnest! What's a bachelor? A mere nothing—he's a chrysalis. He can't be said to live—he exists.

Mar.
What a delightful institution marriage is! Why have we wasted all this time? Why didn't we marry ten years ago?

Tess.
Because you couldn't find anybody nice enough.

Gia.
Because you were waiting for *us.*

Mar.
I suppose that *was* the reason. We were waiting for you without knowing it. (*Don Alhambra comes forward.*)   Hallo!

Don Al.
Good morning.

Giu.
If this gentleman is an undertaker, it's a bad omen.

Don Al.
Ceremony of some sort going on.

Giu. (*aside*).
He *is* an undertaker! (*Aloud.*) No—a little unimportant family gathering. Nothing in *your* line.

Don Al.
Somebody's birthday, I suppose?

Gia.
Yes, mine!

Tess.
And mine!

Mar.
And mine!

Giu.
And mine!

Don Al.
Curious coincidence! And how old may you all be?

Tess.
It's a rude question—but about ten minutes.

Don Al.
Remarkably fine children! But surely you are jesting?

11

Tess.
In other words, we were married about ten minutes since.

Don Al.
Married! You don't mean to say you are married?

Mar.
Oh yes, we are married.

Don Al.
What, both of you?

All.
All four of us.

Don Al. (*aside*).
Bless my heart, how extremely awkward!

Gia.
You don't mind, I suppose?

Tess.
You were not thinking of either of us for yourself, I presume? Oh, Giuseppe, look at him—he was. He's heartbroken!

Don Al.
No, no, I wasn't! I wasn't!

Giu.
Now, my man (*slapping him on the back*), we don't want anything in your line to-day, and if your curiosity's satisfied,—you can go!

Don Al.
You mustn't call me your man. It's a liberty. I don't think you know who I am.

Giu.
Not we, indeed! We are jolly gondoliers, the sons of Baptisto Palmieri, who led the last revolution. Republicans, heart and soul, we hold all men to be equal. As we abhor oppression, we abhor kings: as we detest vain-glory, we detest rank: as we despise effeminacy, we despise wealth. We are Venetian gondoliers—your equals in everything except our calling, and in that at once your masters and your servants.

Don Al.
Bless my heart, how unfortunate! One o you may be Baptisto's son, for anything I know to the contrary; but the other is no less a personage than the only son of the late King of Barataria.

All.
What!

Don Al.
And I trust—I *trust* it was that one who slapped me on the shoulder and called me his man!

Giu.
One of us a king!

Mar.
Not brothers!

Tess.
The King of Barataria!

Gia.
Well, who'd have thought it!

} *Together.*

Mar.
But which is it?

Don Al.
What does it matter? As you are both Republicans, and hold kings in detestation, of course you'll abdicate at once. Good morning! (*going*).

Gia. & Tess.
Oh, don't do that! (*Marco and Giuseppe stop him.*)

Giu.
Well, as to that, of course there are kings and kings. When I say that I detest kings, I mean I detest *bad* kings.

Don Al.
I see. It's a delicate distinction.

Giu.
Quite so. Now I can conceive a kind of king —an ideal king—the creature of my fancy. you know—who would be absolutely unobjectionable. A king, for instance, who would abolish taxes and make everything cheap, except gondolas—

Mar.
And give a great many free entertainments to the gondoliers—

Giu.
And let off fireworks on the Grand Canal. and engage all the gondolas for the occasion—

Mar.
And scramble money on the Rialto among the gondoliers.

Giu.
Such a king would be a blessing to his people, and if I were a king, that is the sort of king I would be.

Mar.
And so would I!

Don Al.
Come, I'm glad to find your objections are not insuperable.

Mar. & Giu.
Oh, they're not insuperable.

Gia. & Tess.
No, they're not insuperable.

Giu.
Besides, we are open to conviction,

Gia.
Yes; they are open to conviction.

Tess.
Oh! they've often been convicted.

Giu.
Our views may have been hastily formed on insufficient grounds. They may be crude, ill-digested, erroneous. I've a very poor opinion of the politician who is not open to conviction.

Tess. (*to Gia.*)
Oh, he's a fine fellow!

Gia.
Yes, that's the sort of politician for *my* money!

Don Al.
Then we'll consider it settled. Now, as the country is in a state of insurrection, it is absolutely necessary that you should assume the reins of Government at once; and, until it is ascertained which of you is to be king, I have arranged that you will reign jointly, so that no question can arise hereafter as to the validity of any of your acts.

Mar.
As one individual?

Don Al.
As one individual.

Giu. (*linking himself with Marco*).
Like this?

Don Al.
Something like that.

Mar.
And we may take our friends with us, and give them places about the Court?

Don Al.
Undoubtedly. That's always done!

Mar.
I'm convinced!

Giu.
So am I!

Tess.
Then the sooner we're off the better.

Gia.
We'll just run home and pack up a few things (*going*)—

Don Al.
Stop, stop—that won't do at all—ladies are not admitted.

All.
What!

Don Al.
Not admitted. Not at present. Afterwards, perhaps. We'll see.

Giu.
Why, you don't mean to say you are going to separate us from our wives!

Don Al. (*aside*).
This is very awkward! (*aloud*) Only for a time—a few months. After all, what is a few months?

Tess.
But we've only been married half an hour!

FINALE, ACT I.
Song.—*Gianetta.*
Kind sir, you cannot have the heart
  Our lives to part

From those to whom an hour ago
  We were united!
Before our flowing hopes you stem,
  Ah, look at them,
And pause before you deal this blow,
  All uninvited!
You men can never understand
  That heart and hand
Cannot be separated when
  We go a-yearning;
You see, you've only women's eyes
  To idolize
And only women's hearts, poor men,
  To set *you* burning!
Ah me, you men will never understand
That woman's heart is one with woman's
  hand!
Some kind of charm you seem to find
  In womankind—
Some source of unexplained delight
  (Unless you're jesting),
But what attracts you, I confess,
  I cannot guess,
To me a woman's face is quite
  Uninteresting!
If from my sister I were torn
  It could be borne—
I should, no doubt, be horrified,
  But I could bear it;—
But Marco's quite another thing—
  He is my King,
He has my heart and none beside
  Shall ever share it!
Ah me, you men will never understand
That woman's heart is one with woman's
  hand! (*Weeps.*)
    Recit.—*Don Alhambra.*
Do not give way to this uncalled-for grief,
Your separation will be very brief.
  To ascertain which is the King
  And which the other,
  To Barataria's Court I'll bring
  His foster-mother;
  Her former nurseling to declare
  She'll be delighted.
  That settled, let each happy pair
  Be reunited.

Mar., Giu., Gia., Tess.
Viva! His argument is strong!
Viva! We'll not be parted long!
Viva! It will be settled soon!
Viva! Then comes our honeymoon!
        [*Exit Don Alhambra.*

Quartet.—*Marco, Giuseppe, Gianetta, Tessa.*
Gia.
Then one of us will be a Queen,
  And sit on a golden throne,
    With a crown instead
    Of a hat on her head,

13

And diamonds all her own!
With a beautiful robe of gold and green,
I've always understood;
   I wonder whether
   She'd wear a feather?
I rather think she should!

All.
Oh 'tis a glorious thing, I ween,
To be a regular Royal Queen!
No half-and-half affair, I mean,
But a right-down regular Royal Queen!

Mar.
She'll drive about in a carriage and pair,
With the King on her left-hand side,
   And a milkwhite horse,
   As a matter of course,
Whenever she wants to ride!
With beautiful silver shoes to wear
Upon her dainty feet;
   With endless stocks
   Of beautiful frocks
And as much as she wants to eat!

All.
Oh 'tis a glorious thing, I ween, &c.

Tess.
Whenever she condescends to walk,
Be sure she'll shine at that,
   With her haughty stare
   And her nose in the air,
Like a well-born aristocrat!
At elegant high society talk
She'll bear away the bell,
   With her "How de do?"
   And her "How are you?"
And "I trust I see you well!"

All.
Oh! 'tis a glorious thing, I ween, &c.

Giu.
And noble lords will scrape and bow,
And double themselves in two,
   And open their eyes
   In blank surprise
At whatever she likes to do.
And everybody will roundly vow
She's fair as flowers in May,
   And say, "How clever!"
   At whatsoever
She condescends to say!

All.
Oh! 'tis a glorious thing, I ween,
To be a regular Royal Queen—
No half-and-half affair, I mean,
But a right-down regular Royal Queen!

Dance.

(*Enter chorus of Gondoliers and Contadine.*)

CHORUS

Now, pray, what is the cause of this remark-
   able hilarity?
   This sudden ebullition of unmitigated
     jollity?
Has anybody blessed you with a sample of
   his charity?
   Or have you been adopted by a gentleman
     of quality?

Mar. and Giu.
Replying, we sing
   As one individual,
As I find I'm a king
   To my kingdom I bid you all.
I'm aware you object
   To pavilions and palaces,
But you'll find I respect
   Your Republican fallacies.

Cho.
As they know we object
   To pavilions and palaces,
How can they respect
   Our Republican fallacies?

Marco and Giuseppe.

Marco.
For every one who feels inclined,
Some post we undertake to find
Congenial with his frame of mind—
   And all shall equal be.

Giu.
The Chancellor in his peruke—
The Earl, the Marquis, and the Dook,
The Groom, the Butler, and the Cook—
   They all shall equal be.

Marco.
The Aristocrat who banks with Coutts,
The Aristocrat who hunts and shoots,
The Aristocrat who cleans our boots—
   They all shall equal be!

Giu.
The Noble Lord who rules the State—
The Noble Lord who cleans the plate—

Marco.
The Noble Lord who scrubs the grate—
   They all shall equal be!

Giu.
The Lord High Bishop orthodox—
The Lord High Coachman on the box—

Marco.
The Lord High Vagabond in the stocks—
   They all shall equal be!

Both.
For every one, &c.
   Sing high, sing low,
   Wherever they go,
   They all shall equal be!

14

Sing high, sing low,
Wherever they go,
  They all shall equal be!
The Earl, the Marquis, and the Dook,
The Groom, the Butler, and the Cook
The Aristocrat who banks with Coutts,
The Aristocrat who cleans the boots,
The Noble Lord who rules the State,
The Noble Lord who scrubs the grate,
The Lord High Bishop orthodox,
The Vagabond in the stocks—

For everyone, etc.
  Sing high, sing low,
  Wherever they go,
    They all shall equal be!

Then hail! O King,
  Whichever you may be,
To you we sing,
  But do not bend the knee.
Then hail! O King.

Marco and Giuseppe (together).

Come, let's away—our island crown awaits
  me—
Conflicting feelings rend my soul apart!
The thought of Royal dignity elates me,
  But leaving thee behind me breaks my
  heart!

(*Addressing Gianetta and Tessa.*)
Gianetta and Tessa (together).

Farewell, my love; on board you must be
  getting!
But while upon the sea you gaily roam,
Remember that a heart for thee is fretting—
The tender little heart you've left at home!

Gia.
Now, Marco dear,
My wishes hear:
  While you're away
It's understood
You will be good,
  And not too gay.
To every trace
Of maiden grace
  You will be blind,
And will not glance
By any chance
  On womankind!
If you are wise,
You'll shut your eyes
  'Till we arrive,
And not address
A lady less
  Than forty-five.
You'll please to frown
On every gown
  That you may see;

And, O my pet,
You won't forget
  You've married me!

And O my darling, O my pet,
Whatever else you may forget,
In yonder isle beyond the sea,
Do not forget you've married me!

Tess.
You'll lay your head
Upon your bed
  At set of sun.
You will not sing
Of anything
  To any one.
You'll sit and mope
All day, I hope
  And shed a tear
Upon the life
Your little wife
  Is passing here.
And if so be
You think of me,
  Please tell the moon!
I'll read it all
In rays that fall
  On the lagoon:
You'll be so kind
As tell the wind
  How you may be,
And send me words
By little birds
  To comfort me!

And O my darling, O my pet,
Whatever else you may forget,
In yonder isle beyond the sea,
Do not forget you've married me!

Quartet.
O my darling, O my pet, &c.

Cho.
(*during which a "Xebeque" is hauled
    alongside the quay*)

Then away we go to an island fair
  That lies in a Southern sea:
We know not where, and we don't much care,
  Wherever that isle may be.

The Men (hauling on boat).
One, two, three,
  Haul!
One, two, three,
  Haul!
One, two, three,
  Haul!
With a will!

All.
When the breezes are blowing
The ship will be going,
  When they don't we shall all stand still!
Then away we go to an island fair,

We know not where, and we don't much care,
  Wherever that isle may be.

SOLO.—*Marco.*

Away we go
  To a balmy isle,
Where the roses blow
  All the winter while.

All (hoisting sail).
  Then away we go to an island fair,
    That lies in a southern sea,
  Then away we go to an island fair,
    Then away, then away, then away!

(*The men embark on the "Xebeque." Marco
  and Giuseppe embracing Gianetta and
  Tessa. The girls wave a farewell to the
  men as the curtain falls.*)

END OF ACT I.

ACT II.

SCENE.—*Pavilion in the Court of Barataria.
Marco and Giuseppe magnificently dressed,
are seated on two thrones occupied in cleaning the crown and the sceptre. The gondoliers are discovered dressed, some as courtiers, officers of rank, &c., and others as
private soldiers and servants of various degrees. All are enjoying themselves without
reference to social distinctions—some playing
cards, others throwing dice, some reading,
others playing cup and ball, "morra," &c.*

Chorus of Men with Marco and Giuseppe.

Of happiness the very pith
  In Barataria you may see:
A monarchy that's tempered with
  Republican Equality.
This form of government we find
The beau ideal of its kind—
A despotism strict, combined
  With absolute equality!

Marco and Giuseppe.

Two kings, of undue pride bereft,
  Who act in perfect unity,
Whom you can order right and left
  With absolute impunity.
Who put their subjects at their ease
By doing all they can to please!
And thus, to earn their bread-and-cheese,
  Seize every opportunity.

Cho.
Of happiness the very pith, &c.

Mar.
  Gentlemen, we are much obliged to you for
your expressions of satisfaction and good
feeling—I say, we are much obliged to you
for your expressions of satisfaction and good
feeling.

All.
  We heard you.

Mar.
  We are delighted, at any time, to fall in with
sentiments so charmingly expressed.

All.
  That's all right.

Giu.
  At the same time there is just one little grievance that we should like to ventilate.

All (angrily).
  What?

Giu.
  Don't be alarmed—it's not serious. It is
arranged that, until it is decided which of us
two is the actual King, we are to act as one
person.

Giorgio.
  Exactly.

Giu.
  Now, although we act as *one* person, we are,
in point of fact, *two* persons.

Annibale.
  Ah, I don't think we can go into that. It is
a legal fiction, and legal fictions are solemn
things. Situated as we are, we can't recognize two independent responsibilities.

Giu.
  No; but you can recognize two independent
appetites. It's all very well to say we act as
one person, but when you supply us with
only one ration between us, I should describe it as a legal fiction carried a little too
far.

Anni.
  It's rather a nice point. I don't like to express an opinion off-hand. Suppose we reserve it for argument before the full Court?

Mar.
  Yes, but what are we to do in the meantime?

Mar. and Giu.
  We want our tea.

Anni.
  I think we may make an interim order for
double rations on their Majesties entering
into the usual undertaking to indemnify in
the event of an adverse decision?

16

Giorgio.

That, I think, will meet the case. But you must work hard—stick to it—nothing like work.

Giu.

Oh, certainly. We quite understand that a man who holds the magnificent position of King should do something to justify it. We are called "Your Majesty," we are allowed to buy ourselves magnificent clothes, our subjects frequently nod to us in the streets, the sentries always return our salutes, and we enjoy the inestimable privilege of heading the subscription lists to all the principal charities. In return for these advantages the least we can do is to make ourselves useful about the Palace.

SONG.—*Giuseppe with Chorus.*

Rising early in the morning,
 We proceed to light the fire,
Then our Majesty adorning
 In its work-a-day attire,
    We embark without delay
    On the duties of the day.

First, we polish off some batches
Of political despatches,
 And foreign politicians circumvent;
Then, if business isn't heavy,
We may hold a Royal *levée,*
 Or ratify some Acts of Parliament.
Then we probably review the household troops—
With the usual "Shalloo humps!" and "Shalloo hoops"
Or receive with ceremonial and state
An interesting Eastern potentate.
 After that we generally
 Go and dress our private *valet*—
(It's a rather nervous duty—he's a touchy little man)—
 Write some letters literary
 For our private secretary—
He is shaky in his spelling, so we help him if we can.
 Then, in view of cravings inner,
 We go down and order dinner;
Then we polish the Regalia and the Coronation Plate—
 Spend an hour in titivating
 All our Gentlemen-in-Waiting:
Or we run on little errands for the Ministers of State.
 Oh, philosophers may sing
 Of the troubles of a King;
Yet the duties are delightful, and the privileges great;
 But the privilege and pleasure
 That we treasure beyond measure

Is to run on little errands for the Ministers of State.

Cho.

Oh! Philosophers may sing, &c.
After luncheon (making merry
On a bun and glass of sherry),
 If we've nothing in particular to do,
We may make a Proclamation,
Or receive a Deputation—
 Then we possibly create a Peer or two.
Then we help a fellow-creature on his path
With the Garter or the Thistle or the Bath.
Or we dress and toddle off in semi-State
To a festival, a function, or a *fête.*
 Then we go and stand as sentry
 At the Palace (private entry),
Marching hither, marching thither, up and down and to and fro,
 While the warrior on duty
 Goes in search of beer and beauty
(And it generally happens that he hasn't far to go).
 He relieves us, if he's able,
 Just in time to lay the table,
Then we dine and serve the coffee, and at half-past twelve or one,
 With a pleasure that's emphatic,
 We retire to our attic.
With the gratifying feeling that our duty has been done!
 Oh, philosophers may sing
 Of the troubles of a King,
But of pleasures there are many and of worries there are none;
 And the culminating pleasure
 That we treasure beyond measure
Is the gratifying feeling that our duty has been done!

Cho.

Oh! Philosophers may sing, &c.
 [*Exeunt all but Marco and Giuseppe.*

Giu.

Yet it really is a very pleasant existence. They're all so singularly kind and considerate. You don't find them wanting to do this, or wanting to do that, or saying "It's my turn now." No, they let us have all the fun to ourselves, and never seem to grudge it.

Mar.

It makes one feel quite selfish. It almost seems like taking advantage of their good nature.

Giu.

How nice they were about the double rations.

Mar.

Most considerate. Ah! there's only one thing wanting to make us thoroughly comfortable.

17

Giu.

And that is?

Mar.

The dear little wives we left behind us three months ago.

Giu.

Yes, it *is* dull without female society. We can do without everything else, but we can't do without that.

Mar.

And if we have that in perfection, we have everything. There is only one recipe for perfect happiness.

Song.—*Marco.*

Take a pair of sparkling eyes,
    Hidden, ever and anon,
        In a merciful eclipse—
Do not heed their mild surprise—
    Having passed the Rubicon.
        Take a pair of rosy lips;
Take a figure trimly planned—
    Such as admiration whets
        (Be particular in this) ;
Take a tender little hand,
    Fringed with dainty fingerettes,
        Press it—in parenthesis ;—
Ah! Take all these, you lucky man—
Take and keep them, if you can!

Take a pretty little cot—
    Quite a miniature affair—
        Hung about with trellised vine,
Furnish it upon the spot
    With the treasures rich and rare
        I've endeavoured to define.
Live to love and love to live—
    You will ripen at your ease,
        Growing on the sunny side—
Fate has nothing more to give.
    You're a dainty man to please
        If you're not satisfied.
Ah! Take my counsel, happy man!
Act upon it, if you can!

(*Enter Chorus of Contadine, running in, led by Fiametta and Vittoria. They are met by all the Ex-Gondoliers, who welcome them heartily.*)

SCENA, *Chorus of Girls, Quartet, Duet and Chorus.*

Here we are, at the risk of our lives,
From ever so far, and we've brought your wives—
And to that end we've crossed the main,
And don't intend to return again

Fia.

Though obedience is strong,
    Curiosity's stronger—
We waited for long,
    Till we couldn't wait longer.

Vit.

It's imprudent, we know,
    But without your society
Existence was slow,
    And we wanted variety—

All.

So here we are, at the risk of our lives,
From ever so far, and we've brought your wives—
And to that end we've crossed the main,
And don't intend to return again!

(*Enter Gianetta and Tessa. They rush to the arms of Marco and Giuseppe.*)

Giu.
    Tessa!
Tessa.
    Giuseppe!
Gia.
    Marco!
Mar.
    Gianetta!

}Embrace.

Tessa and Gianetta.

Tessa.

After sailing to this island—

Gia.

    Tossing in a manner frightful,

Tessa.

We are all once more on dry land—

Gia.

    And we find the change delightful

Tessa.

As at home we've been remaining—
    We've not seen you both for ages,

Gia.

Tell me, are you fond of reigning?—
    How's the food, and what's the wages?

Tessa.

Does your new employment please ye?—

Gia.

    How does Royalizing strike you?

Tessa.

Is it difficult or easy?—

Gia.

    Do you think your subjects like you?

Tessa.

I am anxious to elicit,
    Is it plain and easy steering?

Gia.

Take it altogether, is it—
    Better fun than gondoliering?

Both.

We shall both go on requesting,
    Till you tell us, never doubt it,
Everything is interesting,
    Tell us, tell us all about it!

Chorus.
They will both go on requesting, &c.
Tessa.
Is the populace exacting?
Gia.
Do they keep you at a distance?
Tessa.
All unaided are you acting,
Gia.
Or do they provide assistance?
Tessa.
When you're busy, have you got to
Get up early in the morning?
Gia.
If you do what you ought not to,
Do they give the usual warning?
Tessa.
With a horse do they equip you?
Gia.
Lots of trumpeting and drumming?
Tessa.
Do the Royal tradesmen tip you?
Gia.
Ain't the livery becoming!
Tessa.
Does your human being inner
Feed on everything that nice is?
Gia.
Do they give you wine for dinner;
Peaches, sugar-plums, and ices?
Both.
We shall both go on requesting
Till you tell us, never doubt it;
Everything is interesting,
Tell us, tell us all about it!
Chorus.
They will both go on requesting, &c.
Mar.
This is indeed a most delightful surprise!
Tess.
Yes, we thought you'd like it. You see, it
was like this. After you left we felt very
dull and mopey, and the days crawled by,
and you never wrote; so at last I said to
Gianetta, "I can't stand this any longer;
those two poor Monarchs haven't got any one
to mend their stockings or sew on their but-
tons or patch their clothes—at least, I hope
they haven't—let us all pack up a change and
go and see how they're getting on." And
she said "done," and they all said "done";
and we asked old Giacopo to lend us his
boat, and *he* said "done"; and we've crossed
the sea, and, thank goodness, *that's* done;
and here we are, and—and—*I've* done!
Gia.
And now—which of you is King?

Tess.
And which of us is Queen?
Giu.
That we shan't know until Nurse turns up.
But never mind that—the question is, how
shall we celebrate the commencement of our
honeymoon? Gentlemen, will you allow us
to offer you a magnificent banquet?
All.
We will!
Giu.
Thanks very much; and, ladies, what do you
say to a dance?
Tess.
A banquet *and* a dance! Oh, it's too much
happiness!

CHORUS *and* DANCE.
Dance a cachucha, fandango, bolero,
Xeres we'll drink—Manzanilla, Montero—
Wine, when it runs in abundance, enhances
The reckless delight of that wildest of
dances!
To the pretty pitter-pitter-patter,
And the clitter-clitter-clitter-clatter—
Clitter—clitter—clatter,
Pitter—pitter—pitter,
Patter, patter, patter, patter, we'll dance.
Old Xeres we'll drink—Manzanilla, Mont-
ero;
For wine, when it runs in abundance, en-
hances
The reckless delight of that wildest of
dances!

CACHUCHA.
*The dance is interrupted by the unexpected ap-
pearance of Don Alhambra, who looks on
with astonishment. Marco and Giuseppe ap-
pear embarrassed. The others run off, except
Drummer Boy, who is driven off by Don
Alhambra.*
Don Al.
Good evening. Fancy ball?
Giu.
No, not exactly. A little friendly dance.
That's all. Sorry you're late.
Don Al.
But I saw a groom dancing, and a footman!
Mar.
Yes. That's the Lord High Footman.
Don Al.
And, dear me, a common little drummer boy!
Giu.
Oh no! That's the Lord High Drummer Boy.
Don Al.
But surely, surely the servants'-hall is the
place for these gentry?

Giu.

Oh dear no! *We* have appropriated the servant's-hall. It's the Royal Apartment, and accessible only by tickets obtainable at the Lord Chamberlain's office.

Mar.

We really must have some place that we can call our own.

Don Al. (puzzled)

I'm afraid I'm not quite equal to the intellectual pressure of the conversation.

Giu.

You see, the Monarchy has been remodelled on Republican principles.

Don Al.

What!

Giu.

All departments rank equally, and everybody is at the head of his department.

Don Al.

I see.

Mar.

I'm afraid you're annoyed.

Don Al.

No. I won't say that. It's not quite what I expected.

Giu.

I'm awfully sorry.

Mar.

So am I.

Giu.

By-the-bye, can I offer you anything after your voyage? A plate of maccaroni and a rusk?

Don Al. (pre-occupied).

No, no—nothing—nothing.

Giu.

Obliged to be careful?

Don Al.

Yes—gout. You see, in every Court there are distinctions that must be observed.

Giu. (puzzled).

There are, are there?

Don Al.

Why, of course. For instance, you wouldn't have a Lord High Chancellor play leapfrog with his own cook.

Mar.

Why not?

Don Al.

Why not! Because a Lord High Chancellor is a personage of great dignity, who should never, under any circumstances, place himself in the position of being told to tuck in his tuppenny, except by noblemen of his own rank. A Lord High Archbishop, for instance, might tell a Lord High Chancellor to tuck in his tuppenny, but certainly not a cook, gentlemen, certainly not a cook.

Giu.

Not even a Lord High Cook?

Don Al.

My good friend, that is a rank that is not recognized at the Lord Chamberlain's office. No, no, it won't do. I'll give you an instance in which the experiment was tried.

Song.—*Don Alhambra, with Marco and Giuseppe.*

Don Al.

There lived a King, as I've been told,
In the wonder-working days of old,
When hearts were twice as good as gold,
  And twenty times as mellow.
Good-temper triumphed in his face,
And in his heart he found a place
For all the erring human race
  And every wretched fellow.
When he had Rhenish wine to drink
It made him very sad to think
That some, at junket or at jink,
  Must be content with toddy.

Mar. & Giu.

With toddy, must be content with toddy.

Don Al.

He wished all men as rich as he
(And he was rich as rich could be),
So to the top of every tree
  Promoted everybody.

Mar. & Giu.

Now, that's the kind of King for me—
He wished all men as rich as he,
So to the top of every tree
  Promoted everybody!

Don Al.

Lord Chancellors were cheap as sprats,
And Bishops in their shovel hats
Were plentiful as tabby cats—
  In point of fact, too many.
Ambassadors cropped up like hay,
Prime Ministers and such as they
Grew like asparagus in May,
  And Dukes were three a penny.
On every side Field Marshals gleamed,
Small beer were Lords Lieutenant deemed,
With Admirals the ocean teemed
  All round his wide dominions.

Mar. & Giu.

With Admirals all round his wide dominions.

Don Al.

And Party Leaders you might meet
In twos and threes in every street
Maintaining, with no little heat,
  Their various opinions..

Mar. & Giu.

Now that's a sight you couldn't beat—

20

Two Party Leaders in each street
Maintaining, with no little heat,
　　Their various opinions.

Don Al.
That King, although no one denies
His heart was of abnormal size,
Yet he'd have acted otherwise
　　If he had been acuter.
The end is easily foretold,
When every blessed thing you hold
Is made of silver, or of gold,
　　You long for simple pewter.

When you have nothing else to wear
But cloth of gold and satins rare,
For cloth of gold you cease to care—
　　Up goes the price of shoddy.

Mar. & Giu.
Of shoddy, up goes the price of shoddy.

Don Al.
In short, whoever you may be,
To this conclusion you'll agree,
When everyone is somebodee,
　　Then no one's anybody!

Mar. & Giu.
Now that's as plain as plain can be,
To this conclusion we agree—

All.
When every one is somebodee,
　　Then no one's anybody!

(*Gianetta and Tessa enter unobserved. The two girls, impelled by curiosity, remain listening at the back of the stage.*)

Don Al.
And now I have some important news to communicate. His Grace the Duke of Plaza-Toro, Her Grace the Duchess, and their beautiful daughter Casilda—I say their beautiful daughter Casilda—

Giu.
We heard you.

Don Al.
Have arrived at Barataria, and may be here at any moment.

Mar.
The Duke and Duchess are nothing to us.

Don Al.
But the daughter—the beautiful daughter! Aha! Oh, you're a lucky dog, one of you!

Giu.
I think you're a very incomprehensible old gentleman.

Don Al.
Not a bit—I'll explain. Many years ago when you (whichever you are) were a baby, you (whichever you are) were married to a little girl who has grown up to be the most beautiful young lady in Spain. That beauti-

ful young lady will be here to claim you (whichever you are) in half an hour, and I congratulate that one (whichever it is) with all my heart.

Mar.
Married when a baby!

Giu.
But we were married three months ago!

Don Al.
One of you—only one. The other (whichever it is) is an unintentional bigamist.

Gia. & Tess. (*coming forward*).
Well, upon my word!

Don Al.
Eh? Who are these young people?

Tess.
Who are we? Why, their wives, of course. We've just arrived.

Don Al.
Their wives! Oh dear, this is very unfortunate! Oh, dear, this complicates matters! Dear, dear, what will Her Majesty say?

Gia.
And do you mean to say that one of these Monarchs was already married?

Tess.
And that neither of us will be a Queen?

Don Al.
That is the idea I intended to convey. (*Tessa and Gianetta begin to cry.*)

Giu. (*to Tessa*).
Tessa, my dear, dear child—

Tess.
Get away! perhaps it's you!

Mar. (*to Gia.*).
My poor, poor little woman!

Gia.
Don't! Who knows whose husband you are?

Tess.
And pray, why didn't you tell us all about it before they left Venice?

Don Al.
Because if I had, no earthly temptation would have induced these gentlemen to leave two such extremely fascinating and utterly irresistible little ladies!

Tess.
There's something in that.

Don Al.
I may mention that you will not be kept long in suspense, as the old lady who nursed the Royal child is at present in the Torture Chamber, waiting for me to interview her.

Giu.
Poor old girl. Hadn't you better go and put her out of her suspense?

Don Al.

Oh no—there's no hurry—she's all right. She has all the illustrated papers. However, I'll go and interrogate her, and in the meantime, may I suggest the absolute propriety of your regarding yourselves as single young ladies. Good evening!

[*Exit Don Alhambra.*

Gia.

Well, here's a pleasant state of things!

Mar.

Delightful. One of us is married to two young ladies, and nobody knows which; and the other is married to one young lady whom nobody can identify!

Gia.

And one of us is married to one of you, and the other is married to nobody.

Tess.

But which of you is married to which of us, and what's to become of the other? (*about to cry.*)

Giu.

It's quite simple. Observe. Two husbands have managed to acquire three wives. Three wives—two husbands. (*Reckoning up.*) That's two-thirds of a husband to each wife.

Tess.

O Mount Vesuvius, here we are in arithmetic! My good sir, one can't marry a vulgar fraction!

Giu.

You've no right to call me a vulgar fraction.

Mar.

We are getting rather mixed. The situation is entangled. Let's try and comb it out.

QUARTET.—*Marco, Giuseppe, Gianetta, Tessa.*

In a contemplative fashion,
　And a tranquil frame of mind,
Free from every kind of passion,
　Some solution let us find.
Let us grasp the situation,
　Solve the complicated plot—
Quiet, calm deliberation
　Disentangles every knot.

Tess.

I, no doubt, Giuseppe wedded— *The Others.* That's, of course, a slice of luck. [In a con-
He is rather dunder-headed, 　　[templative
Still distinctly, he's a duck. 　[fashion, &c.

Gia.

I, a victim, too, of Cupid, *The Others.* Let
Marco married—that is clear. [us grasp the
He's particularly stupid, 　　[situation, &c.
Still distinctly, he's a dear.

Mar.

To Gianetta I was mated; *The Others.* In a
I can prove it in a trice: 　[contemplative

Though her charms are overrated 　[fashion,
Still I own she's rather nice. 　　　[&c.

Giu.

I to Tessa, willy-nilly, 　*The Others.* Let us
All at once a victim fell. [grasp the situa-
She is what is called a silly, 　[tion, &c.
Still she answers pretty well.

Mar.

Now when we were pretty babies
　Some one married us, that's clear—

Gia.

And if I can catch her
I'll pinch her and scratch her,
And send her away with a flea in her ear.

Giu.

He whom that young lady married,
　To receive her can't refuse.

Tess.

If I overtake her
I'll warrant I'll make her
To shake in her aristocratical shoes!

Gia. (to Tess.)

If she married your Giuseppe
You and he will have to part—

Tess. (to Gia.)

If I have to do it
I'll warrant she'll rue it—
I'll teach her to marry the man of my heart!

Tess. (to Gia.)

If she married Messer Marco
You're a spinster,

Gia. (to Tess.)

No matter—no matter
If I can get at her
I doubt if her mother will know her again!

All.

Quiet, calm deliberation
　Disentangles every knot!

[*Exeunt, pondering.*

MARCH. *Enter procession of Retainers, heralding approach of Duke, Duchess, and Casilda. All three are now dressed with the utmost magnificence.*

CHORUS *of Men, with Duke and Duchess*

With ducal pomp and ducal pride
　(Announce these comers,
　　O ye kettle-drummers!)
Comes Barataria's high-born bride.
　(Ye sounding cymbals clang!)
She comes to claim the Royal hand—
　(Proclaim their Graces,
　　O ye double basses!)
Of the King who rules this goodly land.
　(Ye brazen brasses bang!)

22

Duke and Duch.
This polite attention touches
Heart of Duke and heart of Duchess,
   Who resign their pet
   With profound regret.
She of beauty was a model
When a tiny tiddle-toddle,
   And at twenty-one
   She's excelled by none!

Chorus.
     She comes to claim the Royal hand, &c.

Duke (to his attendants).
Be good enough to inform His Majesty that
His Grace the Duke of Plaza-Toro, Limited,
has arrived, and begs—

Cas.
Desires—

Duch.
Demands—

Duke.
And demands an audience. (*Exeunt attendants.*) And now, my child, prepare to
receive the husband to whom you were united
under such interesting and romantic circumstances.

Cas.
But which is it? There are two of them!

Duke.
It is true that at present His Majesty is a
double gentleman; but as soon as the circumstances of his marriage are ascertained, he
will, *ipso facto,* boil down to a single gentleman—thus presenting a unique example of
an individual who becomes a single man
and a married man by the same operation.

Duch. (severely).
I have known instances in which the characteristics of both conditions existed concur-
rently in the same individual.

Duke.
Ah, he couldn't have been a Plaza-Toro.

Duch.
Oh! couldn't he, though!

Cas.
Well, whatever happens, I shall, of course,
be a dutiful wife, but I can never love my
husband.

Duke.
I don't know. It's extraordinary what un-
prepossessing people one can love if one gives
one's mind to it.

Duch.
I loved your father.

Duke.
My love—that remark is a little hard, I
think? Rather cruel, perhaps? Somewhat
uncalled for, I venture to believe?

Duch.
It was very difficult, my dear; but I said to
myself, "That man is a Duke, and I *will* love
him." Several of my relations bet me I
couldn't, but I did—desperately!

Song.—*Duchess*

On the day when I was wedded
   To your admirable sire,
I acknowledge that I dreaded
   An explosion of his ire.
I was overcome with panic—
For his temper was volcanic,
   And I didn't dare revolt,
   For I feared a thunderbolt!
I was always very wary,
   For his fury was ecstatic—
His refined vocabulary
   Most unpleasantly emphatic.
     To the thunder
       Of this Tartar
     I knocked under
       Like a martyr;
     When intently
       He was fuming,
     I was gently
       Unassuming—
     When reviling
       Me completely,
     I was smiling
       Very sweetly:
Giving him the very best, and getting back
   the very worst—
That is how I tried to tame your great pro-
   genitor—at first!

But I found that a reliance
   On my threatening appearance,
And a resolute defiance
   Of marital interference,
And a gentle intimation
Of my firm determination
   To see what I could do
   To be wife and husband too,
Was the only thing required
   For to make his temper supple,
And you couldn't have desired
   A more reciprocating couple
     Ever willing
       To be wooing,
     We were billing—
       We were cooing;
     When I merely
       From him parted
     We were nearly
       Broken-hearted—
     When in sequel
       Reunited,
     We were equal-
       Ly delighted.

So with double-shotted guns and colours
    nailed unto the mast,
I tamed your insignificant progenitor—at
    last!

Cas.

My only hope is that when my husband sees
what a shady family he has married into he
will repudiate the contract altogether.

Duke.

Shady? A nobleman shady, who is blazing
in the lustre of unaccustomed pocket-money?
A nobleman shady, who can look back upon
ninety-five quarterings? It is not every
nobleman who is ninety-five quarters in ar-
rear—I mean, who can look back upon
ninety-five of them! And this, just as I have
been floated at a premium! Oh fie!

Duch.

Your Majesty is surely unaware that directly your Majesty's father came before the
public he was applied for over and over
again.

Duke.

My dear, her Majesty's father was in the
habit of being applied for over and over
again—and very urgently applied for, too—
long before he was registered under the
Limited Liability Act.

RECITATIVE.—*Duke.*

To help unhappy commoners, and add to
    their enjoyment,
Affords a man of noble rank congenial em-
    ployment;
Of our attempts we offer you examples illus-
    trative:
The work is light, and, I may add, it's most
    remunerative.

DUET.—*Duke and Duchess.*

Duke.

Small titles and orders
For Mayors and Recorders
    I get—and they're highly delighted—

Duch.

    They're highly delighted!

Duke.

M.P.'s baronetted,
Sham Colonels gazetted,
    And second-rate Aldermen knighted—

Duch.

    Yes, Aldermen knighted.

Duke.

Foundation-stone laying
I find very paying:
    It adds a large sum to my makings—

Duch.

    Large sum to his makings.

Duke.

At charity dinners
The best of speech-spinners,
    I get ten per cent. on the takings—

Duch.

    One-tenth of the takings.

Duke.

I present any lady
Whose conduct is shady
    Or smacking of doubtful propriety—

Duke.

    Doubtful propriety.

Duch.

When Virtue would quash her,
I take and whitewash her,
    And launch her in first-rate society—

Duke.

    First-rate society!

Duch.

I recommend acres
Of clumsy dressmakers—
    Their fit and their finishing touches—

Duke.

    Their finishing touches.

Duch.

A sum in addition.
They pay for permission
    To say that they make for the Duchess—

Duke.

    They make for the Duchess!

Duke.

Those pressing prevailers,
The ready-made tailors,
    Quote me as their great double-barrel—

Duch.

    Their great double-barrel.

Duke.

I allow them to do so,
Though Robinson Crusoe
    Would jib at their wearing apparel!

Duch.

    Such wearing apparel!

Duke.

I sit, by selection,
Upon the direction
    Of several Companies bubble—

Duch.

    All Companies bubble!

Duke.

As soon as they're floated
I'm freely bank-noted—
    I'm pretty well paid for my trouble!

Duch.

    He's paid for his trouble!

Duch.

At middle-class party
I play at *ecarte*—

24

And I'm by no means a beginner—
Duke (*significantly*).

She's not a beginner.

Duch.

To one of my station
The remuneration—
Five guineas a night and my dinner—

Duke.

And wine with her dinner.

Duch.

I write letters blatant
On medicines patent—
And use any other you mustn't—

Duke.

Believe me, you mustn't—

Duch.

And vow my complexion
Derives its perfection
From somebody's soap—which it doesn't—

Duke (*significantly*).

It certainly doesn't!

Duke.

We're ready as witness
To any one's fitness
To fill any place or preferment—

Duch.

A place or preferment.

Duch.

We're often in waiting
At junket or *fêting,*
And sometimes attend an interment—

Duke.

We enjoy an interment.

Both.

In short, if you'd kindle
The spark of a swindle,
Lure simpletons into your clutches—
Yes; into your clutches.
Or hoodwink a debtor
You cannot do better

Duch.

Than trot out a Duke or a Duchess—

Duke.

A Duke or a Duchess!

(*Enter Marco and Giuseppe.*)

Duke.

Ah! their Majesties. Your Majesty! (*Bows with great ceremony.*)

Mar.

The Duke of Plaza-Toro, I believe?

Duke.

The same. (*Marco and Giuseppe offer to shake hands with him. The Duke bows ceremoniously. They endeavour to imitate him.*) Allow me to present—

Giu.

The young lady one of us married?

Marco and Giuseppe offer to shake hands with her. Casilda curtsies formally. They endeavour to imitate her.)

Cas.

Gentlemen, I am the most obedient servant of one of you. (*aside*) Oh, Luiz!

Duke.

I am now about to address myself to the gentleman whom my daughter married; the other may allow his attention to wander if he likes, for what I am about to say does not concern him. Sir, you will find in this young lady a combination of excellences which you would search for in vain in any young lady who had not the good fortune to be my daughter. There is some little doubt as to which of you is the gentleman I am addressing, and which is the gentleman who is allowing his attention to wander; but when that doubt is solved, I shall say (still addressing the attentive gentleman), "Take her, and may she make you happier than her mother has made me."

Duch.

Sir!

Duke.

If possible. And now there is a little matter to which I think I am entitled to take exception. I come here in State with Her Grace the Duchess and Her Majesty, my daughter, and what do I find? Do I find, for instance, a guard of honour to receive me? No.

Mar. and Giu.

No.

Duke.

The town illuminated? No.

Mar. and Giu.

No.

Duke.

Refreshment provided? No.

Mar. and Giu.

No.

Duke.

A Royal salute fired? No.

Mar. and Giu.

No.

Duke.

Triumphal arches erected? No.

Mar. and Giu.

No.

Duke.

The bells set ringing?

Mar. and Giu.

No.

Duke.
Yes—one—the Visitors', and I rang it my-self. It is not enough! It is not enough!

Giu.
Upon my honour, I'm very sorry; but you see, I was brought up in a gondola, and my ideas of politeness are confined to taking off my cap to my passengers when they tip me.

Duch.
That's all very well in its way, but it is not enough.

Giu.
I'll take off anything else in reason.

Duke.
But a Royal Salute to my daughter—it costs so little.

Cas.
Papa, I don't want a Salute.

Giu.
My dear sir, as soon as we know which of us is entitled to take that liberty she shall have as many salutes as she likes.

Mar.
As for guards of honour and triumphal arches, you don't know our people—they wouldn't stand it.

Giu.
They are very off-hand with us—very off-hand indeed.

Duke.
Oh, but you mustn't allow that—you must keep them in proper discipline, you must im-press your Court with your importance. You want deportment—carriage—

Giu.
We've got a carriage.

Duke.
Manner—dignity. There must be a good deal of this sort of thing—(*business*)—and a little of this sort of thing—(*business*)— and possibly just a *soupçon* of this sort of thing!—(*business*)—and so on. Oh, it's very useful, and most effective. Just attend to me. You are a King—I am a subject. Very good—

GAVOTTE.

Duke, Duchess, Casilda, Marco, Giuseppe.
Duke.
I am a courtier grave and serious
   Who is about to kiss your hand:
Try to combine a pose imperious
   With a demeanour nobly bland.

Mar. & Giu.
Let us combine a pose imperious
   With a demeanour nobly bland.

(*Marco and Giuseppe endeavour to carry out his instructions.*)

Duke.
That's, if anything, *too* unbending—
Too aggressively stiff and grand;
   (*They suddenly modify their attitudes.*)
Now to the other extreme you're tending—
Don't be so deucedly condescending!

Duch. & Cas.
Now to the other extreme you're tending—
Don't be so dreadfully condescending!

Mar. & Giu.
Oh, hard to please some noblemen seem!
   At first, if anything, *too* unbending;
Off we go to the other extreme—
   Too confoundedly condescending!

Duke.
Now a gavotte perform sedately—
   Offer your hand with conscious pride;
Take an attitude not too stately,
   Still sufficiently dignified.

Mar. & Giu.
Now for an attitude not too stately,
   Still sufficiently dignified.

(*They endeavour to carry out his instructions.*)

Duke (*beating time*).
Oncely, twicely—oncely, twicely—
   Bow impressively ere you glide. (*They do so.*)
Capital both—you've caught it nicely!
   That is the style of thing precisely!

Duch. & Cas.
Capital both—you've caught it nicely!
   That is the style of thing precisely!

Mar. and Giu.
Oh, sweet to earn a nobleman's praise!
   Capital both—we've caught it nicely!
Supposing he's right in what he says,
   This is the style of thing precisely!

(GAVOTTE. *At the end exeunt Duke and Duchess, leaving Casilda with Marco and Giuseppe.*)

Giu. (*to Marco*).
The old birds have gone away and left the young chickens together. That's called tact.

Mar.
It's very awkward. We really aught to tell her how we are situated. It's not fair to the girl.

Giu.
Then why don't you do it?

Mar.
I'd rather not—you.

Giu.
I don't know how to begin. (*To Casilda.*)
A—Madam—I—we, that is, several of us—

Cas.
Gentlemen, I am bound to listen to you; but it is right to tell you that, not knowing I

was married in infancy, I am over head and ears in love with somebody else.

Giu.
Our case exactly! *We* are over head and ears in love with somebody else! (*Enter Gianetta and Tessa.*) In point of fact, with our wives!

Cas.
Your wives! Then you are married?

Tess.
It's not our fault.

Gia.
We knew nothing about it.

Both.
We are sisters in misfortune.

Cas.
My good girls, I don't blame you. Only before we go any further we must really arrive at some satisfactory arrangement, or we shall get hopelessly complicated.

QUINTET and FINALE.

Marco, Giuseppe, Casilda, Gianette, Tessa.

All.
Here is a case unprecedented!
    Here are a King and Queen ill-starred!
Ever since marriage was first invented
    Never was known a case so hard!

Mar. & Giu.
I may be said to have been bisected,
    By a profound catastrophe!

Cas., Gia., Tess.
Through a calamity unexpected
    I am divisible into three!

All.
        O moralists all,
        How can you call
    Marriage a state of unitee,
When excellent husbands are bisected,
    Wives are divisible into three?
        O moralists all,
        How can you call
    Marriage a state of union true,

Cas., Gia., Tess.
One-third of myself is married to half of ye
    or you?

Mar. and Giu.
When half of myself has married two-thirds
    of ye or you?

(*Enter Don Alhambra, followed by Duke, Duchess, and all the Chorus.*)

FINALE.

RECIT.—*Don Alhambra.*

Now let the loyal lieges gather round—
The Prince's foster-mother has been found!
She will declare, to silver clarion's sound,

The rightful King—let him forthwith be
    crowned!

Cho.
She will declare, &c.

(*Don Alhambra brings forward Inez, the Prince's foster-mother.*)

Tess.
Speak, woman, speak—

Duke.
    We're all attention!

Gia.
The news we seek—

Duch.
    This moment mention.

Cas.
To us they bring—

Don Al.
    His foster-mother.

Mar.
Is he the King?

Giu.
    Or this my brother?

All.
Speak, woman, speak, &c.

RECIT.—*Inez.*

The Royal Prince was by the King entrusted
To my fond care, ere I grew old and crusted!
When traitors came to steal his son reputed,
My own small boy I deftly substituted!
The villains fell into the trap completely—
I hid the Prince away—still sleeping sweetly:
I called him "son" with pardonable slyness—
His name, Luiz! Behold his Royal Highness!

(*Sensation. Luiz ascends the throne, crowned and robed as King.*)

Cas. (*rushing to his arms*).
Luiz!

Luiz.
    Casilda! (*Embrace.*)

All.
Is this indeed the King,
    Oh, wondrous revelation!
Oh, unexpected thing!
    Unlooked-for situation!

Marco, Gianetta, Giuseppe, Tessa.
This statement we receive
    With sentiments conflicting;
Our hearts rejoice and grieve,
    Each other contradicting;
To those whom we adore
    We can be reunited—
On one point rather sore,
    But, on the whole, delighted!

Luiz.
When others claimed thy dainty hand,
    I waited—waited—waited.

27

Duke.

    As prudence (so I understand)
        Dictated—tated—tated.

Cas.

    By virtue of our early vow
        Recorded—corded—corded.

Duch.

    Your pure and patient love is now
        Rewarded—warded—warded.

All.

    Then hail, O King of a Golden Land,
    And the high-born bride who claims his
        hand!
    The past is dead, and you gain your own,
    A royal crown and a golden throne!

(All kneel: Luiz crowns Casilda.)

All.

    Once more *gondolieri*,
    Both skilful and wary,
    Free from this quandary
        Contented are we.
    From Royalty flying,
    Our gondolas plying
    And merrily crying
        Our *"premé," "stali!"*

    So good-bye Cachucha, fandango, bolero,
      We'll dance a farewell to that measure—
    Old Xeres, adieu—Manzanilla—Montero—
      We leave you with feelings of pleasure!

CURTAIN

28

THE PIRATES OF PENZANCE;

OR,

THE SLAVE OF DUTY.

▼▼▼▼▼▼▼

ACT I.

SCENE.—*A rocky sea-shore on the coast of Cornwall. In the distance is a calm sea, on which a schooner is lying at anchor. As the curtain rises groups of pirates are discovered—some drinking, some playing cards. Samuel, the pirate lieutenant, is going from one group to another, filling the cups from a flask. Frederic is seated in a despondent attitude at the back of the scene. Ruth kneels at his feet.*

OPENING CHORUS

Pour, oh pour the pirate sherry;
  Fill, oh fill the pirate glass;
And, to make us more than merry,
  Let the pirate bumper pass.

Sam.
For to-day our pirate 'prentice
  Rises from indenture freed;
Strong his arm and keen his scent is,
  He's a pirate now indeed!

All.
Here's good luck to Frederic's ventures!
Frederic's out of his indentures.

Sam.
Two-and-twenty now he's rising,
  And alone he's fit to fly,
Which we're bent on signalizing
  With unusual reve*lry*.

All.
Here's good luck to Frederic's ventures!
Frederic's out of his indentures.
Pour! oh pour the pirate sherry, &c.
(*Frederic rises and comes forward with Pirate King, who enters.*)

King.
Yes, Frederic, from to-day you rank as a full-blown member of our band.

All.
Hurrah!

Fred.
My friends, I thank you all, from my heart, for your kindly wishes. Would that I could repay them as they deserve!

King.
What do you mean?

Fred.
Today I am out of my indentures, and to-day I leave you for ever.

King.
But this is quite unaccountable; a keener hand at scuttling a Cunarder or cutting out a P. and O. never shipped a handspike.

Fred.
Yes, I have done my best for you. And why? It was my duty under my indentures, and I am the slave of duty. As a child I was regularly apprenticed to your ban. It was through an error—no matter, the mistake was ours, not yours, and I was in honour bound by it.

Sam.
An error? What error? (*Ruth rises and comes forward.*)

Fred.
I may not tell you; it would reflect upon my well-loved Ruth.

Ruth.
Nay, dear master, my mind has long been gnawed by the cankering tooth of mystery. Better have it out at once.

SONG.—*Ruth.*

When Frederic was a little lad he proved so
  brave and daring,
His father thought he'd 'prentice him to some
  career seafaring
I was, alas! his nurserymaid, and so it fell
  to *my* lot
To take and bind the promising boy apprentice to a *pilot*.
A life not bad for a hardy lad, though surely
  not a high lot,
Though I'm a nurse, you might do worse,
  than make your boy a pilot.

I was a stupid nurserymaid, on breakers always steering,
And I did not catch the word aright, through
  being hard of hearing;
Mistaking my instructions, which within my
  brain did gyrate,
I took and bound this promising boy apprentice to a *pirate*.

A sad mistake it was to make and doom him
    to a vile lot,
I bound him to a pirate—you—instead of to
    a pilot.

I soon found out, beyond all doubt, the scope
    of this disaster,
But I hadn't the face to return to my place,
    and break it to my master.
A nurserymaid is not afraid of what you peo-
    ple *call* work,
So I made up my mind to go as a kind of
    piratical maid-of-all-work.
And that is how you find me now, a member
    of your shy lot,
Which you wouldn't have found, had he been
    bound apprentice to a pilot.

Ruth.
Oh, pardon! Frederic, pardon! (*Kneels.*)

Fred.
Rise, sweet one, I have long pardoned you.

Ruth (rises).
The two words were so much alike!

Fred.
They were. They still are, though years
have rolled over their heads. But this afternoon my obligation ceases: Individually, I
love you all with affection unspeakable, but,
collectively, I look upon you with a disgust
that amounts to absolute detestation. Oh!
pity me, my beloved friends, for such is my
sense of duty that, once out of my indentures, I shall feel myself bound to devote
myself heart and soul to your extermination!

All.
Poor lad—poor lad! (*All weep.*)

King.
Well, Frederic, if you conscientiously feel
that it is your duty to destroy us, we cannot
blame you for acting on that conviction. Always act in accordance with the dictates of
your conscience, my boy, and chance the consequences.

Sam.
Besides, we can offer you but little temptation to remain with us. We don't seem to
make piracy pay. I'm sure I don't know
why, but we don't.

Fred.
I know why, but, alas! I mustn't tell you; it
wouldn't be right.

King.
Why not, my boy? It's only half-past eleven,
and you are one of us until the clock strikes
twelve.

Sam.
True, and until then you are bound to pro-
tect our interests.

All.
Hear, hear!

Fred.
Well, then, it is my duty, as a pirate, to tell
you that you are too tender-hearted. For
instance, you make a point of never attacking
a weaker party than yourselves, and when
you attack a stronger party you invariably
get thrashed.

King.
There is some truth in that.

Fred.
Then, again, you make a point of never mo-
lesting an orphan!

Sam.
Of course: we are orphans ourselves, and
know what it is.

Fred.
Yes, but it has got about, and what is the
consequence? Every one we capture says
he's an orphan. The last three ships we
took proved to be manned entirely by orphans, and so we had to let them go. One
would think that Great Britain's mercantile
navy was recruited solely from her orphan
asylums—which we know is not the case.

Sam.
But, hang it all! You wouldn't have us absolutely merciless?

Fred.
There's my difficulty; until twelve o'clock I
would, after twelve I wouldn't. Was ever a
man placed in so delicate a situation?

Ruth.
And Ruth, your own Ruth, whom you love so
well, and who has won her middle-aged way
into your boyish heart, what is to become of
her?

King.
Oh, he will take you with him. (*Hands
Ruth to Frederic.*)

Fred.
Well, Ruth, I feel some little difficulty about
you. It is true that I admire you very much,
but I have been constantly at sea since I was
eight years old, and yours is the only woman's face I have seen during that time. I
think it is a sweet face.

Ruth.
It is—oh, it is!

Fred.
I say I *think* it is! that is my impression.
But as I have never had an opportunity of
comparing you with other women, it is just
possible I may be mistaken.

King.
True.

Fred.
What a terrible thing it would be if I were to marry this innocent person, and then find out that she is, on the whole, plain!

King.
Oh, Ruth is very well, very well indeed.

Sam.
Yes, there are the remains of a fine woman about Ruth.

Fred.
Do you really think so?

Sam.
I do.

Fred.
Then I will not be so selfish as to take her from you. In justice to her and in consideration for you, I will leave her behind. (*Hands Ruth to King.*)

King.
No, Frederic, this must not be. We are rough men who lead a rough life, but we are not so utterly heartless as to deprive thee of thy love. I think I am right in saying that there is not one here who would rob thee of this inestimable treasure for all the world holds dear.

All (loudly).
Not one!

King.
No, I thought there wasn't. Keep thy love, Frederic, keep thy love. (*Hands her back to Frederic.*)

Fred.
You're very good, I'm sure.   [*Exit Ruth.*

King.
Well, it's the top of the tide, and we must be off. Farewell, Frederic. When your process of extermination begins, let our deaths be as swift and painless as you can conveniently make them.

Fred.
I will! By the love I have for you, I swear it! Would that you could render this extermination unnecessary by accompanying me back to civilization!

King.
No, Frederic, it cannot be. I don't think much of our profession, but, contrasted with respectability, it is comparatively honest. No, Frederic, I shall live and die a Pirate King.

SONG.—*Pirate King.*
Oh, better far to live and die
Under the brave black flag I fly,
Than play a sanctimonious part,
With a pirate head and a pirate heart.
Away to the cheating world go you,
Where pirates all are well to do;
But I'll be true to the song I sing,

And live and a die a Pirate King.
    For I am a Pirate King.

All.
    You are!
Hurrah for our Pirate King!

King.
And it is, it is a glorious thing
To be a Pirate King.

All.
    It is!
Hurrah for our Pirate King!

King.
When I sally forth to seek my prey,
I help myself in a royal way:
I sink a few more ships, it's true,
Than a well-bred monarch ought to do;
But many a king on a first-class throne,
If he wants to call his crown his own,
Must manage somehow to get through
More dirty work than ever *I* do,
    For I am a Pirate King.

All.
    You are!
Hurrah for our Pirate King!

King.
And it is, it is a glorious thing
To be a Pirate King!

All.
    It is!
Hurrah for our Pirate King!
                [*Exeunt all except Frederic.
                Enter Ruth.*

Ruth.
Oh, take me with you. I cannot live if I am left behind.

Fred.
Ruth, I will be quite candid with you. You are very dear to me, as you know, but I must be circumspect. You see you are considerably older than I. A lad of twenty-one usually looks for a wife of seventeen.

Ruth.
A wife of seventeen! You will find me a wife of a thousand!

Fred.
No, but I shall find you a wife of forty-seven, and that is quite enough. Ruth, tell me candidly, and without reserve, compared with other women—how are *you?*

Ruth.
I will answer you truthfully, master—I have a slight cold, but otherwise I am quite well.

Fred.
I am sorry for your cold, but I was referring rather to your personal appearance. Compared with other women, are you beautiful?

Ruth (bashfully).
I have been told so, dear master.

Fred.

Ah, but lately?

Ruth.

Oh, no, years and years ago.

Fred.

What do you think of yourself?

Ruth.

It is a delicate question to answer, but I think I am a fine woman.

Fred.

That is your candid opinion?

Ruth.

Yes, I should be deceiving you if I told you otherwise.

Fred.

Thank you, Ruth, I believe you, for I am sure you would not practise on my inexperience; I wish to do the right thing, and if— I say *if*—you are really a fine woman, your age shall be no obstacle to our union! (*Chorus of girls heard in the distance.*) Hark! Surely I hear voices! Who has ventured to approach our all but inaccessible lair? Can it be Custom House? No, it does not sound like Custom House.

Ruth (aside).

Confusion! it is the voices of young girls! If he should see them I am lost.

Fred (looking off).

By all that's marvellous, a bevy of beautiful maidens!

Ruth (aside).

Lost! lost! lost!

Fred.

How lovely! how surpassingly lovely is the plainest of them! What grace—what delicacy—what refinement! And Ruth—Ruth told me she was beautiful!

RECIT.

Fred.

Oh, false one, you have deceived me!

Ruth.

I have deceived you?

Fred.

Yes, deceived me!

(*Denouncing her.*)

DUET.—*Fred and Ruth.*

Fred.

You told me you were fair as gold!

Ruth (wildly).

And, master am I not so?

Fred.

And now I see you're plain and old,

Ruth.

I am sure I am not a jot so.

Fred.

Upon my innocence you play,

Ruth.

I'm not the one to plot so.

Fred.

Your face is lined, your hair is grey.

Ruth.

It's gradually got so.

Fred.

Faithless woman to deceive me,
I who trusted so!

Ruth.

Master, master, do not leave me,
Hear me, ere you go!
My love without reflecting—
Oh, do not be rejecting,
Take a maiden tender—her affection raw and green,
At very highest rating,
Has been accumulating
Summers seventeen—summers seventeen.

ENSEMBLE.

Ruth.

Don't, beloved master,
Crush me with disaster.
What is such a dower to the dower
I have here?
My love unabating
Has been accumulating
Forty-seven year—forty-seven year!

Fred.

Yes, your former master
Saves you from disaster.
Your love would be uncomfortably fervid,
it is clear.
If, as you are stating
It's been accumulating
Forty-seven year—forty-seven year!

(*At the end he renounces her, and she goes off in despair.*)

RECIT.—*Fred.*

What shall I do? Before these gentle maidens
I dare not show in this alarming costume.
No, no, I must remain in close concealment
Until I can appear in decent clothing!
(*Hides in cave as they enter climbing over the rocks.*)

Girls.

Climbing over rocky mountain,
Skipping rivulet and fountain,
Passing where the willows quiver
By the ever-rolling river,
Swollen with the summer rain:
Threading long and leafy mazes
Dotted with unnumbered daisies;
Scaling rough and rugged passes,
Climb the hardy little lasses,
Till the bright sea-shore they gain!

Edith.

Let us gaily tread the measure,
Make the most of fleeting leisure;
Hail it as a true ally,
Though it perish by-and-bye.

All.

Hail it as a true ally,
Though it perish by-and-bye.

Edith.

Every moment brings a treasure
Of its own especial pleasure,
Though the moments quickly die,
Greet them gaily as they fly.

All.

Though the moments quickly die, &c.

Kate.

Far away from toil and care,
Revelling in fresh sea air,
Here we live and reign alone
In a world that's all our own.
Here in this our rocky den
Far away from mortal men
We'll be queens, and make decrees—
They may honour them who please.

All.

Let us gaily tread the measure, &c.

Kate.

What a picturesque spot! I wonder where
we are!

Edith.

And a wonder where papa is. We have left
him ever so far behind.

Isabel.

Oh, he will be here presently! Remember
poor papa is not as young as we are, and
we come over a rather difficult country.

Kate.

But how thoroughly delightful it is to be so
entirely alone! Why, in all probability we
are the first human beings who ever set foot
on this enchanting spot.

Isabel.

Except the mermaids—it's the very place for
mermaids.

Kate.

Who are only human beings down to the
waist!

Edith.

And who can't be said strictly to set *foot*
anywhere. Tails they may, but feet they
cannot.

Kate.

But what shall we do until papa and the
servants arrive with the luncheon?

Edith.

We are quite alone, and the sea is as smooth
as glass. Suppose we take off our shoes and
stockings and paddle?

All.

Yes, yes! The very thing! (*They prepare
to carry out the suggestion. They have all
taken off one shoe, when Frederic comes forward from cave.*)

Fred. (*recitative*).

Stop, ladies, pray!

All (*hopping on one foot*).

A man!

Fred.

I had intended
Not to intrude myself upon your notice
In this effective but alarming costume,
But under these peculiar circumstances
It is my bounden duty to inform you
That your proceedings will not be unwit-
nessed!

Edith.

But who are you, sir? Speak! (*All hopping.*)

Fred.

I am a pirate!

All (*recoiling, hopping*).

A pirate! Horror!

Fred.

Ladies, do not shun me!
This evening I renounce my wild profession;
And to that end, oh, pure and peerless
maidens!
Oh, blushing buds of ever-blooming beauty!
I, sore at heart, implore your kind assistance.

Edith.

How pitiful his tale!

Kate.

How rare his beauty!

All.

How pitiful his tale! How rare his beauty!

Song.—*Fred..*

Oh, is there not one. maiden breast
Which does not feel the moral beauty
Of making worldly interest
Subordinate to sense of duty?
Who would not give up willingly
All matrimonial ambition,
To rescue such an one as I
From his unfortunate position?

All.

Alas! there's not one maiden breast
Which seems to feel the moral beauty
Of making worldly interest
Subordinate to sense of duty!

Fred.

Oh, is there not one maiden here
Whose homely face and bad complexion
Have caused all hopes to disappear
Of ever winning man's affection?
To such an one, if such there be,

I swear by Heaven's arch above you,
If you will cast your eyes on me— .
However plain you be—I'll love you!

All.
Alas! there's not one maiden here
Whose homely face and bad complexion
Have caused all hope to disappear
Of ever winning man's affection!

Fred. (in despair).
Not one?

All.
No, no—not one!

Fred.
Not one?

All.
No, no!

Mabel enters.

Mabel.
Yes, one!

All.
'Tis Mabel!

Mabel.
Yes, 'tis Mabel!

RECIT.—*Mabel.*

Oh, sisters, deaf to pity's name,
For shame!
It's true that he has gone astray,
But pray
Is that a reason good and true
Why you
Should all be deaf to pity's name?

All (aside).
The question is, had he not been
A thing of beauty,
Would she be swayed by quite as keen
A sense of duty?

Mabel.
For shame, for shame, for shame!

SONG.—*Mabel.*

Poor wandering one!
Though thou hast surely strayed,
Take heart of grace,
Thy steps retrace,
Poor wandering one!
Poor wandering one!
If such poor love as mine
Can help thee find
True peace of mind—
Why, take it, it is thine!
Take heart, fair days will shine;
Take any heart—take mine!

All.
Take heart, no danger lowers;
Take any heart—but ours!

[*Exit Mabel and Frederic.*

(*Edith beckons her sisters, who form in a semi-circle around her.*)

EDITH.

What ought we to do,
Gentle sisters, say!
Propriety, we know,
Says we ought to stay;
While sympathy .exclaims,
"Free them from your tether—
Play at other games—
Leave them here together."

KATE.

Her case may, any day,
Be yours, my dear, or mine.
Let her make her hay
While the sun doth shine.
Let us compromise
(Our hearts are not of leather),
Let us shut our eyes,
And talk about the weather.

Girls.
Yes, yes, let's talk about the weather.

CHATTERING CHORUS.
How beautifully blue the sky,
The glass is rising very high,
Continue fine I hope it may,
And yet it rained but yesterday.
Tomorrow it may pour again,
(I hear the country wants some rain),
Yet people say, I know not why,
That we shall have a warm July.

Enter Mabel and Frederic.
(*During Mabel's solo the Girls continue chatter pianissimo, but listening eagerly all the time.*)

SOLO.—*Mabel.*

Did ever maiden wake
From dream of homely duty,
To find her daylight break
With such exceeding beauty?
Did ever maiden close
Her eyes on waking sadness,
To dream of such exceeding gladness?

Fred.
Ah, yes! ah, yes! this is exceeding gladness.

Girls.
How beautifully blue the sky, &c.

SOLO.—*Fred.*
(*During this, Girls continue their chatter pianissimo as before, but listening intently all the time.*)

Did ever pirate roll
His soul in guilty dreaming,
And wake to find that soul
With peace and virtue beaming?

36

ENSEMBLE.

Mabel.
Did ever maiden wake, &c.

Fred.
Did ever pirate loathed, &c.

Girls.
How beautifully blue the sky, &c.

RECIT.—*Fred.*
Stay, we must not lose our senses,
Men who stick at no offences
  Will anon be here.
Piracy their dreadful trade is,
Pray you get you hence, young ladies,
  While the coast is clear.

        [*Frederic and Mabel retire*

Girls.
No, we must not lose our senses,
If they stick at no offences
  We should not be here.
Piracy their dreadful trade is—
Nice companions for young ladies!
  Let us disappear.

(*During this chorus the Pirates have entered
stealthily, and formed in a semi-circle behind
the Girls. As the Girls move to go off each
Pirate seizes a girl. King seizes Edith and
Isabel, Samuel seizes Kate.*)

Girls.
Too late!

Pirates.
  Ha! Ha!

Girls.
  Too late!

Pirates.
  Ha! Ha!
Ha! ha! ha! ha! Ha! ha! ha! ha!

ENSEMBLE.

Pirates.
Here's a first-rate opportunity
To get married with impunity,
And indulge in the felicity
Of unbounded domesticity.
You shall quickly be parsonified,
Conjugally matrimonified,
By a doctor of divinity,
Who resides in this vicinity.

Ladies.
We have missed our opportunity
Of escaping with impunity;
So farewell to the felicity
Of our maiden domesticity!
We shall quickly be parsonified,
Conjugally matrimonified,
By a doctor of divinity,
Who resides in this vicinity.

Mabel (*coming forward*).

RECIT.
Hold, monsters! Ere your pirate caravan-
  serai
Proceed, against our will, to wed us all.
Just bear in mind that we are Wards in
  Chancery,
And father is a Major-General!

Sam. (*cowed*).
We'd better pause, or danger may befall,
Their father is a Major-General.

Girls.
Yes, yes; he is a Major-General! (*The
Major-General has entered unnoticed, on
rock.*)

Gen.
Yes, yes—I am a Major-General!

Sam.
For he is a Major-General!

All.
He is! Hurrah for the Major-General!

Gen.
And it is—it is a glorious thing
To be a Major-General!

All.
It is!
  Hurrah for the Major-General!

SONG.—*Major-General.*
I am the very model of a modern Major-
  General,
I've information vegetable, animal and min-
  eral;
I know the kings of England, and I quote the
  fights historical,
From Marathon to Waterloo, in order cate-
  gorical;
I'm very well acquainted too with matters
  mathematical,
I understand equations, both the simple and
  quadratical,
About binominal theorem I'm teeming with a
  lot o' news—
With many cheerful facts about the square of
  the hypotenuse.

All.
With many cheerful facts, &c.

Gen.
I'm very good at integral and differential
  calculus,
I know the scientific names of beings animal-
  culous;
In short, in matters vegetable, animal, and
  mineral,
I am the very model of a modern Major-
  General.

All.
> In short, in matters, vegetable, animal, and mineral,
> He is the very model of a modern Major-General.

Gen.
> I know our mythic history, King Arthur's and Sir Caradoc's,
> I answer hard acrostics, I've a pretty taste for paradox.
> I quote in elegiacs all the crimes of Heliogabalus,
> In conics I can floor peculiarities parabolus.
> I can tell undoubted Raphaels from Gerard Dows and Zoffanies,
> I know the croaking chorus from the "Frogs" of Aristophanes.
> Then I can hum a fugue of which I've heard the music's din afore,
> And whistle all the airs from that infernal nonsense "Pinafore."

All.
> And whistle all the airs, &c.

Gen.
> Then I can write a washing bill in Babylonic cuneiform,
> And tell you every detail of Caractacus's uniform;
> In short, in matters vegetable, animal, and mineral,
> I am the very model of a modern Major-General.

All.
> In short, in matters vegetable, animal, and mineral,
> He is the very model of a modern Major-General.

Gen.
> In fact, when I know what is meant by "mamelon" and "ravelin,"
> When I can tell at sight a mauser rifle from a javelin,
> When such affairs as sorties and surprises I'm more wary at,
> And when I know precisely what is meant by commissariat,
> When I have learnt what progress has been made in modern gunnery,
> When I know more of tactics than a novice in a nunnery;
> In short, when I've a smattering of elemental strategy,
> You'll say a better Major-General has never sat a gee—

All.
> You'll say a better, &c.

Gen.
> For my military knowledge, though I'm plucky and adventury,

Has only been brought down to the beginning of the century;
> But still in matters vegetable, animal, and mineral,
> I am the very model of a modern Major-General.

All.
> But still in matters vegetable, animal, and mineral,
> He is the very model of a modern Major-General.

Gen.
And now that I've introduced myself I should like to have some idea of what's going on.

Kate.
Oh, papa—we—

Sam.
Permit me, I'll explain in two words: we propose to marry your daughters.

Gen.
Dear me!

Girls.
Against our wills, papa—against our wills!

Gen.
Oh, but you mustn't do that! May I ask—this is a picturesque uniform, but I'm not familiar with it. What are you?

King.
We are all single gentlemen.

Gen.
Yes, I gathered that—anything else?

King.
No, nothing else.

Edith.
Papa, don't believe them; they are pirates—the famous Pirates of Penzance!

Gen.
The Pirates of Penzance! I have often heard of them.

Mabel.
All except this gentleman—(*indicating Frederic*)—who was a pirate once, but who is out of his indentures to-day, and who means to lead a blameless life evermore.

Gen.
But wait a bit. I object to pirates as sons-in-law.

King.
We object to Major-Generals as fathers-in-law. But we waive that point. We do not press it. We look over it.

Gen. (*aside*).
Hah! an idea! (*Aloud.*) And do you mean to say that you would deliberately rob me of these, the sole remaining props of my old age, and leave me to go through the remainder of my life unfriended, unprotected, and alone?

King.
Well, yes, that's the idea.

Gen.
Tell me, have you ever known what it is to be an orphan?

Pirates (disgusted).
Oh, dash it all!

King.
Here we are again!

Gen.
I ask you, have you ever known what it is to be an orphan?

King.
Often!

Gen.
Yes, orphan. Have you ever known what it is to be one?

King.
I say, often.

All (disgusted).
Often, often, often.

Gen.
I don't think we quite understand one another. I ask you, have you ever known what it is to be an orphan, and you say "orphan." As I understand you, you are merely repeating the word "orphan" to show that you understand me.

King.
I didn't repeat the word often.

Gen.
Pardon me, you did indeed.

King.
I only repeated it once.

Gen.
True, but you repeated it.

King.
But not often.

Gen.
Stop: I think I see where we are getting confused. When you said "orphan," did you mean "orphan"—a person who has lost his parents, or "often"—frequently!

King.
Ah! I beg pardon—I see what you mean—frequently.

Gen.
Ah! you said often—frequently.

King.
No, only once.

Gen. (irritated).
Exactly—you said often, frequently, only once.

RECIT.—*General.*

Oh, men of dark and dismal fate,
  Forego your cruel employ,

Have pity on my lonely state,
  I am an orphan boy!

King and Sam.
An orphan boy?

Gen.
An orphan boy!

Pirates.
How sad—an orphan boy!

Solo.—*General.*
These children whom you see
  Are all that I can call my own!

Pirates.
          Poor fellow!

Gen.
Take them away from me
  And I shall be indeed alone.

Pirates.
          Poor fellow!

Gen.
If pity you can feel,
  Leave me my sole remaining joy—
See, at your feet they kneel;
Your hearts you cannot steel
Against the sad, sad tale of the lonely orphan boy!

Pirates (sobbing).
          Poor fellow!
See at our feet they kneel;
  Our hearts we cannot steel
Against the sad, sad tale of the lonely orphan boy!

King.
The orphan boy!

Sam.
The orphan boy!

All.
The lonely orphan boy! Poor fellow!

Ensemble.

General (aside).
I'm telling a terrible story,
But it doesn't diminish my glory;
For they would have taken my daughters
Over the billowy waters.
If I hadn't in elegant diction,
Indulged in an innocent fiction;
Which is not in the same category
As a regular terrible story.

Girls (aside).
He's telling a terrible story,
Which will tend to diminish his glory;
Though they would have taken his daughters
Over the billowy waters,
It's easy, in elegant diction,
To call it an innocent fiction,
But it comes in the same category
As a regular terrible story.

39

Pirates (aside).
  If he's telling a terrible story,
  He shall die by a death that is gory,
  One of the cruellest slaughters
  That ever were known in these waters;
  It's easy, in elegant diction,
  To call it an innocent fiction,
  But it comes in the same category
  If he's telling a terrible story.

King.
  Although our dark career
    Sometimes involves the crime of stealing,
  We rather think that we're
    Not altogether void of feeling.
  Although we live by strife,
    We're always sorry to begin it,
  For what, we ask, is life
    Without a touch of Poetry in it?

All (kneeling).
  Hail Poetry, thou heaven-born maid!
  Thou gildest e'en the pirate's trade:
  Hail flowing fount of sentiment,
  All hail Divine Emollient! (*All rise.*)

King.
  You may go, for you're at liberty, our pirate
    rules protect you,
  And honorary members of our band we do
    elect you!

Sam.
  For he is an orphan boy.

Chorus.
  He is! Hurrah for the orphan boy!

Gen.
  And it sometimes is a useful thing
    To be an orphan boy.

Chorus.
  It is! Hurrah for the orphan boy!

Ensemble.

Oh, happy day, with joyous glee
We ⎱
They ⎰ will away and married be;
Should it befall auspiciously,
My ⎱
Her ⎰ sisters all will bridesmaids be!

Ruth enters and appeals to Frederic.

Ruth.
  Oh, master, hear one word, I do implore you!
  Remember Ruth, your Ruth, who kneels be-
    fore you!
  (*Pirates.*) Yes, yes, remember Ruth, who
  kneels before you!

Fred.
  Away, you did deceive me!
  (*Pirates threatening Ruth.*) Away, you did
  deceive him!

Ruth.
  Oh, do not leave me!
  (*Pirates.*) Oh, do not leave her!

Fred.
  Away, you grieve me!
  (*Pirates.*) Away, you grieve him!

Fred.
  I wish you'd leave me!
      (*Frederic casts Ruth from him.*)

Pirates.
  We wish you'd leave him!

Ensemble.

Pray observe the magnanimity
We ⎱
They ⎰ display to lace and dimity!
Never was such opportunity
To get married with impunity,
But ⎰ we ⎱ give up the felicity
    ⎱ they ⎰
Of unbounded domesticity,
Though a doctor of divinity
Resides in this vicinity.

[*Girls and General go up rocks, while Pirates
indulge in a wild dance of delight on stage.
The General produces a British flag, and the
Pirate King produces a black flag with skull
and cross-bones. Enter Ruth, who makes a
final appeal to Frederic, who casts her from
him.*

End of Act I.

▼▼▼▼▼▼▼

ACT II.

Scene.—*A Ruined Chapel by Moonlight.
Ruined Gothic windows at back. General
Stanley discovered seated pensively, sur-
rounded by his daughters.*

Chorus.

Oh, dry the glistening tear

  That dews that martial cheek,
Thy loving children hear,
  In them thy comfort seek.
With sympathetic care
  Their arms around thee creep,
For oh, they cannot bear
  To see their father weep!

Enter Mabel.

SOLO.—*Mabel.*

Dear father, why leave your bed
  At this untimely hour,
When happy daylight is dead,
  And darksome dangers lower?
See, heaven has lit her lamp,
  The midnight hour is past,
And the chilly night air is damp,
  The dew is falling fast!
Dear father, why leave your bed
When happy daylight is dead?

CHORUS.

Oh, dry the glistening tear, &c.

Frederic enters.

Mabel.

Oh, Frederic, cannot you, in the calm excellence of your wisdom, reconcile it with your conscience to say something that will relieve my father's sorrow?

Fred.

I will try, dear Mabel. But why does he sit, night after night, in this draughty old ruin?

Gen.

Why do I sit here? To escape from the pirates' clutches, I described myself as an orphan, and, heaven help me, I am no orphan! I came here to humble myself before the tombs of my ancestors, and to implore their pardon for having brought dishonour on the family escutcheon.

Fred.

But you forget, sir, you only bought the property a year ago, and the stucco in your baronial hall is scarcely dry.

Gen.

Frederic, in this chapel are ancestors: you cannot deny that. With the estate, I bought the chapel and its contents. I don't know whose ancestors they *were*, but I know whose ancestors they *are*, and I shudder to think that their descendant by purchase (if I may so describe myself) should have brought disgrace upon what, I have no doubt, was an unstained escutcheon.

Fred.

Be comforted. Had you not acted as you did, these reckless men would assuredly have called in the nearest clergyman, and have married your large family on the spot.

Gen.

I thank you for your proffered solace, but it is unavailing. I assure you, Frederic, that such is the anguish and remorse I feel at the abominable falsehood by which I escaped these easily deluded pirates, that I would go to their simple-minded chief this very night and confess all, did I not fear that the consequences would be most disastrous to myself. At what time does your expedition march against these scoundrels?

Fred.

At eleven, and before midnight I hope to have atoned for my involuntary association with the pestilent scourges by sweeping them from the face of the earth—and then, dear Mabel, you will be mine!

Gen.

Are your devoted followers at hand?

Fred.

They are, they only wait my orders.

RECIT.—*General.*

Then, Frederic, let your escort lion-hearted
Be summoned to receive a general's blessing,
Ere they depart upon their dread adventure.

Fred.

Dear sir, they come.

Enter Police, marching in single file. They form in line, facing audience.

SONG.—*Sergeant.*

When the foeman bares his steel,
  Tarantara! tarantara!
We uncomfortable feel,
  Tarantara!
And we find the wisest thing,
  Tarantara! tarantara!
Is to slap our chests and sing-
  Tarantara!
For when threatened with emeutes,
  Tarantara! tarantara!
And your heart is in your boots,
  Tarantara!
There is nothing brings it round,
Like the trumpet's martial sound,
  Tarantara! tarantara!
Tarantara, ra-ra-ra-ra!

Police.

Tarantara, ra-ra-ra-ra!

Mabel.

Go, ye heroes, go to glory,
Though ye die in combat gory,
Ye shall live in song and story.
  Go to immortality!
Go to death, and go to slaughter;
Die, and every Cornish daughter
With her tears your grave shall water.
  Go, ye heroes, go and die!

Girls.

  Go, ye heroes, go and die!

Police.

Though to us it's evident,
  Tarantara! tarantara!
These attentions are well meant.
  Tarantara!

Such expressions don't appear,
　Tarantara! tarantara!
Calculated men to cheer,
　Tarantara!
Who are going to meet their fate
In a highly nervous state,
　Tarantara!
Still to us it's evident
These attentions are well meant,
　Tarantara!

Edith.

Go and do your best endeavour,
And before all links we sever,
We will say farewell for ever.
　Go to glory and the grave!

Girls.

For your foes are fierce and ruthless,
False, unmerciful, and truthless,
Young and tender, old and toothless,
　All in vain their mercy crave.

Serg.

We observe too great a stress
On the risks that on us press,
And of reference alack
To our chance of coming back.
Still, perhaps it would be wise
Not to carp or criticise,
For it's very evident
These attentions are well meant.

Police.

Yes, it's very evident
These attentions are well meant.
　Tarantara-ra-ra-ra-ra!

ENSEMBLE.

Chorus of all but Police.

Go, ye heroes, go to glory;
Though ye die in combat gory,
Ye shall live in song and story,
　Go to immortality!
Go to death and go to slaughter;
Die, and every Cornish daughter
With her tears your grave shall water.
　Go, ye heroes, go and die!

Chorus of Police.

When the foeman bares his steel,
　Tarantara, tarantara!
We uncomfortable feel,
　Tarantara!
And we find the wisest thing,
　Tarantara, tarantara!
Is to slap our chests and sing,
　Tarantara!
For when threatened with emeutes,
　Tarantara, tarantara!
And your heart is in your boots,
　Tarantara!
There is nothing brings it round
Like the trumpet's martial sound,
　Tarantara, tarantara!

Gen.

Away, away!

Police (without moving).

Yes, yes, we go.

Gen.

These pirates slay.

Police.

　Tarantara!

Gen.

Then do not stay.

Police.

　Tarantara!

Gen.

Then why this delay?

Police.

　All right—we go.
Yes, forward on the foe!

Gen.

Yes, but you *don't* go!

Police.

We go, we go!
Yes, forward on the foe!

Gen.

Yes, but you *don't* go!

All.

At last they really go. (*Exeunt Police.*)

(*Mabel tears herself from Frederic and exit,
followed by the General and her sisters, con-
soling her. Frederic remains.*)

RECIT.—*Fred.*

Now for the pirates' lair! Oh, joy un-
　　bounded!
Oh, sweet relief! Oh, rapture unexampled!
At last I may atone, in some slight measure,
For the repeated acts of theft and pillage
Which, at a sense of duty's stern dictation,
I, circumstance's victim, have been guilty

(*King and Ruth appear at the window,
armed.*)

King.

Young Frederic! (*Covering him with pistol.*)

Fred.

　Who calls?

King.

　Your late commander!

Ruth.

And I, your little Ruth! (*Covering him
with postol.*)

Fred.

　Oh, mad intruders,
How dare ye face me? Know ye not, oh
　rash ones,
That I have doomed you to extermination?

(*King and Ruth hold a pistol to each ear.*)

42

King.
Have mercy on us, hear us, ere you slaughter.
Fred.
I do not think I ought to listen to you.
Yet, mercy should alloy our stern resentment,
And so I will be merciful—say on!

TRIO.—*Ruth, King, and Fred.*

Ruth.
When you had left our pirate fold,
  We tried to raise our spirits faint,
According to our custom old,
  With quips and quibbles quaint.
But all in vain, the quips we heard,
  We lay and sobbed upon the rocks,
Until to somebody occurred
  A startling paradox.

Fred.
    A paradox?
Ruth.
        A paradox,
  A most ingenious paradox!
We've quips and quibbles heard in flocks,
But none to beat this paradox!
All.
  A paradox, a most ingenious paradox!
    Ha! ha! ha! ha! Ho! ho! ho! ho!
King.
We knew your taste for curious quips,
  For cranks and contradictions queer,
And with the laughter on our lips,
  We wished you there to hear.
We said, "If we could tell it him,
  How Frederic would the joke enjoy,"
And so we've risked both life and limb
  To tell it to our boy.

Fred (interested).
That paradox?
King.
      That paradox,
(*Laughing*). That most ingenious paradox!
We've quips and quibbles heard in flocks,
But none to beat that paradox!
All.
  A paradox, a most ingenious paradox!
    Ha! ha! ha! ha! Ho! ho! ho! ho!

CHANT.—*King.*

For some ridiculous reason, to which, however, I've no desire to be disloyal.
Some person in authority, I don't know who,
  very likely the Astronomer Royal,
Has decided that, although for such a beastly
  month as February, twenty-eight days as
  a rule are plenty,
One year in every four his days shall be
  reckoned as nine-and-twenty.
Through some singular coincidence—I
  shouldn't be surprised if it were owing to
  the agency of an ill-natured fairy—

You are the victim of this clumsy arrangement, having been born in leap-year, on
  the twenty-ninth of February.
And so, by a simple arithmetical process,
  you'll easily discover,
That though you've lived twenty-one years,
  yet, if we go by birthdays, you're only five
  and a little bit over!

Ruth.
Ha! ha! ha! ha!
King.
Ho! ho! ho! ho!
Fred.
Dear me!
Let's see! (*counting on fingers.*)
Yes, yes; with yours my figures do agree!
All.
Ha! ha! ha! ha! Ho! ho! ho! ho! (*Fred-
eric more amused than any.*)
Fred.
How quaint the ways of Paradox!
At common sense she gaily mocks!
Though counting in the usual way,
  Years twenty-one I've been alive,
Yet reckoning by my natal day,
  I am a little boy of five!
All.
He is a little boy of five! Ha! ha!
A paradox, a paradox,
A most ingenious paradox!
  Ha! ha! ha! ha!
All.
Ho! ho! ho! ho! (*Ruth and King throw
themselves back on seats, exhausted with
laughter.*)

Fred.
Upon my word, this is most curious—most
absurdly whimsical. Five and a quarter!
No one would think it to look at me!
Ruth.
You are glad now, I'll be bound, that you
spared us. You would never have for-
given yourself when you discovered that you
had killed *two of your comrades.*
Fred.
My comrades?
King (rises).
I'm afraid you don't appreciate the delicacy
of your position. You were apprenticed to
us—
Fred.
Until I reached my twenty-first year.
King.
No, until you reached your twenty-first birth-
day (*producing document*), and, going by
birthdays, you are as yet only five and a
quarter.

43

Fred.
You don't mean to say you are going to hold me to that?

King.
No, we merely remind you of the fact, and leave the rest to your sense of duty.

Ruth (rises).
Your sense of duty!

Fred. (wildly).
Don't put it on that footing! As I was merciful to you just now, be merciful to me! I implore you not to insist on the letter of your bond just as the cup of happiness is at my lips!

Ruth.
We insist on nothing; we content ourselves with pointing out to you *your duty.*

King.
Your duty!

Fred. (after a pause).
Well, you have appealed to my sense of duty, and my duty is only too clear. I abhor your infamous calling; I shudder at the thought that I have ever been mixed up with it; but duty is before all—at any price I will do my duty.

King.
Bravely spoken! Come, you are one of us once more.

Fred.
Lead on, I follow. (*Suddenly.*) Oh, horror!

King.
Ruth.　What is the matter?

Fred.
Ought I to tell you? No, no, I cannot do it; and yet, as one of your band—

King.
Speak out, I charge you by that sense of conscientiousness to which we have never yet appealed in vain.

Fred.
General Stanley, the father of my Mabel—

King.
Ruth.　Yes, yes!

Fred.
He escaped from you on the plea that he was an orphan!

King.
He did!

Fred.
It breaks my heart to betray the honoured father of the girl I adore, but as your apprentice I have no alternative. It is my duty to tell you that General Stanley is no orphan!

King.
Ruth.　What!

Fred.
More than that, he never was one!

King.
Am I to understand that, to save his contemptible life, he dared to practise on our credulous simplicity? (*Frederic nods as he weeps.*) Our revenge shall be swift and terrible. We will go and collect our band and attack Tremorden Castle this very night.

Fred.
But—stay—

King.
Not a word! He is doomed!

TRIO.

King and Ruth.
Away, away! my heart's on fire,
　I burn this base deception to repay,
This very night my vengeance dire
　Shall glut itself in gore.
　　Away, away!

Fred.
Away, away! ere I expire—
　I find my duty hard to do to-day!
My heart is filled with anguish dire,
　It strikes me to the core.
　　Away, away!

King.
With falsehood foul
He tricked us of our brides.
　Let vengeance howl;
The Pirate so decides.
　Our nature stern
He softened with his lies,
　And, in return,
To-night the traitor dies.

All.
Yes, yes! to-night the traitor dies!

Ruth.
To-night he dies!

King.
Yes, or early to-morrow.

Fred.
His girls likewise?

Ruth.
They will welter in sorrow.

King.
　The one soft spot

Ruth.
In their natures they cherish—

Fred.
　And all who plot

King.
To abuse it shall perish!

All.
　To-night he dies—
　Away, away! &c.

[*Exeunt King and Ruth.*

44

Enter Mabel.

RECIT.—*Mabel.*

All is prepared, your gallant crew await you.
My Frederic in tears? It cannot be
That lion-heart quails at the coming conflict?

Fred.

No, Mabel, no. A terrible disclosure
Has just been made! Mabel, my dearly-
    loved one,
I bound myself to serve the pirate captain
Until I reached my one and twentieth birth-
    day—

Mabel.

But you *are* twenty-one?

Fred.

            I've just discovered
That I was born in leap-year, and that birth-
    day
Will not be reached by me till 1940.

Mabel.

Oh, horrible! catastrophe appalling!

Fred.

And so, farewell!

Mabel.

No, no! Ah, Frederic, hear me.

DUET.—*Mabel and Fred.*

Mabel.

Stay, Frederic, stay!
    They have no legal claim,
    No shadow of a shame
    Will fall upon thy name.
Stay, Frederic, stay!

Fred.

Nay, Mabel, nay!
    To-night I quit these walls,
    The thought my soul appals,
    But when stern Duty calls,
I must obey.

Mabel.

Stay, Frederic, stay!

Fred.

Nay, Mabel, nay!

Mabel.

They have no claim—

Fred.

    But Duty's name!
    The thought my soul appals,
    But when stern Duty calls,
I must obey.

BALLAD.—*Mabel.*

Ah, leave me not to pine
    Alone and desolate;
No fate seemed fair as mine,
    No happiness so great!
And nature, day by day,
    Has sung, in accents clear,

This joyous roundelay,
    "He loves thee—he is here.
    Fa-la, la-la, Fa-la."

Fred.

Ah, must I leave thee here
    In endless night to dream,
Where joy is dark and drear,
    And sorrow all supreme!
Where nature, day by day,
    Will sing, in altered tone,
This weary roundelay,
    "He loves thee—he is gone.
    Fa-la, la-la, Fa-la."

Both.

        Fa-la, la-la, Fa-la!

Fred.

In 1940 I of age shall be,
I'll then return, and claim you—I declare it!

Mabel.

        It seems so long!

Fred.

Swear that, till then, you will be true to me.

Mabel.

        Yes, I'll be strong!
By all the Stanleys dead and gone, I swear it!

ENSEMBLE.

Oh, here is love, and here is truth,
    And here is food for joyous laughter
He } will be faithful to } his } sooth
She }   } her }
Till we are wed, and even after.

[*Frederic rushes to window and leaps out.*

Mabel (almost fainting).

No, I am brave! Oh, family descent,
How great thy charm, thy sway how ex-
    cellent!
Come, one and all, undaunted men in blue,
A crisis, now, affairs are coming to!

Enter Police, marching in single file.

Serg.

Though in body and in mind,
    Tarantara, tarantara!
We are timidly inclined,
    Tarantara!
And anything but blind,
    Tarantara, tarantara!
To the danger that's behind,
    Tarantara!
Yet, when the danger's near,
    Tarantara, tarantara!
We manage to appear,
    Tarantara!
As insensible to fear
As anybody here.
    Tarantara, tarantara-ra-ra-ra-ra!

45

Mabel.

Sergeant, approach! Young Frederic was to have led you to death and glory.

All.

That is not a pleasant way of putting it.

Mabel.

No matter; he will not so lead you, for he has allied himself once more with his old associates.

All.

He has acted shamefully!

Mabel.

You speak falsely. You know nothing about it. He has acted nobly.

All.

He has acted nobly!

Mabel.

Dearly as I loved him before, his heroic sacrifice to his sense of duty has endeared him to me tenfold. He has done his duty. I will do mine. Go ye and do yours.

[*Exit Mabel.*

All.

Right oh!

Serg.

This is perplexing.

All.

We cannot understand it at all.

Serg.

Still, as he is actuated by a sense of duty—

All.

That makes a difference, of course. At the same time we repeat, we cannot understand it at all.

Serg.

No matter; our course is clear. We must do our best to capture these pirates alone. It is most distressing to us to be the agents whereby our erring fellow creatures are deprived of that liberty which is so dear to all— but we should have thought of that before we joined the force.

All.

We should!

Serg.

It is too late now!

All.

It is!

Song.—*Serg.*

When a felon's not engaged in his employment—

All.

His employment,

Or maturing his felonious little plans—

All.

Little plans,

Serg.

His capacity for innocent enjoyment—

All.

'Cent enjoyment

Serg.

Is just as great as any honest man's—

All.

Honest man's.

Serg.

Our feelings we with difficulty smother—

All.

'Culty smother

Serg.

When constabulary duty's to be done—

All.

To be done.

Serg.

Ah, take one consideration with another—

All.

With another,

Serg.

A policeman's lot is not a happy one.

All.

When constabulary duty's to be done—
To be done,
The policeman's lot is not a happy one.

Serg.

When the enterprising burglar's not a-burgling—

All.

Not a-burgling,

Serg.

When the cut-throat isn't occupied in crime—

All.

'Pied in crime,

Serg.

He loves to hear the little brook a-gurgling—

All.

Brook a-gurgling,

Serg.

And listen to the merry village chime—

All.

Village chime.
When the coster's finished jumping on his mother—

All.

On his mother,

Serg.

He loves to lie a-basking in the sun—

All.

In the sun.

Serg.

Ah, take one consideration with another—

All.

With another,

Serg.
The policeman's lot is not a happy one.

All.
When constabulary duty's to be done—
　　To be done,
The policeman's lot is not a happy one—
　　Happy one.

(*Chorus of Pirates without, in the distance.*)
A rollicking band of pirates we,
Who, tired of tossing on the sea,
Are trying their hand at a burglaree,
　　With weapons grim and gory.

Serg.
Hush, hush! I hear them on the manor
　　poaching,
With stealthy step the pirates are approach-
　　ing.

(*Chorus of Pirates, resumed nearer.*)
We are not coming for plate or gold—
A story General Stanley's told—
We seek a penalty fifty-fold,
　　For General Stanley's story.

Police.
They seek a penalty—

Pirates (*without*).
　　Fifty-fold,
We seek a penalty—

Police.
　　Fifty-fold,

All. {We　} seek a penalty fifty-fold,
　　　 {They}
　　For General Stanley's story.

Serg.
· They come in force, with stealthy stride,
　　Our obvious course is now—to hide.

(*Police conceal themselves. As they do so,
the Pirates are seen appearing at ruined window. They enter cautiously, and come down
stage. Samuel is laden with burglarious tools
and pistols, &c.*)

　　CHORUS.—*Pirates* (*very loud*).

With cat-like tread,
　　Upon our prey we steal,
In silence dread
　　Our cautious way we feel,
No sound at all.
　　We never speak a word,
A fly's foot-fall
　　Would be distinctly heard—

Police (*pianissimo*).
　　Tarantara, tarantara!

Pirates.
So stealthily the pirate creeps,
While all the household soundly sleeps.
Come, friends, who plough the sea,
　　Truce to navigation,
　　Take another station;

Let's vary piracee
With a little burglaree!

Police (*pianissimo*).
　　Tarantara, tarantara!

Sam. (*distributing implements to various mem-
bers of the gang*).
Here's your crowbar and your centrebit,
Your life preserver—you may want to hit;
Your silent matches, your dark lantern seize,
Take your file and your skeletonic keys.

　　Enter King, Frederic, and Ruth.

All (*fortissimo*).
With cat-like tread, &c.

　　　　　RECIT.
Fred.
Hush, hush, not a word! I see a light inside!
The Major-General comes, so quickly hide!

Pirates.
Yes, yes, the Major-General comes! (*Pirates
conceal themselves.*)
[*Exeunt King, Frederic, Samuel, and Ruth.*

Police.
Yes, yes, the Major-General comes!

Gen. (*entering in dressing gown, carrying a
light*).
Yes, yes, the Major General comes!

　　　SOLO.—*General.*
Tormented with the anguish dread
　　Of falsehood unatoned,
I lay upon my sleepless bed,
　　And tossed and turned and groaned.
The man who finds his conscience ache
　　No peace at all enjoys,
And as I lay in bed awake
　　I thought I heard a noise.

Pirates.) He thought he heard a noise—ha! ha!
Police.) He thought he heard a noise—ha! ha!
Gen.
　No, all is still
　In dale, on hill;
My mind is set at ease.
　So still the scene—
　It must have been
The sighing of the breeze.
　　　BALLAD.—*General.*
Sighing softly to the river
　　Comes the loving breeze,
Setting nature all a-quiver,
　　Rustling through the trees—

All.
　　Through the trees.

Gen.
　And the brook, in rippling measure,
　　Laughs for very love,
While the poplars, in their pleasure,
　　Wave their arms above.

Police and Pirates.
Yes, the trees, for very love,
Wave their leafy arms above,
River, river, little river,
May thy loving prosper e'er.
Heaven speed thee, poplar tree,
May thy wooing happy be.

Gen.
Yet, the breeze is but a rover,
When he wings away!
Brook and poplar mourn a lover!
Sighing well-a-day!

All.
Well-a-day!

Gen.
Ah! the doing and undoing,
That the rogue could tell,
When the breeze is out a-wooing,
Who can woo so well?

Police and Pirates.
Shocking tales the rogue could tell,
Nobody can woo so well.
Pretty brook, thy dream is over,
For thy love is but a rover!
Sad the lot of poplar trees,
Courted by the fickle breeze!

Enter the General's daughters, all in white peignoires and night-caps, and carrying lighted candles.

Girls.
Now what is this, and what is that, and why
does father leave his rest
At such a time of night as this, so very incompletely dressed?
Dear father is, and always was, the most
methodical of men!
It's his invariable rule to go to bed at half-past ten.
What strange occurrence can it be that calls
dear father from his rest
At such a time of night as this, so very incompletely dressed?
Enter King, Samuel, and Frederic.

King.
Forward, my men, and seize that General
there! (*They seize the General.*)

Girls.
The pirates! the pirates! Oh, despair!

Pirates (springing up).
Yes, we're the pirates, so despair!

Gen.
Frederic here! Oh, joy! Oh, rapture!
Summon your men and effect their capture!

Mabel.
Frederic, save us!

Fred.
Beautiful Mabel,
I would if I could, but I am not able.

Pirates.
He's telling the truth, he is not able.

King.
With base deceit
You worked upon our feelings!
Revenge is sweet,
And flavours all our dealings!
With courage rare
And resolution manly,
For death prepare,
Unhappy General Stanley!

Mabel (wildly).
Is he to die, unshriven—unannealed?

Girls.
Oh, spare him!

Mabel.
Will no one in his cause a weapon wield?

Girls.
Oh, spare him!

Police (springing up).
Yes, we are here, though hitherto concealed!

Girls.
Oh, rapture!

Police.
So to Constabulary, pirates yield!

Girls.
Oh, rapture!

(*A struggle ensues between Pirates and Police. Eventually the Police are overcome, and fall prostrate, the Pirates standing over them with drawn swords.*)

Chorus of Police and Pirates.

You⎱
We⎰ triumph now, for well we trow

Our ⎱
Your⎰ mortal career's cut short,

No pirate band will take its stand
At the Central Criminal Court.

Serg.
To gain a brief advantage you've contrived,
But your proud triumph will not be long-lived.

King.
Don't say you are orphans, for we know that
game.

Serg.
On your allegiance we've a stronger claim—
We charge you yield, in Queen Victoria's
name!

King (baffled).
You do!

Police.
We do!
We charge you yield, in Queen Victoria's
name!

(*Pirates kneel, Police stand over them triumphantly.*)

King.
We yield at once, with humbled mien,
Because, with all our faults, we love our
  Queen.

Police.
Yes, yes, with all their faults, they love their
  Queen

All.
Yes, yes, with all, &c.

(Police holding Pirates by the collar, take out handkerchiefs and weep.)

Gen.
Away with them, and place them at the bar!

Enter Ruth.

Ruth.
One moment! let me tell you who they are.
They are no members of the common throng;
They are all noblemen, who have gone
  wrong!

Girls.
They are all noblemen, who have gone wrong.

Gen.
No Englishman unmoved that statement
  hears,

Because, with all our faults, we love our
  House of Peers.

RECIT.—*General.*

I pray you pardon me, ex-Pirate King,
Peers will be peers, and youth will have its
  fling.
Resume your ranks, and legislative duties,
And take my daughters, all of whom are
  beauties.

FINALE.

Poor wandering ones!
  Though ye have surely strayed,
  Take heart of grace,
  Your steps retrace,
Poor wandering ones!
Poor wandering ones!
  If such poor love as ours
  Can help you find
  True peace of mind,
Why, take it, it is yours!

All.
Poor wandering ones! &c.

HAIL POETRY

A POLICEMAN'S LOT

Authentic Libretto
of the new
GILBERT AND SULLIVAN LIBRARY

IOLANTHE;

OR,

THE PEER AND THE PERI

BY

Sir W. S. GILBERT

AND

Sir ARTHUR S. SULLIVAN

The Bass Publishers

IOLANTHE;

OR,

THE PEER AND THE PERI.

Dramatis Personae

THE LORD CHANCELLOR

EARL OF MOUNTARARAT

EARL TOLLOLLER

PRIVATE WILLIS (*of the Grenadier Guards*)

STREPHON (*an Arcadian Shepherd*)

QUEEN OF THE FAIRIES

IOLANTHE (*a Fairy, Strephon's Mother*)

CELIA }

LEILA } *Fairies*

FLETA }

PHYLLIS (*an Arcadian Shepherdess and Ward in Chancery*)

CHORUS OF DUKES, MARQUISES, EARLS, VISCOUNTS, BARONS, AND FAIRIES.

ACT I.—An Arcadian Landscape.

ACT. II.—Palace Yard, Westminster.

Date—between 1700 and 1882.

IOLANTHE;

OR,

THE PEER AND THE PERI.

▼▼▼▼▼▼▼

ACT I.

Scene.—*An Arcadian Landscape. A river runs around the back of the Stage.*
A rustic bridge crosses the river.

Enter Fairies, led by Leila, Celia, and Fleta. They trip around the stage, singing as they dance.

CHORUS.

Tripping hither, tripping thither,
Nobody knows why or whither;
We must dance and we must sing,
Round about our fairy ring!

Solo.—*Celia.*

We are dainty little fairies,
  Ever singing, ever dancing;
We indulge in our vagaries
  In a fashion most intrancing.
If you ask the special function
  Of our never-ceasing motion,
We reply, without compunction,
  That we haven't any notion!

CHORUS.

No, we haven't any notion!
Tripping hither, &c.

Solo.—*Leila.*

If you ask us how we live,
Lovers all essentials give—
  We can ride on lovers' sighs,
  Warm ourselves in lovers' eyes,
  Bathe ourselves in lovers' tears,
  Clothe ourselves with lovers' fears,
  Arm ourselves with lovers' darts,
  Hide ourselves in lovers' hearts.
When you know us, you'll discover
That we almost live on lover!

CHORUS.

Yes! we live on lover!
  Tripping hither, &c.

(*At the end of chorus, all sigh wearily.*)

Celia. Ah, it's all very well, but since our Queen banished Iolanthe, fairy revels have not been what they were!

Leila. Iolanthe was the life and soul of Fairyland. Why, she wrote all our songs and arranged all our dances! We sing her songs and we trip her measures, but we don't enjoy ourselves!

Fleta. To think that five-and-twenty years have elapsed since she was banished! What could she have done to have deserved so terrible a punishment?

Leila. Something awful! She married a mortal!

Fleta. Oh! Is it injudicious to marry a mortal?

Leila. Injudicious? It strikes at the root of the whole fairy system! By our laws, the fairy who marries a mortal, dies!

Celia. But Iolanthe didn't die!

Enter Fairy Queen.

Queen. No, because your Queen, who loved her with a surpassing love, commuted her sentence to penal servitude for life, on condition that she left her husband and never communicated with him again!

Leila. That sentence of penal servitude she is now working out, on her head, at the bottom of that stream!

Queen. Yes, but when I banished her, I gave her all the pleasant places of the earth to dwell in. I'm sure, I never intended that she should go and live at the bottom of a stream! It makes me perfectly wretched to think of the discomfort she must have undergone!

Leila. Think of the damp! And her chest was always delicate.

Queen. And the frogs! Ugh! I never shall enjoy any peace of mind until I know why Iolanthe went to live among the frogs!

Fleta. Then why not summon her and ask her?

Queen. Why? Because if I set eyes on her I should forgive her at once!

Celia. Then why not forgive her? Twenty-five years—it's a long time!

Leila. Think how we loved her!

Queen. Loved her? What was your love to mine? Why, she was invaluable to me! Who taught me to curl myself inside a buttercup? Iolanthe! Who taught me to swing upon a cobweb? Iolanthe! Who taught me to dive into a dewdrop—to nestle in a nutshell—to gambol upon gossamer? Iolanthe!

Leila. She certainly did surprising things!

Fleta. Oh, give her back to us, great Queen, for your sake if not for ours! (*All kneel in supplication.*)

Queen (*irresolute*). Oh, I should be strong, but I am weak! I should be marble, but I am clay! Her punishment has been heavier than I intended. I did not mean that she should live among the frogs—and—well, well, it shall be as you wish—it shall be as you wish!

INVOCATION.—*Queen.*
Iolanthe!
From thy dark exile thou art summoned!
    Come to our call—
    Come, Iolanthe!

Celia. Iolanthe!

Leila. Iolanthe!

All. Come to our call,
    Iolanthe! Come!

Iolanthe rises from the water. She is clad in water-weeds. She approaches the Queen with head bent and arms crossed.

Iolanthe. With humbled breast
    And every hope laid low,
To thy behest,
    Offended queen, I bow!

Queen. For a dark sin against our fairy laws,
We sent thee into life-long banishment;
But mercy holds her sway within our hearts—
Rise—thou art pardoned!

Iol. Pardoned!

All. Pardoned!

(*Her weeds fall from her, and she appears clothed as a fairy. The Queen places a diamond coronet on her head, and embraces her. The others also embrace her.*)

CHORUS.
Welcome to our hearts again,
    Iolanthe! Iolanthe!
We have shared thy bitter pain,
    Iolanthe! Iolanthe!
Every heart and every hand
In our loving little band
Welcome thee to Fairyland.
    Iolanthe!

Queen. And now, tell me, with all the world to choose from, why on earth did you decide to live at the bottom of that stream?

Iol. To be near my son, Strephon.

Queen. Bless my heart, I didn't know you had a son.

Iol. He was born soon after I left my husband by your royal command—but he does not even know of his father's existence.

Fleta. How old is he?

Iol. Twenty-four.

Leila. Twenty-four! No one, to look at you, would think you had a son of twenty-four! But that's one of the advantages of being immortal. We never grow old! Is he pretty?

Iol. He's extremely pretty, but he's inclined to be stout.

All (*disappointed*). Oh!

Queen. I see no objection to stoutness, in moderation.

Celia. And what is he?

Iol. He's an Arcadian shepherd—and he loves Phyllis, a Ward in Chancery.

Celia. A mere shepherd! and he half a fairy!

Iol. He's a fairy down to the waist—but his legs are mortal.

All. Dear me!

Queen. I have no reason to suppose that I am more curious than other people, but I confess I should like to see a person who is a fairy down to the waist, but whose legs are mortal.

Iol. Nothing easier, for here he comes!

Enter Strephon, singing and dancing and playing on a flageolet. He does not see the Fairies, who retire up stage as he enters.

SONG.—*Strephon.*
Good morrow, good mother!
    Good mother, good morrow!
By some means or other,
    Pray banish your sorrow!
        With joy beyond telling
        My bosom is swelling,
        So join in a measure
        Expressive of pleasure.
For I'm to be married to-day—to-day—
    Yes, I'm to be married to-day!

Chorus (*aside*).
    Yes, he's to be married to-day—to-day—
    Yes, he's to be married to-day!

Iol. Then the Lord Chancellor has at last given his consent to your marriage with his beautiful ward, Phyllis?

Streph. Not he, indeed. To all my tearful prayers he answers me, "A shepherd lad is no fit helpmate for a ward of Chancery." I stood in court, and there I sang him songs of Arcadee; with flageolet accompaniment—in vain. At first he seemed amused, so did the bar; but quickly wearying of my song and pipe, bade me get out. A servile usher then, in crumpled bands and rusty bombazine, led me, still singing, into Chancery Lane! I'll go no more; I'll marry her to-day, and brave the upshot, be it what it may! (*Sees Fairies.*) But who are these?

Iol. Oh, Strephon! rejoice with me, my Queen has pardoned me!

Streph. Pardoned you, mother? This is good news indeed.

Iol. And these ladies are my beloved sisters.

Streph. Your sisters! Then they are—my aunts!

Queen. A pleasant piece of news for your bride on her wedding day!

Streph. Hush! My bride knows nothing of my fairyhood. I dare not tell her, lest it frighten her. She thinks me mortal, and prefers me so.

Leila. Your fairyhood doesn't seem to have done you much good.

Streph. Much good! My dear aunt—it's the curse of my existence! What's the use of being half a fairy? My body can creep through a keyhole, but what's the good of that when my legs are left kicking behind? I can make myself invisible down to the waist, but that's of no use when my legs remain exposed to view? My brain is a fairy brain, but from the waist downwards I'm a gibbering idiot. My upper half is immortal, but my lower half grows older every day, and some day or other must die of old age. What's to become of my upper half when I've buried my lower half I really don't know!

Fairies. Poor fellow!

Queen. I see your difficulty, but with a fairy brain you should seek an intellectual sphere of action. Let me see. I've a borough or two at my disposal. Would you like to go into Parliament?

Iol. A fairy Member! That would be delightful!

Streph. I'm afraid I should do no good there—you see, down to the waist I'm a Tory of the most determined description, but my legs are a couple of confounded Radicals, and, on a division, they'd be sure to take me into the wrong lobby. You see, they're two to one, which is a strong working majority.

Queen. Don't let that distress you; you shall be returned as a Liberal-Conservative, and your legs shall be our peculiar care.

Streph. (*bowing.*) I see your Majesty does not do things by halves.

Queen. No, we are fairies down to the feet.

Ensemble.

Queen.
Fare thee well, attractive stranger.
Fairies.
Fare thee well, attractive stranger.

Queen.
Shouldst thou be in doubt or danger,
Peril or perplexitee,
Call us, and we'll come to thee!

Fairies.
Aye! Call us, and we'll come to thee!
Tripping hither, tripping thither,
Nobody knows why or whither;
We must now be taking wing
To another fairy ring!

(*Fairies and Queen trip off. Iolanthe, who takes an affectionate farewell of her son, going off last.*)

Enter Phyllis, singing and dancing, and accompanying herself on a flageolet.

Song.—*Phyllis.*
Good morrow, good lover!
    Good lover, good morrow!
I prithee discover,
    Steal, purchase, or borrow,
        Some means of concealing
        The care you are feeling,
    And join in a measure
    Expressive of pleasure,
For we're to be married to-day—to-day!
    Yes, we're to be married to-day!

Both.
    Yes, we're to be married, &c.

Streph. (*embracing her*). My Phyllis! And to-day we are to be made happy for ever.

Phyl. Well, we're to be married.

Streph. It's the same thing.

Phyl. I suppose it is. But, oh, Strephon, I tremble at the step I'm taking! I believe it's penal servitude for life to marry a Ward of Court without the Lord Chancellor's consent! I shall be of age in two years. Don't you think you could wait two years?

Streph. Two years. Have you ever looked in the glass?

Phyl. No, never.

Streph. Here, look at that (*showing her a pocket mirror*), and tell me if you think it rational to expect me to wait two years?

Phyl. (*looking at herself*). No. You're quite right—it's asking too much. One must be reasonable.

Streph. Besides, who knows what will happen in two years? Why, you might fall in love with the Lord Chancellor himself by that time!

Phyl. Yes. He's a clean old gentleman.

Streph. As it is, half the House of Lords are sighing at your feet.

Phyl. The House of Lords are certainly extremely attentive.

Streph. Attentive? I should think they were! Why did five-and-twenty Liberal Peers come down to shoot over your grass-plot last autumn? It couldn't have been the sparrows. Why did five-and-twenty Conservative Peers come down to fish your pond? Don't tell me it was the gold-fish! No, no—delays are dangerous, and if we are to marry, the sooner the better.

DUET.—*Strephon and Phyllis.*

Phyllis.
None shall part us from each other,
    One in life and death are we;
All in all to one another—
    I to thee and thou to me!

Both.
Thou the tree and I the flower—
    Thou the idol; I the throng—
Thou the day and I the hour—
    Thou the singer; I the song!

Streph.
All in all since that fond meeting,
    When, in joy, I woke to find
Mine the heart within thee beating,
    Mine the love that heart enshrined!

Both.
Thou the stream and I the willow—
    Thou the sculptor; I the clay—
Thou the ocean; I the billow—
    Thou the sunrise; I the day!

(*Exeunt Strephon and Phyllis together.*)
March. Enter Procession of Peers.

CHORUS.

Loudly let the trumpet bray!
    Tantantara!
Proudly bang the sounding brasses!
    Tzing! Boom!
As upon its lordly way
    This unique procession passes,
    Tantantara! Tzing! Boom!
Bow, bow, ye lower middle classes!
Bow, bow, ye tradesmen, bow, ye masses!
Blow the trumpets bang the brasses!
    Tantantara! Tzing! Boom!
We are peers of highest station
Paragons of legislation,
Pillars of the British nation!
    Tantantara! Tzing! Boom!

Enter the Lord Chancellor, followed by his train-bearer.

SONG.—*Lord Chancellor.*

The Law is the true embodiment
Of everything that's excellent,
It has no kind of fault or flaw,
And I, my lords, embody the Law.
The constitutional guardian I
Of pretty young Wards in Chancery,
All very agreeable girls—and none
Are over the age of twenty-one,
A pleasant occupation for
A rather susceptible Chancellor!

All.   A pleasant, &c.

But though the compliment implied
Inflates me with legitimate pride,
It nevertheless can't be denied
That it has its inconvenient side.
For I'm not so old, and not so plain,
And I'm quite prepared to marry again,
But there'd be the deuce to pay in the Lords
If I fell in love with one of my Wards!
    Which rather tries my temper, for
    I'm *such* a susceptible Chancellor!

All.   Which rather, &c.

And every one who'd marry a Ward
Must come to me for my accord,
And in my court I sit all day,
Giving agreeable girls away,
With one for him—and one for he—
And one for you—and one for ye—
And one for thou—and one for thee—
But never, oh never a one for me!
    Which is exasperating, for
    A highly susceptible Chancellor!

All.   Which is, &c.
    Enter Lord Tolloller.

Lord Toll. And now, my Lords, to the business of the day.

Lord Ch. By all means. Phyllis, who is a Ward of Court, has so powerfully affected your Lordships, that you have appealed to me in a body to give her to whichever one of you she may think proper to select, and a noble Lord has just gone to her cottage to request her immediate attendance. It would be idle to deny that I, myself, have the misfortune to be singularly attracted by this young person. My regard for her is rapidly undermining my constitution. Three months ago I was stout man. I need say no more. If I could reconcile it with my duty, I should unhesitatingly award her to myself, for I can conscientiously say that I know no man who is so well fitted to render her exceptionally happy. (Peers: Hear, hear!) But such an award would be open to misconstruction, and therefore, at whatever personal inconvenience, I waive my claim.

Lord Toll. My Lord, I desire, on the part of this House, to express its sincere sympathy with your Lordship's most painful position.

Lord Ch. I thank your Lordships. The feelings of a Lord Chancellor who is in love with a Ward of Court are not to be envied. What is his position? Can he give his own consent to his own marriage with his own Ward? Can he marry his own Ward without his own consent? And if he marries his own Ward, without his own consent, can he commit himself for contempt of his own Court? And if he commit himself for contempt of his own Court, can he appear by counsel before himself, to move for arrest of his own judgment? Ah, my Lords, it is indeed painful to have to sit upon a woolsack which is stuffed with such thorns as these!

Enter Lord Mountararat.

Lord Mount. My Lords, I have much pleasure in announcing that I have succeeded in inducing the young person to present herself at the Bar of this House.

Enter Phyllis.

Recit.—*Phyl.*

My well-loved Lord and Guardian dear,
You summoned me, and I am here!

Chorus of Peers.

Oh, rapture, how beautiful!
How gentle—how dutiful!

Solo.—*Lord Tolloller.*

Of all the young ladies I know
  This pretty young lady's the fairest;
Her lips have the rosiest show,
  Her eyes are the richest and rarest.
Her origin's lowly, it's true,
  But of birth and position I've plenty;
I've grammar and spelling for two,
  And blood and behaviour for twenty!
    Her origin's lowly it's true,
     I've grammar and spelling for two;
Chorus. Of birth and position he's plenty,
    With blood and behaviour for twenty!

Solo.—*Lord Mountararat.*

Though the views of the House have diverged
  On every conceivable motion,
All questions of Party are merged
  In a frenzy of love and devotion;
If you ask us distinctly to say
  What Party we claim to belong to,
We reply, without doubt or delay,
  The Party we're singing this song to!
    If you ask us distinctly to say,
    We reply, without doubt or delay,
    The Party we claim to belong to
    Is the Party we're singing this song to!

Solo.—*Phyllis.*

I'm very much pained to refuse,
  But I'll stick to my pipes and my tabors;
I can spell all the words that I use,
  And my grammar's as good as my neighbours'.
As for birth—I was born like the rest,
  My behaviour is rustic but hearty,
And I know where to turn for the best,

When I want a particular Party!
Chorus. Though her station is none of the best,
  I suppose she was born like the rest;
  She knows where to look for her hearty,
  When she wants a particular Party!

Recit.—*Phyllis.*

Nay, tempt me not.
  To wealth I'll not be bound:
In lowly cot
  Alone is virtue found!

Chorus. No, no; indeed high rank will never hurt you,
  The Peerage is not destitute of virtue.

Ballad.—*Lord Tolloller.*

Spurn not the nobly born
  With love affected,
Nor treat with virtuous scorn
  The well connected.
High rank involves no shame—
We boast an equal claim
With him of humble name
  To be respected!
Blue blood! Blue blood!
  When virtuous love is sought
  Thy power is naught,
Though dating from the flood,
  Blue blood!
Chorus. When virtuous love is sought, &c.

Spare us the bitter pain
  Of stern denials,
Nor with lowborn disdain
  Augment our trials.
Hearts just as pure and fair
May beat in Belgrave Square
As in the lowly air
  Of Seven Dials!
Blue blood! Blue blood!
  Of what avail art thou
  To serve us now?
Though dating from the flood,
  Blue blood!
Chorus. Of what avail art thou, &c.

Recit.—*Phyllis.*

My Lords, it may not be.
  With grief my heart is riven!
You waste your time on me,
  For ah! my heart is given!
All. Given!
Phyl. Yes, given!
All. Oh, horror!!!

Recit.—*Lord Chancellor.*

And who has dared to brave our high displeasure,
  And thus defy our definite command?

56

Enter Strephon.

Streph. 'Tis I—young Strephon! mine this
priceless treasure!
Against the world I claim my darling's hand!

(*Phyllis rushes to his arms.*)

A shepherd I—
All.   A shepherd he!
Streph. Of Arcady—
All.   Of Arcadee!
Streph. Bethrothed are we!
All.   Bethrothed are they—
Streph. And mean to be—
All.   Espoused to-day!

ENSEMBLE.

Streph. A shepherd I
Of Arcady,
Bethrothed are we,
And mean to be
Espoused to-day!

The Others. A shepherd he
Of Arcadee,
Betrothed is he,
And means to be
Espoused to-day!

DUET.—*Lord Mountararat and Lord Tolloller*
(*aside to each other*).

'Neath this blow,
Worse than stab of dagger—
Though we mo-
Mentarily stagger,
In each heart
Proud are we innately—
Let's depart,
Dignified and stately!

All.   Let's depart,
Dignified and stately!

Chorus of Peers.

Though our hearts she's badly bruising,
In another suitor choosing,
Let's pretend it's most amusing,
Ha! ha! ha! Tan-ta-ra!

(*Exeunt all the Peers, marching round stage
with much dignity. Lord Chancellor separates
Phyllis from Strephon and orders her off.
She follows Peers. Manent Lord Chancellor
and Strephon.*)

Lord Ch. Now, sir, what excuse have you to
offer for having disobeyed an order of the
Court of Chancery?

Streph. My Lord, I know no Courts of
Chancery; I go by Nature's Acts of Parliament.
The bees—the breeze—the seas—the rooks—
the brooks—the gales—the vales—the fountains
and the mountains, cry "You love this maiden—
take her, we command you!" 'Tis writ in heaven
by the bright barbed dart that leaps forth into
lurid light from each grim thundercloud. The
very rain pours forth her sad and sodden sympathy! When chorussed Nature bids me take
my love, shall I reply, "Nay, but a certain
Chancellor forbids it"? Sir, you are England's
Lord High Chancellor, but are you Chancellor
of birds and trees, King of the winds and
Prince of thunderclouds?

Lord Ch. No. It's a nice point. I don't
know that I ever met it before. But my difficulty is that at present there's no evidence before the Court that chorussed Nature has interested herself in the matter.

Streph. No evidence! You have my word
for it. I tell you that she bade me take my love.

Lord Ch. Ah! but, my good sir, you mustn't
tell us what she told you—it's not evidence.
Now an affidavit from a thunderstorm, or a
few words on oath from a heavy shower, would
meet with all the attention they deserve.

Streph. And have you the heart to apply the
prosaic rules of evidence to a case which bubbles over with poetical emotion?

Lord Ch. Distinctly. I have always kept
my duty strictly before my eyes, and it is to
that fact that I owe my advancement to my
present distinguished position.

SONG.—*Lord Chancellor.*

When I went to the Bar as a very young
man,
    (Said I to myself—said I,)
I'll work on a new and original plan,
    (Said I to myself—said I,)
I'll never assume that a rogue or a thief
Is a gentleman worthy implicit belief,
Because his attorney has sent me a brief,
    (Said I to myself—said I!)
Ere I go into court I will read my brief
through,
    (Said I to myself—said I,)
And I'll never take work I'm unable to do,
    (Said I to myself—said I,)
My learned profession I'll never disgrace
By taking a fee with a grin on my face,
When I haven't been there to attend to the
case,
    (Said I to myself—said I!)
I'll never throw dust in a juryman's eyes,
    (Said I to myself—said I,)
Or hoodwink a judge who is not over-wise,
    (Said I to myself—said I,)
Or assume that the witnesses summoned in
force
In Exchequer, Queen's Bench, Common
Pleas, or Divorce,
Have perjured themselves as a matter of
course,
    (Said I to myself—said I!)
In other professions in which men engage,
    (Said I to myself—said I,)

The Army, the Navy, the Church, and the
    Stage,
  (Said I to myself—said I,)
Professional licence, if carried too far,
Your chance of promotion will certainly
    mar—
And I fancy the rule might apply to the Bar,
  (Said I to myself—said I!)

                    [*Exit Lord Chancellor.*

        Enter Iolanthe.

Streph. Oh, Phyllis, Phyllis! To be taken
from you just as I was on the point of making
you my own! Oh, it's too much—it is too
much!

Iol. (*to Strephon, who is in tears*). My son
in tears—and on his wedding day!

Streph. My wedding day! Oh, mother, weep
with me, for the Law has interposed between
us, and the Lord Chancellor has separated us
for ever!

Iol. The Lord Chancellor! (*Aside.*) Oh,
if he did but know!

Streph. (*overhearing her*). If he did but
know what?

Iol. No matter! The Lord Chancellor has
no power over you. Remember you are half a
fairy. You can defy him—down to the waist.

Streph. Yes, but from the waist downwards
he can commit me to prison for years! Of
what avail is it that my body is free, if my legs
are working out seven years' penal servitude?

Iol. True. But take heart—our Queen has
promised you her special protection. I'll go
to her and lay your peculiar case before her.

Streph. My beloved mother! how can I repay the debt I owe you?

        FINALE.—*Quartet.*

(*As it commences, the Peers appear at the
back, advancing unseen and on tiptoe. Lord
Mountararat and Lord Tolloller lead Phyllis
between them, who listens in horror to what
she hears.*)

Streph. (*to Iolanthe*). When darky looms
    the day,
  And all is dull and grey,
  To chase the gloom away,
    On thee I'll call!

Phyl. (*speaking, aside to Lord Mountararat*).
What was that?

Lord Mount. (*aside to Phyllis*). I think I
heard him say,
  That on a rainy day,
  To while the time away,
    On her he'd call!

Chorus. We think we heard him say, &c.

(*Phyllis, much agitated at her lover's sup-
    posed faithlessness.*)

Iol. (*to Strephon*). When tempests wreck thy
    bark,
  And all is drear and dark,
  If thou shouldst need an Ark,
    I'll give thee one!

Phyl. (*speaking aside to Lord Tolloller*).
What was that?

Lord Toll. (*aside to Phyllis*). I heard the
    minx remark,
  She'd meet him after dark,
  Inside St. Jame's Park,
    And give him one!

Chorus. We heard the minx remark, &c.

Phyl. The prospect's very bad,
  My heart so sore and sad
  Will never more be glad
    As summer's sun.

Iol., Lord Toll., Streph., Lord Mount.
  The prospect's not so bad,
  $\begin{Bmatrix} My \\ Thy \end{Bmatrix}$ heart so sore and sad
  May very soon be glad
    As summer's sun;

Phyl., Iol., Lord Toll., Streph., Lord Mount.
  For when the sky is dark,
  And tempests wreck $\begin{Bmatrix} my \\ thy \\ his \end{Bmatrix}$ bark,
  If $\begin{Bmatrix} He\ should \\ I\ should \\ thou\ shouldst \end{Bmatrix}$ need an Ark,
  $\begin{Bmatrix} She'll \\ I'll \end{Bmatrix}$ give $\begin{Bmatrix} him \\ me \\ thee \end{Bmatrix}$ one!

Phyl. (*revealing herself*). Ah!

(*Iolanthe and Strephon much confused.*)

Phyl. Oh, shameless one, tremble!
  Nay, do not endeavour
  Thy fault to dissemble,
  We part—and for ever!
  I worshipped him blindly,
  He worships another—

Streph. Attend to me kindly,
  This lady's my mother!

Toll. This lady's his *what?*

Streph. This lady's my mother!

Tenors. This lady's his *what?*

Basses. He says she's his mother!

(*They point derisively to Iolanthe, laughing heartily at her. She goes for protection to
Strephon.*)

  Enter Lord Chancellor. Iolanthe veils herself.

Lord Ch. What means this mirth unseemly,
  That shakes the listening earth?

Lord Toll. The joke is good extremely,
  And justifies our mirth.

Lord Mount. This gentleman is seen,
  With a maid of seventeen,
  A-taking of his *dolce far niente;*
  And wonders he'd achieve,
  For he asks us to believe.
She's his mother—and he's nearly five-and-
  twenty!

Lord Ch. (*sternly*). Recollect yourself, I
  pray,
  And be careful what you say—
As the ancient Romans said, *festina lente,*
  For I really do not see
  How so young a girl could be
The mother of a man of five-and-twenty.

All.   Ha! ha! ha! ha! ha!

Streph. My Lord, of evidence I have no
  dearth—
She is—has been—my mother from my birth!

BALLAD.

  In babyhood
Upon her lap I lay,
  With infant food
She moistenèd my clay;
  Had she withheld
The succour she supplied,
  By hunger quelled,
Your Strephon might have died!

Lord Ch. (*much moved*).
  Had that refreshment been denied,
  Indeed our Strephon might have died!

All (*much affected*).
  Had that refreshment been denied,
  Indeed our Strephon might have died!

Lord Mount. But as she's not
    His mother, it appears,
  Why weep these hot
    Unnecessary tears?
  And by what laws
    Should we, so joyously
  Rejoice, because
    Our Strephon did not die?
Oh, rather let us pipe our eye
Because our Strephon did not die!

All. That's very true—let's pipe our eye
Because our Strephon did not die!

(*All weep. Iolanthe, who has succeeded in
hiding her face from the Lord Chancellor, es-
capes unnoticed.*)

Phyl. Go, traitorous one—for ever we must
  part:
To one of you, my Lords, I give my heart!

All.   Oh, rapture!

Streph. Hear me, Phyllis, ere you leave me,

Phyl. Not a word—you did deceive me,

All. Not a word—you did deceive her.

(*Exit Strephon.*)
BALLAD —*Phyllis.*

For riches and rank I do not long—

Their pleasures are false and vain;
I gave up the love of a lordly throng
  For the love of a simple swain.
But now that simple swain's untrue,
With sorrowful heart I turn to you—
  A heart that's aching,
  Quaking, breaking,
As sorrowful hearts are wont to do!
The riches and rank that you befall
  Are the only baits you use,
So the richest and rankiest of you all
  My sorrowful heart shall choose.
As none are so noble—none so rich
As this couple of lords, I'll find a niche
  In my heart that's aching,
  Quaking, breaking,
For one of you two—and I don't care
  which!

ENSEMBLE.

Phyl. (*to Lord Mountararat and Lord Tolloller*).
  To you I give my heart so rich!

All (*puzzled*). To which?

Phyl. I do not care!
  To you I yield—it is my doom!

All. To whom?

Phyl. I'm not aware!
  I'm yours for life if you but choose.

All. She's whose?

Phyl. That's your affair;
  I'll be a countess, shall I not?

All. Of what?

Phyl. I do not care!

All. Lucky little lady!
  Strephon's lot is shady;
  Rank, it seems, is vital,
  "Countess" is the title,
  But of what I'm not aware!

Enter Strephon.

Streph. Can I inactive see my fortunes
  fade?
    No, no!

Peers. Ho! Ho!

Streph. Mighty protectress, hasten to my
aid!

(*Enter Fairies, tripping, headed by Celia,
Leila, and Fleta, and followed by Queen.*)

CHORUS OF FAIRIES.

Tripping hither, tripping thither,
Nobody knows why or whither;
Why you want us we don't know,
But you've summoned us, and so
  Enter all the little fairies
    To their usual tripping measure!
To oblige you all our care is—
    Tell us, pray, what is your pleasure!

Streph. The lady of my love has caught me talking to another—

Peers. Oh, fie! young Strephon is a rogue!

Streph. I tell her very plainly that the lady is my mother—

Peers. Taradiddle, taradiddle, tol lol lay!

Streph. She won't believe my statement, and declares we must be parted,
Because on a career of double-dealing I have started,
Then gives her hand to one of these, and leaves me broken-hearted—

Peers. Taradiddle, taradiddle, tol lol lay!

Queen. Ah, cruel ones, to separate two lovers from each other!

Fairies. Oh, fie! our Strephon's not a rogue!

Queen. You've done him an injustice, for the lady *is* his mother!

Fairies. Taradiddle, taradiddle, tol lol lay!

Lord Ch. That fable perhaps may serve his turn as well as any other.

(*aside*). I didn't see her face, but if they fondled one another,
And she's but seventeen—I don't believe it was his mother!

(*aloud*). Taradiddle, taradiddle.

Fairies. Tol lol lay!

Lord Toll. I have often had a use
For a thorough-bred excuse
Of a sudden (which is English for *"re-pentè"*),
But of all I ever heard
This is much the most absurd,
For she's seventeen, and he is five-and-twenty!

All. Though she is seventeen, and he is only five-and-twenty!

Peers. Oh, fie! young Strephon is a rogue!

Fairies. Oh, fie! our Strephon's not a rogue.

Lord Mount. Now listen, pray, to me,
For this paradox will be
Carried, nobody at all *contradicentc.*
Her age, upon the date
Of his birth, was *minus* eight,
If she's seventeen, and he is five-and-twenty!

All. To say she is his mother is an utter bit of folly!

Peers. Oh, fie! young Strephon is a rogue!

Fairies. Oh, fie! our Strephon's not a rogue.

All. Perhaps his brain is addled, and it's very melancholy!
Taradiddle, taradiddle, tol lol lay!
I wouldn't say a word that could be reckoned as injurious,
But to find a mother younger than her son is very curious,

And that's a kind of mother that is usually spurious.
Taradiddle, taradiddle, tol lol lay!

Lord Ch. Go away, madam;
I should say, madam,
You display, madam,
Shocking taste.

It is rude, madam,
To intrude, madam,
With your brood, madam,
Brazen-faced!

You come here, madam,
Interfere, madam,
With a peer, madam.
(I am one.)

You're aware, madam,
What you dare, madam,
So take care, madam,
And begone!

ENSEMBLE.

Fairies (to Queen).
Let us stay, madam;
I should say, madam,
They display madam,
Shocking taste.

It is rude madam,
To allude, madam,
To your brood, madam,
Brazen-faced!

We don't fear, madam,
Any peer, madam,
Though, my dear madam,
This is one.

They will stare, madam,
When aware, madam,
What they dare, madam—
What they've done!

Peers.

Go away, madam;
I should say, madam,
You display, madam,
Shocking taste.

It is rude, madam,
To intrude, madam,
With your brood, madam,
Brazen-faced!

You come here, madam,
Interfere, madam,
With a peer, madam,
(I am one.)

You're aware, madam,

What you dare, madam
So take care, madam,
And begone!

Queen (aside, furiously).
Bearded by these puny mortals!
I will launch from fairy portals
All the most terrific thunders
In my armoury of wonders!

Phyl. (aside).
Should they launch terrific wonders,
All would then repent their blunders.
Surely these must be immortals.

                    [Exit Phyllis.

Queen. Oh! Chancellor unwary,
It's highly necessary
    Your tongue to teach
    Respectful speech—
Your attitude to vary!
Your badinage so airy,
Your manner arbitrary,
    Are out of place
    When face to face
With an influential Fairy.

All the Peers (aside).
    We never knew
    We were talking to
An influential Fairy!

Lord Ch. A plague on this vagary
I'm in a nice quandary!
    Of hasty tone
    With dames unknown;
I ought to be more chary.
It seems that she's a fairy
From Andersen's library,
    And I took her for
    The proprietor
Of a Ladies' Seminary!

Peers.   We took her for
    The proprietor
Of a Ladies' Seminary!

Queen. When next your Houses do assemble,
You may tremble!

Celia. Our wrath, when gentlemen offend us,
Is tremendous!

Leila. They meet, who underrate our calling,
Doom appalling!

Queen. Take down our sentence as we speak it,
And *he* shall wreak it! *(Indicating Strephon.*

Peers. Oh, spare us!

Queen. Henceforth, Strephon, cast away
Crooks and pipes and ribbons so gay—
Flocks and herds that bleat and low!
Into Parliament you shall go!

All. Into Parliament he shall go!

Backed by {our / their} supreme authority,
    He'll command a large majority;
Into Parliament he shall go!

Queen. In the Parliamentary hive,
Liberal or Conservative—
Whig or Tory—I don't know—
But into Parliament you shall go!

Fairies. Into Parliament, &c.

Queen (speaking through music).
Every bill and every measure
That may gratify his pleasure,
Though your fury it arouses,
Shall be passed by both your Houses!

Peers. Oh!
You shall sit, if he sees reason,
Through the grouse and salmon season:

Peers. No!
He shall end the cherished rights
You enjoy on Friday nights:

Peers. No! No!
He shall prick that annual blister,
Marriage with deceased wife's sister:

Peers. Mercy!
Titles shall ennoble, then,
All the Common Councilmen:

Peers. Spare us!
Peers shall teem in Christendom,
    And a Duke's exalted station
Be attainable by Competitive Examination!

[Exeunt. Lord Chancellor, Lord Mountararat and Lord Tolloller.]

Peers. Oh, horror!

Fairies. Their horror!
They can't dissemble
Nor hide the fear that makes them tremble!

ENSEMBLE.

Peers.
Young Strephon is the kind of lout
We do not care a fig about!
    We cannot say
    What evils may
Result in consequence.
But lordly vengeance will pursue
All kinds of common people who
    Oppose our views,
    Or boldly choose
    To offer us offence.
Your powers we dauntlessly pooh-pooh:
A dire revenge will fall on you
    If you besiege
    Our high *prestige*
(The word "*prestige*" is French.)

Fairies, Queen and Strephon.
With Strephon for your foe, no doubt,
A fearful prospect opens out,
    And who shall say

What evils may
  Result in consequence?
A hideous vengeance will pursue
All noblemen who venture to
  Oppose his views,
  Or boldly choose
To offer him offence.
'Twill plunge them into grief and shame;
His kind forbearance they must claim,
  If they'd escape
  In any shape
A very painful wrench.
Although our threats you now pooh-pooh,
A dire revenge will fall on you,
  Should he besiege
  Your high *prestige*
(The word "*prestige*" is French.)

Peers. Our lordly style
    You shall not quench
  With base *canaille!*

Fairies. (That word is French.)

Peers. Distinction ebbs
    Before a herd
  Of vulgar *plebs!*

Fairies. (A Latin word.)

Peers. 'Twould fill with joy,
    And madness stark
  The οἱ πολλοί

Fairies. (A Greek remark.)

Peers. One Latin word, one Greek remark.
    And one that's French.

Fairies.   Your lordly style
    We'll quickly quence
  With base *canaille!*

Peers.   (That word is French.)

Fairies. Distinction ebbs
    Before a herd
  Of vulgar *plebs!*

Peers.   (A Latin word.)

Fairies. 'Twill fill with joy
    And madness stark
  · The οἱ πολλοί

Peers.   (A Greek remark.)

Fairies. One Latin word, one Greek remark,
    And one that's French.

Peers. You needn't wait,
    Away you fly!
  Your threatened hate
  We thus defy!

Fairies. We will not wait,
    We go sky-high!
  Our threatened hate
  You won't defy!

(*Fairies threaten Peers with their wands.
Enter Phyllis followed by Lord Chancellor,
Lord Mountararat and Lord Tolloller. She
implores Strephon to relent; he casts her from
him, and she falls fainting into the arms of
Lord Mountararat and Lord Tolloller.*)

END OF ACT I.

ACT II.

SCENE.—*Palace Yard, Westminster. Westminster Hall,* L. *Clocktower up,* R.C. *Private
Willis discovered on sentry,* R. *Moonlight.*

SONG.—*Private Willis.*

When all night long a chap remains
  On sentry-go, to chase monotony
He exercises of his brains,
  That is, assuming that he's got any.
Though never nurtured in the lap
  Of luxury, yet I admonish you,
I am an intellectual chap,
  And think of things that would astonish
    you.
    I often think it's comical—Fal, lal, la, la!
    How Nature always does contrive—Fal,
        lal, la, la!
    That every boy and every gal
      That's born into the world alive
    Is either a little Liberal
      Or else a little Conservative!
        Fal, lal, la!
When in that house M.P.'s divide,
  If they've a brain and cerebellum, too,
They've got to leave that brain outside,
  And vote just as their leaders tell 'em to.
But then the prospect of a lot
  Of dull M.P.'s in close proximity,
All thinking for themselves, is what
  No man can face with equanimity.
    Then let's rejoice with loud Fal, lal, la,
        la!
    That Nature always does contrive—Fal,
        lal, la, la!
    That every boy and every gal
      That's born into the world alive
    Is either a little Liberal
      Or else a little Conservative!
        Fal, lal, la!

*Enter Fairies with Celia, Leila, and Fleta.
They trip round stage.*

CHORUS OF FAIRIES.

Strephon's a Member of Parliament!
  Carries every Bill he chooses.
To his measures all assent;—
  Showing that fairies have their uses.
    Whigs and Tories
    Dim their glories,
Giving an ear to all his stories—
Lords and Commons are both in the blues:
Strephon makes them shake in their shoes!
    Shake in their shoes!
    Shake in their shoes!
Strephon makes them shake in their shoes!

Enter Peers from Westminster Hall.

Strephon's a Member of Parliament!
    Running a-muck of all abuses.
His unqualified assent
    Somehow· nobody now refuses.
        Whigs and Tories
        Dim their glories,
Giving an ear to all his stories—
Carrying every Bill he may wish;
Here's a pretty kettle of fish!
        Kettle of fish!
        Kettle of· fish!
Here's a pretty kettle of fish!

*Enter Lord Mountararat and Lord Tolloller
from Westminster Hall.*

Celia. You seem annoyed.

Lord Mount. Annoyed! I should think so!
Why, this ridiculous *protégé* of yours is playing the deuce with everything! To-night is the
second reading of his Bill to throw the Peerage
open to Competitive Examination!

Lord Toll. And he'll carry it, too!

Lord Mount. Carry it? Of course he will!
He's a Parliamentary Pickford—he carries
everything!

Leila. Yes. If you please, that's our fault!

Lord Mount. The deuce it is!

Ceila. Yes; we influence the members, and
compel them to vote just as he wishes them
to.

Leila. It's our system. It shortens the de-
bates.

Lord Toll. Well, but think what it all
means. I don't so much mind for myself, but
with a House of Peers with no grandfathers
worth mentioning, the country must go to the
dogs!

Leila. I suppose it must!

Lord Mount. I don't want to say a word
against brains—I've a great respect for brains
—I often wish I had some myself—but with a
House of Peers composed exclusively of people
of intellect, what's to become of the House of
Commons?

Leila. I never thught of that!

Lord Mount. This comes of women inter-
fering in politics. It so happens that if there
is an institution in Great Britain which is not
susceptible of any improvement at all: it is the
House of Peers!

SONG.—*Lord Mountararat.*

When Britain really ruled the waves—
    (In good Queen Bess's time)
The House of Peers made no pretence
To intellectual eminence,
    Or scholarship sublime;
Yet Britain won her proudest bays
In good Queen Bess's glorious days!

Chorus. Yes, Britain won, &c.
When Wellington thrashed Bonaparte,
    As every child can tell,
The House of Peers, throughout the war,
Did nothing in particular,·
    And did it very well:
Yet Britain set the world a-blaze
In good King George's glorious days!

Chorus. Yes, Britain set, &c.
And while the House of Peers withholds
    Its legislative hand,
And noble statesmen do not itch
To interfere with matters which
    They do not understand,
As bright will shine Great Britain's rays
As in King George's glorious days!

Chorus. As bright will shine, &c.

*Leila (who has been much attracted by the
Peers during this song).* Charming persons,
are they not?

Celia. Distinctly. For self-contained dignity,
combined with airy condescension, give me a
British Representative Peer!

Lord Toll. Then pray stop this *protégé* of
yours before it's too late. Think of the mis-
chief you're doing!

Leila. But we *can't* stop him now. (*Aside
to Celia.*) Aren't they lovely! (*Aloud.*) Oh,
why did you go and defy us, you great geese!

DUET.—*Leila and Celia.*

Leila. In vain to us you plead—
            Don't go!
        Your prayers we do not heed—
            Don't go!
        It's true we sigh,
            But don't suppose
        A tearful eye
            Forgiveness shows. .
                Oh, no!
        We've very cross indeed—
            Don't go!

Fairies. It's true we sigh, &c.

Celia. Your disrespectful sneers—
            Don't go!
        Call forth indignant tears—
            Don't go!
        You break our laws—
            You are our foe:
        We cry, because
            We hate you so!
                You know!
        You very wicked Peers!
            Don't go!
                Fairies.
You break our laws.
    You are our foe:
We cry because
    We hate you so!
        You know!

You very wicked peers!
    Don't go!

Lords Mount. and Toll.

Our disrespectful sneers,
    Ha, ha!
Call forth indignant tears,
    Ha, ha!
If that's the case, my dears—
Fairies. Don't go!
Peers. We'll go!

[*Exeunt Lord Mountararat, Lord Tolloller
and Peers. Fairies gaze wistfully after them.*]
        Enter Fairy Queen.

Queen. Oh, shame—shame upon you! Is
this your fidelity to the laws you are bound to
obey? Know ye not that it is death to marry
a mortal?

Leila. Yes, but it's not death to *wish* to
marry a mortal!

Fleta. If it were, you'd have to execute us
all!

Queen. Oh, this is weakness! Subdue it!
Celia. We know it's weakness, but the weakness is so strong!

Leila. We are not all as tough as you are!
Queen. Tough! Do you suppose that I am
insensible to the effect of manly beauty? Look
at that man! (*Referring to sentry.*) A perfect
picture. (*To sentry.*) Who are you, sir?

Willis (*coming to "attention"*). Private Willis, B Company, 1st Grenadier Guards.

Queen. You're a very fine fellow, sir.
Willis. I am generally admired.

Queen. I can quite understand it. (*To
Fairies*). Now here is a man whose physical
attributes are simply godlike. That man has
a most extraordinary effect upon me. If I
yielded to a natural impulse, I should fall down
and worship that man. But I mortify this in-
clination. I wrestle with it, and it lies beneath my feet! That is how I treat my regard
for that man!

        SONG.—*Fairy Queen.*

Oh, foolish fay,
    Think you, because
His brave array
    My bosom thaws.
I'd disobey
    Our fairy laws?
Because I fly
    In realms above,
In tendency
    To fall in love,
Resemble I
    The amorous dove?
    Oh, amorous dove!
        Type of Ovidius Naso!

    This heart of mine
    Is soft as thine,
    Although I dare not say so!

Chorus. Oh, amorous dove, &c.
On fire that glows
    With heat intense
I turn the hose
    Of common sense,
And out it goes
    At small expense!
We must maintain
    Our fairy law;
That is the main
    On which to draw—
In that we gain
    A Captain Shaw!
    Oh, Captain Shaw!
        Type of true love kept under!
        Could thy Brigade
        With cold cascade
        Quench my great love, I wonder!

Chorus. Oh, Captain Shaw! &c.
[*Exeunt Fairies and Fairy Queen, sorrowfully.*]

        Enter Phyllis.

Phyl. (*half crying*). I can't think why I'm
not in better spirits. I'm engaged to two noblemen at once. That ought to be enough to make
any girl happy. But I'm miserable! Don't
suppose it's because I care for Strephon, for I
hate him! No girl *could* care for a man who
goes about with a mother considerably younger
than himself!

Enter Lord Mountararat and Lord Tolloller.
Lord Mount. Phyllis! My darling!
Lord Toll. Phyllis! My own!

Phyl. Don't! How dare you? Oh, but per-
haps you're the two noblemen I'm engaged to?
Lord Mount. I am one of them.
Lord Toll. I am the other.

Phyl. Oh, then, my darling! (*to Lord
Mountararat*). My own! (*to Lord Tolloller.*)
Well, have you settled which it's to be?

Lord Toll. Not altogether. It's a difficult
position. It would be hardly delicate to toss up.
On the whole we would rather leave it to you.

Phyl. How can it possibly concern me?
You are both Earls, and you are both rich, and
you are both plain.

Lord Mount. So we are. At least I am.
Lord Toll. So am I.
Lord Mount. No, no!
Lord Toll. I am indeed. Very plain.
Lord Mount. Well, well—perhaps you are.

Phyl. There's really nothing to choose between you. If one of you would forego his
title and distribute his estates among his Irish

tenantry, why then I should then see a reason for accepting the other.

Lord Mount. Tolloller, are you prepared to make this sacrifice?

Lord Toll. No!

Lord Mount. Not even to oblige a lady?

Lord Toll. No! not even to oblige a lady.

Lord Mount. Then, the only question is, which of us shall give way to the other? Perhaps, on the whole, she would be happier with me. I don't know. I may be wrong.

Lord Toll. No. I don't know that you are. I really believe she would. But the awkward part of the thing is that if you rob me of the girl of my heart, we must fight, and one of us must die. It's a family tradition that I have sworn to respect. It's a painful position, for I have a very strong regard for you, George.

Lord Mount. (*much effected*). My dear Thomas!

Lord Toll. You are very dear to me, George. We were boys together—at least *I* was. If I were to survive you, my existence would be hopelessly embittered.

Lord Mount. Then, my dear Thomas, you must not do it. I say it again and again—if it will have this effect upon you, you must not do it. No, no. If one of us is to destroy the other, let it be me!

Lord Toll. No, no!

Lord Mount. Ah, yes!—by our boyish friendship I implore you!

Lord Toll. (*much moved*). Well, well, be it so. But, no—no!—I cannot consent to an act which would crush you with unavailing remorse.

Lord Mount. But it would not do so. I should be very sad at first—oh, who would not be?—but it would wear off. I like you *very much*—but not, perhaps, as much as you like me.

Lord Toll. George, you're a noble fellow, but that tell-tale tear betrays you. No, George; you are very fond of me, and I cannot consent to give you a week's uneasiness on my account.

Lord Mount. But, dear Thomas, it would not last a week! Remember, you lead the House of Lords! on your demise I shall take your place! Oh, Thomas, it would not last a day!

Phyl. (*coming down*). Now I do hope you're not going to fight about me, because it's really not worth while.

Lord Toll. (*looking at her*). Well, I don't believe it is!

Lord Mount. Nor I. The sacred ties of Friendship are paramount.

QUARTET.—*Lord Mountararat, Lord Tolloller, Phyllis, and Private Willis.*

Lord Toll.
Though p'r'aps I may incur your blame,
  The things are few
  I would not do
In Friendship's name!

Lord Mount.
And I may say I think the same;
  Not even love
  Should rank above
True Friendship's name!

Phyl.
Then free me, pray; be mine the blame;
  Forget your craze
  And go your ways
In Friendship's name!

All.
Oh, many a man, in Friendship's name,
Has yielded fortune, rank and fame!
But no one yet, in the world so wide,
Has yielded up a promised bride!

Willis.
Accept, oh Friendship, all the same,

All.
This sacrifice to thy dear name!

[*Excunt Lord Mountararat and Lord Tolloller, lovingly, in one direction, and Phyllis in another. Exit Sentry.*]

Enter Lord Chancellor, very miserable.

RECIT.—*Lord Chancellor.*

Love, unrequited, robs me of my rest;
  Love, hopeless love, my ardent soul encumbers;
Love, nightmare like, lies heavy on my chest,
  And weaves itself into my midnight slumbers!

SONG.—*Lord Chancellor.*

When you're lying awake with a dismal headache, and repose is taboo'd by anxiety,
I conceive you may use any language you choose to indulge in, without impropriety;
For your brain is on fire—the bedclothes conspire of usual slumber to plunder you:
First your counterpane goes, and uncovers your toes, and your sheet slips demurely from under you;
Then the blanketing tickles—you feel like mixed pickles—so terribly sharp is the pricking,
And you're hot, and you're cross, and you tumble and toss till there's nothing 'twixt you and the ticking.
Then the bedclothes all creep to the ground in a heap, and you pick 'em all up in a tangle;

Next your pillow resigns and politely declines to remain at its usual angle!

Well, you get some repose in the form of a doze, with hot eye-balls and head ever aching.

But your slumbering teems with such horrible dreams that you'd very much better be waking;

For you dream you are crossing the Channel, and tossing about in a steamer from Harwich—

Which is something between a large bathing machine and a very small second-class carriage—

And you're giving a treat (penny ice and cold meat) to a party of friends and relations—

They're a ravenous horde—and they all came on board at Sloane Square and South Kensington Stations.

And bound on that journey you find your attorney (who started that ·morning from Devon);

He's a bit undersized, and you don't feel surprised when he tells you he's only eleven.

Well, you're driving like mad with this singular lad (by-the-bye the ship's now a four-wheeler),

And you're playing round games, and he calls you bad names when you tell him that "ties pay the dealer";

But this you can't stand, so you throw up your hand, and you find you're as cold as an icicle,

In your shirt and your socks (the black-silk with gold clocks), crossing Salisbury Plain on a bicycle:

And he and the crew are on bicycles too—which they've somehow or other invested in—

And he's telling the tars, all the particulars of a company he's interested in—

It's a scheme of devices, to get at low prices all goods from cough mixtures to cables

(Which tickled the sailors) by treating retailers, as though they were all vegetables—

You get a good spadesman to plant a small tradesman (first take off his boots with a boot-tree),

And his legs will take root, and his fingers will shoot, and they'll blossom and bud like a fruit-tree,

From the greengrocer tree you get grapes and green pea, cauliflower, pineapple, and cranberries,

While the pastrycook plant, cherry brandy will grant, apple puffs, and three-corners, and Banburys—

The shares are a penny, and ever so many are taken by Rothschild and Baring,

And just as a few are allotted to you, you awake with a shudder despairing—

You're a regular wreck, with a crick in your neck, and no wonder you snore, for your head's on the floor, and you've needles and pins from your soles to your shins, and your flesh is a-creep, for your left leg's asleep, and you've cramp in your toes, and a fly on your nose, and some fluff in your lung, and a feverish tongue, and a thirst that's intense, and a general sense that you haven't been sleeping in clover;

But the darkness has passed, and it's daylight at last, and the night has been long—ditto ditto my song—and thank goodness· they're both of them over!

(*Lord Chancellor falls exhausted on a seat*)

Enter Lords Mountararat and Tolloller.

Lord Mount. I am much distressed to see your Lordship in this condition.

Lord Ch. Ah, my Lords, it is seldom that a Lord Chancellor has reason to envy the position of another, but I am free to confess that I would rather be two Earls engaged to Phyllis than any other half-dozen noblemen upon the face of the globe.

Lord Toll. (*without enthusiasm*). Yes. It's an enviable position when you're the only one.

Lord Mount. Oh yes, no doubt—most enviable. At the same time, seeing you thus, we naturally say to ourselves, "This is very sad. His Lordship is constitutionally as blithe as a bird—he trills upon the bench like a thing of song and gladness. His series of judgments in F sharp minor, given *andante* in six-eight time, are among the most remarkable effects ever produced in a Court of Chancery. He is, perhaps, the only living instance of a judge whose decrees have received the honour of a double *encore*. How can we bring ourselves to do that which will deprive the Court of Chancery of one of its most attractive features?"

Lord Ch. I feel the force of your remarks, but I am here in two capacities, and they clash, my Lords, they clash! I deeply grieve to say that in declining to entertain my last application to myself, I presumed to address myself in terms which render it impossible for me ever to apply to myself again. It was a most painful scene, my Lords—most painful!

Lord Toll. This is what it is to have two capacities! Let us be thankful that we are persons of no capacity whatever.

Lord Mount. Come, come. Remember you are a very just and kindly old gentleman, and you need have no hesitation in approaching yourself, so that you do so respectfully and with a proper show of deference.

Lord Ch. Do you really think so?

Lord Mount. I do.

Lord Ch. Well, I will nerve myself to another effort, and, if that fails, I resign myself to my fate!

Trio.—*Lord Chancellor, Lords Mountararat and Tolloller.*

Lord Mount.
> If you go in
> You're sure to win—
> Yours will be the charming maidie:
> Be your law
> The ancient saw,
> "Faint heart never won fair lady!"

All.
> Faint heart never won fair lady!
> Every journey has an end—
> When at the worst affairs will mend—
> Dark the dawn when day is nigh—
> Hustle your horse and don't say die!

Lord Toll.
> He who shies
> At such a prize
> Is not worth a maravedi,
> Be so kind
> To bear in mind—
> Faint heart never won fair lady!

All.
> Faint heart never won fair lady!
> While the sun shines make your hay—
> Where a will is, there's a way—
> Beard the lion in his lair—
> None but the brave deserve the fair!

Lord Ch.
> I'll take heart
> And make a start—
> Though I fear the prospect's shady—
> Much I'd spend
> To gain my end—
> Faint heart never won fair lady!

All.
> Faint heart never won fair lady!
> Nothing venture, nothing win—
> Blood is thick, but water's thin—
> In for a penny, in for a pound—
> It's Love that makes the world go round!

(*Dance, and exeunt arm-in-arm together.*)

Enter Strephon, in very low spirits.

Streph. I suppose one ought to enjoy oneself in Parliament, when one leads both Parties, as I do! But I'm miserable, poor, broken-hearted fool that I am! Oh, Phyllis, Phyllis!—

Enter Phyllis.

Phyl. Yes.

Streph. (*surprised*). Phyllis! But I suppose I should say "My Lady." I have not yet been informed which title your ladyship has pleased to select?

Phyl. I—I haven't quite decided. You **see** I have no *mother* to advise *me!*

Streph. No. I have.

Phyl. Yes; a *young* mother.

Streph. Not very—a couple of centuries or so.

Phyl. Oh! She wears well.

Streph. She does. She's a fairy.

Phyl. I beg your pardon—a what?

Streph. Oh, I've no longer any reason to conceal the fact—she's a fairy.

Phyl. A fairy! Well, but—that would account for a good many things! Then—I suppose *you're* a fairy?

Streph. I'm half a fairy.

Phyl. Which half?

Streph. The upper half—down to the waistcoat.

Phyl. Dear me! (*Prodding him with her fingers.*) There is nothing to show it!

Streph. Don't do that.

Phyl. But why didn't you tell me this before?

Streph. I thought you would take a dislike to me. But as it's all off, you may as well know the truth—I'm only half a mortal!

Phyl. But I'd rather have half a mortal I do love than half a dozen I don't!

Streph. Oh, I think not—go to your half-dozen.

Phyl. It's only two! and I hate 'em! Please forgive me!

Streph. I don't think I ought to. Besides, all sorts of difficulties will arise. You know, my grandmother looks quite as young as my mother. So do all my aunts.

Phyl. I quite understand. Whenever I see you kissing a very young lady I shall know it's an elderly relative.

Streph. You will? Then, Phyllis, I think we shall be very happy! (*embracing her.*)

Phyl. We won't wait long.

Streph. No. We might change our minds. We'll get married first.

Phyl. And change our minds afterwards?

Streph. That's the usual course.

Duet.—*Strephon and Phyllis.*

Streph.
> If we're weak enough to tarry
> Ere we marry,
> You and I,
> Of the feeling I inspire,
> You may tire
> By-and-bye.
> For peers with flowing coffers
> Press their offers—

That is why
I am sure we should not tarry
Ere we marry,
You and I!

Phyl.
If we're weak enough to tarry
Ere we marry,
You and I,
With a more attractive maiden,
Jewel-laden,
You may fly.
If by chance we should be parted,
Broken-hearted
I should die—
So I think we will not tarry
Ere we marry,
You and I.

Phyl. But does your mother know you're—
I mean, is she aware of our engagement?

Enter Iolanthe.

Iol. She is; and thus she welcomes her
daughter-in-law! (*Kisses her.*)
But the Lord Chancellor?

Phyl. She kisses just like other people!

Streph. I forgot him! Mother, none can
resist your fairy eloquence; you will go to him
and plead for us?

Iol. (*much agitated*). No, no, impossible!

Streph. But our happiness—our very lives
—depend upon our obtaining his consent!

Phyl. Oh, madam, you cannot refuse to do
this!

Iol. You know not what you ask! The Lord
Chancellor is—my husband!

Streph. and Phyl. Your husband!

Iol. My husband and your father! (*Addressing Strephon, who is much moved.*)

Phyl. Then our course is plain; on his learning that Strephon is his son, all objection to our
marriage will be at once removed!

Iol. No; he must never know! He believes
me to have died childless, and, dearly as I love
him, I am bound, under penalty of death, not to
undeceive him. But see—he comes! Quick—
my veil!

(*Iolanthe veils herself. Strephon and Phyllis
go off on tip-toe.*)

Enter Lord Chancellor.

Lord Ch. Victory! Victory! Success has
crowned my efforts, and I may consider myself
engaged to Phyllis! At first I wouldn't hear
of it—it was out of the question. But I took
heart. I pointed out to myself that I was no
stranger to myself; that, in point of fact, I had
been personally acquainted with myself for
some years. This had its effect. I admitted
that I had watched my professional advancement with considerable interest, and I handsomely added that I yielded to no one in admiration for my private and professional vir-
tues. This was a great point gained. I then
endeavoured to work upon my feelings. Conceive my joy when I distinctly perceived a tear
glistening in my own eye! Eventually, after a
severe struggle with myself, I reluctantly—
most reluctantly—consented.

(*Iolanthe comes down veiled.*)

RECIT.—*Iolanthe.*

My lord, a suppliant at your feet I kneel,
Oh, listen to a mother's fond appeal!
Hear me to-night! I come in urgent need—
'Tis for my son, young Strephon, that I
plead!

BALLAD.—*Iolanthe.*

He loves! If in the bygone years
Thine eyes have ever shed
Tears—bitter, unavailing tears,
For one untimely dead—
If, in the eventide of life
Sad thoughts of her arise,
Then let the memory of thy wife
Plead for my boy—he dies!
He dies! If fondly laid aside
In some old cabinet,
Memorials of thy long-dead bride
Lie, dearly treasured yet,
Then let her hallowed bridal dress—
Her little dainty gloves—
Her withered flowers—her faded tress—
Plead for my boy—he loves!

(*The Lord Chancellor is moved by this appeal. After a pause* :)

Lord Ch. It may not be—for so the fates decide!

Learn thou that Phyllis is my promised bride.

Iol. (*in horror*). Thy bride! No! no!

Lord Ch. It shall be so!
Those who would separate us woe betide.

Iol. My doom thy lips have spoken—
I plead in vain!

Chorus of Fairies (*without*).
Forbear! forbear!

Iol. A vow already broken
I break again!

Chorus of Fairies (*without*).
Forbear! forbear!

Iol. For him—for her—for thee
I yield my life.
Behold—it may not be!
I am thy wife. (*Kneels.*)

Chorus of Fairies (*without*).
Aiaiah! Aiaiah! Willaloo!

Lord Ch. (*recognising her*). Iolanthe! thou
livest?

Iol. Aye!
I live! Now let me die!

Enter Fairy Queen and Fairies.

Queen. Once again thy vows are broken:
Thou thyself thy doom hath spoken!

Chorus of Fairies.
　Aiaiah! Aiaiah!
　Willahalah! Willaloo!
　Willahalah! Willaloo!

Queen. Bow thy head to Destiny:
Death thy doom, and thou shalt die!

Chorus of Fairies.
　Aiaiah! Aiaiah! &c.

The Queen raises her spear. Peers and Sentry enter.

Leila. Hold! If Iolanthe must die, so must we all! for, as she has sinned, so have we!

Queen. What!

Celia. We are all fairy duchesses, marchionesses, countesses, viscountesses, and baronesses.

Lord Mount. It's our fault. They couldn't help themselves.

Queen. It seems they *have* helped themselves, and pretty freely, too! (*After a pause.*) You have all incurred death; but I can't slaughter the whole company! And yet (*unfolding a scroll*) the law is clear—every fairy must die who marries a mortal!

Lord Ch. Allow me, as an old equity draughtsman, to make a suggestion. The subtleties of the legal mind are equal to the emergency. The thing is really quite simple—the insertion of a single word will do it. Let it stand that every fairy shall die who don't marry a mortal, and there you are, out of your difficulty at once!

Queen. We like your humour. Very well! (*Altering the MS. in pencil.*) Private Willis!

Sentry (*coming forward*). Ma'am!

Queen. To save my life, it is necessary that I marry at once. How would you like to be a fairy guardsman?

Sentry. Well, ma'am, I don't think much of the British soldier who wouldn't ill-convenience himself to save a female in distress.

Queen. You are a brave fellow. You're a fairy from this moment. (*Wings spring from Sentry's shoulders.*) And you, my Lords, how say you, Will you join our ranks?

(*Phyllis and Strephon enter.*)

(*Fairies kneel to Peers and implore them to do so.*)

Lord Mount. (*to Lord Tolloller*). Well, now that the Peers are to be recruited entirely from persons of intelligence, I really don't see what use *we* are down here, do you, Tolloller?

Lord Toll. None whatever.

Queen. Good! (*Wings spring from shoulders of Peers.*) Then away we go to Fairyland.

FINALE.

Phyl. 　Soon as we may,
　　Off and away!
　We'll commence our journey airy—
　　Happy are we—
　　As you can see,
　Every one is now a fairy!

All. 　Every one is now a fairy!

Iol., Queen and Phyl. Though, as a general rule, we know
Two strings go to every bow,
Make up your minds that grief 'twill bring
If you've two beaux to every string,

All. Though, as a general rule, &c.

Lord Ch. Up in the sky,
　Ever so high,
Pleasures come in endless series;
　We will arrange
　Happy exchange—
House of Peers for House of Peris!

All. House of Peers for House of Peris!

Lords Ch., Mount. and Toll. Up in the air, sky-high, sky-high.

$\left\{\begin{array}{l}\text{I}\\\text{He}\end{array}\right\}$ will be surely happier, for

$\left\{\begin{array}{l}\text{I'm}\\\text{He's}\end{array}\right\}$ such a susceptible Chancellor.

All. Up in the air, &c.

CURTAIN.

A PLEASANT OCCUPATION

Allegro vivace. LORD CHAN.

The Law is the true em - bo - di - ment Of ev - 'ry - thing that's ex - cel - lent. It has no kind of fault or flaw, And I, my lords, em - bo - dy the Law. The con - sti - tu - tion - al guar - dian I Of pret - ty young Wards in Chan - ce - ry. All ve - ry a - gree - a - ble girls and none Are o - ver the age of twen - ty one. A

CHORUS OF PEERS

plea - sant oc - cu - pa - tion for A ra - ther sus - cep - ti - ble Chan - cel - lor! A plea - sant oc - cu - pa - tion for A ra - ther sus - cep - ti - ble Chan - cel - lor! But though the com - pli - ment im - plied In - flates me with le - gi - ti - mate pride, It ne - ver - the - less can't be de - nied, That it has its in - con - ve - ni - ent side. For I'm not so old, and

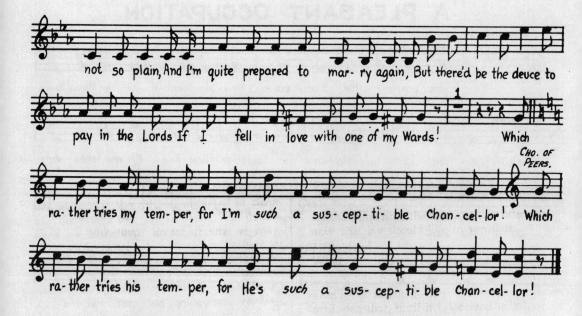

not so plain, And I'm quite prepared to mar-ry again, But there'd be the deuce to pay in the Lords If I fell in love with one of my Wards! Which

ra-ther tries my tem-per, for I'm such a sus-cep-ti-ble Chan-cel-lor! Which

ra-ther tries his tem-per, for He's such a sus-cep-ti-ble Chan-cel-lor!

GOOD MORROW - GOOD LOVER!

Allegretto. PHYLLIS.

Good-morrow, good lo-ver!... Good lo-ver, good mor-row!__ I

pri-thee dis-co-ver, Steal, pur-chase, or bor-row, Some means of con-ceal-ing The

care you are feel-ing, And join in a mea-sure Ex-pres-sive of plea-sure, For

STREPHON & PHYLLIS.

we're to be mar-ried to-day, to-day, Yes, we're to be mar-ried to-day!... Yes,

we're to be mar-ried to-day, to-day, Yes, we're to be mar-ried to-day!...

OH, FOOLISH FAY!

Oh, fool-ish fay, Think you, be-cause His brave ar-ray My bo-som thaws, I'd dis-o-bey Our fai-ry laws? Be-cause I fly In realms a-bove, In ten-den-cy To fall in love, Re-sem-ble I The am-'rous dove? Re-sem-ble I the am-'rous dove? Oh, am-'rous dove! Type of O-vi-dius Na-so! This heart of mine Is soft as thine, Al-though I dare not say so! Oh, am-'rous dove! Type of O-vi-dius Na-so! This heart of mine Is soft as thine, Al-though I dare not say so!

FAINT HEART NE'ER WON FAIR LADY

Authentic Libretto
of the new
GILBERT AND SULLIVAN LIBRARY

H.M.S. PINAFORE

OR

THE LASS THAT LOVED A SAILOR.

BY

Sir W. S. GILBERT

AND

Sir ARTHUR S. SULLIVAN

The Bass Publishers

H.M.S. PINAFORE

Dramatis Personae

THE RT. HON. SIR JOSEPH PORTER, K.C.B.
   (*First Lord of the Admiralty*)

CAPTAIN CORCORAN (*Commanding H.M.S. Pinafore*)

RALPH RACKSTRAW (*Able Seaman*)

DICK DEADEYE (*Able Seaman*)

BILL BOBSTAY (*Boatswain's Mate*)

BOB BECKET (*Carpenter's Mate*)

TOM TUCKER (*Midshipmite*)

SERGEANT OF MARINES

JOSEPHINE (*the Captain's Daughter*)

HEBE (*Sir Joseph's First Cousin*)

MRS. CRIPPS (LITTLE BUTTERCUP)
   (*a Portsmouth Bumboat Woman*)

First Lord's Sisters, his Cousins, his Aunts, Sailors, Marines, etc.

SCENE—QUARTER-DECK OF H.M.S. PINAFORE, OFF PORTSMOUTH

ACT I.—NOON.   ACT II.—NIGHT.

H.M.S. PINAFORE

OR

THE LASS THAT LOVED A SAILOR.

ACT I.

SCENE.—*Quarter-deck of H.M.S. Pinafore. Sailors, led by Boatswain, discovered cleaning brasswork, splicing rope, &c.*

CHORUS.

We sail the Ocean blue,
And our saucy ship's a beauty;
We're sober men and true,
And attentive to our duty.
When the balls whistle free
O'er the bright blue sea,
We stand to our guns all day;
When at anchor we ride
On the Portsmouth tide,
We've plenty of time for play.
Ahoy! Ahoy! Ahoy!

(*Enter Little Buttercup, with large basket on her arm.*)

RECIT.

Hail, men-o'-wars' men—safeguards of your nation,
Here is an end, at last, of all privation;
You've got your pay—spare all you can afford
To welcome Little Buttercup on board.

ARIA.

I'm called Little Buttercup—dear Little Buttercup,
Though I could never tell why,
But still I'm called Buttercup—poor Little Buttercup,
Sweet Little Buttercup I!

I've snuff and tobaccy, and excellent jacky,
I've scissors, and watches, and knives;
I've ribbons and laces to set off the faces
Of pretty young sweethearts and wives.

I've treacle and toffee, I've tea and I've coffee,
Soft tommy and succulent chops;
I've chickens and conies, and pretty polonies,
And excellent peppermint drops.

Then buy of your Buttercup—dear Little Buttercup,
Sailors should never be shy;
So buy of your Buttercup—poor Little Buttercup,
Come, of your Buttercup buy!

Boat. Aye, Little Buttercup—and well called—for you're the rosiest, the roundest, and the reddest beauty in all Spithead.

All. Aye! Aye!

But. Red, am I? and round—and rosy! May be, for I have dissembled well! But hark ye, my merry friend—hast ever thought that beneath a gay and frivolous exterior there may lurk a canker-worm which is slowly but surely eating its way into one's very heart?

Boat. No, my lass, I can't say I've ever thought that.

(*Enter Dick Deadeye. He pushes through sailors, and comes down.*)

Dick. I've thought it often. (*All recoil from him.*)

But. Yes, you look like it! What's the matter with the man? Isn't he well?

Boat. Don't take no heed of *him,* that's only poor Dick Deadeye.

Dick. I say—it's a beast of a name, ain't it. Dick Deadeye.

But. It's not a nice name.

Dick I'm ugly too, ain't I?

But. You are certainly plain.

Dick. And I'm three-cornered too, ain't I?

But. You are rather triangular.

Dick. Ha! Ha! That's it. I'm ugly, and they hate me for it; for you all hate me, don't you?

All. We do!

Dick. There!

Boat. Well, Dick, we wouldn't go for to hurt any fellow creature's feelings, but you can't expect a chap with such a name as Dick Deadeye to be a popular character—now can you?

Dick. No.

Boat. It's asking too much, ain't it?

Dick. It is. From such a face and form as mine the noblest sentiments sound like the black utterances of a depraved imagination. It is human nature, I'm resigned.

RECIT.

But. (*Looking down hatchway from* R.)
But, tell me—who's the youth whose faltering feet

With difficulty bear him on his course?

Boat. That is the smartest lad in all the fleet—
Ralph Rackstraw!

But. Ralph! That name! Remorse! remorse!

(Enter Ralph from hatchway.)

MADRIGAL.—*Ralph.*

The Nightingale
Sighed for the moon's bright ray,
And told his tale
In his own melodious way!
He sang "Ah, well-a-day!"

All. He sang "Ah, well-a-day!"

The lowly vale
For the mountain vainly sighed,
To his humble wail
The echoing hills replied.
They sang "Ah, well-a-day!"

All. They sang "Ah, well-a-day!"

RECIT.

I know the value of a kindly chorus,
But choruses yield little consolation,
When we have pain and sorrow too before us!
I love—and love, alas, above my station!

But. (*Aside.*) He loves—and loves a lass above his station.

All. (*Aside.*) Yes, yes, the lass is much above his station.

BALLAD.—*Ralph.*

A maiden fair to see,
The pearl of minstrelsy,
A bud of blushing beauty;
For whom proud nobles sigh,
And with each other vie
To do her menial's duty.

All. To do her menial's duty.

A suitor, lowly born,
With hopeless passion torn,
And poor beyond denying,
Has dared for her to pine,
At whose exalted shrine
A world of wealth is sighing.

All. A world of wealth is sighing!

Unlearned he in aught
Save that which love has taught,
(For love had been his tutor);
Oh, pity, pity me—
Our captain's daughter, she,
And I that lowly suitor!

All. And he that lowly suitor!

Boat. Ah, my poor lad, you've climbed too high; our worthy captain's child won't have nothin' to say to a poor chap like you. Will she, lads?

All. No, no!

Dick. No, no, captain's daughters don't marry foremost hands.

All. (*Recoiling from him.*) Shame! shame!

Boat. Dick Deadeye, them sentiments o' yourn are a disgrace to our common natur.

Ralph. But it's a strange anomaly, that the daughter of a man who hails from the quarter-deck may not love another who lays out on the fore-yard arm. For a man is but a man, whether he hoists his flag at the main truck or his slacks on the main-deck.

All. Aye! aye!

Dick. Ah, it's a queer world!

Ralph. Dick Deadeye, I have no desire to press hardly on you, but such a revolutionary sentiment is enough to make an honest sailor shudder. (*All shudder.*)

Boat. My lads, our gallant captain has come on deck, let us greet him as so brave an officer and so gallant a seaman deserves.

(Enter Captain Corcoran.)

RECIT.

Capt. My gallant crew, good morning.

All. (*Saluting.*) Sir, good morning!

Capt. I hope you're all quite well.

All. (*As before.*) Quite well; and you, sir?

Capt. I am in reasonable health, and happy
To meet you all once more.

All. (*As before.*) You do us proud, sir!

SONG.—*Capt.*

Capt. I am the Captain of the Pinafore!

All. And a right good captain, too!

Capt. You're very, very good,
And be it understood,
I command a right good crew.

All. We're very, very good,
And be it understood,
He commands a right good crew.

Capt. Though related to a peer,
I can hand, reef, and steer,
Or ship a selvagee;
I am never known to quail
At the fury of a gale,
And I'm never, never sick at sea!

All. What, never?

Capt. No, never!

All. What, *never?*

Capt. Hardly ever!

All. He's hardly ever sick at sea!
Then give three cheers, and one cheer more,
For the hardy Captain of the Pinafore!

Capt. I do my best to satisfy you all—

All. And with you we're quite content.

Capt. You're exceedingly polite,
       And I think it only right
   To return the compliment.

All.   We're exceedingly polite,
       And he thinks it only right
   To return the compliment.

Capt. Bad language or abuse,
       I never, never use,
   Whatever the emergency;
       Though, "bother it," I may
       Occasionally say,
       I never use a big, big D—

All.   What, never?
Capt. No, never!
All.   What, *never?*
Capt. Hardly ever!
All. Hardly ever swears a big, big D—
       Then give three cheers, and one cheer
           more,
       For the well-bred Captain of the Pina-
           fore!

(After song exeunt all but Captain. Enter Little Buttercup.)

But.
   Sir, you are sad! The silent eloquence
   Of yonder tear, that trembles on your eye-
       lash,
   Proclaims a sorrow far more deep than com-
       mon;
   Confide in me—fear not—I am a mother!

Capt.
   Yes, Little Buttercup, I'm sad and sorry—
   My daughter, Josephine, the fairest flower
   That ever blossomed on ancestral timber,
   Is sought in marriage by Sir Joseph Porter,
   Our Admiralty's First Lord, but for some
       reason
   She does not seem to tackle kindly to it.

But. (with emotion.)
   Ah, poor Sir Joseph. Ah, I know too well
   The anquish of a heart that loves but vainly!
   But see, here comes your most attractive
       daughter.
   I go—Farewell;   *(Exit.)*
Capt. (looking after her). A plump and pleasing person!   *(Exit.)*
(Enter Josephine, twining some flowers which she carries in a small basket.)

BALLAD.—*Josephine.*

Sorry her lot who loves too well,
   Heavy the heart that hopes but vainly,
Sad are the sighs that own the spell,
   Uttered by eyes that speak too plainly;
   Heavy the sorrow that bows the head
   When love is alive and hope is dead!

Sad is the hour when sets the sun—
   Dark is the night to earth's poor daughters,
When to the ark the wearied one
   Flies from the empty waste of waters!

Heavy the sorrow that bows the head
When love is alive and hope is dead! !

(Enter Captain.)

Capt. My child, I grieve to see that you are a prey to melancholy. You should look your best to-day, for Sir Joseph Porter, K.C.B., will be here this afternoon to claim your promised hand.

Jos. Ah, father, your words cut me to the quick. I can esteem—reverence—venerate Sir Joseph, for he is a great and good man; but oh, I cannot love him! My heart is already given.

Capt. (Aside.) It is then as I feared. *(Aloud.)* Given? And to whom? Not to some gilded lordling?

Jos. No, father—the object of my love is no lordling. Oh, pity me, for he is but a humble sailor on board your own ship!

Capt. Impossible!

Jos. Yes, it is true—too true;

Capt. A common sailor? Oh fie!

Jos. I blush for the weakness that allows me to cherish such a passion. I hate myself when I think of the depth to which I have stooped in permitting myself to think tenderly of one so ignobly born, but I love him! I love him! I love him! *(Weeps.)*

Capt. Come, my child, let us talk this over. In a matter of the heart I would not coerce my daughter—I attach but little value to rank or wealth, but the line must be drawn somewhere. A man in that station may be brave and worthy, but at every step he would commit solecisms that society would never pardon.

Jos. Oh, I have thought of this night and day. But fear not, father, I have a heart, and therefore I love; but I am your daughter, and therefore I am proud. Though I carry my love with me to the tomb, he shall never, never know it.

Capt. You *are* my daughter after all. But see, Sir Joseph's barge approaches, manned by twelve trusty oarsmen and accompanied by the admiring crowd of sisters, cousins and aunts that attend him wherever he goes. Retire, my daughter, to your cabin—take this, his photograph, with you—it may help to bring you to a more reasonable frame of mind.

Jos. My own thoughtful father!

(Exit Josephine. Captain remains and ascends the poop-deck.)

BARCAROLLE *(invisible).*

   Over the bright blue sea
Comes Sir Joseph Porter, K.C.B.,
   Wherever he may go
Bang-bang the loud nine pounders go!
   Shout o'er the bright blue sea
For Sir Joseph Porter, K.C.B.

(During this the crew have entered on tiptoe, listening attentively to the song.)

Sir Joseph's barge is seen,
 And its crowd of blushing beauty,
We hope he'll find us clean,
 And attentive to our duty.
We sail, we sail the ocean blue,
 And our saucy ship's a beauty,
We're sober, sober men and true,
 And attentive to our duty.
We're smart and sober men,
 And quite devoid of fe-ar,
  In all the Royal N.
 None are so smart as we are.

(*Enter Sir Joseph's Female Relatives. They dance round stage.*)

Rel. Gaily tripping,
  Lightly skipping,
Flock the maidens to the shipping.

Sailors.
Flags and guns and pennants dipping!
All the ladies love the shipping.

Rel. Sailors sprightly,
  Always rightly
Welcome ladies so politely,

Sailors.
Ladies who can smile so brightly,
Sailors welcome most politely.

Capt. (*from poop*).
Now give three cheers, I'll lead the way.
Hurrah! hurrah!

All. Hurray! hurray! hurray!

(*Enter Sir Joseph with Cousin Hebe.*)

SONG.—*Sir Joseph.*

I am the monarch of the sea,
 The ruler of the Queen's Navee.
Whose praise Great Britain loudly chants.

Cousin Hebe.
And we are his sisters, and his cousins, and
 his aunts!

Rel.
And we are his sisters, and his cousins, and
 his aunts!

Sir Joseph.
When at anchor here I ride,
 My bosom swells with pride,
And I snap my fingers at a foeman's taunts;

Cousin Hebe.
And so do his sisters, and his cousins, and
 his aunts!

All.
And so do his sisters, and his cousins, and
 his aunts!

Sir Joseph.
But when the breezes blow,
 I generally go below,
And seek the seclusion that a cabin grants!

Cousin Hebe.
And so do his sisters, and his cousins, and
 his aunts!

All.
And so do his sisters, and his cousins, and his
 aunts!
His sisters and his cousins,
 Whom he reckons up by dozens,
  And his aunts!

SONG.—*Sir Joseph.*

Solo.
When I was a lad I served a term
As office boy to an Attorney's firm,
I cleaned the windows and I swept the floor,
And I polished up the handle of the big front
 door.
  CHORUS.—He polished, etc.

Solo.
 I polished up that handle so carefullee
 That now I am the ruler of the Queen's
  Navee!
  CHORUS.—He polished, etc.

Solo.
As office boy I made such a mark
That they gave me the post of a junior clerk.
I served the writs with a smile so bland,
And I copied all the letters in a big round
 hand—
  CHORUS.—He copied, etc.

Solo.
 I copied all the letters in a hand so free,
 That now I am the ruler of the Queen's
  Navee!
  CHORUS.—He copied, etc.

Solo.
In serving writs I made such a name
That an articled clerk I soon became;
I wore clean collars and a bran new suit
For the pass examination at the Institute.
  CHORUS.—For the pass, etc.

Solo.
That pass examination did so well for me,
That now I am the ruler of the Queen's
 Navee!
  CHORUS.—That pass examination, etc.

Solo.
Of legal knowledge I acquired such a grip
That they took me into the partnership
And that junior partnership I ween
Was the only ship that I ever had seen.
  CHORUS.—Was the only ship, etc.

Solo.
But that kind of ship so suited me,
That now I am the ruler of the Queen's
 Navee!
  CHORUS.—But that kind, etc.

Solo.
I grew so rich that I was sent
By a pocket borough into Parliament.
I always voted at my party's call,
And I never thought of thinking for myself
 at all.
  CHORUS.—He never thought, etc.

Solo.

    I thought so little, they rewarded me,
    By making me the ruler of the Queen's
        Navee!

      Chorus.—He thought so little, etc.

Solo.

    Now landsmen all, whoever you may be,
    If you want to rise to the top of the tree,
    If your soul isn't fettered to an office stool,
    Be careful to be guided by this golden rule—

        Chorus.—Be careful, etc.

Solo.

    Stick close to your desks and never go to
      sea,
    And you all may be rulers of the Queen's
        Navee!

        Chorus.—Stick close, etc.

Sir Joseph. You've a remarkably fine crew, Captain Corcoran.

Capt. It *is* a fine crew, Sir Joseph.

Sir Joseph. (*Examining a very small midshipman.*) A British sailor is a splendid fellow, Captain Corcoran.

Capt. A splendid fellow indeed, Sir Joseph.

Sir Joseph. I hope you treat your crew kindly, Captain Corcoran.

Capt. Indeed I hope so, Sir Joseph.

Sir Joseph. Never forget that they are the bulwarks of England's greatness, Captain Corcoran.

Capt. So I have always considered them, Sir Joseph.

Sir Joseph. No bullying, I trust—no strong language of any kind, eh?

Capt. Oh, never, Sir Joseph.

Sir Joseph. What, *never?*

Capt. Well! hardly ever, Sir Joseph. They are an excellent crew, and do their work thoroughly without it.

Sir Joseph. Don't patronize them, sir—pray don't patronize them.

Capt. Certainly not, Sir Joseph.

Sir Joseph. That you are their Captain is an accident of birth. I cannot permit these noble fellows to be patronized because an accident of birth has placed you above them and them below you.

Capt. I am the last person to insult a British sailor, Sir Joseph.

Sir Joseph. You are the last person who did, Captain Corcoran. Desire that splendid seaman to step forward.

      (*Dick comes forward.*)

Sir Joseph. No, no, the other splendid seaman.

Capt. Ralph Rackstraw, three paces to the front—march!

Sir Joseph. (*Sternly.*) If what?

Capt. I beg your pardon—I don't think I understand you.

Sir Joseph. If you *please.*

Capt. Oh, yes, of course. If you please. (*Ralph steps forward.*)

Sir Joseph. You're a remarkably fine fellow.

Ralph. Yes, your honour.

Sir Joseph. And a first-rate seaman, I'll be bound.

Ralph. There's not a smarter topman in the navy, your honour, though I say it who shouldn't.

Sir Joseph. Not at all. Proper self-respect, nothing more. Can you dance a hornpipe?

Ralph. No, your honour.

Sir Joseph. That's a pity; all sailors should dance hornpipes. I will teach you one this evening, after dinner. Now tell me—don't be afraid—how does your Captain treat you, eh?

Ralph. A better Captain don't walk the deck, your honour.

All. Aye! Aye!

Sir Joseph. Good. I like to hear you speak well of your commanding officer; I dare say he don't deserve it, but still it does you credit. Can you sing?

Ralph. I can hum a little, your honour.

Sir Joseph. Then hum this at your leisure. (*Giving him MS. music.*) It is a song that I have composed for the use of the Royal Navy. It is designed to encourage independence of thought and action in the lower branches of the service, and to teach the principle that a British sailor is any man's equal, excepting mine. Now, Captain Corcoran, a word with you in your cabin on a tender and sentimental subject.

Capt. Aye, aye, Sir Joseph. (*Crossing.*) Boatswain, in commemoration of this joyous occasion, see that extra grog is served out to the ship's company at seven bells.

Boat. Beg pardon. If what, your honour?

Capt. If what? I don't think I understand you.

Boat. If you *please,* your honour.

Capt. What!

Sir Joseph. The gentleman is quite right. If you *please.*

Capt. (*Stamping his foot impatiently.*) If you *please!*   [*Exit.*

Sir Joseph.

    For I hold that on the seas
    The expression, "if you please,"
      A particularly gentlemanly tone implants.

Cousin Hebe.

    And so do his sisters, and his cousins, and his
        aunts!

All.

    And so do his sisters, and his cousins, and his
        aunts!

    (*Exeunt Sir Joseph and Relatives.*)

Boat. Ah! Sir Joseph's a true gentleman; courteous and considerate to the very humblest.

Ralph. True, Boatswain, but we are not the very humblest. Sir Joseph has explained our true position to us. As he says, a British seaman is any man's equal excepting his, and if Sir Joseph says that, is it not our duty to believe him?

All. Well spoke! well spoke!

Dick. You're on a wrong tack, and so is he. He means well, but he don't know. When people have to obey other people's orders, equality's out of the question.

All. (*Recoiling.*) Horrible! horrible!

Boat. Dick Deadeye, if you go for to infuriate this here ship's company too far, I won't answer for being able to hold 'em in. I'm shocked! that's what I am—shocked!

Ralph. Messmates, my mind's made up. I'll speak to the captain's daughter, and tell her, like an honest man, of the honest love I have for her.

All. Aye, aye!

Ralph. Is not my love as good as another's? Is not my heart as true as another's? Have I not hands and eyes and ears and limbs like another?

All. Aye, aye!

Ralph. True, I lack birth—

Boat. You've a berth on board this very ship.

Ralph. Well said—I had forgotten that. Messmates—what do you say? do you approve my determination?

All. We do.

Dick. I don't.

Boat. What is to be done with this here hopeless chap? Let us sing him the song that Sir Joseph has kindly composed for us. Perhaps it will bring this here miserable creetur to a proper state of mind.

GLEE.—*Ralph, Boatswain, Carpenter's Mate, and Chorus.*

A British tar is a soaring soul,
   As free as a mountain bird,
His energetic fist should be ready to resist
   A dictatorial word.
His nose should pant and his lip should curl,
His cheeks should flame and his brow should
   furl,
His bosom should heave and his heart should
   glow,
And his fist be ever ready for a knock-down
   blow.

CHORUS.—His nose should pant, etc.

His eyes should flash with an inborn fire,
   His brow with scorn be rung;
He never should bow down to a domineering
   frown,

Or the tang of a tyrant tongue.
His foot should stamp and his throat should
   growl,
His hair should twirl and his face should
   scowl;
His eyes should flash and his breast protrude,
And this should be his customary attitude!—
   (*Pose.*)

CHORUS.—His foot should stamp, etc.

(*All dance off excepting Ralph, who remains, leaning pensively against bulwark.*)

(*Enter Josephine from Cabin.*)

Jos. It is useless—Sir Joseph's attentions nauseate me. I know that he is a truly great and good man, for he told me so himself, but to me he seems tedious, fretful and dictatorial. Yet his must be a mind of no common order, or he would not dare to teach my dear father to dance a hornpipe on the cabin table. (*Sees Ralph.*) Ralph Rackstraw! (*Overcome by emotion.*)

Ralph. Aye, lady—no other than poor Rackstraw!

Jos. (*Aside.*) How my heart beats! (*Aloud.*) And why poor, Ralph?

Ralph. I am poor in the essence of happiness, lady—rich only in never-ending unrest. In me there meet a combination of antithetical elements which are at eternal war with one another. Driven hither by objective influences—thither by subjective emotions—wafted one moment into blazing day, by mocking hope—plunged the next into the Cimmerian darkness of tangible despair, I am but a living ganglion of irreconcilable antagonisms. I hope I make myself clear, lady?

Jos. Perfectly. (*Aside.*) His simple eloquence goes to my heart. Oh, if I dared—but no, the thought is madness! (*Aloud.*) Dismiss these foolish fancies, they torture you but needlessly. Come, make one effort.

Ralph. (*Aside.*) I will—one. (*Aloud.*) Josephine!

Jos. (*Indignantly.*) Sir!

Ralph. Aye, even though Jove's armoury were launched at the head of the audacious mortal whose lips, unhallowed by relationship, dared to breathe that precious word, yet would I breathe it once, and then perchance be silent evermore. Josephine, in one brief breath I will concentrate the hopes, the doubts, the anxious fears of six weary months. Josephine, I am a British sailor, and I love you!

Jos. Sir, this audacity! (*Aside.*) Oh, my heart, my beating heart. (*Aloud.*) This unwarrantable presumption on the part of a common sailor! (*Aside.*) Common! oh, the irony of the word! (*Crossing, aloud.*) Oh, sir, you forget the disparity in our ranks.

Ralph. I forget nothing, haughty lady. I love you desperately, my life is in your hand—I lay it at your feet! Give me hope, and what I lack in education and polite accomplishments, that I will endeavour to acquire. Drive me to despair, and in death alone I shall look for consolation. I am proud and cannot stoop to implore. I have spoken and I wait your word.

Jos. You shall not wait long. Your proffered love I haughtily reject. Go, sir, and learn to cast your eyes on some village maiden in your own poor rank—they should be lowered before your captain's daughter.

DUET.—*Josephine and Ralph.*

Jos. Refrain, audacious tar,
  Your suit from pressing,
  Remember what you are,
  And whom addressing!
 (Aside.)
  I'd laugh my rank to scorn
  In union holy,
  Were he more highly born
  Or I more lowly!

Ralph. Proud lady, have your way,
  Unfeeling beauty!
  You speak and I obey,
  It is my duty!
  I am the lowliest tar
  That sails the water,
  And you, proud maiden, are
  My captain's daughter!
 (Aside.)
  My heart with anguish torn
  Bows down before her,
  She laughs my love to scorn,
  Yet I adore her!

(Repeat Refrain, Ensemble, then Exit Josephine into cabin.)

Ralph. (Recit.)
  Can I survive this overbearing
  Or live a life of mad despairing,
  My proffered love despised, rejected?
  No, no, it's not to be expected!
   (Calling off.)
  Messmates, ahoy!
  Come here! Come here!

(Enter Sailors, Hebe, Relatives and Buttercup.)

All. Aye, aye, my boy,
  .What cheer, what cheer?
  Now tell us, pray,
  Without delay
  What does she say—
  What cheer, what cheer?

Ralph (to Cousin Hebe.)
 The maiden treats my suit with scorn,
  Rejects my humble gift, my lady;
 She says I am ignobly born,
  And cuts my hopes adrift, my lady.

All. Oh, cruel one.

Dick.
  She spurns your suit? Oho! Oho!
  I told you so, I told you so.

Sailors and Relatives.
 Shall $\begin{Bmatrix} \text{we} \\ \text{they} \end{Bmatrix}$ submit? Are $\begin{Bmatrix} \text{we} \\ \text{they} \end{Bmatrix}$ but slaves;
  Love comes alike to high and low—
  Britannia's sailors rule the waves,
   And shall they stoop to insult? No!

Dick.
  You must submit, you are but slaves;
   A lady she! Oho! Oho!
  You lowly toilers of the waves,
   She spurns you all—I told you so!

Ralph.
  My friends, my leave of life I'm taking,
  For oh, my heart, my heart is breaking.
  When I am gone, oh, prithee tell
  The maid that, as I died, I loved her well!

All. (Turning away, weeping.)
  Of life, alas! his leave he's taking,
  For ah! his faithful heart is breaking,
  When he is gone we'll surely tell
  The maid that, as he died, he loved her well!

(During Chorus Boatswain has loaded pistol, which he hands to Ralph.)

Ralph.
  Be warned, my messmates all
   Who love in rank above you—
  For Josephine I fall!

(Puts pistol to his head. All the sailors stop their ears.)

   (Enter Josephine on deck.)

Jos. Ah! stay your hand! I love you!
All. Ah! stay your hand—she loves you!
Ralph. (Incredulously.) Loves me?
Jos.   Loves you!
All. Yes, yes—ah, yes—she loves you!

Josephine, Hebe and Ralph.

Oh joy, oh rapture unforeseen,
For now the sky is all serene,
The god of day—the orb of love,
Has hung his ensign high above,
 The sky is all a-blaze.
With wooing words and loving song,
We'll chase the lagging hours along,
And if $\begin{Bmatrix} \text{I find} \\ \text{we find} \end{Bmatrix}$ the maiden coy,
$\begin{Bmatrix} \text{I'll} \\ \text{We'll} \end{Bmatrix}$ murmur forth decorous joy
 In dreamy roundelays!

Dick Deadeye.

He thinks he's won his Josephine,
But though the sky is now serene,
A frowning thunderbolt above
May end their ill-assorted love
 Which now is all a-blaze.
Our captain, ere the day is gone,
Will be extremely down upon
The wicked men who art employ

To make his Josephine less coy
  In many various ways. (*Exit Dick.*)
ENSEMBLE.

Jos.   This very night,
Hebe. With bated breath
Ralph. And muffled oar—
Jos.   Without a light,
Hebe. As still as death,
Ralph. We'll steal ashore,
Jos.   A clergyman
Ralph. Shall make us one
Boat. At half past ten,
Jos.   And then we can
Ralph. Return, for none
Boat. Can part them then!
All.   This very night, etc.
    (*Dick appears at Hatchway.*)

Dick.
Forbear, nor carry out the scheme you've
  planned,
She is a lady—you a foremast hand!
Remember, she's your gallant captain's
  daughter,
And you the meanest slave that crawls the
  water!
All. Back, vermin, back,
    Nor mock us!
  Back, vermin, back,
    You shock us!   (*Exit Dick.*)
Let's give three cheers for the sailor's bride
Who casts all thought of rank aside—

And gives up home and fortune, too,
For the honest love of a sailor true!
  Tra la la la la la la

Rel. For a British tar is a soaring soul
    As free as a mountain bird!
    His energetic fist should be ready to
      resist
    A dictatorial word!
His eyes should flash with an inborn fire,
  His brow with scorn be wrung;
He never should bow down to a domineering
  frown,
  Or the tang of a tyrant tongue.

Sails.
His nose should pant and his lip should curl,
His cheeks should flame and his brow should
  furl,
His bosom should heave and his heart should
  glow,
And his fist be ever ready for a knock-down
  blow.

ENSEMBLE.

His foot should stamp and his throat should
  growl,
His hair should twirl and his face should
  scowl,
His eyes should flash and his breast protrude,
And this should be his customary attitude.
    (*Pose.*)

GENERAL DANCE.

END OF ACT I.

ACT II.

Same Scene. Night. Moonlight.
Captain discovered singing, and accompanying
himself on a Guitar. Little Buttercup, seated
on quarter-deck, gazing sentimentally at him.

SONG.—Captain.

Fair moon, to thee I sing,
  Bright regent of the heavens,
Say, why is everything
  Either at sixes or at sevens?
I have lived hitherto
  Free from the breath of slander,
Beloved by all my crew—
  A really popular commander.
But now my kindly crew rebel,
  My daughter to a tar is partial,
Sir Joseph storms, and, sad to tell,
  He threatens a court martial!
    Fair moon, to thee I sing,
      Bright regent of the heavens,
    Say, why is everything
      Either at sixes or at sevens?

But. How sweetly he carols forth his melody to the unconscious moon! Of whom is he

thinking? Of some high born beauty? It may
be! Who is poor Little Buttercup that she
should expect his glance to fall on one so lowly!
And yet if he knew—if he only knew!
  Capt. (*Coming down.*) Ah! Little Buttercup, still on board? That is not quite right,
little one. It would have been more respectable
to have gone on shore at dusk.
  But. True, dear captain—but the recollec-
tion of your sad pale face seemed to chain me
to the ship. I would fain see you smile before
I go.
  Capt. Ah! Little Buttercup, I fear it will
be long before I recover my accustomed cheer-
fulness, for misfortunes crowd upon me, and
all my old friends seem to have turned against
me!
  But. Oh, no—do not say "all," dear Captain. That were unjust to one, at least.
  Capt. True, for you are staunch to me.
(*Aside.*) If ever I gave my heart again, methinks it would be to such a one as this!
(*Aloud.*) I am touched to the heart by your
innocent regard for me, and were we differently

79

situated, I think I could have returned it. But, as it is, I fear I can never be more to you than a friend.

But. I understand! You hold aloof from me because you are rich and lofty—and I, poor and lowly. But take care! The poor bumboat woman has gipsy blood in her veins, and she can read destinies.

Capt. Destinies!

But. There is a change in store for you!

Capt. A change!

But. Aye—be prepared!

DUET.—*Little Buttercup and Captain.*

But.
Things are seldom what they seem,
Skim milk masquerades as cream;
Highlows pass as patent leathers;
Jackdaws strut in peacock's feathers.

Capt. (*Puzzled.*) Very true,
　　　　　　　　　So they do.

But.
Black sheep dwell in every fold;
All that glitters is not gold;
Storks turn out to be but logs;
Bulls are but inflated frogs.

Capt. (*Puzzled.*) So they be,
　　　　　　　　　　Frequentlee.

But.
Drops the wind and stops the mill;
Turbot is ambitious brill;
Gild the farthing if you will,
Yet it is a farthing still.

Capt. (*Puzzled.*) Yes, I know,
　　　　　　　　　　That is so.
Though to catch your drift I'm striving,
　It is shady—it is shady;
I don't see at what you're driving,
　Mystic lady—mystic lady,
(*Aside.*)
Stern convictions o'er me stealing,
That the mystic lady's dealing
In oracular revealing.

But. (*Aside.*)
Stern convictions o'er him stealing
That the mystic lady's dealing
In oracular revealing.

Capt. Yes, I know—
But.　That is so!
Capt.
Though I'm anything but clever,
I could talk like that for ever;
Once a cat was killed by care;
Only brave deserve the fair.

But. Very true,
　　　　So they do.
Capt.
Wink is often good as nod;
Spoils the child who spares the rod;

Thirsty lambs run foxy dangers;
Dogs are found in many mangers.

But. Frequentlee,
　　　I agree.

Capt.
Paw of cat the chestnut snatches;
Worn out garments show new patches;
Only count the chick that hatches;
Men are grown up catchy-catchies.

But. Yes, I know,
　　　That is so.

(*Aside.*)
Though to catch my drift he's striving,
　I'll dissemble—I'll dissemble;
When he sees at what I'm driving,
　Let him tremble—let him tremble!

ENSEMBLE.

Though a mystic tone { I / you } borrow,

{ I shall / He will } learn the truth with sorrow,

Here to-day and gone to-morrow;

Both. Yes, I know—
　　　　That is so!

(*At the end, exit Little Buttercup, melo-dramatically.*)

Capt. Incomprehensible as her utterances are, I nevertheless feel that they are dictated by a sincere regard for me. But to what new misery is she referring! Time alone can tell!

(*Enter Sir Joseph.*)

Sir Joseph. Captain Corcoran, I am much disappointed with your daughter. In fact, I don't think she will do.

Capt. She won't do, Sir Joseph!

Sir Joseph. I'm afraid not. The fact is, that although I have urged my suit with as much eloquence as is consistent with an official utterance, I have done so hitherto without success. How do you account for this!

Capt. Really, Sir Joseph, I hardly know. Josephine is of course sensible of your condescension.

Sir Joseph. She naturally would be.

Capt. But perhaps your exalted rank dazzles her.

Sir Joseph. You think it does?

Capt. I can hardly say; but she is a modest girl, and her social position is far below your own. It may be that she feels she is not worthy of you.

Sir Joseph. That is really a very sensible suggestion, and displays more knowledge of human nature than I had given you credit for.

Capt. See, she comes. If your lordship would kindly reason with her and assure her officially that it is a standing rule at the Admiralty that love levels all ranks, her respect for an official utterance might induce her to look upon your offer in its proper light.

Sir Joseph. It is not unlikely. I will adopt your suggestion. But soft, she is here. Let us withdraw, and watch our opportunity.

(*Enter Josephine from Cabin. Sir Joseph and Captain retire.*)

SCENA.—*Josephine.*

The hours creep on apace,
    My guilty heart is quaking!
Oh, that I might retrace
    The step that I am taking.
Its folly it were easy to be showing,
What I am giving up and whither going.
On the one hand, papa's luxurious home,
    Hung with ancestral armour and old
        brasses,
Carved oak and tapestry from distant Rome,
    Rare "blue and white", Venetian finger
        glasses,
Rich oriental rugs, luxurious sofa pillows,
And everything that isn't old, from Gillow's.
And on the other, a dark and dingy room,
    In some back street with stuffy children
        crying,
Where organs yell, and clacking housewives
    fume,
    And clothes are hanging out all day
        a-drying.
With one cracked looking-glass to see your
    face in,
And dinner served up in a pudding basin!
A simple sailor, lowly born,
    Unlettered and unknown,
Who toils for bread from early morn
    Till half the night has flown!
No golden rank can he impart—
    No wealth of house or land—
No fortune save his trusty heart,
    And honest brown right hand!
    And yet he is so wondrous fair,
    That love for one so passing rare,
    So peerless in his manly beauty,
    Were little else than solemn duty!
Oh, god of love, and god of reason, say,
Which of you twain shall my poor heart
    obey!

(*Sir Joseph and Captain enter.*)

Sir Joseph. Madam, it has been represented to me that you are appalled by my exalted rank. I desire to convey to you officially my assurance, that if your hesitation is attributable to that circumstance, it is uncalled for.

Jos. Oh, then your lordship is of opinion that married happiness is *not* inconsistent with discrepancy in rank?

Sir Joseph. I am officially of that opinion.

Jos. That the high and the lowly may be truly happy together, provided that they truly love one another?

Sir Joseph. Madam, I desire to convey to

you officially my opinion that love is a platform upon which all ranks meet.

Jos. I thank you, Sir Joseph. I *did* hesitate, but I will hesitate no longer. (*Aside.*) He little thinks how eloquently he has pleaded his rival's cause!

TRIO.—*Sir Joseph, Captain, and Josephine.*

Capt.
    Never mind the why and wherefore,
    Love can level ranks, and therefore,
    Though his lordship's station's mighty,
        Though stupendous be his brain,
    Though her tastes are mean and flighty
        And her fortune poor and plain,
Capt. and Sir Joseph.
    Ring the merry bells on board-ship,
        Rend the air with warbling wild,
    For the union of $\begin{cases} his \\ my \end{cases}$ lordship
        With a humble captain's child!
Capt. For a humble captain's daughter—
Jos. For a gallant captain's daughter—
Sir Joseph. And a lord who rules the water—
Jos. (*Aside.*)
    And a *tar* who ploughs the water!
All.
    Let the air with joy be laden,
        Rend with songs the air above,
    For the union of a maiden
        With the man who owns her love!
Sir Joseph.
    Never mind the why and wherefore,
    Love can level ranks, and therefore,
    Though your nautical relation (*alluding to
        Capt.*)
        In my set could scarcely pass—
    Though you occupy a station
        In the lower middle class—
Capt. and Sir Joseph.
    Ring the merry bells on board-ship,
        Rend the air with warbling wild,
    For the union of $\begin{cases} my \\ his \end{cases}$ lordship
        With a humble captain's child!
Capt. For a humble captain's daughter—
Jos. For a gallant captain's daughter—
Sir Joseph. And a lord who rules the water—
Jos. (*Aside.*) And a *tar* who ploughs the water!
All.
    Let the air with joy be laden,
        Rend with songs the air above,
    For the union of a maiden
        With the man who owns her love!
Jos.
    Never mind the why and wherefore,
    Love can level ranks, and therefore
    I admit the jurisdiction:
        Ably have you played your part,
    You have carried firm conviction
        To my hesitating heart.

81

Capt. and Sir Joseph.
Ring the merry bells on board-ship,
Rend the air with warbling wild,

For the union of $\begin{Bmatrix} my \\ his \end{Bmatrix}$ lordship
With a humble captain's child!

Capt. For a humble captain's daughter—
Jos. For a gallant captain's daughter—
Sir Joseph. And a lord who rules the water—
Jos. (Aside.) And a *tar* who ploughs the water!
(Aloud.) Let the air with joy be laden.
Capt. and Sir Joseph. Ring the merry bells
  on board-ship—
Jos. For the union of a maiden—
Capt. and Sir Joseph. For her union with his
  lordship.
All.
Rend with songs the air above
For the man who owns her love!

(*Exit Jos.*)

Capt. Sir Joseph, I cannot express to you
my delight at the happy result of your eloquence. Your argument was unanswerable.

Sir Joseph. Captain Corcoran, it is one of
the happiest characteristics of this glorious
country that official utterances are invariably
regarded as unanswerable. (*Exit Sir Joseph.*)

Capt. At last my fond hopes are to be
crowned. My only daughter is to be the bride
of a Cabinet Minister. The prospect is Elysian.
(*During this speech Dick Deadeye has entered.*)

Dick. Captain.

Capt. Deadeye! You here? Don't! (*Recoiling from him.*)

Dick. Ah, don't shrink from me, Captain.
I'm unpleasant to look at, and my name's agin
me, but I ain't as bad as I seem.

Capt. What would you with me?

Dick. (*Mysteriously.*) I'm come to give
you warning.

Capt. Indeed! do you propose to leave the
Navy then?

Dick. No, no, you misunderstand me; listen!

DUET.—*Captain and Dick Deadeye.*

Dick.
Kind Captain, I've important information,
  Sing hey, the kind commander that you
    are,
About a certain intimate relation,
  Sing hey, the merry maiden and the tar.
Both. The merry maiden and the tar.
Capt.
Good fellow, in conundrums you are speak-
    ing,
  Sing hey, the mystic sailor that you are,
The answer to them vainly I am seeking;
  Sing hey, the merry maiden and the tar.
Both. The merry maiden and the tar.

Dick.
Kind Captain, your young lady is a sighing.
  Sing hey, the simple captain that you are,
This very night with Rackstraw to be flying;
  Sing hey, the merry maiden and the tar.
Both. The merry maiden and the tar.
Capt.
Good fellow, you have given timely warning,
  Sing hey, the thoughtful sailor that you
    are,
I'll talk to Master Rackstraw in the morning:
  Sing hey, the cat-o-nine-tails and the tar!
            (*Producing a "cat."*)
Both. The merry cat-o-nine tails and the tar!
Capt. Dick Deadeye—I thank you for your
warning—I will at once take means to arrest
their flight. This boat cloak will afford me
ample disguise—So! (*Envelopes himself in a
mysterious cloak, holding it before his face.*)
Dick. Ha, ha! They are foiled—foiled—
foiled!

(*Enter Crew on tiptoe, with Ralph and Boatswain meeting Josephine, who enters from Cabin on tiptoe, with bundle of necessaries, and accompanied by Little Buttercup.*)

ENSEMBLE.
Carefully on tiptoe stealing,
  Breathing gently as we may,
Every step with caution feeling,
  We will softly steal away.

(*Captains stamps.*)—*Chord.*
All. (*Much alarmed.*)
Goodness me—
  Why, what was that?
Dick.
Silent be,
  It was the cat!
All. (*Reassured.*)
It was—it was the cat!
Capt. (*Producing cat-o-nine tails.*) They're
                right, it was the cat!
  Pull ashore in fashion steady,
    Hymen will defray the fare,
  For a clergyman is ready
    To unite the happy pair!
      (*Stamp as before, and Chord.*)
All. Goodness me,
  Why, what was that?
Dick.
Silent be,
  Again the cat!
All. It was again the cat!
Capt. (*Aside.*)
They're right, it was the cat!
Capt. (*Throwing off cloak.*) Hold! (*All start.*)
  Pretty daughter of mine,
    I insist upon knowing
    Where you may be going
  With these sons of the brine,
    For my excellent crew,

82

Though foes they could thump any,
Are scarcely fit company,
My daughter, for you.
Crew. Now, hark at that, do!
Though foes we could thump any,
We're scarcely fit company
For a lady like you!
Ralph.
Proud officer, that haughty lip uncurl!
Vain man, suppress that supercilious sneer,
For I have dared to love your matchless girl,
A fact well known to all my messmates
here!
Capt. Oh, horror!
Ralph and Jos.
$\left\{ \begin{array}{l} \text{I,} \\ \text{He,} \end{array} \right\}$ humble, poor, and lowly born,
The meanest in the port division—
The butt of epauletted scorn—
The mark of quarter-deck derision—
$\left. \begin{array}{l} \text{Have} \\ \text{Has} \end{array} \right\}$ dared to raise $\left\{ \begin{array}{l} \text{my} \\ \text{his} \end{array} \right\}$ wormy eyes,
Above the dust to which you'd mould$\left\{ \begin{array}{l} \text{me} \\ \text{him} \end{array} \right.$
In manhood's glorious pride to rise,
$\left. \begin{array}{l} \text{I am} \\ \text{He is} \end{array} \right\}$ an Englishman—behold $\left\{ \begin{array}{l} \text{me!} \\ \text{him!} \end{array} \right.$
All. He is an Englishman!
Boat. He is an Englishman!
For he himself has said it,
And it's greatly to his credit,
That he is an Englishman!
All. That he is an Englishman!
Boat. For he might have been a Roosian,
A French, or Turk or Proosian,
Or perhaps Itali-an!
All. Or perhaps Itali-an!
Boat. But in spite of all temptations
To belong to other nations,
He remains an Englishman!
All. For in spite of all temptations, etc.
(*Capt. trying to repress his anger.*)
In uttering a reprobation
To any British Tar,
I try to speak with moderation,
But you have gone too far.
I'm very sorry to disparage
A humble foremast lad,
But to seek your captain's child in mar-
riage
Why, damme, it's too bad!
(*During this Cousin Hebe and Female Rela-
tives have entered.*)
All. (*Shocked.*)   Oh!
Capt. Yes, damme, it's too bad!
All.   Oh!
Capt. and Dick Deadeye. Yes, damme, it's too
bad.
(*During this Sir Joseph has appeared on
poop-deck. He is horrified at the bad language.*)
Hebe.

Did you hear him—did you hear him?
Oh, the monster overbearing!
Don't go near him—don't go near him—
He is swearing—he is swearing—
Sir Joseph.
My pain and my distress,
I find it is not easy to express;
My amazement—my surprise—
You may learn from the expression of my
eyes!
Capt.
My lord—one word—the facts are not before
you,
The word was injudicious, I allow—
But hear my explanation, I implore you,
And you will be indignant, too, I vow!
Sir Joseph.
I will hear of no defence,
Attempt none if you're sensible.
That word of evil sense
Is wholly indefensible.
Go ribald, get you hence
To your cabin with celerity.
This is the consequence
Of ill-advised asperity!
(*Exit Captain, disgraced, followed by
Josephine.*)
All.
This is the consequence,
Of ill-advised asperity!
Sir Joseph.
For I'll teach you all, ere long,
To refrain from language strong.
For I haven't any sympathy for ill-bred
taunts!
Hebe. No more have his sisters, nor his
cousins, nor his aunts.
All. For he is an Englishman, etc. (*Re-en-
ter Josephine.*)
Sir Joseph. Now, tell me, my fine fellow—
for you *are* a fine fellow—
Ralph. Yes, your honour.
Sir Joseph. How came your captain so far
to forget himself? I am quite sure you had
given him no cause for annoyance.
Ralph. Please, your honour, it was thus
wise. You see I'm only a top-man—a mere
foremast hand—
Sir Joseph. Don't be ashamed of that. Your
position as a top-man is a very exalted one.
Ralph. Well, your honour, love burns as
brightly in the fo'c's'le as it does on the quarter-deck, and Josephine is the fairest bud that
ever blossomed upon the tree of a poor fellow's
wildest hopes.
(*Josephine rushes to Ralph's arms.*)
Jos. Darling! (*Sir Joseph horrified.*)
Ralph. She is the figurehead of my ship of
life—the bright beacon that guides me into my
port of happiness—the rarest, the purest gem

that ever sparkled on a poor but worthy fellow's trusting brow!

All. Very pretty, very pretty!

Sir Joseph. Insolent sailor, you shall repent this outrage. Seize him! (*Two Marines seize him and handcuff him.*)

Jos. Oh, Sir Joseph, spare him, for I love him tenderly.

Sir Joseph. Pray don't. I will teach this presumptuous mariner to discipline his affections. Have you such a thing as a dungeon on board?

All. We have!

Dick. They have!

Sir Joseph. Then load him with chains and take him there at once!

OCTETTE.

Ralph.
Farewell, my own,
    Light of my life, farewell!
For crime unknown
    I go to a dungeon cell.

Jos.
I will atone,
    In the meantime farewell!
And all alone
    Rejoice in your dungeon cell!

Sir Joseph.
A bone, a bone
    I'll pick with this sailor fell;
Let him be shown
    At once to his dungeon cell.

Boatswain, Dick Deadeye and Cousin Hebe.
He'll hear no tone
    Of the maiden he loves so well!
No telephone
    Communicates with his cell!

But. (*mysteriously.*)
But when is known
    The secret I have to tell,
Wide will be thrown
    The door of his dungeon cell.

All.
For crime unknown
    He goes to a dungeon cell!
        (*Ralph is led off in custody.*)

Sir Joseph.
My pain and my distress
Again it is not easy to express,
My amazement, my surprise
Again you may discover from my eyes!

All.
How terrible the aspect of his eyes!

But.
Hold! Ere upon your loss
    You lay much stress,
A long-concealed crime
    I would confess.

SONG.—Buttercup.

A many years ago,
    When I was young and charming,
As some of you may know,
    I practised baby-farming.

All.
Now this is most alarming!
When she was young and charming,
She practised baby-farming,
    A many years ago.

But.
Two tender babes I nussed,
    One was of low condition,
The other, upper crust,
    A regular patrician.

All. (*Explaining to each other.*)
Now, this is the position.
One was of low condition,
The other a patrician,
    A many years ago.

But.
Oh, bitter is my cup!
    However could I do it?
I mixed those children up,
    And not a creature knew it!

All.
However could you do it,
Some day, no doubt, you'll rue it,
Although no creature knew it,
    So many years ago.

But.
In time each little waif
    Forsook his foster mother,
The well-born babe was Ralph—
    Your captain was the other!!!

All.
They left their foster mother,
The one was Ralph, our brother,
Our captain was the other,
    A many years ago.

Sir Joseph. Then I am to understand that Captain Corcoran and Ralph were exchanged in childhood's happy hours—that Ralph is really the Captain, and the Captain is Ralph?

But. That is the idea I intended to convey, officially!

Sir Joseph. And very well you have conveyed it, Miss Buttercup!

But. Aye! Aye! yer 'onour.

Sir Joseph. Dear me! Let them appear before me at once!

(*Ralph enters as Captain; Captain as a common sailor. Josephine rushes to his arms.*)

Jos. My father—a common sailor!

Capt. It is hard, is it not, my dear?

Sir Joseph. This is a very singular occurrence; I congratulate you both. (*To Ralph.*) Desire that remarkably fine seaman to step forward.

Ralph. Concoran. Three paces to the front —march!

Capt. If what?

Ralph. I don't understand.

Capt. If you please!

84

Ralph. What!

Sir Joseph. Perfectly right. If you *please.*

Ralph. Oh. If you *please.* (*Captain steps forward.*)

Sir Joseph. (*To Captain.*) You are an extremely fine fellow.

Capt. Yes, your honour.

Sir Joseph. So it seems that you were Ralph, and Ralph was you.

Capt. So it seems, your honour.

Sir Joseph. Well, I need not tell you that after this change in your condition, a marriage with your daughter will be out of the question.

Capt. Don't say that, your honour—love levels all ranks.

Sir Joseph. It does to a considerable extent, but it does not level them as much as that.

Sir Joseph. (*Handing Josephine to Ralph.*) Here—take her, sir, and mind you treat her kindly.

Ralph and Jos. Oh bliss, oh rapture!

Capt. and But. Oh rapture. oh bliss!

Sir Joseph. Sad my lot and sorry, what shall I do? I cannot live alone!

Hebe. Fear nothing—while I live I'll not desert you. I'll sooth and comfort your declining days.

Sir Joseph. No, don't do that.

Hebe. Yes, but indeed I'd rather—

Sir Joseph. (*Resigned.*) Oh! very well, then!
> To-morrow morn our vows shall all be
>   plighted,
> Three loving pairs on the same day united!

QUARTETTE.—*Josephine, Hebe, Ralph and Deadeye.*
> Oh joy, oh rapture unforeseen,
> The clouded sky is now serene,
> The god of day—the orb of love,
> Has hung his ensign high above,
>   The sky is all ablaze.
> With wooing words and loving song,
> We'll chase the lagging hours along,
> And if { he finds / I find } the maiden coy,
> We'll murmur forth decorous joy
>   In dreamy roundelays.

Capt.
> For he's the Captain of the "Pinafore."

All. And a right good captain, too!

Capt.
> And though before my fall
> I was captain of you all,
>   I'm a member of the crew.

All.
> And though before his fall, etc.

Capt.
> I shall marry with a wife,
> In my humble rank of life! (*turning to But.*)
>   And you, my own, are she—
> I must wander to and fro,
> But wherever I may go,
>   I shall never be untrue to thee!

All. What never?

Capt. No never!

All. What *never?*

Capt. Hardly ever!

All. Hardly ever be untrue to thee.
> Then give three cheers, and one cheer more,
> For the former Captain of the "Pinafore."

But.
> For he loves little Buttercup, dear little But-
>   tercup,
> Though I could never tell why;
> But still he loves Buttercup, poor little But-
>   tercup,
> Sweet little Buttercup, aye!

All. For he loves, etc.

Sir Joseph.
> I'm the monarch of the sea,
>   And when I've married thee (*to Hebe*),
> I'll be true to the devotion that my love im-
>   plants,

Hebe.
> Then good-bye to your sisters, and your
>   cousins, and your aunts,
> Especially your cousins,
> Whom you reckon up by dozens.

All. Then good-bye, etc.
> For he is an Englishman,
>   And he himself hath said it,
>   And it's greatly to his credit
> That he is an Englishman!

CURTAIN.

I'M CALLED LITTLE BUTTERCUP.

SONG. MRS. CRIPPS.

I'm called lit - tle But - ter - cup, Dear lit - tle But - ter - cup, Tho' I could nev - er tell why,

But still I'm call'd But - ter - cup, Poor lit - tle But - ter - cup, Sweet lit - tle But - ter - cup, I.

I've snuff and to - bac - cy, And ex - cel - lent jack - y; I've scis - sors and watch - es and knives.

I've rib - bons and la - ces to set off the fa - ces of pret - ty young sweethearts and wives.

But - ter - cup, Poor lit - tle But - ter - cup, Come, of your But - ter - cup buy. . . .

colla voce.

I AM THE MONARCH OF THE SEA.

SIR JOSEPH, COUSIN HEBE, BOATSWAIN AND CHORUS.

(*Enter* Sir Joseph *with* Cousin Hebe.)

SIR J. PORTER. (*Advancing to front of stage.*)

Vivace.

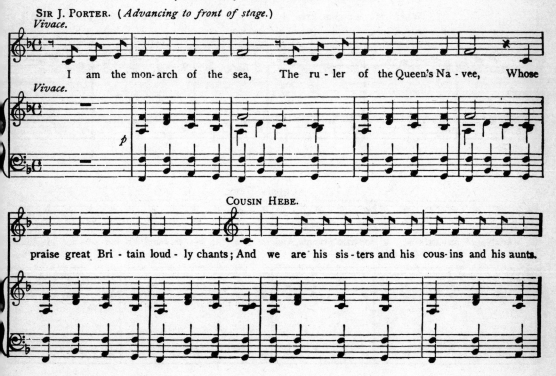

I am the mon - arch of the sea, The ru - ler of the Queen's Na - vee, Whose

Vivace.

COUSIN HEBE.

praise great Bri - tain loud - ly chants; And we are his sis - ters and his cous - ins and his aunts.

THE MIKADO

OR,

THE TOWN OF TITIPU.

BY

Sir W. S. GILBERT

AND

Sir ARTHUR S. SULLIVAN

THE MIKADO

Dramatis Personae

THE MIKADO OF JAPAN

NANKI-POO (*his Son, disguised as a wandering minstrel, and in love with* YUM-YUM)

KO-KO (*Lord High Executioner of Titipu*)

POOH-BAH (*Lord High Everything Else*)

PISH-TUSH (*a Noble Lord*)

YUM-YUM
PITTI-SING } *Three Sisters—Wards of* KO-KO
PEEP-BO

KATISHA (*an elderly Lady, in love with* NANKI-POO)

CHORUS OF SCHOOL-GIRLS, NOBLES, GUARDS, AND COOLIES.

ACT I.—Court-yard of Ko-Ko's Official Residence.

ACT II.—Ko-Ko's Garden.

THE MIKADO

OR,

THE TOWN OF TITIPU

▼▼▼

ACT I.

SCENE.—*Court-yard of Ko-Ko's Palace in Titipu. Japanese nobles discovered standing and sitting in attitudes suggested by native drawings.*

CHORUS OF NOBLES.

If you want to know who we are,
We are gentlemen of Japan:
On many a vase and jar—
On many a screen and fan,
  We figure in lively paint:
  Our attitudes queer and quaint—
You're wrong if you think it ain't, oh!

If you think we are worked by strings,
Like a Japanese marionette,
You don't understand these things:
It is simply Court etiquette.
  Perhaps you suppose this throng
  Can't keep it up all day long?
  If that's your idea, you're wrong, oh!

Enter Nanki-Poo in great excitement. He carries a native guitar on his back and a bundle of ballads in his hand.

RECIT.—*Nanki-Poo.*

Gentlemen, I pray you tell me
Where a gentle maiden dwelleth,
Named Yum-Yum, the ward of Ko-Ko?
In pity speak—oh, speak, I pray you!

A Noble. Why, who are you who ask this question?

Nank. Come gather round me, and I'll tell you.

SONG AND CHORUS.—*Nanki-Poo.*

A wandering minstrel I—
  A thing of shreds and patches,
  Of ballads, songs and snatches,
And dreamy lullaby!

My catalogue is long,
  Through every passion raging,
  And to your humours changing
I tune my supple song!

Are you in sentimental mood?
  I'll sigh with you,
    Oh, sorrow, sorrow!
On maiden's coldness do you brood?
I'll do so, too—
    Oh, sorrow, sorrow!
I'll charm your willing ears
With songs of lovers' fears,
While sympathetic tears
  My cheeks bedew—
    Oh, sorrow, sorrow!

But if patriotic sentiment is wanted,
  I've patriotic ballads cut and dried;
For where'er our country's banner may be planted,
  All other local banners are defied!
Our warriors, in serried ranks assembled,
  Never quail—or they conceal it if they do—
And I shouldn't be surprised if nations trembled
  Before the mighty troops of Titipu!

Chorus. We shouldn't be surprised, &c.
Nank. And if you call for a song of the sea,
  We'll heave the capstan round,
  With a yeo heave ho, for the wind is free,
  Her anchor's a-trip and her helm's a-lee,
    Hurrah for the homeward bound!
Chorus.   Yeo-ho—heave ho—
    Hurrah for the homeward bound!

To lay aloft in a howling breeze
  May tickle a landsman's taste,
But the happiest hour a sailor sees
  Is when he's down
  At an inland town,
With his Nancy on his knees, yeo ho!
And his arm around her waist!

Chorus. Then man the capstan—off we go,
  As the fiddler swings us round,
With a yeo heave ho,
And a rum below,
  Hurrah for the homeward bound!

A wandering minstrel I, &c.

Enter Pish-Tush.

Pish. And what may be your business with Yum-Yum?

Nank. I'll tell you. A year ago I was a member of the Titipu town band. It was my duty to take the cap round for contributions. While discharging this delicate office I saw Yum-Yum. We loved each other at once, but she was betrothed to her guardian Ko-Ko, a cheap tailor, and I saw that my suit was hopeless. Overwhelmed with despair I quitted the town. Judge of my delight when I heard, a month ago, that Ko-Ko had been condemned to death for flirting! I hurried back at once, in the hope of finding Yum-Yum at liberty to listen to my protestations.

Pish. It is true that Ko-Ko was condemned to death for flirting, but he was reprieved at the last moment, and raised to the exalted rank of Lord High Executioner under the following reable circumstances :—

SONG.—*Pish-Tush and Chorus.*

Our great Mikado, virtuous man,
When he to rule our land began,
    Resolved to try
    A plan whereby
Young men might best be steadied.
So he decreed, in words succinct,
That all who flirted, leered or winked,
(Unless connubially linked,)
    Should forthwith be beheaded.
      And I expect you'll all agree
      That he was right to so decree.
      And I am right,
      And you are right,
      And all is right as right can be!

Chorus.   And you are right,
          And we are right, &c.

This stern decree, you'll understand,
Caused great dismay throughout the land!
    For young and old
    And shy and bold
Were equally affected.
The youth who winked a roving eye,
Or breathed a non-connubial sigh,
Was thereupon condemned to die—
    He usually objected.
      And you'll allow, as I expect,
      That he was right to so object.
      And I am right.
      And you are right,
      And everything is quite correct!

Chorus.   And you are right,
          And we are right, &c.

And so we straight let out on bail
A convict from the county jail,
    Whose head was next

    On some pretext
Condemned to be mown off,
And made *him* Headsman, for we said,
    Who's next to be decapited
Cannot cut off another's head
    Until he's cut his own off."

      And we are right, I think you'll say,
      To argue in this kind of way
      And I am right,
      And you are right,
      And all is right—too-looral-lay!

Chorus.   And you are right,
          And we are right, &c.

              [*Exeunt Chorus.*

    Enter Pooh-Bah.

Nank. Ko-Ko, the cheap tailor, Lord High Executioner of Titipu! Why, that's the highest rank a citizen can attain!

Pooh. It is. Our logical Mikado, seeing no moral difference between the dignified judge, who condemns a criminal to die, and the industrious mechanic who carries out the sentence, has rolled the two offices into one, and every judge is now his own executioner.

Nank. But how good of you (for I see that you are a nobleman of the highest rank) to condescend to tell all this to me, a mere strolling minstrel!

Pooh. Don't mention it. I am, in point of fact, a particularly haughty and exclusive person, of pre-Adamite ancestral descent. You will understand this when I tell you that I can trace my ancestry back to a protoplasmal primordial atomic globule. Consequently, my family pride is something inconceivable. I can't help it. I was born sneering. But I struggle hard to overcome this defect. I mortify my pride continually. When all the great officers of State resigned in a body, because they were too proud to serve under an ex-tailor, did I not unhesitatingly accept all their posts at once?

Pish. And the salaries attached to them? You did.

Pooh. It is consequently my degrading duty to serve this upstart as First Lord of the Treasury, Lord Chief Justice, Commander-in-Chief, Lord High Admiral, Master of the Buckhounds, Groom of the Back Stairs, Archbishop of Titipu, and Lord Mayor, both acting and elect, all rolled into one. And at a salary! A Pooh-Bah paid for his services! I a salaried minion! But I do it! It revolts me, but I do it!

Nank. And it does you credit.

Pooh. But I don't stop at that. I go and dine with middle-class people on reasonable terms. I dance at cheap suburban parties for a moderate fee. I accept refreshment at any hands, however lowly. I also retail State secrets at a very low figure. For instance, any further information about Yum-Yum would come under the head of a State secret. (*Nanki-Poo takes the hint, and gives him money.*) (*Aside.*) Another insult, and I think a light one!

SONG.—*Pooh-Bah with Nanki-Poo and Pish.*

Young man, despair,
　　Likewise go to,
　　Yum-Yum the fair
　　You must not woo.
　　It will not do:
　　I'm sorry for you,
You very imperfect ablutioner!
　　This very day
　　From school Yum-Yum
Will wend her way,
　　And homeward come,
　　With beat of drum
　　And a rum-tum-tum,
To wed the Lord High Executioner!
　　And the brass will crash,
　　And the trumpets bray,
　　And they'll cut a dash
　　On their wedding day.
She'll toddle away, as all aver,
With the Lord High Executioner!

Nank. and Pooh.　And the brass will crash, &c.

　　It's a hopeless case,
　　As you may see,
And in your place
　　Away I'd flee;
　　But don't blame me—
　　I'm sorry to be
Of your pleasure a diminutioner.
　　They'll vow their pact
　　Extremely soon,
In point of fact
　　This afternoon
　　Her honeymoon
　　With that buffoon
At seven. commences, so *you* shun her!

All.　And the brass will crash, &c.

[*Exit Pish-Tush.*

RECIT.—*Nanki-Poo and Pooh-Bah.*

Nank.
And have I journeyed for a month, or nearly.
To learn that Yum-Yum, whom I love so dearly,
This day to Ko-Ko is to be united!

Pooh.
The fact appears to be as you've recited:
But here he comes, equipped as suits his station;
He'll give you any further information.

[*Exeunt Pooh-Bah and Nanki-Poo.*
Enter Chorus of Nobles.

Behold the Lord High Executioner!
A personage of noble rank and title—
A dignified and potent officer,
Whose functions are particularly vital!

Defer, defer,
To the Lord High Executioner!
Enter Ko-Ko attended.
SOLO.—*Ko-Ko.*

Taken from the county jail
　　By a set of curious chances;
Liberated then on bail,
　　On my own recognizances;
Wafted by a favouring gale
　　As one sometimes is in trances,
To a height that few can scale,
　　Save by long and weary dances;
Surely, never had a male
　　Under such like circumstances
So adventurous a tale,
　　Which may rank with most romances.

Chorus.　　Defer, defer,
To the Lord High Executioner, &c.

Ko. Gentlemen, I'm much touched by this reception. I can only trust that by strict attention to duty I shall ensure a continuance of those favours which it will ever be my study to deserve. If I should ever be called upon to act professionally, I am happy to think that there will be no difficulty in finding plenty of people whose loss will be a distinct gain to society at large.

SONG.—*Ko-Ko with Chorus of Men.*

As some day it may happen that a victim must be found,
　　I've got a little list—I've got a little list
Of society offenders who might well be underground,
　　And who never would be missed—who never would be missed!
There's the pestilential nuisances who write for autographs—
All people who have flabby hands and irritating laughs—
All children who are up in dates, and floor you with 'em flat—
All persons who in shaking hands, shake hands with you like *that*—
And all third persons who on spoiling *tête-à-têtes* insist—
They'd none of 'em be missed—they'd none of 'em be missed!

Chorus.　He's got 'em on the list—he's got 'em on the list;
　　And they'll none of 'em be missed—they'll none of 'em be missed.

There's the nigger serenader, and the others of his race,
And the piano organist—I've got him on the list!
And the people who eat peppermint and puff it in your face,
They never would be missed—they never would be missed!
Then the idiot who praises, with enthusiastic tone,

93

All centuries but this, and every country but
    his own;
And the lady from the provinces, who dresses
    like a guy,
And "who doesn't think she dances, but would
    rather like to try";
And that singular anomaly, the lady novelist—
    I don't think she'd be missed—I'm *sure* she'd
    not be missed!
Chorus. He's got her on the list—he's got her
    on the list;
        And I don't think she'll be missed—
        I'm *sure* she'll not be missed!
And that *Nisi Prius* nuisance, who just now is
    rather rife,
    The Judicial humorist—I've got *him* on the
    list!
All funny fellows, comic men, and clowns of
    private life—
    They'd none of 'em be missed—they'd none
    of 'em be missed
And apologetic statesmen of a compromising
    kind,
Such as—what d'ye call him—Thing'em-bob,
    and likewise—Never mind,
And 'St—'st—'st—and What's-his-name, and
    also You-know-who—
The task of filling up the blanks I'd rather leave
    to *you.*
But it really doesn't matter whom you put upon
    the list,
    For they'd none of 'em be missed—they'd
    none of 'em be missed!
Chorus. You may put 'em on the list—you
    may put 'em on the list;
        And they'll none of 'em be missed—
        they'll none of 'em be missed!
                                    [*Exeunt Chorus.*
            Enter Pooh-Bah.
Ko. Pooh-Bah, it seems that the festivities
in connection with my approaching marriage
must last a week. I should like to do it handsomely, and I want to consult you as to the
amount I ought to spend upon them.
Pooh. Certainly. In which of my capacities? As First Lord of the Treasury, Lord
Chamberlain, Attorney-General, Chancellor of
the Exchequer, Privy Purse, or Private Secretary?
Ko. Suppose we say as Private Secretary.
Pooh. Speaking as your Private Secretary,
I should say that as the city will have to pay
for it, don't stint yourself, do it well.
Ko. Exactly—as the city will have to pay
for it. That is your advice.
Pooh. As Private Secretary. Of course you
will understand that, as Chancellor of the Exchequer, I am bound to see that due economy is
observed.
Ko. Oh! But you said just now "don't
stint yourself, do it well."

Pooh. As Private Secretary.
Ko. And now you say that due economy
must be observed.
Pooh. As Chancellor of the Exchequer.
Ko. I see. Come over here, where the
Chancellor can't hear us. (*They cross the
stage.*) Now, as my Solicitor, how do you ad-
vise me to deal with this difficulty?
Pooh. Oh, as your Solicitor, I should have
no hesitation in saying "chance it—"
Ko. Thank you. (*Shaking his hand.*) I
will.
Pooh. If it were not that, as Lord Chief
Justice, I am bound to see that the law isn't
violated.
Ko. I see. Come over here where the Chief
Justice can't hear us. (*They cross the stage.*)
Now, then, as First Lord of the Treasury?
Pooh. Of course, as First Lord of the
Treasury, I could propose a special vote that
would cover all expenses, if it were not that,
as Leader of the Opposition, it would be my
duty to resist it, tooth and nail. Or, as Pay-
master-General, I could so cook the accounts
that as Lord High Auditor, I should never discover the fraud. But then, as Archbishop of
Titipu, it would be my duty to denounce my
dishonesty and give myself into my own custody as First Commissioner of Police.
Ko. That's extremely awkward.
Pooh. I don't say that all these distinguished
people couldn't be squared; but it is right to
tell you that they wouldn't be sufficiently de-
graded in their own estimation unless they are
insulted with a very considerable bribe.
Ko. The matter shall have my careful consideration. But my bride and her sisters approach, and any little compliment on your part,
such as an abject grovel in a characteristic Japanese attitude, would be esteemed a favour.
                                    [*Exeunt together.*
    *Enter procession of Yum-Yum's schoolfel-
lows, heralding Yum-Yum, Peep-Bo, and Pitti-
Sing.*

            CHORUS OF GIRLS.

Comes a train of little ladies
    From scholastic trammels free,
Each a little bit afraid is,
    Wondering what the world can be!

Is it but a world of trouble—
    Sadness set to song?
Is its beauty but a bubble
    Bound to break ere long?

Are its palaces and pleasures
    Fantasies that fade?
And the glory of its treasures
    Shadow of a shade?

Schoolgirls we, eighteen and under,

94

From scholastic trammels free,
And we wonder—how we wonder!—
What on earth the world can be!

TRIO.—*Yum-Yum, Peep-Bo, and Pitti-Sing,*
with Chorus of Girls.

The Three.
Three little maids from school are we,
Pert as a school-girl well can be,
Filled to the brim with girlish glee,
Three little maids from school!
Yum-Yum.
Everything is a source of fun. (*Chuckle.*)
Peep-Bo.
Nobody's safe, for we care for none!
(*Chuckle.*)
Pitti-Sing.
Life is a joke that's just begun!
(*Chuckle.*)
The Three. Three little maids from school!
All (*dancing*).
Three little maids who, all unwary,
Come from a ladies' seminary,
Freed from its genius tutelary—
The Three (*suddenly demure*). Three little
maids from school!
Yum-Yum.
One little maid is a bride, Yum-Yum—
Peep-Bo.
Two little maids in attendance come—
Pitti-Sing.
Three little maids is the total sum.
The Three. Three little maids from school!
Yum-Yum.
From three little maids take one away.
Peep-Bo. Two little maids remain, and they—
Pitti-Sing.
Won't have to wait very long, they say—
The Three. Three little maids from school!
All (*dancing*).
Three little maids who, all unwary,
Come from a ladies' seminary,
Freed from its genius tutelary—
The Three (*suddenly demure*). Three little
maids from school!

(*Enter Ko-Ko and Pooh-Bah.*)

Ko. At last, my bride that is to be! (*About
to embrace her.*)
Yum. You're not going to kiss me before all
these people?
Ko. Well, that was the idea.
Yum. (*aside to Peep-Bo*). It seems odd,
doesn't it?
Peep. It's rather peculiar.
Pitti. Oh, I expect it's all right. Must have
a beginning, you know.
Yum. Well, of course I know nothing about
these things; but I've no objection if it's usual.
Ko. Oh, it's quite usual, I think. Eh, Lord
Chamberlain? (*Appealing to Pooh-Bah.*)
Pooh. I have known it done. (*Ko-Ko em-
braces her.*)

Yum. Thank goodness that's over! (*Sees
Nanki-Poo and rushes to him.*) Why, that's
never you? (*The Three Girls rush to him and
shake his hands, all speaking at once.*)

Yum. Oh, I'm so glad! I haven't seen
you for ever so long, and I'm right at the
top of the school, and I've got three prizes
and I've come home for good, and I'm not
going back any more!
Peep. And have you got an engagement?
Yum-Yum's got one, but she doesn't like it,
and she'd ever so much rather it was you!
I've come home for good, and I'm not going
back any more!
Pitti. Now tell us all the news, because
you go about everywhere, and we've been at
school, but, thank goodness, that's all over
now, and we've come home for good, and
we're not going back any more!

(*These three speeches are spoken together
in one breath.*)

Ko. I beg your pardon. Will you present
me?
Yum. Oh, this is the musician who used—
Peep. Oh, this is the gentleman who used—
Pitti. Oh, it is only Nanki-Poo who used—
Ko. One at a time, if you please.
Yum. Oh, if you please he's the gentleman
who used to play so beautifully on the—on
the—
Pitti. On the Marine Parade.
Yum. Yes, I think that was the name of the
instrument.
Nank. Sir, I have the misfortune to love
your ward, Yum-Yum—oh, I know I deserve
your anger!
Ko. Anger! not a bit, my boy. Why, I love
her myself. Charming little girl, isn't she?
Pretty eyes, nice hair. Taking little thing, al-
together. Very glad to hear my opinion backed
by a competent authority. Thank you very
much. Good-bye. (*To Pish-Tush.*) Take him
away. (*Pish-Tush removes him.*)
Pitti (*who has been examining Pooh-Bah.*)
I beg your pardon, but what is this? Customer
come to try on?
Ko. That is a Tremendous Swell.
Pitti. Oh, it's alive. (*She starts back in
alarm.*)
Pooh. Go away, little girls. Can't talk to
little girls like you. Go away, there's dears.
Ko. Allow me to present you, Pooh-Bah.
These are my three wards. The one in the mid-
dle is my bride elect.
Pooh. What do you want me to do to them?
Mind, I *will not* kiss them.
Ko. No, no, you shan't kiss them; a little
bow—a mere nothing—you needn't mean it, you
know.
Pooh. It goes against the grain. They are
not young ladies, they are young persons.

Ko. Come, come, make an effort, there's a good nobleman.

Pooh (aside to Ko-Ko). Well, I shan't mean it. (*With a great snort.*) How de do, little girls, how de do? (*Aside.*) Oh, my protoplasmal ancestor!

Ko. That's very good. (*Girls indulge in suppressed laughter.*)

Pooh. I see nothing to laugh at. It is very painful to me to have to say "How de do, little girls, how de do?" to young persons. I'm not in the habit of saying "How de do, little girls, how de do?" to anybody under the rank of a Stockbroker.

Ko. (*aside to girls*). Don't laugh at him, he can't help it—he's under treatment for it. (*Aside to Pooh-Bah.*) Never mind them, they don't understand the delicacy of your position.

Pooh. We know how delicate it is, don't we?

Ko. I should think we did! How a nobleman of your importance can do it at all is a thing I never can, never shall understand.

(*Ko-Ko retires up and goes off.*)

Quartet and Chorus of Girls.—*Yum-Yum, Peep-Bo, Pitti-Sing, and Pooh-Bah.*

Yum., Peep. and Pitti.

So please you, Sir, we much regret
If we have failed in etiquette
Towards a man of rank so high—
W shall know better by and by.

Yum.

But youth, of course, must have its fling,
      So pardon us,
      So pardon us,

Pitti.

And don't, in girlhood's happy spring,
      Be hard on us,
      Be hard on us,
If we're inclined to dance and sing.
      Tra la la, &c. (*Dancing.*)

Chorus of Girls. But youth, of course, &c.

Pooh.

I think you ought to recollect
You cannot show too much respect
Towards the highly titled few;
But nobody does, and why should you!
That youth at us should have its fling,
      Is hard on us,
      Is hard on us;
To our prerogative we cling—
      So pardon us,
      So pardon us,
If we decline to dance and sing.
      Tra la la, &c. (*Dancing.*)

Chorus of Girls. But youth, of course, must have its fling, &c.

(*Exeunt all but Yum-Yum.*)

Enter Nanki-Poo.

Nank. Yum-Yum, at last we are alone! I have sought you night and day for three weeks, in the belief that your guardian was beheaded, and I find that you are about to be married to him this afternoon!

Yum. Alas, yes!

Nank. But you do not love him?

Yum. Alas, no!

Nank. Modified rapture! But why do you not refuse him?

Yum. What good would that do? He's my guardian, and he wouldn't let me marry you!

Nank. But I would wait until you were of age!

Yum. You forget that in Japan girls do not arrive at years of discretion until they are fifty.

Nank. True; from seventeen to forty-nine are considered years of indiscretion.

Yum. Besides—a wandering minstrel, who plays a wind instrument outside tea-houses, is hardly a fitting husband for the ward of a Lord High Executioner.

Nank. But—(*Aside.*) Shall I tell her? Yes! She will not betray me! (*Aloud.*) What if it should prove that, after all, I am no musician!

Yum. There! I was certain of it, directly I heard you play!

Nank. What if it should prove that I am no other than the son of his Majesty the Mikado?

Yum. The son of the Mikado! But why is your Highness disguised? And what has your Highness done? And will your Highness promise never to do it again?

Nank. Some years ago I had the misfortune to captivate Katisha, an elderly lady of my father's Court. She misconstrued my customary affability into expressions of affection, and claimed me in marriage, under my father's law. My father, the Lucius Junius Brutus of his race, ordered me to marry her within a week, or perish ignominiously on the scaffold. That night I fled his Court, and, assuming the disguise of a Second Trombone, I joined the band in which you found me when I had the happiness of seeing you! (*Approaching her.*)

Yum (retreating). If you please, I think your Highness had better not come too near. The laws against flirting are excessively severe.

Nank. But we are quite alone, and nobody can see us.

Yum. Still, that doesn't make it right. To flirt is capital.

Nank. It *is* capital!

Yum. And we must obey the law.

Nank. Deuce take the law!

Yum. I wish it would, but it won't!

Nank. If it were not for that, how happy we might be!

Yum. Happy indeed!

Nank. If it were not for the law, we should now be sitting side by side, like that. (*Sits by her.*)

Yum. Instead of being obliged to sit half a

mile off, like that. (*Crosses and sits at other side of stage.*)

Nank. We should be gazing into each other's eyes, like that. (*Gazing at her sentimentally.*)

Yum. Breathing sighs of unutterable love—like that. (*Sighing and gazing lovingly at him.*)

Nank. With our arms round each other's waists, like that. (*Embracing her.*)

Yum. Yes, if it wasn't for the law.

Nank. If it wasn't for the law.

Yum. As it is, of course we couldn't do anything of the kind.

Nank. Not for worlds!

Yum. Being engaged to Ko-Ko, you know!

Nank. Being engaged to Ko-Ko!

DUET.—*Yum-Yum and Nanki-Poo.*

Nank.

Were you not to Ko-Ko plighted,
    I would say in tender tone,
"Loved one, let us be united—
    Let us be each other's own!"
I would merge all rank and station,
    Worldly sneers are nought to us,
And, to mark my admiration,
    I would kiss you fondly thus—(*Kisses her.*)

Both.

{ I }
{ He } would kiss { you } { me } fondly thus—(*Kiss.*)

Yum.

But as I'm engaged to Ko-Ko,
    To embrace you thus, *con fuoco,*
Would distinctly be no *gioco,*
    And for yam I should get toco—

Both. Toco, toco, toco, toco!

Nank.

So, in spite of all temptation,
    Such a theme I'll not discuss,
And on no consideration
    Will I kiss you fondly thus—(*Kissing her.*)
Let me make it clear to you,
    This is what I'll never do!
    This, oh this, oh this, oh this—(*Kissing her.*)

Together. This, oh this, &c.

[*Exeunt in opposite directions*
Enter Ko-Ko.

Ko. (*looking after Yum-Yum*). There she goes! To think how entirely my future happiness is wrapped up in that little parcel! Really, it hardly seems worth while! Oh, matrimony!—(*Enter Pooh-Bah and Pish-Tush.*) Now then, what is it? Can't you see I'm soliloquizing? You have interrupted an apostrophe, sir!

Pish. I am the bearer of a letter from his Majesty, the Mikado.

Ko. (*taking it from him reverentially*). A letter from the Mikado! What in the world can he have to say to me? (*Reads letter.*) Ah, here it is at last! I thought it would come sooner or later! The Mikado is struck by the fact that no executions have taken place in Titipu for a year, and decrees that unless somebody is beheaded within one month the post of Lord High Executioner shall be abolished, and the city reduced to the rank of a village!

Pish. But that will evolve us all in irretrievable ruin!

Ko. Yes. There is no help for it, I shall have to execute somebody at once. The only question is, who shall it be?

Pooh. Well, it seems unkind to say so, but as you're already under sentence of death for flirting, everything seems to point to *you.*

Ko. To me? What are you talking about? I can't execute myself.

Pooh. Why not?

Ko. Why not? Because, in the first place, self-decapitation is an extremely difficult, not to say dangerous, thing to attempt; and, in the second, it's suicide, and suicide is a capital offence.

Pooh. That is so, no doubt.

Pish. We might reserve that point.

Pooh. True, it could be argued six months hence, before the full Court.

Ko. Besides, I don't see how a man *can* cut off his own head.

Pooh. A man might try.

Pish. Even if you only succeeded in cutting it half off, that would be something.

Pooh. It would be taken as an earnest of your desire to comply with the Imperial will.

Ko. No. Pardon me, but there I am adamant. As official Headsman, my reputation is at stake, and I can't consent to embark on a professional operation unless I see my way to a successful result.

Pooh. This professional conscientiousness is highly creditable to *you,* but it places us in a very awkward position.

Ko. My good sir, the awkwardness of your position is grace itself compared with that of a man engaged in the act of cutting off his own head.

Pish. I am afraid that, unless you can obtain a substitute—

Ko. A substitute? Oh, certainly—nothing easier. (*To Pooh-Bah.*) Pooh-Bah, I appoint you Lord High Substitute.

Pooh. I should be delighted. Such an appointment would realize my fondest dreams. But no, at any sacrifice, I must set bounds to my insatiable ambition!

TRIO.

Ko-Ko.

My brain it teems
    With endless schemes
Both good and new
    For Titipu;

But if I flit,
The benefit
That I'd diffuse
The town would lose!
Now every man
To aid his clan
Should plot and plan
    And so,
    Although
I'm ready to go,
Yet recollect
'Twere disrespect
Did I neglect
To thus effect
This aim direct,
So I object—
So I object—
So I object—

Pooh-Bah. I am so proud,
If I allowed
My family pride
To be my guide,
I'd volunteer
To quit this sphere
Instead of you,
In a minute or two.
But family pride
Must be denied,
And set aside,
And mortified.
    And so,
    Although
I wish to go.
And greatly pine
To brightly shine,
And take the line
Of a hero fine,
With grief condign
I must decline—
I must decline—
I must decline—

Pish-Tush. I heard one day
A gentleman say
That criminals who
Are cut in two
Can hardly feel
The fatal steel,
And so are slain
Without much pain.
If this is true,
It's jolly for you;
Your courage screw
To bid us adieu,
    And go
    And show
Both friend and foe
How much you dare.
I'm quite aware
It's your affair,
Yet I declare

I'd take your share,
But I don't much care—
I don't much care—
I don't much care—

All.
To sit in solemn silence in a dull, dark dock,
In a pestilential prison, with a life-long lock,
Awaiting the sensation of a short, sharp shock,
From a cheap and chippy chopper on a big black block.

        [*Exeunt Pooh, and Pish.*

Ko. This is simply appalling! I, who allowed myself to be respited at the last moment, simply in order to benefit my native town, am now required to die within a month, and that by a man whom I have loaded with honours! Is this public gratitude? Is this—(*Enter Nanki-Poo, with a rope in his hands.*) Go away, sir! How dare you? Am I never to be permitted to soliloquize?

Nank. Oh, go on—don't mind me.

Ko. What are you going to do with that rope?

Nank. I'm about to terminate an unendurable existence.

Ko. Terminate your existence? Oh, nonsense! What for?

Nank. Because you are going to marry the girl I adore.

Ko. Nonsense, sir. I won't permit it. I am a humane man, and if you attempt anything of the kind I shall order your instant arrest. Come, sir, desist at once, or I summon my guard.

Nank. That's absurd. If you attempt to raise an alarm, I instantly perform the Happy Despatch with this dagger.

Ko. No, no, don't do that. This is horrible! (*Suddenly.*) Why you cold-blooded scoundrel, are you aware that, in taking your life, you are committing a crime which—which—which is—Oh! (*Struck by an idea.*) Substitute!

Nank. What's the matter?

Ko. Is it *absolutely certain* that you are resolved to die?

Nank. Absolutely!

Ko. Will *nothing* shake your resolution?

Nank. Nothing.

Ko. Threats, entreaties, prayers—all useless?

Nank. All! My mind is made up.

Ko. Then, if you really mean what you say, and if you are absolutely resolved to die, and if nothing whatever will shake your determination—don't spoil yourself by committing suicide, but be beheaded handsomely at the hands of the Public Executioner!

Nank. I don't see how that would benefit me.

Ko. You don't? Observe: you'll have a

month to live, and you'll live like a fighting cock at my expense. When the day comes there'll be a grand public ceremonial—you'll be the central figure—no one will attempt to deprive you of that distinction. There'll be a procession—bands—dead march—bells tolling—all the girls in tears—Yum-Yum distracted—then, when it's all over, general rejoicings, and a display of fireworks in the evening. *You* won't see them, but they'll be there all the same.

Nank. Do you think Yum-Yum would really be distracted at my death?

Ko. I am convinced of it. Bless you, she's the most tenderhearted little creature alive.

Nank. I should be sorry to cause her pain. Perhaps, after all, if I were to withdraw from Japan, and travel in Europe for a couple of years, I might contrive to forget her.

Ko. Oh, I don't think you could forget Yum-Yum so easily; and, after all, what is more miserable than a love-blighted life?

Nank. True.

Ko. Life without Yum-Yum—why, it seems absurd!

Nank. And yet there are a good many people in the world who have to endure it.

Ko. Poor devils, yes! You are quite right not to be of their number.

Nank (*suddenly*). I *won't* be of their number!

Ko. Noble fellow!

Nank. I'll tell you how we'll manage it. Let me marry Yum-Yum to-morrow, and in a month you may behead me.

Ko. No, no. I draw the line at Yum-Yum.

Nank. Very good. If you can draw the line, so can I. (*Preparing rope.*)

Ko. Stop, stop—listen one moment—be reasonable. How can I consent to your marrying Yum-Yum if I'm going to marry her myself?

Nank. My good friend, she'll be a widow in a month, and you can marry her then.

Ko. That's true, of course. I quite see that But, dear me! my position during the next month will be most unpleasant—most unpleasant.

Nank. Not half so unpleasant as my position at the end of it.

Ko. But—dear me!—well—I agree—after all, it's only putting off my wedding for a month. But you won't prejudice her against me, will you? You see, I've educated her to be my wife; she's been taught to regard me as a wise and good man. Now I shouldn't like her views on that point disturbed.

Nank. Trust me, she shall never learn the truth from me.

FINALE.

Enter Chorus, Pooh-Bah, and Pish-Tush.

CHORUS.

With aspect stern

And gloomy stride,
We come to learn
How you decide.

Don't hesitate
Your choice to name,
A dreadful fate
You'll suffer all the same.

Pooh. To ask you what you mean to do we punctually appear.

Ko. Congratulate me, gentlemen, I've found a Volunteer!

All. The Japanese equivalent for **Hear, Hear, Hear!**

Ko. (*presenting him*). 'Tis Nanki-Poo!

All. Hail, Nanki-Poo!

Ko. I think he'll do?

All. Yes, yes, he'll do!

Ko.

He yields his life if I'll Yum-Yum surrender.
Now I adore that girl with passion tender,
And could not yield her with a ready will,
Or her allot,
If I did not
Adore myself with passion tenderer still!

Enter Yum-Yum, Peep-Boo, and Pitti-Sing.

All. Ah, yes!

He loves himself with passion tenderer still!

Ko. (*to Nanki-Poo*). Take her—she's yours!

[*Exit Ko-Ko.*

ENSEMBLE.

Nanki-Poo.

The threatened cloud has passed away,

Yum-Yum.

And brightly shines the dawning day;

Nanki-Poo.

What though the night may come too soon,

Yum-Yum.

There's yet a month of afternoon!

Nanki-Poo, Pooh-Bah, Pish-Tish, Yum-Yum,
Pitti-Sing and Peep-Bo.

Then let the throng
Our joy advance,
With laughing song
And merry dance,

Chorus. With joyous shout and ringing cheer,
Inaugurate our brief career! &c.

Pitti-Sing. A day, a week, a month, a year—

Yum. Or far or near, or far or near,

Pooh. Life's eventime comes much too soon,

Pitti-Sing. You'll live at least a honeymoon!

All. Then let the throng, &c.

Chorus. With joyous shout, &c.

SOLO.—*Pooh-Bah.*

As in a month you've got to die,
If Ko-Ko tells us true,
'Twere empty compliment to cry
"Long life to Nanki-Poo!"
But as one month you have to live
As fellow-citizen,

99

This toast with three times three we'll give—
  "Long life to you—till then!"
                [*Exit Pooh-Bah.*

Chorus.   May all good fortune prosper you,
    May you have health and riches, too,
    May you succeed in all you do!
      Long life to you—till then!
        (*Dance.*)

    Enter Katisha melodramatically.

Kat.   Your revels cease! Assist me, all of you!
Chorus.   Why, who is this whose evil eyes
      Rain blight on our festivities?
Kat.   I claim my perjured lover, Nanki-Poo!
    Oh fool! to shun delights that never cloy!
Chorus.   Go, leave thy deadly work undone!
Kat.   Come back, oh shallow fool! come back
    to joy!
Chorus.   Away, away! ill-favoured one!
Nank. (*aside to Yum-Yum.*)   Ah!
    'Tis Katisha!
    The maid of whom I told you. (*About to go.*)
Kat. (*detaining him.*)   No!
    You shall not go,
    These arms shall thus enfold you!
        SONG.—*Katisha.*
Kat. (*addressing Nanki-Poo*).
    Oh fool, that fleest
      My hallowed joys!
    Oh blind, that seest
      No equipoise!
    Oh rash, that judgest
      From half, the whole!
    Oh base, that grudgest
      Love's lightest dole!
      Thy heart unbind,
      Oh fool, oh blind!
      Give me my place,
      Oh rash, or base!
Chorus.   If she's thy bride, restore her place,
    Oh fool, oh blind, oh rash, oh base!
Kat. (*addressing Yum-Yum*).
    Pink cheek, that rulest
      Where wisdom serves!
    Bright eye, that foolest
      Heroic nerves!
    Rose lip, that scornest
      Lore-laden years!
    Smooth tongue, that warnest
      Who rightly hears!
      Thy doom is nigh,
      Pink cheek, bright eye!
      Thy knell is rung,
      Rose lip, smooth tongue!
Chorus.   If true her tale, thy knell is rung,
    Pink cheek, bright eye, rose lip,
                smooth tongue!
Pitti-Sing.
    Away, nor prosecute your quest—
    From our intention, well expressed,
      You cannot turn us!
    The state of your connubial views

    Towards the person you accuse
      Does not concern us!
    For he's going to marry Yum-Yum—
All.   Yum-Yum!
Pitti.   Your anger pray bury,
    For all will be merry,
    I think you had better succumb—
All.   Cumb—cumb!
Pitti.   And join our expressions of glee.
    On this subject I pray you be dumb—
All.   Dumb—dumb.
Pitti.   You'll find there are many
    Who'll wed for a penny—
    The word for your guidance is "Mum"—
All.   Mum—mum!
Pitti.   There's lots of good fish in the sea!
All.   On this subject we pray you be dumb,
    &c.

       SOLO.—*Katisha.*
    The hour of gladness
      Is dead and gone;
    In silent sadness
      I live alone!
    The hope I cherished
      All lifeless lies,
    And all has perished
      Save love, which never dies!
  Oh, faithless one, this insult you shall rue!
  In vain for mercy on your knees you'll sue.
    I'll tear the mask from your disguising!
Nank. (*aside*).   Now comes the blow!
Kat.   Prepare yourselves for news surprising!
Nank. (*aside*).   How foil my foe?
Kat.   No minstrel he, despite bravado!
Yum. (*aside, struck by an idea*).
             Ha! Ha! I know!
Kat.   He is the son of your—
    (*Nanki-Poo, Yum-Yum, and Chorus, inter-*
rupting, sing Japanese words, to drown her
voice.)
      O ni! bikkuri shakkuri to!
Kat.   In vain you interrupt with this tornado!
    He is the only son of your—
All.   O ni! bikkuri shakkuri to!
Kat.   I'll spoil—
All.   O ni! bikkuri shakkuri to!
Kat.   Your gay gambado!
    He is the son—
All.   O ni! bikkuri shakkuri to!
Kat.   Of your—
All.   O ni! bikkuri shakkuri to!
Kat.   The son of your—
All.   O ni! bikkuri shakkuri to! oya! oya!

        ENSEMBLE.
Katisha.
    Ye torrents roar!
      Ye tempests howl!
    Your wrath outpour
      With angry growl!
  Do ye your worst, my vengeance call
  Shall rise triumphant over all!

Prepare for woe,
  Ye haughty lords,
At once I go
  Mikado-wards,
My wrongs with vengeance shall be crowned!
My wrongs with vengeance shall be crowned!
The Others.
  We'll hear no more,
    Ill-omened owl,
  To joy we soar,
    Despite your scowl!

The echoes of our festival
Shall rise triumphant over all!
  Away you go,
    Collect your hordes;
  Proclaim your woe
    In dismal chords;
We do not heed their dismal sound,
For joy reigns everywhere around.
(*Katisha rushes furiously up stage clearing
the crowd away right and left, finishing on steps
at the back of stage.*)

END OF ACT I.

ACT II.

SCENE.—*Ko-Ko's Garden.*

*Yum-Yum discovered seated at her bridal
toilet, surrounded by maidens, who are dressing
her hair and painting her face and lips, as she
judges of the effect in a mirror.*

SOLO.—*Pitti-Sing and Chorus of Girls.*

Chorus. Braid the raven hair—
  Weave the supple tress—
Deck the maiden fair
  In her loveliness—
Paint the pretty face—
  Dye the coral lip—
Emphasize the grace
  Of her ladyship!
Art and nature, thus allied,
Go to make a pretty bride.
  SOLO.—*Pitti-Sing.*
Sit with downcast eye—
  Let it brim with dew—
Try if you can cry—
  We will do so, too.
When you're summoned, start
  Like a frightened roe—
Flutter, little heart,
  Colour, come and go!
Modesty at marriage tide
Well becomes a pretty bride!
    CHORUS.
Braid the raven hair, &c.

[*Exeunt Pitti-Sing, Peep-Bo and Chorus.*

Yum. Yes, I am indeed beautiful! Sometimes I sit and wonder, in my artless Japanese
way, why it is that I am so much more attractive than anybody else in the whole world. Can
this be vanity? No! Nature is lovely and
rejoices in her loveliness. I am a child of Nature, and take after my mother.

    SONG.—*Yum-Yum.*
The sun, whose rays
Are all ablaze
  With ever-living glory,
Does not deny
His majesty—
  He scorns to tell a story!

He don't exclaim
  "I blush for shame,
  So kindly be indulgent."
But, fierce and bold,
In fiery gold,
  He glories all effulgent!

I mean to rule the earth,
  As he the sky—
We really know our worth,
  The sun and I!

Observe his flame,
That placid dame,
  The moon's Celestial Highness;
There's not a trace
Upon her face
  Of diffidence or shyness:
She borrows light
That, through the night,
  Mankind may all acclaim her!
And, truth to tell,
She lights up well,
  So I, for one, don't blame her!

Ah, pray make no mistake,
  We are not shy;
We're very wide awake,
  The moon and I!

Enter Pitti-Sing and Peep-Bo.

Yum. Yes, everything seems to smile upon
me. I am to be married to-day to the man I
love best, and I believe I am the very happiest
girl in Japan!

Peep. The happiest girl indeed, for she is
indeed to be envied who has attained happiness
in all but perfection.

Yum. In "all but" perfection?

Peep. Well, dear, it can't be denied that
the fact that your husband is to be beheaded
in a month is, in its way, a drawback. It does
seem to take the top off it, you know.

101

Pitti. I don't know about that. It all depends!

Peep. At all events, *he* will find it a drawback.

Pitti. Not necessarily. Bless you, it all depends!

Yum. (*in tears*). I think it very indelicate of you to refer to such a subject on such a day. If my married happiness *is* to be—to be—

Peep. Cut short.

Yum. Well, cut short—in a month, can't you let me forget it? (*Weeping.*)

Enter Nanki-Poo, and Pish-Tush.

Nank. Yum-Yum in tears—and on her wedding morn!

Yum. (*sobbing*). They've been reminding me that in a month you're to be beheaded! (*Bursts into tears.*)

Pitti. Yes, we've been reminding her that you're to be beheaded. (*Bursts into tears.*)

Peep. It's quite true, you know, you *are* to be beheaded! (*Bursts into tears.*)

Nank. (*aside*). Humph! How some bridegrooms would be depressed by this sort of thing! (*Aloud.*) A month? Well, what's a month? Bah! These divisions of time are purely arbitrary. Who says twenty-four hours make a day?

Pitti. There's a popular impression to that effect.

Nank. Then we'll efface it. We'll call each second a minute—each minute an hour—each hour a day—and each day a year. At that rate we've about thirty years of married happiness before us!

Peep. And, at that rate, this interview has already lasted four hours and three-quarters! (*Exit Peep-Bo.*)

Yum. (*Still sobbing*). Yes. How time flies when one is thoroughly enjoying oneself!

Nank. That's the way to look at it! Don't let's be downhearted! There's a silver lining to every cloud.

Yum. Certainly. Let's—let's be perfectly happy! (*Almost in tears.*)

Pish. By all means. Let's—let's thoroughly enjoy ourselves.

Pitti. It's—it's absurd to cry! (*Trying to force a laugh.*)

Yum. Quite ridiculous! (*Trying to laugh.*) (*All break into a forced and melancholy laugh.*)

MADRIGAL.—*Yum-Yum, Pitti-Sing, Nanki-Poo, and Pish-Tush.*

Brightly dawns our wedding day;
　Joyous hour, we give thee greeting!
　Whither, whither art thou fleeting?
Fickle moment, prithee stay!
　What though mortal joys be hollow?
　Pleasures come, if sorrows follow:
Though the tocsin sound, ere long
　Ding dong! Ding dong!

Yet until the shadows fall
Over one and over all,
Sing a merry madrigal—
　　　　　A madrigal!
Fal-la—fal-la! &c. (*Ending in tears.*)

Let us dry the ready tear,
　Though the hours are surely creeping,
　Little need for woeful weeping,
Till the sad sundown is near.
　All must sip the cup of sorrow—
　I to-day and thou to-morrow;
This the close of every song—
　Ding dong! Ding dong!
What, though solemn shadows fall,
Sooner, later, over all?
Sing a merry madrigal—
　　　　　A madrigal!
Fal-la—fal-la! &c. (*Ending in tears.*)
　　[*Exeunt Pitti-Sing and Pish-Tush.*
(*Nanki-Poo embraces Yum-Yum. Enter Ko-Ko. Nanki-Poo releases Yum-Yum.*)

Ko. Go on—don't mind me.

Nank. I'm afraid we're distressing you.

Ko. Never mind, I must get used to it. Only please do it by degrees. Begin by putting your arm round her waist. (*Nanki-Poo does so.*) There; let me get used to that first.

Yum. Oh, wouldn't you like to retire? It must pain you to see us so affectionate together!

Ko. No, I must learn to bear it! Now oblige me by allowing her head to rest on your shoulder.

Nank. Like that? (*He does so. Ko-Ko much affected.*)

Ko. I am much obliged to you. Now—kiss her! (*He does so. Ko-Ko writhes with anguish.*) Thank you—it's simple torture!

Yum. Come, come, bear up. After all, it's only for a month.

Ko. No. It's no use deluding oneself with false hopes.

Nank. } What do you mean?
Yum. }

Ko. (*to Yum-Yum*). My child—my poor child! (*Aside.*) How shall I break it to her? (*Aloud.*) My little bride that was to have been—

Yum. (*delighted*). Was to have been?

Ko. Yes, you never can be mine!

Nank. } (*in ecstasy*). {What!
Yum. } {I'm so glad!

Ko. I've just ascertained that, by the Mikado's law, when a married man is beheaded his wife is buried alive.

Nank. } Buried alive!
Yum. }

Ko. Buried alive. It's a most unpleasant death.

Nank. But whom did you get that from?

Ko. Oh, from Pooh-Bah. He's my solicitor.

Yum. But he may be mistaken!

Ko. So I thought; so I consulted the Attorney-General, the Lord Chief Justice, the Master of the Rolls, the Judge Ordinary, and the Lord Chancellor. They're all of the same opinion. Never knew such unanimity on a point of law in my life!

Nank. But stop a bit! This law has never been put in force.

Ko. Not yet. You see, flirting is the only crime punishable with decapitation, and married men never flirt.

Nank. Of course, they don't. I quite forgot that! Well, I suppose I may take it that my dream of happiness is at an end!

Yum. Darling—I don't want to appear selfish, and I love you with all my heart—I don't suppose I shall ever love anybody else half as much—but when I agreed to marry you—my own—I had no idea—pet—that I should have to be buried alive in a month!

Nank. Nor I! It's the very first I've heard of it!

Yum. It—it makes a difference, doesn't it?

Nank. It *does* make a difference, of course.

Yum. You see—burial alive—it's such a stuffy death.

Nank. I call it a beast of a death.

Yum. You see my difficulty, don't you?

Nank. Yes, and I see my own. If I insist on your carrying out your promise, I doom you to a hideous death; if I release you, you marry Ko-Ko at once!

TRIO.—*Yum-Yum, Nanki-Poo, and Ko-Ko.*

Yum.   Here's a how-de-do!
          If I marry you,
When your time has come to perish,
Then the maiden whom you cherish
          Must be slaughtered, too!
          Here's a how-de-do!

Nank.   Here's a pretty mess!
          In a month, or less,
I must die without a wedding!
Let the bitter tears I'm shedding
          Witness my distress,
          Here's a pretty mess!

Ko.   Here's a state of things!
          To her life she clings!
Matrimonial devotion
Doesn't seem to suit her notion—
          Burial it brings!
          Here's a state of things!

ENSEMBLE.

Yum-Yum and Nanki-Poo.
          With a passion that's intense
          I worship and adore,
          But the laws of common sense
          We oughtn't to ignore.
          If what he says is true,

'Tis death to marry you!
          Here's a pretty state of things!
          Here's a pretty how-de-do!

Ko-Ko.   With a passion that's intense
          You worship and adore,
          But the laws of common sense
          You oughtn't to ignore.
          If what I say is true,
'Tis death to marry you!
          Here's a pretty state of things!
          Here's a pretty how-de-do!
                         [*Exit Yum-Yum.*

Ko. (*going up to Nanki-Poo*). My poor boy, I'm really very sorry for you.

Nank. Thanks, old fellow. I'm sure you are.

Ko. You see I'm quite helpless.

Nank. I quite see that.

Ko. I can't conceive anything more distressing than to have one's marriage broken off at the last moment. But you shan't be disappointed of a wedding—you shall come to mine.

Nank. It's awfully kind of you, but that's impossible.

Ko. Why so?

Nank. To-day I die.

Ko. What do you mean?

Nank. I can't live without Yum-Yum. This afternoon I perform the Happy Despatch.

Ko. No, no—pardon me—I can't allow that.

Nank. Why not?

Ko. Why, hang it all, you're under contract to die by the hand of the Public Executioner in a month's time! If you kill yourself, what's to become of me? Why, I shall have to be executed in your place!

Nank. It would certainly seem so!

            Enter Pooh-Bah.

Ko. Now then, Lord Mayor, what is it?

Pooh. The Mikado and his suite are approaching the city, and will be here in ten minutes.

Ko. The Mikado! He's coming to see whether his orders have been carried out! (*To Nanki-Poo.*) Now look here, you know—this is getting serious—a bargain's a bargain, and you really mustn't frustrate the ends of justice by committing suicide. As a man of honour and a gentleman, you are bound to die ignominiously by the hands of the Public Executioner.

Nank. Very well, then—behead me.

Ko. What, now?

Nank. Certainly; at once.

Pooh. Chop it off! Chop it off!

Ko. My good sir, I don't go about prepared to execute gentlemen at a moment's notice. Why, I never even killed a blue-bottle!

Pooh. Still, as Lord High Executioner—

Ko. My good sir, as Lord High Executioner I've got to behead him in a month. I'm not ready yet. I don't know how it's done.

I'm going to take lessons. I mean to begin with a guinea pig, and work my way through the animal kingdom till I come to a Second Trombone. Why, you don't suppose that, as a humane man, I'd have accepted the post of Lord High Executioner if I hadn't thought the duties purely nominal? I *can't* kill you—I will kill anything! I can't kill anybody! (*Weeps*.)

Nank. Come, my poor fellow, we all have unpleasant duties to discharge at times; after all, what is it? If I don't mind, why should you? Remember, sooner or later it must be done.

Ko. (*springing up suddenly*). *Must it?* I'm not so sure about that!

Nank. What do you mean?

Ko. Why should I kill you when making an affidavit that you've been executed will do just as well? Here are plenty of witnesses—the Lord Chief Justice, Lord High Admiral, Commander-in-Chief, Secretary of State for the Home Department, First Lord of the Treasury, and Chief Commissioner of Police.

Nank. But where are they?

Ko. There they are. They'll all swear to it —won't you? (*To Pooh-Bah*.)

Pooh. Am I to understand that all of us high Officers of State are required to perjure ourselves to ensure your safety!

Ko. Why not? You'll be grossly insulted, as usual.

Pooh. Will the insult be cash down, or at a date?

Ko. It will be a ready-money transaction.

Pooh. (*Aside*.) Well, it will be a useful discipline. (*Aloud*.) Very good. Choose your fiction, and I'll endorse it! (*Aside*.) Ha! ha! Family Pride, how do you like *that*, my buck?

Nank. But I tell you that life without Yum-Yum—

Ko. Oh, Yum-Yum, Yum-Yum! Bother Yum-Yum! Here, Commissionaire (*to Pooh-Bah*), go and fetch Yum-Yum. (*Exit Pooh-Bah*.) Take Yum-Yum and marry Yum-Yum, only go away and never come back again. (*Enter Pooh-Bah with Yum-Yum*.) Here she is. Yum-Yum, are you particularly busy?

Yum. Not particularly.

Ko. You've five minutes to spare?

Yum. Yes.

Ko. Then go along with his Grace the Archbishop of Titipu; he'll marry you at once.

Yum. But if I'm to be buried alive?

Ko. Now, don't ask any questions, but do as I tell you, and Nanki-Poo will explain all.

Nank. But one moment—

Ko. Not for worlds. Here comes the Mikado, no doubt to ascertain whether I've obeyed his decree, and if he finds you alive I shall have the greatest difficulty in persuading him that I've beheaded you. (*Exeunt Nanki-Poo and Yum-Yum, followed by Pooh-Bah*.) Close thing that, for here he comes!

[*Exit Ko-Ko*.

MARCH.—*Enter procession, heralding Mikado, with Katisha.*

ENTRANCE *of Mikado and Katisha.*
("*March of the Mikado's troops.*")

Chorus.   Miya sama, miya sama,
          On n'm-ma no mayé ni
          Pira-Pira suru no wa
          Nan gia na
          Toko tonyaré tonyaré na?

DUET.—*Mikado and Katisha.*

Mik. From every kind of man
          Obedience I expect;
     I'm the Emperor of Japan—

Kat. And I'm his daughter-in-law elect!
          He'll marry his son
          (He's only got one)
     To his daughter-in-law elect.

Mik. My morals have been declared
          Particularly correct;

Kat. But they're nothing at all, compared
     With those of his daughter-in-law
                              elect!

          Bow—Bow—
     To his daughter-in-law elect!

All.   Bow—Bow—
     To his daughter-in-law elect.

Mik. In a fatherly kind of way
     I govern each tribe and sect,
     All cheerfully own my sway—

Kat. Except his daughter-in-law elect!
          As tough as a bone,
          With a will of her own,
     Is his daughter-in-law elect!

Mik. My nature is love and light—
          My freedom from all defect—

Kat. Is significant quite,
     Compared with his daughter-in-law
                              elect!

          Bow—Bow—
     To his daughter-in-law elect!

All.   Bow—Bow—
     To his daughter-in-law elect!

SONG.—*Mikado and Chorus.*

A more humane Mikado never
Did in Japan exist,
     To nobody second,
     I'm certainly reckoned
A true philanthropist.
It is my very humane endeavour
To make, to some extent,
     Each evil liver
     A running river
Of harmless merriment.

     My object all sublime
     I shall achieve in time—
To let the punishment fit the crime—
     The punishment fit the crime;

And make each prisoner pent
Unwillingly represent
A source of innocent merriment!
Of innocent merriment!

All prosy dull society sinners,
Who chatter and bleat and bore,
Are sent to hear sermons
From mystical Germans
Who preach from ten till four.
The amateur tenor, whose vocal villanies
All desire to shirk,
Shall, during off-hours,
Exhibit his powers
To Madame Tussaud's waxwork.

The lady who dies a chemical yellow,
Or stains her grey hair puce,
Or pinches her figger,
Is blacked like a nigger
With permanent walnut juice.
The idiot who, in railway carriages,
Scribbles on window-panes,
We only suffer
To ride on a buffer
In Parliamentary trains.
My object all sublime, &c.

Chorus. His object all sublime, &c.

The advertising quack who wearies
With tales of countless cures,
His teeth, I've enacted,
Shall all be extracted
By terrified amateurs.
The music-hall singer attends a series
Of masses and fugues and "ops"
By Bach, interwoven
With Spohr and Beethoven,
At classical Monday Pops.
The billiard sharp whom any one catches,
His doom's extremely hard—
He's made to dwell—
In a dungeon cell
On a spot that's always barred.
And there he plays extravagant matches
In fitless finger-stalls
On a cloth untrue,
With twisted cue
And elliptical billiard balls!
My object all sublime, &c.

Chorus. His object all sublime, &c.

*Enter Pooh-Bah, Ko-Ko and Pitti-Sing. All
kneel. (Pooh-Bah hands a paper to Ko-Ko.)*
Ko. I am honoured in being permitted to
welcome your Majesty. I guess the object of
your Majesty's visit—your wishes have been attended to. The execution has taken place.
Mik. Oh, you've had an execution, have
you?

Ko. Yes. The Coroner has just handed me
his certificate.
Pooh. I am the Coroner. (*Ko-Ko hands
certificate to Mikado.*)
Mik. And this is the certificate of his death.
(*Reads.*) "At Titipu, in the presence of the
Lord Chancellor, Lord Chief Justice, Attorney
General, Secretary of State for the Home De-
partment, Lord Mayor, and Groom of the Sec-
ond Floor Front—"
Pooh. They were all present, your Majesty.
I counted them myself.
Mik. Very good house. I wish I'd been in
time for the performance.
Ko. A tough fellow he was, too—a man of
gigantic strength. His struggles were terrific.
It was really a remarkable scene.
Mik. Describe it.

Trio and Chorus.—*Pitti-Sing, Ko-Ko, Pooh-
Bah, and Chorus.*

Ko. The criminal cried, as he dropped him
down,
In a state of wild alarm—
With a frightful, frantic, fearful frown.
I bared my big right arm.
I seized him by his little pig-tail,
And on his knees fell he,
As he squirmed and struggled,
And gurgled and guggled,
I drew my snickersnee!
Oh, never shall I
Forget the cry,
Or the shriek that shriekèd he,
As I gnashed my teeth,
When from its sheath
I drew my snickersnee!

CHORUS.
We know him well,
He cannot tell
Untrue or groundless tales—
He always tries
To utter lies,
And every time he fails.

Pitti. He shivered and shook as he gave the
sign
For the stroke he didn't deserve;
When all of a sudden his eye met mine,
And it seemed to brace his nerve;
For he nodded his head and kissed his
hand,
And he whistled an air, did he,
As the sabre true
Cut cleanly through
His cervical vertebræ!
When a man's afraid,
A beautiful maid
Is a cheering sight to see;
And it's oh, I'm glad
That moment sad
Was soothed by sight of me!

CHORUS.
Her terrible tale
You can't assail,
With truth it quite agrees!
Her taste exact
For faultless fact
Amounts to a disease.

Pooh. Now though you'd have said that head
was dead
(For its owner dead was he),
It stood on its neck, with a smile well
bred,
And bowed three times to me!
It was none of your impudent off-hand
nods,
But as humble as could be;
For it clearly knew
The deference due
To a man of pedigree!
And it's oh, I vow,
This deathly bow
Was a touching sight to see;
Though trunkless, yet
It couldn't forget,
The deference due to me!

CHORUS.
This haughty youth,
He speaks the truth
Whenever he finds it pays:
And in this case
It all took place
Exactly as he says!

[*Exeunt Chorus.*

Mik. All this is very interesting, and I should like to have seen it. But we came about a totally different matter. A year ago my son, the heir to the throne of Japan, bolted from our Imperial Court.

Ko. Indeed! Had he any reason to be dissatisfied with his position?

Kat. None whatever. On the contrary, I was going to marry him—yet he fled!

Pooh. I am surprised that he should have fled from one so lovely!

Kat. That's not true.

Pooh. No!

Kat. You hold that I am not beautiful because my face is plain. But you know nothing; you are still unenlightened. Learn, then, that it is not in the face alone that beauty is to be sought. My face is unattractive!

Pooh. It is.

Kat. But I have a left shoulder-blade that is a miracle of loveliness. People come miles to see it. My right elbow has a fascination that few can resist.

Pooh. Allow me!

Kat. It is on view Tuesdays and Fridays, on presentation of visiting card. As for my circulation, it is the largest in the world.

Ko. And yet he fled!

Mik. And is now masquerading in this town, disguised as a Second Trombone.

Ko.
Pooh. } A Second Trombone!
Pitti.

Mik. Yes; would it be troubling you too much if I asked you to produce him? He goes by the name of—

Kat. Nanki-Poo.

Mik. Nanki-Poo.

Ko. It's quite easy. That is, it's rather difficult. In point of fact, he's gone abroad!

Mik. Gone abroad? His address.

Ko. Knightsbridge!

Kat. (*who is reading certificate of death*). Ha!

Mik. What's the matter?

Kat. See here—his name—Nanki-Poo—beheaded this morning. Oh, where shall I find another? Where shall I find another?

(*Ko-Ko, Pooh-Bah, and Pitti-Sing fall on their knees.*)

Mik. (*looking at paper.*) Dear, dear, dear! this is very tiresome. (*To Ko-Ko.*) My poor fellow, in your anxiety to carry out my wishes you have beheaded the heir to the throne of Japan!

Ko. I beg to offer an unqualified apology.

Pooh. I desire to associate myself with that expression of regret.

Pitti. We really hadn't the least notion—

Mik. Of course you hadn't. How could you? Come, come, my good fellow, don't distress yourself—it was no fault of yours. If a man of exalted rank chooses to disguise himself as a Second Trombone, he must take the consequences. It really distresses me to see you take on so. I've no doubt he thoroughly deserved all he got. (*They rise.*)

Ko. We are infinitely obliged to your Majesty—

Pitti. Much obliged, your Majesty.

Pooh. Very much obliged, your Majesty.

Mik. Obliged? not a bit. Don't mention it. How *could* you tell?

Pooh. No, of course we couldn't tell who the gentleman really was.

Pitti. It wasn't written on his forehead, you know.

Ko. It might have been on his pocket-handkerchief, but Japanese don't use pocket-handkerchiefs! Ha! ha! ha!

Mik. Ha! ha! ha! (*To Katisha.*) I forget the punishment for compassing the death of the Heir Apparent.

Ko.
Pooh. } Punishment. (*They drop down on*
Pitti. *their knees again.*)

Mik. Yes. Something lingering, with boiling oil in it, I fancy. Something of that sort. I think boiling oil occurs in it, but I'm not sure. I know it's something humorous, but lingering, with either boiling oil or melted lead. Come, come don't fret—I'm not a bit angry.

Ko. (*in abject terror.*) If your Majesty will accept our assurance, we had no idea—

Mik. Of course—

Pitti. I knew nothing about it.

Pooh. I wasn't there.

Mik. That's the pathetic part of it. Unfortunately, the fool of an Act says "compassing the death of the Heir Apparent." There's not a word about a mistake—

Ko., Pitti. and Pooh. No!

Mik. Or not knowing—

Ko. No!

Mik. Or having no notion—

Pitti. No!

Mik. Or not being there—

Pooh. No!

Mik. There should be, of course—

Ko., Pitti. and Pooh. Yes!

Mik. But there isn't.

Ko., Pitti. and Pooh. Oh!

Mik. That's the slovenly way in which these Acts are always drawn. However, cheer up, it'll be all right. I'll have it altered next session. Now, let's see about your execution—will after luncheon suit you? Can you wait till then?

Ko., Pitti. and Pooh. Oh, yes—we can wait till then!

Mik. Then we'll make it after luncheon.

Pooh. I don't want any lunch.

Mik. I'm really very sorry for you all, but it's an unjust world, and virtue is triumphant only in theatrical performances.

Glee.—*Pitti-Sing, Katisha, Ko-Ko, Pooh-Bah, and Mikado.*

Mik. See how the Fates their gifts allot,
  For A is happy—B is not.
  Yet B is worthy, I dare say,
  Of more prosperity than A!

Ko., Pooh., and Pitti. Is B more worthy?

Kat.   I should say
  He's worth a great deal more than A.

Ensemble.
{
  Yet A is happy!
   Oh, so happy!
  Laughing, Ha! ha!
  Chaffing, Ha! ha!
  Nectar quaffing, Ha! ha! ha!
  Ever joyous, ever gay,
   Happy, undeserving A!
}

Ko., Pooh., and Pitti.
  If I were Fortune—which I'm not—
  B should enjoy A's happy lot,
  And A should die in miserie—
  That is, assuming I am B.

Mik. and Kat. But *should* A perish?

Ko., Pooh., and Pitti. That should he
  (Of course, assuming I am B).
   B should be happy!
   Oh, so happy!

  Laughing, Ha! ha!
  Chaffing, Ha! Ha!
  Nectar quaffing, Ha! ha! ha!
  But condemned to die is he,
  Wretched meritorious B!

[*Exeunt Mikado and Katisha.*

Ko. Well, a nice mess you've got us into, with your nodding head and the deference due to a man of pedigree!

Pooh. Merely corroborative detail, intended to give artistic verisimilitude to an otherwise bald and unconvincing narrative.

Pitti. Corroborative detail indeed! Corroborative fiddlestick!

Ko. And you're just as bad as he is with your cock-and-a-bull stories about catching his eye and his whistling an air. But that's so like you! You must put in your oar!

Pooh. But how about your big right arm?

Pitti. Yes, and your snickersnee!

Ko. Well, well, never mind that now. There's only one thing to be done. Nanki-Poo hasn't started yet—he must come to life again at once. (*Enter Nanki-Poo and Yum-Yum prepared for journey.*) Here he comes. Here, Nanki-Poo, I've good news for you—you're reprieved.

Nank. Oh, but it's too late. I'm a dead man, and I'm off for my honeymoon.

Ko. Nonsense! A terrible thing has just happened. It seems you're the son of the Mikado.

Nank. Yes, but that happened some time ago.

Ko. Is this a time for airy persiflage? Your father is here, and with Katisha!

Nank. My father! And with Katisha.

Ko. Yes, he wants you particularly.

Pooh. So does she.

Yum. Oh, but he's married now.

Ko. But, bless my heart! what has that to do with it?

Nank. Katisha claims me in marriage, but I can't marry her because I'm married already—consequently she will insist on my execution, and if I'm executed, my wife will have to be buried alive.

Yum. You see our difficulty.

Ko. Yes. I don't know what's to be done.

Nank. There's one chance for you. If you could persuade Katisha to marry you, she would have no further claim on me, and in that case I could come to life without any fear of being put to death.

Ko. I marry Katisha!

Yum. I really think it's the only course.

Ko. But, my good girl, have you seen her? She's something appalling!

Pitti. Ah! that's only her face. She has a left elbow which people come miles to see!

Pooh. I am told that her right heel is much admired by connoisseurs.

Ko. My good sir, I decline to pin my heart upon any lady's right heel.

Nank. It comes to this: While Katisha is single, I prefer to be a disembodied spirit. When Katisha is married, existence will be as welcome as the flowers in spring.

DUET.—*Nanki-Poo and Ko-Ko.*
(With Yum-Yum, Pitti-Sing, and Pooh-Bah.)
Nank.

The flowers that bloom in the spring,
    Tra la,
  Breathe promise of merry sunshine—
As we merrily dance and we sing,
    Tra la,
We welcome the hope that they bring,
    Tra la,
  Of a summer of roses and wine.
    And that's what we mean when we say
      that a thing
  Is welcome as flowers that bloom in the
      spring.
    Tra la la la la la, &c.

All. Tra la la la, &c.
Ko.

The flowers that bloom in the spring,
    Tra la,
  Have nothing to do with the case.
I've got to take under my wing,
    Tra la,
A most unattractive old thing,
    Tra la,
  With a caricature of a face.
    And that's what I mean when I say, or
      I sing,
  "Oh, bother the flowers that bloom in
    the spring."
    Tra la la la la la, &c.

All.   Tra la la la, Tra la la la, &c.
(*Dance and exeunt Nanki-Poo, Yum-Yum,*
  Pooh-Bah, Pitti-Sing, and Ko-Ko.)
    Enter Katisha.

RECITATIVE AND SONG.—*Katisha.*
Alone, and yet alive! Oh, sepulchre!
My soul is still my body's prisoner!
Remote the peace that Death alone can give—
My doom, to wait! my punishment, to live!
    SONG.
  Hearts do not break!
  They sting and ache
  For old love's sake,
    But do not die,
  Though with each breath
  They long for death
  As witnesseth
    The living I!
      Oh, living I!
      Come, tell me why,
      When hope is gone
      Dost thou stay on?

      Why linger here,
      Where all is drear?
      Oh, living I!
      Come, tell me why,
      When hope is gone,
      Dost thou stay on?
    May not a cheated maiden die?

Ko. (*entering and approaching her timidly*). Katisha!

Kat. The miscreant who robbed me of my love! But vengeance pursues—they are heating the cauldron!

Ko. Katisha—behold a suppliant at your feet! Katisha—mercy!

Kat. Mercy? Had you mercy on him? See here, you! You have slain my love. He did not love *me*, but he would have loved me in time. I am an acquired taste—only the educated palate can appreciate *me*. I was educating *his* palate when he left me. Well, he is dead, and where shall I find another? It takes years to train a man to love me. Am I to go through the weary round again, and, at the same time, implore mercy for you who robbed me of my prey—I mean my pupil—just as his education was on the point of completion? Oh, where shall I find another?

Ko. (*suddenly, and with great vehemence*). Here!—Here!

Kat. What!!!

Ko. (*with intense passion*). Katisha, for years I have loved you with a white-hot passion that is slowly but surely consuming my very vitals! Ah, shrink not from me! If there is aught of woman's mercy in your heart, turn not away from a love-sick suppliant whose every fibre thrills at your tiniest touch! True it is that, under a poor mask of disgust, I have endeavoured to conceal a passion whose inner fires are broiling the soul within me! But the fire will not be smothered—it defies all attempts at extinction, and, breaking forth, all the more eagerly for its long restraint, it declares itself in words that will not be weighed—that cannot be schooled—that should not be too severely criticised. Katisha, I dare not hope for your love—but I will not live without it! Darling!

Kat. You, whose hands still reek with the blood of my bethrothed, dare to address words of passion to the woman you have so foully wronged!

Ko. I do—accept my love, or I perish on the spot!

Kat. Go to! Who knows so well as I that no one ever yet died of a broken heart!

Ko. You know not what you say. Listen!

    SONG.—*Ko-Ko.*
On a tree by a river a little tom-tit
  Sang "Willow, titwillow, titwillow!"
And I said to him, "Dicky-bird, why do you
    sit

Singing 'Willow, titwillow, titwillow'?
"Is it weakness of intellect, birdie?" I cried,
"Or a rather tough worm in your little in-
side?"
With a shake of his poor little head, he re-
plied,
"Oh, willow, titwillow, titwillow!"
He slapped at his chest, as he sat on that
bough,
Singing "Willow titwillow, titwillow!"
And a cold perspiration bespangled his brow,
Oh, willow, titwillow, titwillow!
He sobbed and he sighed, and a gurgle he
gave,
Then he plunged himself into the billowy
wave,
And an echo arose from the suicide's grave—
"Oh, willow, titwillow, titwillow!"
Now I feel just as sure as I'm sure that my
name
Isn't Willow, titwillow, titwillow,
That 'twas blighted affection that made him
exclaim,
"Oh, willow, titwillow, titwillow!"
And if you remain callous and obdurate, I
Shall perish as he did, and you will know
why,
Though I probably shall not exclaim as I die,
"Oh, willow, titwillow, titwillow!"

(*During this song Katisha has been greatly
affected, and at the end is almost in tears.*)

Kat. (*whimpering*). Did he really die of
love?

Ko. He really did.

Kat. All on account of a cruel little hen?

Ko. Yes.

Kat. Poor little chap!

Ko. It's an affecting tale, and quite true.
I knew the bird intimately.

Kat. Did you? He must have been very
fond of her.

Ko. His devotion was something extraordinary.

Kat. (*still whimpering*). Poor little chap!
And—and if I refuse you, will you go and do
the same?

Ko. At once.

Kat. No, no—you mustn't! Anything but
that! (*Falls on his breast.*) Oh, I'm a silly
little goose!

Ko. (*making a wry face*). You are!

Kat. And you won't hate me because I'm
just a little teeny weeny wee bit bloodthirsty,
will you?

Ko. Hate you? Oh, Katisha! is there not
beauty even in bloodthirstiness?

Kat. My idea exactly.

DUET.—*Katisha and Ko-Ko.*

Kat.
There is beauty in the bellow of the blast,

There is grandeur in the growling of the
gale,
There is eloquent outpouring
When the lion is a-roaring,
And the tiger is a-lashing of his tail!
Ko. Yes, I like to see a tiger
From the Congo or the Niger,
And especially when lashing of his tail!
Kat.
Volcanoes have a splendour that is grim,
And earthquakes only terrify the dolts,
But to him who's scientific
There's nothing that's terrific
In the falling of a flight of thunderbolts!
Ko. Yes, in spite of all my meekness,
If I have a little weakness,
It's a passion for a flight of thunderbolts!
Both. If that is so,
Sing derry down derry!
It's evident, very,
Our tastes are one.
Away we'll go,
And merrily marry,
Nor tardily tarry
Till day is done!

Ko.
There is beauty in extreme old age—
Do you fancy you are elderly enough?
Information I'm requesting
On a subject interesting:
Is a maiden all the better when she's tough?
Kat. Throughout this wide dominion
It's the general opinion
That she'll last a good deal longer when
she's tough.
Ko.
Are you old enough to marry, do you think?
Won't you wait till you are eighty in the
shade?
There's a fascination frantic
In a ruin that's romantic;
Do you think you are sufficiently de-
cayed?
Kat. To the matter that you mention
I have given some attention,
And I think I am sufficiently decayed.
Both. If that is so,
Sing derry down derry!
It's evident, very,
Our tastes are one!
Away we'll go,
And merrily marry,
Nor tardily tarry
Till day is done!
[*Exeunt together.*
*Flourish. Enter the Mikado, attended by
Pish-Tush and Court.*
Mik. Now then, we've had a capital lunch,
and we're quite ready. Have all the painful
preparations been made?
Pish. Your Majesty, all is prepared.

Mik. Then produce the unfortunate gentleman and his two well-meaning but misguided accomplices.

Enter Katisha, Ko-Ko, Pitti-Sing and Pooh-Bah. They throw themselves at the Mikado's feet.

Kat. Mercy! Mercy for Ko-Ko! Mercy for Pitti-Sing! Mercy even for Pooh-Bah!

Mik. I beg your pardon, I don't think I quite caught that remark.

Pooh. Mercy even for Pooh-Bah.

Kat. Mercy! My husband that was to have been is dead, and I have just married this miserable object.

Mik. Oh! You've not been long about it!

Ko. We were married before the Registrar.

Pooh. I am the Registrar.

Mik. I see. But my difficulty is that, as you have slain the Heir Apparent—

Enter Nanki-Poo and Yum-Yum. They kneel.

Nanki. The Heir Apparent is *not* slain.

Mik. Bless my heart, my son!

Yum. And your daughter-in-law elected!

Kat. (*seizing Ko-Ko*). Traitor, you have deceived me!

Mik. Yes, you are entitled to a little explanation, but I think he will give it better whole than in pieces.

Ko. Your Majesty, it's like this: It is true that I stated that I had killed Nanki-Poo—

Mik. Yes, with most affecting particulars.

Pooh. Merely corroborative detail intended to give artistic verisimilitude to a bald and—

Ko. *Will* you refrain from putting in your oar? (*To Mikado.*) It's like this: When your Majesty says, "Let a thing be done," it's as good as done—practically, it *is* done—because your Majesty's will is law. Your Majesty says, "Kill a gentleman," and a gentle-

man is told off to be killed. Consequently, that gentleman is as good as dead—practically, he *is* dead—and if he is dead, why not say so?

Mik. I see. Nothing could possibly be more satisfactory!

FINALE.

Pitti. For he's gone and married Yum-Yum—

All. Yum-Yum!

Pitti. Your anger pray bury,
For all will be merry,
I think you had better succumb—

All. Cumb—cumb!

Pitti. And join our expressions of glee!

Ko. On this subject I pray you be dumb—

All. Dumb—dumb!

Ko. Your notions, though many,
Are not worth a penny,
The word for your guidance is "Mum"—

All. Mum—mum!

Ko. You've a very good bargain in me.

All. On this subject we pray you be dumb—
Dumb—dumb!
We think you had better succumb—
Cumb—cumb!
You'll find there are many
Who'll wed for a penny,
There are lots of good fish in the sea.

Yum. and Nank.

The threatened cloud has passed away,
And fairly shines the dawning day;
What though the night may come too soon,
We've years and years of afternoon!

All. Then let the throng
Our joy advance,
With laughing song
And merry dance,
With joyous shout and ringing cheer,
Inaugurate their new career!
Then let the throng, &c.

CURTAIN.

A WANDERING MINSTREL
(NANKI-POOH)

TIT-WILLOW
(KO-KO)

VOICE

PIANO

Andante espressivo

KO-KO

1. On a tree by a riv-er a lit-tle tom-tit Sang "Wil-low, tit-wil-low, tit - wil-low!" And I said to him, Dick-y-bird why do you sit Sing-ing "Wil-low, tit-wil-low, tit-wil-low?" "Is it weak-ness of in-tel-lect, bird-ie?" I cried, "Or a rath-er tough worm in your lit-tle in-side?" With a shake of his poor lit-tle head he re-plied, "Oh, wil-low, tit-wil-low, tit - wil-low!

THE YEOMEN OF THE GUARD;

OR,

THE MERRYMAN AND HIS MAID.

▼▼▼

ACT I.

SCENE.—*Tower Green.*
Phœbe discovered spinning.

SONG.—*Phœbe.*

When maiden loves, she sits and sighs,
  She wanders to and fro;
Unbidden tear drops fill her eyes,
And to all questions she replies,
  With a sad "heigho!"
  'Tis but a little word—"heigho!"
So soft, 'tis scarcely heard—"heigho!"
  An idle breath—
  Yet life and death
May hang upon a maid's "heigho!"

When maiden loves, she mopes apart,
  As owl mopes on a tree;
Although she keenly feels the smart,
She cannot tell what ails her heart,
  With its sad "Ah me!"
  'Tis but a foolish sigh—"Ah me!"
Born but to droop and die—"Ah me!"
  Yet all the sense
  Of eloquence
Lies hidden in a maid's "Ah me!"

(*weeps*).

Enter Wilfred.

Wil. Mistress Meryll!

Phœ. (*looking up*). Eh! Oh! it's you, is it?
You may go away, if you like. Because I don't
want you, you know.

Wil. Haven't you anything to say to me?

Phœ. Oh yes! Are the birds all caged? The
wild beasts all littered down? All the locks,
chains, bolts, and bars in good order? Is the
Little Ease sufficiently uncomfortable? The
racks, pincers, and thumbscrews all ready for
work? Ugh! you brute!

Wil. These allusions to my professional duties are in doubtful taste. I didn't become a
head-jailer because I like head-jailing. I didn't
become an assistant-tormentor because I like
assistant-tormenting. We can't *all* be sorcerers,
you know. (*Phœbe annoyed.*) Ah! you
brought that upon yourself.

Phœ. Colonel Fairfax is *not* a sorcerer.
He's a man of science and an alchemist.

Wil. Well, whatever he is, he won't be one

long, for he's to be beheaded to-day for dealings with the devil. His master nearly had him
last night, when the fire broke out in the Beauchamp Tower.

Phœ. Oh! how I wish he had escaped in the
confusion! But take care; there's still time for
a reply to his petition for mercy.

Wil. Ah! I'm content to chance that. This
evening at half-past-seven—ah!

Phœ. You're a cruel monster to speak so
unfeelingly of the death of a young and handsome soldier.

Wil. Young and handsome! How do *you*
know he's young and handsome?

Phœ. Because I've seen him every day for
weeks past taking his exercise on the Beauchamp Tower.

Wil. Curse him!

Phœ. There, I believe you're jealous of
him, now. Jealous of a man I've never spoken
to! Jealous of a poor soul who's to die in an
hour!

Wil. I am! I'm jealous of everybody and
everything. I'm jealous of the very words I
speak to you—because they reach your ears—
and I mustn't go near 'em!

Phœ. How unjust you are! Jealous of the
words you speak to me! Why, you know as
well as I do that I don't even like them.

Wil. You used to like 'em.

Phœ. I used to *pretend* I liked them. It
was mere politeness to comparative strangers.

[*Exit Phœbe, with spinning wheel.*

Wil. I don't believe you know what jealousy
is! I don't believe you know how it eats into
a man's heart—and disorders his digestion—
and turns his interior into boiling lead. Oh,
you are a heartless jade to trifle with the delicate organization of the human interior.

[*Exit Wilfred.*

*Enter crowd of Men and Women, followed
by Yeomen of the Guard.*

CHORUS (*as Yeomen march on*).

  Tower Warders,
  Under orders,
Gallant pikemen, valiant sworders!
  Brave in bearing,
  Foemen scaring,
In their bygone days of daring!

Ne'er a stranger
There to danger—
Each was o'er the world a ranger;
To the story
Of our glory
Each à bold contributory!

CHORUS OF YEOMEN.

In the autumn of our life,
Here at rest in ample clover,
We rejoice in telling over
Our impetuous May and June.
In the evening of our day,
With the sun of life declining,
We recall without repining
All the heat of bygone noon.

SOLO.—Second Yeoman.

This the autumn of our life,
This the evening of our day;
Weary we of battle strife,
Weary we of mortal fray.
But our year is not so spent,
And our days are not so faded,
But that we with one consent,
Were our loved land invaded,
Still would face a foreign foe,
As in days of long ago.

Chorus. Still would face a foreign foe.
As in days of long ago.
People. Tower Warders,
Under orders, etc.
Yeomen. This the autumn of our life, &c.
[*Exeunt Crowd. Manent Yeomen.
Enter Dame Carruthers.*

Dame. A good-day to you!
2nd Yeoman. Good-day, Dame Carruthers.
Busy to-day?
Dame. Busy, aye! the fire in the Beauchamp
last night has given me work enough. A dozen
poor prisoners—Richard Colfax, Sir Martin
Byfleet, Colonel Fairfax, Warren the preacher-
poet, and half-a-score others—all packed into
one small cell, not six feet square. Poor Colonel Fairfax, who's to die to-day, is to be removed to No. 14 in the Cold Harbour that he
may have his last hour alone with his confessor;
and I've to see to that.
2nd Yeo. Poor gentleman! He'll die bravely. I fought under him two years since, and
he valued his life as it were a feather!
Phœ. He's the bravest, the handsomest, and
the best young gentleman in England! He
twice saved my father's life; and it's a cruel
thing, a wicked thing, and a barbarous thing
that so gallant a hero should lose his head—for
it's the handsomest head in England!
Dame. For dealings with the devil. Aye!
if all were beheaded who dealt with *him,* there'd
be busy doings on Tower Green.
Phœ. You know very well that Colonel
Fairfax is a student of alchemy—nothing more,

and nothing less; but this wicked Tower, like
a cruel giant in a fairy-tale, must be fed with
blood, and that blood must be the best and bravest in England, or it's not good enough for the
old Blunderbore. Ugh!
Dame. Silence, you silly girl; you know not
what you say. I was born in the old keep, and
I've grown grey in it, and, please God, I shall
die and be buried in it; and there's not a stone
in its walls that is not as dear to me as my own
right hand.

SONG, WITH CHORUS.—*Dame Carruthers and
Yeomen.*

When our gallant Norman foes
Made our merry land their own,
And the Saxons from the Conqueror
were flying,
At his bidding it arose,
In its panoply of stone,
A sentinel unliving and undying.
Insensible, I trow,
As a sentinel should be,
Though a queen to save her head should
come a-suing,
There's a legend on its brow
That is eloquent to me,
And it tells of duty done and duty doing.

"The screw may twist and the rack may
turn,
And men may bleed and men may burn,
O'er London town and its golden hoard
I keep my silent watch and ward!"

Chorus. The screw may twist, &c.

Within its wall of rock
The flower of the brave
Have perished with a constancy un-
shaken.
From the dungeon to the block,
From the scaffold to the grave,
Is a journey many gallant hearts have
taken.
And the wicked flames may hiss
Round the heroes who have fought
For conscience and for home in all its
beauty,
But the grim old fortalice
Takes little heed of aught
That comes not in the measure of its
duty.

"The screw may twist and the rack may
turn,
And men may bleed and men may burn.
O'er London town and its golden hoard
I keep my silent watch and ward!"

Chorus. The screw may twist, &c.
[*Exeunt all but Phœbe. Enter Sergeant Meryll.*

Phœ. Father! Has no reprieve arrived for the poor gentleman?

Mer. No, my lass; but there's one hope yet. Thy brother Leonard, who, as a reward for his valour in saving his standard and cutting his way through fifty foes who would have hanged him, has been appointed a Yeoman of the Guard, will arrive this morning; and as he comes straight from Windsor, where the Court is, it may be—it *may* be—that he will bring the expected reprieve with him.

Phœ. Oh, that he may!

Mer. Amen to that! For the Colonel twice saved my life, and I'd give the rest of my life to save his! And wilt thou not be glad to welcome thy brave brother, with the fame of whose exploits all England is a-ringing?

Phœ. Aye, truly, if he brings the reprieve.

Mer. And not otherwise?

Phœ. Well, he's a brave fellow indeed, and I love brave men.

Mer. *All* brave men?

Phœ. Most of them, I verily believe! But I hope Leonard will not be too strict with me—they say he is a very dragon of virtue and circumspection! Now, my dear old father is kindness itself, and——

Mer. And leaves thee pretty well to thine own ways, eh? Well, I've no fears for thee; thou hast a feather-brain, but thou'rt a good lass.

Phœ. Yes, that's all very well, but if Leonard is going to tell me that I may not do this and I may not do that, and I must not talk to this one, or walk with that one, but go through the world with my lips pursed up and my eyes cast down, like a poor nun who has renounced mankind—why, as I have *not* renounced mankind, and don't mean to renounce mankind, I won't have it—there!

Mer. Nay, he'll not check thee more than is good for thee, Phœbe! He's a brave fellow, and bravest among brave fellows, and yet it seems but yesterday that he robbed the Lieutenant's orchard.

Enter Leonard Meryll.

Leon. Father!

Mer. Leonard! my brave boy! I'm right glad to see thee, and so is Phœbe!

Phœ. Aye—hast thou brought Colonel Fairfax's reprieve?

Leon. Nay, I have here a despatch for the Lieutenant, but no reprieve for the Colonel!

Phœ. Poor gentleman! poor gentleman!

Leon. Aye, I would I had brought better news. I'd give my right hand—nay, my body —my life, to save his!

Mer. Dost thou speak in earnest, my lad?

Leon. Aye, father—I'm no braggart. Did he not save thy life? and am I not his foster-brother?

Mer. Then hearken to me. Thou hast come to join the Yeomen of the Guard!

Leon. Well?

Mer. None has seen thee but ourselves?

Leon. And a sentry, who took but scant notice of me.

Mer. Now to prove thy words. Give me the despatch, and get thee hence at once! Here is money, and I'll send thee more. Lie hidden for a space, and let no one know. I'll convey a suit of Yeoman's uniform to the Colonel's cell—he shall shave off his beard, so that none shall know him, and I'll own him as my son, the brave Leonard Meryll, who saved his flag and cut his way through fifty foes who thirsted for his life. He will be welcomed without question by my brother-yeomen, I'll warrant that. Now, how to get access to the Colonel's cell? (*To Phœbe.*) The key is with thy sour-faced admirer, Wilfred Shadbolt.

Phœ. (*demurely*). I think—I say, I *think*—I can get anything I want from Wilfred. I think —mind I say, I *think*—you may leave that to me.

Mer. Then get thee hence at once, lad— and bless thee for this sacrifice.

Phœ. And take my blessing, too, dear, dear Leonard!

Leon. And thine, eh? Humph! Thy love is new-born; wrap it up carefully, lest it take cold and die.

TRIO.—*Phœbe, Leonard, Meryll.*

Phœ. Alas! I waver to and fro!
Dark danger hangs upon the deed!

All. Dark danger hangs upon the deed!

Leon. The scheme is rash and well may fail,
But ours are not the hearts that quail—
The hands that shrink, the cheeks that pale
In hours of need!

All. No, ours are not the hearts that quail,
The hands that shrink, the cheeks that pale
In hours of need!

Mer. The air I breathe to him I owe:
My life is his—I count it naught!

Phœ. and Leon.
That life is his—so count it naught!

Mer. And shall I reckon risks I run
When services are to be done
To save the life of such an one?
Unworthy thought!

Phœ. and Leon.
And shall we reckon risks we run
To save the life of such an one?

All. Unworthy thought!
We may succeed—who can foretell?
May heaven help our hope—farewell!

(Leonard embraces Meryll and Phœbe, and then exit.)

Phœbe weeping.

Mer. Nay, lass, be of good cheer, we may save him yet.

Phœ. Oh! see, father—they bring the poor gentleman from the Beauchamp! Oh, father! his hour is not yet come?

Mer. No. no,—they lead him to the Cold Harbour Tower to await his end in solitude. But softly—the Lieutenant approaches! He should not see thee weep.

Enter Fairfax, guarded. The Lieutenant enters, meeting him.

Lieut. Halt! Colonel Fairfax, my old friend, we meet but sadly.

Fair. Sir, I greet you with all good-will; and I thank you for the zealous care with which you have guarded me from the pestilent dangers which threaten human life outside. In this happy little community, Death, when he comes, doth so in punctual and business-like fashion; and, like a courtly gentleman, giveth due notice of his advent, that one may not be taken unawares.

Lieut. Sir, you bear this bravely, as a brave man should.

Fair. Why, sir, it is no light boon to die swiftly and surely at a given hour and in a given fashion! Truth to tell, I would gladly have my life; but if that may not be, I have the next thing to it, which is death. Believe me, sir, my lot is not so much amiss!

Phœ. (*aside to Meryll*). Oh, father, father, I cannot bear it!

Mer. My poor lass!

Fair. Nay, pretty one, why weepest thou? Come, be comforted. Such a life as mine is not worth weeping for. (*Sees Meryll.*) Sergeant Meryll, is it not? (*To Lieut.*) May I greet my old friend. (*Shakes Meryll's hand.*) Why, man, what's all this? Thou and I have faced the grim old king a dozen times, and never has his majesty come to me in such goodly fashion. Keep a stout heart, good fellow—we are soldiers, and we know how to die, thou and I. Take my word for it, it is easier to die well than to live well—for, in sooth, I have tried both.

BALLAD.—*Fairfax.*

Is life a boon?
   If so, it must befall
   That Death, whene'er he call,
Must call too soon.
   Though fourscore years he give,
   Yet one would pray to live
Another moon!
   What kind of plaint have I,
   Who perish in July?
I might have had to die,
Perchance, in June!

Is life a thorn?
   Then count it not a whit!
   Man is well done with it;
Soon as he's born
   He should all means essay
   To put the plague away;
And I, war-worn,
   Poor captured fugitive,
   My life most gladly give—
I might have had to live
Another morn!

[*At the end, Phœbe is led off, weeping, by Meryll.*

Fair. And now, Sir Richard, I have a boon to beg. I am in this strait for no better reason than because my kinsman, Sir Clarence Poltwhistle, one of the Secretaries of State, has charged me with sorcery, in order that he may succeed to my estate, which devolves to him provided I die unmarried.

Lieut. As thou wilt most surely do.

Fair. Nay, as I will most surely *not* do, by your worship's grace! I have a mind to thwart this good cousin of mine.

Lieut. How?

Fair. By marrying forthwith, to be sure!

Lieut. But heaven ha' mercy, whom wouldst thou marry?

Fair. Nay, I am indifferent on that score. Coming Death hath made of me a true and chivalrous knight, who holds all womankind in such esteem that the oldest, and the meanest, and the worst favoured of them is good enough for him. So, my good Lieutenant, if thou wouldst serve a poor soldier who has but an hour to live, find me the first that comes—my confessor shall marry us, and her dower shall be my dishonoured name and a hundred crowns to boot. No such poor dower for an hour of matrimony!

Lieut. A strange request. I doubt that I should be warranted in granting it.

Fair. There never was a marriage fraught with so little of evil to the contracting parties. In an hour she'll be a widow, and I—a bachelor again for aught I know!

Lieut. Well, I will see what can be done, for I hold thy kinsman in abhorrence for the scurvy trick he has played thee.

Fair. A thousand thanks, good sir; we meet again on this spot in an hour or so. I shall be a bridegroom then, and your worship will wish me joy. Till then, farewell. (*To guard*)—I am ready, good fellows.

[*Exit with Guard into Cold Harbour Tower.*

Lieut. He is a brave fellow, and it is a pity that he should die. Now, how to find him a bride at such short notice? Well, the task should be easy! [*Exit.*

Enter Jack Point and Elsie Maynard, pursued by a crowd of men and women. Point and Elsie are much terrified; Point, however, assuming an appearance of self-possession.

CHORUS.

Here's a man of jollity,
Jibe, joke, jollify!
Give us of your quality,
Come fool, follify!

If you vapour vapidly,
River runneth rapidly,
Into it we fling
Bird who doesn't sing!

Give us an experiment
In the art of merriment;
Into it we throw
Cock who doesn't crow!

Banish your timidity,
And with all rapidity
Give us quip and quiddity—
Willy-nilly, O!

River none can mollify;—
Into it we throw
Fool who doesn't follify,
Cock who doesn't crow!

Point (alarmed). My masters, I pray you bear with us, and we will satisfy you, for we are merry folk who would make all merry as ourselves. For, look you, there is humour in all things, and the truest philosophy is that which teaches us to find it and to make the most of it.

Elsie (struggling with one of the crowd). Hands off, I say, unmannerly fellow!

Point (to 1st Citizen). Ha! Didst thou hear her say, "Hands off"?

First Cit. Aye, I heard her say it, and I felt her do it! What then?

Point. Thou dost not see the humour of that?

First Cit. Nay, if I do, hang me!

Point. Thou dost not? Now observe. She said "Hands off!" Whose hands? Thine. Off whom? Off *her.* Why? Because she is a woman. Now had she *not* been a woman, thine hands had not been set upon her at all. So the reason for the laying on of hands is the reason for the taking off of hands, and therein is contradiction contradicted! It is the very marriage of *pro* with *con;* and no such opsided union either, as times go, for *pro* is not more unlike *con* than man is unlike woman —yet men and women marry every day with none to say, "Oh, the pity of it!" but I and fools like me! Now wherewithal shall we please you? We can rhyme you couplet, triolet, quatrain, sonnet, rondolet, ballade, what you will. Or we can dance you saraband, gondolet, carole, pimpernel, or Jumping Joan.

Elsie. Let us give them the singing farce of the Merryman and his Maid—therein is song and dance too.

All. Aye, the Merryman and his Maid!

DUET.—*Elsie and Point.*

Point. I have a song to sing, O!
Elsie.   Sing me your song, O!
Point. It is sung to the moon
       By a love-lorn loon,
   Who fled from the mocking throng, O!
It's the song of a merryman, moping mum,
Whose soul was sad, and whose glance was
                              glum,
Who sipped no sup, and who craved no
                              crumb,
   As he sighed for the love of a ladye.
          Heighdy! heighdy!
          Misery me, lackadaydee!
He sipped no sup, and he craved no crumb,
As he sighed for the love of a ladye.
Elsie. I have a song to sing, O!
Point. What is your song, O?
Elsie.   It is sung with the ring
          Of the songs maids sing
   Who love with a love life-long, O!
It's the song of a merrymaid, peerly proud,
Who loved a lord, and who laughed aloud
At the moan of the merryman, moping mum,
Whose soul was sad, and whose glance was
                              glum,
Who sipped no sup, and who craved no
                              crumb,
   As he sighed for the love of a ladye!
          Heighdy! heighdy!
          Misery me, lackadaydee!
          He sipped no sup, &c.
Point. I have a song to sing, O!
Elsie. Sing me your song, O!
Point.   It is sung to the knell
       Of a churchyard bell,
   And a doleful dirge, ding dong, O!
It's a song of a popinjay, bravely born,
Who turned up his noble nose with scorn
At the humble merrymaid, peerly proud
Who loved a lord, and who laughed aloud
At the moan of the merryman, moping mum
Whose soul was sad, and whose glance was
                              glum,
Who sipped no sup, and who craved no
                              crumb,
   As he sighed for the love of a ladye!
          Heighdy! heighdy!
          Misery me, lackadaydee!
          He sipped no sup, &c.
Elsie. I have a song to sing, O!
Point. Sing me your song, O!
Elsie.   It is sung with a sigh
          And a tear in the eye,
   For it tells of a righted wrong, O!
It's a song of the merrymaid, once so gay,
Who turned on her heel and tripped away

119

From the peacock popinjay, bravely born,
Who turned up his noble nose with scorn
At the humble heart that he did not prize:
So she begged on her knees, with downcast
    eyes,
For the love of the merryman, moping mum,
Whose soul was sad and whose glance was
    glum,
Who sipped no sup, and who craved no
    crumb,
  As he sighed for the love of a ladye!
Both.   Heighdy! heighdy!
         Misery me, lackadaydee!
His pains were o'er, and he sighed no more,
For he lived in the love of a ladye!
1st Cit. Well sung and well danced!
2nd Cit. A kiss for that, pretty maid!
All. Aye, a kiss all round.
Elsie (drawing dagger). Best beware! I
am armed!
Point. Back, sirs—back! This is going too
far.
2nd Cit. Thou dost not see the humour of
it, eh? Yet there is humour in all things—even
in this. (*Trying to kiss her.*)
Elsie. Help! help!
*Enter Lieutenant with guard. Crowd falls
back.*
Lieut. What is this pother?
Elsie. Sir, we sang to these folk, and they
would have repaid us with gross courtesy, but
for your honour's coming.
Lieut. (*to Mob*). Away with ye! Clear the
rabble. (*Guards push crowd off, and go off
with them.*) Now, my girl, who are you, and
what do you here?
Elsie. May it please you, sir, we are two
strolling players, Jack Point and I, Elsie Maynard, at your worship's service. We go from
fair to fair, singing, and dancing, and playing
brief interludes; and so we make a poor living.
Lieut. You two, eh? Are ye man and
wife?
Point. No, sir; for though I'm a fool, there
is a limit to my folly. Her mother, old Bridget
Maynard, travels with us (for Elsie is a good
girl), but the old woman is a-bed with fever,
and we have come here to pick up some silver,
to buy an electuary for her.
Lieut. Hark ye, my girl! Your mother is
ill?
Elsie. Sorely ill, sir.
Lieut. And needs good food, and many things
that thou canst not buy?
Elsie. Alas! sir, it is too true.
Lieut. Wouldst thou earn an hundred
crowns?
Elsie. An hundred crowns! They might
save her life!
Lieut. Then listen! A worthy but unhappy
gentleman is to be beheaded in an hour on this
very spot. For sufficient reasons, he desires
to marry before he dies, and he hath asked me
to find him a wife. Wilt thou be that wife?
Elsie. The wife of a man I have never seen!
Point. Why, sir, look you. I am concerned
in this; for though I am not yet wedded to Elsie
Maynard, time works wonders, and there's no
knowing what may be in store for us. Have
we your worship's word for it that this gentleman will die to-day?
Lieut. Nothing is more certain, I grieve to
say.
Point. And that the maiden will be allowed
to depart the very instant the ceremony is at an
end?
Lieut. The very instant. I pledge my hon-
our that it shall be so.
Point. An hundred crowns?
Lieut. An hundred crowns!
Point. For my part, I consent. It is for
Elsie to speak.

    Trio.—*Elsie, Point, and Lieutenant.*

Lieut.
How say you, maiden, will you wed
A man about to lose his head?
    For half an hour
      You'll be a wife,
    And then the dower
      Is yours for life.
A headless bridegroom why refuse?
    If truth the poets tell,
Most bridegrooms, ere they marry, lose
    Both head and heart as well!

Elsie.
A strange proposal you reveal,
It almost makes my senses reel.
Alas! I'm very poor indeed,
And such a sum I sorely need.
    My mother, sir, is like to die,
      This money life may bring,
    Bear this in mind I pray, if I
      Consent to do this thing!
Point.
Though as a general rule of life
I don't allow my promised wife,
My lovely bride that is to be,
To marry anyone but me,
    Yet if the fee is promptly paid,
      And he, in well earned grave,
    Within the hour is duly laid,
      Objection I will waive!
      Yes, objection I will waive!

All.
Temptation, oh temptation,
  Were we, I pray, intended
To shun, whate'er our station,
  Your fascinations splendid;
Or fall, whene'er we view you,

Head over heels into you!
Temptation, oh temptation, &c.
(*During this, the Lieutenant has whispered to Wilfred, who has entered. Wilfred binds Elsie's eyes with a kerchief, and leads her into the Cold Harbour Tower.*)

Lieut. And so, good fellow, you are a jester?

Point. Aye, sir, and, like some of my jests, out of place.

Lieut. I have a vacancy for such an one. Tell me, what are your qualifications for such a post?

Point. Marry, sir, I have a pretty wit. I can rhyme you extempore; I can convulse you with quip and conundrum; I have the lighter philosophies at my tongue's tip; I can be merry, wise, quaint, grim, and sardonic, one by one, or all at once; I have a pretty turn for anecdote; I know all the jests—ancient and modern—past, present, and to come; I can riddle you from dawn of day to set of sun, and, if that content you not, well on to midnight and and the small hours. Oh, sir, a pretty wit, I warrant you—a pretty, pretty wit!

RECITATIVE AND SONG.—*Point.*

I've jibe and joke
    And quip and crank
For lowly folk
    And men of rank.
I ply my craft
    And know no fear,
But aim my shaft
    At prince or peer.
At peer or prince—at prince or peer,
I aim my shaft and know no fear!
I've wisdom from the East and from the West,
    That's subject to no academic rule;
You may find it in the jeering of a jest,
    Or distil it from the folly of a fool.
I can teach you with a quip, if I've a mind;
    I can trick you into learning with a laugh;
Oh winnow all my folly, and you'll find
    A grain or two of truth among the chaff!

I can set a braggart quailing with a quip,
    The upstart I can wither with a whim;
He may wear a merry laugh upon his lip,
    But his laughter has an echo that is grim!
When they're offered to the world in merry guise,
    Unpleasant truths are swallowed with a will—
For he who'd make his fellow-creatures wise
    Should always gild the philosophic pill!

Lieut. And how came you to leave your last employ?

Point. Why, sir, it was in this wise. My Lord was the Archbishop of Canterbury, and it was considered that one of my jokes was unsuited to His Grace's family circle. In truth I ventured to ask a poor riddle, sir—Wherein lay the difference between His Grace and poor Jack Point? His Grace was pleased to give it up, sir. And thereupon I told him that whereas His Grace was paid £10,000 a year for being good, poor Jack Point was good—for nothing. 'Twas but a harmless jest, but it offended His Grace, who whipped me and set me in the stocks for a scurril rogue, and so we parted. I had as lief not take post again with the dignified clergy.

Lieut. But I trust you are very careful not to give offence. I have daughters.

Point. Sir, my jests are most carefully selected, and anything objectionable is expunged. If your honour pleases, I will try them first on your honour's chaplain.

Lieut. Can you give me an example? Say that I had sat me down hurriedly on something sharp?

Point. Sir, I should say that you had sat down on the spur of the moment.

Lieut. Humph! I don't think much of that. Is that the best you can do?

Point. It has always been much admired, sir, but we will try again.

Lieut. Well then, I am at dinner, and the joint of meat is but half cooked.

Point. Why then, sir, I should say—that what is *under*done cannot be helped.

Lieut. I see. I think that manner of thing would be somewhat irritating.

Point. At first, sir, perhaps; but use is everything, and you would come in time to like it.

Lieut. We will suppose that I caught you kissing the kitchen wench under my very nose.

Point. Under *her* very nose, good sir—not under yours! *That* is where *I* would kiss her. Do you take me? Oh, sir, a pretty wit—a pretty, pretty wit!

Lieut. The maiden comes. Follow me, friend, and we will discuss this matter at length in my library.

Point. I am your worship's servant. That is to say, I trust I soon shall be. But, before proceeding to a more serious topic, can you tell me, sir, why a cook's brain-pan is like an overwound clock?

Lieut. A truce to this fooling—follow me.

Point. Just my luck; my best conundrum wasted!   [*Exeunt.*

Enter Elsie from Tower, led by Wilfred, who removes the bandage from her eyes, and exit.

RECITATIVE AND SONG.—*Elsie.*

'Tis done! I am a bride! Oh, little ring,
    That bearest in thy circle all the gladness

That lovers hope for, and that poets sing,
    What bringest thou to me but gold and
        sadness?
A bridegroom all unknown, save in this wise,
To-day he dies! To-day, alas, he dies!

    Though tear and long-drawn sigh
        Ill fit a bride,
    No sadder wife than I
    The whole world wide!
        Ah me! Ah me!
    Yet maids there be
    Who would consent to lose
    The very rose of youth,
        The flower of life,
        To be, in honest truth,
        A wedded wife,
            No matter whose!

    Ah me! what profit we,
    O maids that sigh,
Though gold, though gold should live
    If wedded love must die?
Ere half an hour has rung,
    A widow I!
Ah heaven, he is too young,
    Too brave to die!
        Ah me! Ah me!
    Yet wives there be
    So weary worn, I trow,
    That they would scarce complain,
        So that they could
    In half an hour attain
        To widowhood,
            No matter how!

    O weary wives
    Who widowhood would win,
    Rejoice that ye have time
        To weary in.
        [*Exit Elsie as Wilfred re-enters.*

Wil. (*looking after Elsie*). 'Tis an odd freak, for a dying man and his confessor to be closeted alone with a strange singing girl. I would fain have espied them, but they stopped up the keyhole. *My* keyhole!

Enter Phœbe with Meryll. Meryll remains in the background, unobserved by Wilfred.

Phœ. (*aside*). Wilfred—and alone!

Wil. Now what could he have wanted with her? That's what puzzles me!

Phœ. (*aside*). Now to get the keys from him. (*Aloud.*) Wilfred—has no reprieve arrived?

Wil. None. Thine adored Fairfax is to die.

Phœ. Nay, thou knowest that I have naught but pity for the poor condemned gentleman.

Wil. I know that he who is about to die is more to thee than I, who am alive and well.

Phœ. Why, that were out of reason, dear Wilfred. Do they not say that a live ass is better than a dead lion? No, I don't mean that

Wil. Oh, they say that, do they?

Phœ. It's unpardonably rude of them, but believe they put it in that way. Not that applies to thee, who art clever beyond all telling!

Wil. Oh, yes; as an assistant tormentor

Phœ. Nay, as a wit, as a humorist, as a most philosophic commentator on the vanity of human resolution.

(*Phœbe slyly takes bunch of keys from Wilfred's waistband, and hands them to Meryll who enters the Tower, unnoticed by Wilfred.*

Wil. Truly, I have seen great resolution give way under my persuasive methods (*working a small thumbscrew*). In the nice regulation of a thumbscrew—in the hundredth part of a single revolution lieth all the difference between stony reticence and a torrent of impulsive unbosoming that the pen can scarcely follow Ha! ha! I am a mad wag.

Phœ. (*with a grimace*). Thou art a most light-hearted and delightful companion, Master Wilfred. Thine anecdotes of the torture chamber are the prettiest hearing.

Wil. I'm a pleasant fellow and I choose. believe I am the merriest dog that barks. A we might be passing happy together—

Phœ. Perhaps. I do not know.

Wil. For thou wouldst make a most tender and loving wife.

Phœ. Aye, to one whom I really loved. For there is a wealth of love within this little hear —saving up for—I wonder whom? Now, o all the world of men, I wonder whom? T think that he whom I am to wed is now aliv and somewhere! Perhaps far away, perhap close at hand! And I know him not! I seemeth that I am wasting time in not knowing him.

Wil. Now say that it is I—nay! suppose for the nonce. Say that we are wed—suppose it only—say that thou art my very bride and I thy cheery, joyous, bright, frolicsom husband—and that the day's work being done and the prisoners stored away for the night thou and I are alone together—with a long long evening before us!

Phœ. (*with a grimace*). It is a pretty picture—but I scarcely know. It cometh so unexpectedly—and yet—and yet—*were* I th bride—

Wil. Aye!—wert thou my bride—?

Phœ. Oh, how I would love thee!

SONG.—*Phœbe.*

    Were I thy bride,
  Then all the world beside
    Were not too wide
      To hold my wealth of love—
    Were I thy bride!

Upon thy breast
My loving head would rest,
As on her nest
   The tender turtle dove—
Were I thy bride!

This heart of mine
Would be one heart with thine,
And in that shrine
   Our happiness would dwell—
Were I thy bride!

And all day long
Our lives should be a song:
No grief, no wrong
   Should make my heart rebel—
Were I thy bride!

The silvery flute,
The melancholy lute,
Were night owl's hoot
   To my low-whispered coo—
Were I thy bride!

The skylark's trill
Were but discordance shrill
To the soft thrill
   Of wooing as I'd woo—
Were I thy bride!

Meryll re-enters; gives keys to Phœbe, who replaces them at Wilfred's girdle, unnoticed by him. Exit Meryll.

The rose's sigh
Were as a carrion's cry
To lullaby
   Such as I'd sing to thee,
Were I thy bride!

A feather's press
Were leaden heaviness
To my caress.
   But then, of course, you see
I'm not thy bride!   [*Exit Phœbe.*
Wil. No, thou'rt not—not yet! But, Lord, how she woo'd me! I should be no mean judge of wooing, seeing that I have been more hotly woo'd than most men. I have been woo'd by maid, widow, and wife. I have been woo'd boldly, timidly, tearfully, shyly—by direct assault, by suggestion, by implication, by inference, and by innuendo. But this wooing is not of the common order: it is the wooing of one who must needs woo me, if she die for it!
                    [*Exit Wilfred.*
Enter Meryll, cautiously, from Tower.
Mer. (*looking after them*). The dead is, so far, safely accomplished. The slyboots, how she wheedled him! What a helpless ninny is a love-sick man! He is but as a lute in a wom-an's hands—she plays upon him whatever tune she will. But the Colonel comes. I' faith, he's just in time, for the Yeomen parade here for his execution in two minutes!

Enter Fairfax, without beard and moustache, and dressed in Yeoman's uniform.

Fair. My good and kind friend, thou runnest a grave risk for me!

Mer. Tut, sir, no risk. I'll warrant none here will recognise you. You make a brave Yeoman, sir! So—this ruff is too high; so—and the sword should hang thus. Here is your halbert, sir; carry it thus. The Yeomen come. Now remember, you are my brave son, Leonard Meryll.

Fair. If I may not bear mine own name, there is none other I would bear so readily.

Mer. Now, sir, put a bold face on it; for they come.

FINALE.—ACT I.

Enter Yeomen of the Guard.

CHORUS.

Oh, Sergeant Meryll, is it true—
   The welcome news we read in orders?
Thy son, whose deeds of derring-do
Are echoed all the country through,
   Has come to join the Tower Warders?
If so, we come to meet him,
That we may fitly greet him,
And welcome his arrival here
With shout on shout and cheer on cheer.
   Hurrah! Hurrah! Hurrah!
   RECITATIVE—*Sergeant Meryll.*
Ye Tower Warders, nursed in war's alarms,
   Suckled on gunpowder and weaned on
      glory,
Behold my son, whose all-subduing arms
   Have formed the theme of many a song
      and story!
      Forgive his aged father's pride; nor jeer
      His aged father's sympathetic tear!
                 (*Pretending to weep.*)

CHORUS.

Leonard Meryll!
Leonard Meryll!
Dauntless he in time of peril!
   Man of power,
   Knighthood's flower,
Welcome to the grim old Tower,
To the Tower, welcome thou!
   RECITATIVE.—*Fairfax.*
Forbear, my friends, and spare me this
      ovation,
I have small claim to such consideration;
The tales that of my prowess are narrated
Have been prodigiously exaggerated!

CHORUS.

'Tis ever thus!
Wherever valour true is found,
True modesty will there abound.

COUPLETS.

1st Yeoman.
Didst thou not, oh, Leonard Meryll!
Standard lost in last campaign,
Rescue it at deadly peril—
Bear it safely back again?
Chorus.
Leonard Meryll, at his peril,
Bore it safely back again!
2nd Yeoman.
Didst thou not, when prisoner taken,
And debarred from all escape,
Face, with gallant heart unshaken,
Death in most appalling shape?
Chorus.
Leonard Meryll faced his peril,
Death in most appalling shape!
Fair. (aside).
Truly I was to be pitied,
Having but an hour to live,
I reluctantly submitted,
I had no alternative!
(Aloud.)
Oh! the tales that are narrated
Of my deeds of derring-do
Have been much exaggerated,
Very much exaggerated,
Scarce a word of them is true!
Chorus.
They are not exaggerated, &c.
Enter Phœbe. She rushes to Fairfax.
Enter Wilfred.

RECITATIVE.

Phœ. Leonard!
Fair. (puzzled). I beg your pardon?
Phœ. Don't you know me? I'm little Phœbe!
Fair. (still puzzled). Phœbe? Is this Phœbe?
What! little Phœbe? *(Aside.)* Who the
deuce may *she* be?
It can't be Phœbe, surely?
Wil. Yes, 'tis Phœbe—
Your sister Phœbe! Your own little sister!
All. Aye, he speaks the truth; 'Tis Phœbe!
Fair. (pretending to recognise her). Sister
Phœbe!
Phœ. Oh, my brother!
Fair. Why, how you've grown! I did not rec-
ognise you!
Phœ. So many years! Oh, my brother!
Fair. Oh, my sister!
Wil. Aye, hug him, girl! There are three
thou mayst hug—Thy father and thy brother
and—myself!
Fair. Thyself, forsooth? And who art thou
thyself?

Wil. Good sir, we are betrothed. *(Fairfax
turns enquiringly to Phœbe.)*
Phœ. Or more or less—
But rather less than more!
Wil. To thy fond care
I do commend thy sister. Be to her
An ever-watchful guardian—eagle-eyed!
And when she feels (as sometimes she does
feel)
Disposed to indiscriminate caress,
Be thou at hand to take those favours from
her!
All.
Be thou at hand to take those favours from
her!
Phœ. Yes, yes.
Be thou at hand to take those favours from
me!
TRIO.—*Wilfred, Fairfax, and Phœbe.*
Wil.
To thy fraternal care
Thy sister I commend;
From every lurking snare
Thy lovely charge defend:
And to achieve this end,
Oh! grant, I pray, this boon—
She shall not quit thy sight:
From morn to afternoon—
From afternoon to night—
From seven o'clock to two—
From two to eventide—
From dim twilight to 'leven at night
She shall not quit thy side!
All. From morn to afternoon, &c.
Phœ.
So amiable I've grown,
So innocent as well,
That if I'm left alone
The consequences fell
No mortal can foretell.
So grant, I pray, this boon—
I shall not quit thy sight:
From morn to afternoon—
From afternoon to night—
From seven o'clock to two—
From two to eventide—
From dim twilight to 'leven at night
I shall not quit thy side.
All. From morn to afternoon, &c.
Fair.
With brotherly readiness,
For my fair sister's sake,
At once I answer "Yes"—
That task I undertake—
My word I never break.
I freely grant that boon,
And I'll repeat my plight.
From morn to afternoon—   *(kiss)*
From afternoon to night—   *(kiss)*
From seven o'clock to two—   *(kiss)*
From two to evening meal—   *(kiss)*

From dim twilight to 'leven at night
  That compact I will seal.   (*kiss*)
All. From morn to afternoon, &c.
(*The bell of St. Peter's begins to toll. Exit
Wilfred. The crowd enters; the block is
brought on to the stage, and the headsman takes
his place. The Yeomen of the Guard form
up. The Lieutenant enters and takes his place,
and tells off Fairfax and two others to bring
the prisoner to execution. Fairfax, and two
Yeomen exeunt to Tower.*)
    CHORUS (*to tolling accompaniment*).
The prisoner comes to meet his doom;
The block, the headsman, and the tomb.
The funeral bell begins to toll—
May Heaven have mercy on his soul!
        SOLO.—*Elsie, with Chorus.*
Oh, Mercy, thou whose smile has shone
So many a captive heart upon;
Of all immured within these walls,
To-day the very worthiest falls!
*Enter Fairfax and two other Yeomen from
Tower in great excitement.*
Fair.
  My Lord! I know not how to tell
    The news I bear!
  I and my comrades sought the prisoner's
    cell—
    He is not there!
All. He is not there!
  They sought the prisoner's cell—he is not
      there!
    TRIO.—*Fairfax and Two Yeomen.*
As escort for the prisoner
  We sought his cell, in duty bound;
The double gratings open were,
  No prisoner at all we found!

We hunted high, we hunted low,
  We hunted here, we hunted there—
The man we sought with anxious care
  Had vanished into empty air!
              [*Exit Lieutenant.*
Girls.
  Now, by my troth, the news is fair,
  The man has vanished into air!
All.
  As escort for the prisoner
    They sought his cell in duty bound, &c.

Enter Wilfred, followed by Lieutenant.
Lieut. Astounding news! The prisoner fled!
(*To Wilfred.*) Thy life shall forfeit be instead!
              (*Wilfred is arrested.*)
Wilfred.
  My lord, I did not set him free,
  I hate the man—my rival he!
              (*Wilfred is taken away.*)
Meryll.
  The prisoner gone—I'm all agape!
  Who could have helped him to escape?
Phœbe.
  Indeed I can't imagine who!
  I've no idea at all—have you?
          Enter Jack Point.
Dame.
  Of his escape no traces lurk
  Enchantment must have been at work!
Elsie (*aside to Point*).
  What have I done! Oh, woe is me!
  I am his wife, and he is free!
Point.
  Oh, woe is *you?* Your anguish sink!
  Oh, woe is *me*, I rather think!
  Oh, woe is *me*, I rather think!
  Yes, woe is *me*, I rather think!
    Whate'er betide
    You are his bride,
    And I am left
    Alone—bereft!
  Yes, woe is *me*, I rather think!
  Yes, woe is *me*, I rather think!
    ENSEMBLE.—*Lieutenant and Chorus.*

All frenzied with despair $\left\{ \begin{matrix} I \\ they \end{matrix} \right\}$ rave,
  The grave is cheated of its due.
Who is the misbegotten knave
  Who hath contrived this deed to do?
Let search be made throughout the land,

Or $\left\{ \begin{matrix} his \\ my \end{matrix} \right\}$ vindictive anger dread—

A thousand marks to him $\left\{ \begin{matrix} he'll \\ I'll \end{matrix} \right\}$ hand
  Who brings him here, alive or dead.
(*At the end, Elsie faints in Fairfax's arms;
all the Yeomen and populace rush off the stage
in different directions, to hunt for the fugitive,
leaving only the Headsman on the stage, and
Elsie insensible in Fairfax's arms.*)

END OF ACT I.

ACT II.

SCENE.—*The same.—Moonlight.*
  Two days have elapsed.
Women and Yeomen of the Guard discovered.
          CHORUS.
Women.
  Night has spread her pall once more,
  And the prisoner still is free:

Open is his dungeon door,
  Useless his dungeon key!
He has shaken off his yoke—
  How, no mortal man can tell!
Shame on loutish jailer-folk—
  Shame on sleepy sentinel!

  Enter Dame Carruthers and Kate.

SOLO.—*Dame Carruthers.*

Warders are ye?
　　Whom do ye ward?
Bolt, bar, and key,
　　Shackle and cord,
Fetter and chain,
　　Dungeon of stone,
All are in vain—
　　Prisoner's flown!
Spite of ye all, he is free—he is free!
Whom do ye ward? Pretty warders are ye!
Chorus of Women. Pretty warders are ye, &c.

CHORUS.

Yeomen.

Up and down, and in and out,
Here and there, and round about;
Every chamber, every house,
Every chink that holds a mouse,
Every crevice in the keep,
Where a beetle black could creep,
Every outlet, every drain,
Have we searched, but all in vain.

Women.

Warders are ye? Whom do ye ward? &c.
　　　　　　　　　　　　　[*Exeunt all.*
*Enter Jack Point, in low spirits, reading from
a huge volume.*

Point (*reads*). "The Merrie Jestes of Hugh
Ambrose. No. 7863. The Poor Wit and the
Rich Councillor. A certayne poor wit, being
an-hungered, did meet a well-fed councillor.
'Marry, fool,' quoth the councillor, 'whither
away?' 'In truth,' said the poor wag, 'in that
I have eaten naught these two dayes I do
wither away, and that right rapidly!' The
councillor laughed hugely, and gave him a
sausage." Humph! The councillor was easier
to please than my new master the Lieutenant.
I would like to take post under that councillor.
Ah! 'tis but melancholy mumming when poor
heartbroken, jilted Jack Point must needs turn
to Hugh Ambrose for original light humour!
Enter Wilfred, also in low spirits.

Wil. (*sighing*). Ah, Master Point!
Point (*changing his manner*). Ha! friend
jailer! Jailer that wast—jailer that never shalt
be more! Jailer that jailed not, or that jailed,
if jail he did, so unjailerly that 'twas but jerry-
jailing, or jailing in joke—though no joke to
him who, by unjailerlike jailing, did so jeopar-
dise his jailership. Come, take heart, smile,
laugh, wink, twinkle, thou tormentor that tor-
mentest none—thou racker that rackest not—
thou pincher out of place—come, take heart,
and be merry, as I am!—(*aside, dolefully*)—
as I am!
Wil. Aye, it's well for thee to laugh. Thou
hast a good post, and hast cause to be merry.
Point (*bitterly*). Cause? Have we not all
cause? Is not the world a big butt of humour,

into which all who will may drive a **gimlet**
See, I am a salaried wit; and is there augh
in nature more ridiculous? A poor, dull, heart
broken man, who must needs be merry, or h
will be whipped; who must rejoice, lest h
starve; who must jest you, jibe you, quip you
crank you, wrack you, riddle you, from hou
to hour, from day to day, from year to year
lest he dwindle, perish, starve, pine, and die
Why, when there's naught else to laugh at,
laugh at myself till I ache for it!
Wil. Yet I have often thought that a jester'
calling would suit me to a hair.
Point. Thee? Would suit *thee*, thou death'
head and crossbones?
Wil. Aye, I have a pretty wit—a light, airy
joysome wit, spiced with anecdotes of prison
cells and the torture chamber. Oh, a very delicate wit! I have tried it on many a prisoner
and there have been some who smiled. Now i
is not easy to make a prisoner smile. And i
should not be difficult to be a good jester, seeing
that thou art one.
Point. Difficult? Nothing easier. Nothing
easier. Attend, and I will prove it to thee!

SONG.—*Point.*

Oh! a private buffoon is a light-hearted loon,
　　If you listen to popular rumour;
From the morn to the night he's so joyous
　　　　and bright,
　　And he bubbles with wit and good humour!
He's so quaint and so terse, both in prose and
　　　　in verse;
　　Yet though people forgive his transgres-
　　　　sion,
There are one or two rules that all family
　　　　fools
　　Must observe, if they love their profession.
　　　There are one or two rules,
　　　　　Half a dozen, may be,
　　　That all family fools,
　　　　　Of whatever degree,
　　Must observe, if they love their profession.

If you wish to succeed as a jester, you'll need
　　To consider each person's auricular:
What is all right for B would quite scandalise
　　　　C
　　(For C is so very particular);
And D may be dull, and E's very thick skull
　　Is as empty of brains as a ladle;
While F is F sharp, and will cry with a carp,
　　That he's known your best joke from his
　　　　cradle!
　　When your humour they flout,
　　　　You can't let yourself go;
　　And it *does* put you out
　　　　When a person says, "Oh,
　　I have known that old joke from my
　　　　cradle!"

126

If your master is surly, from getting up early
  (And tempers are short in the morning),
An inopportune joke is enough to provoke
  Him to give you, at once, a month's warning.
Then if you refrain, he is at you again,
  For he likes to get value for money;
He'll ask then and there, with an insolent stare,
  "If you know that you're paid to be funny?"
    It adds to the task
      Of a merryman's place,
    When your principal asks,
      With a scowl on his face,
If you know that you're paid to be funny?

Comes a Bishop, maybe, or a solemn D.D.—
  Oh, beware of his anger provoking!
Better not pull his hair—don't stick pins in his chair;
  He don't understand practical joking.
If the jests that you crack have an orthodox smack,
  You may get a bland smile from these sages;
But should they, by chance, be imported from France,
  Half-a-crown is stopped out of your wages!
    It's a general rule,
      Though your zeal it may quench,
    If the family fool
      Tells a joke that's too French,
Half-a-crown is stopped out of his wages!

Though your head it may rack with a bilious attack,
  And your senses with toothache you're losing,
Don't be mopy and flat—they don't fine you for that,
  If you're properly quaint and amusing!
Though your wife ran away with a soldier that day,
  And took with her your trifle of money;
Bless your heart, they don't mind—they're exceedingly kind—
  They don't blame you—as long as you're funny!
    It's a comfort to feel
      If your partner should flit,
    Though *you* suffer a deal,
      They don't mind it a bit—
They don't blame you—so long as you're funny!

Point.—And so thou wouldst be a jester, eh?"

Wil. Aye!

Point. Now, listen! My sweetheart, Elsie Maynard, was secretly wed to this **Fairfax** half an hour ere he escaped.

Wil. She did well.

Point. She did nothing of the kind, so hold thy peace and perpend. Now, while he liveth she is dead to me and I to her, and so, my jibes and jokes notwithstanding, I am the saddest and the sorriest dog in England!

Wil. Thou art a very dull dog indeed.

Point. Now, if thou wilt swear that thou didst shoot this Fairfax while he was trying to swim across the river—it needs but the discharge of an arquebus on a dark night—and that he sank and was seen no more, I'll make thee the very Archbishop of jesters, and that in two days' time! Now, what sayest thou?

Wil. I am to lie?

Point. Heartily. But thy lie must be a lie of circumstance, which I will support with the testimony of eyes, ears, and tongue.

Wil. And thou wilt qualify me as a jester?

Point. As a jester among jesters. I will teach thee all my original songs, my self-constructed riddles, my own ingenious paradoxes; nay, more, I will reveal to thee the source whence I get them. Now, what sayest thou?

Wil. Why, if it be but a lie thou wantest of me, I hold it cheap enough, and I say yes, it is a bargain!

DUET.—*Point and Wilfred.*

Both. Hereupon we're both agreed,
    All that we two
    Do agree to
  We'll secure by solemn deed,
    To prevent all
    Error mental.

Point. I on Elsie am to call
    With a story
    Grim and gory;

Wil. How this Fairfax died, and all
    I declare to
    You're to swear to

Both.   Tell a tale of cock and bull,
    Of convincing detail full
      Tale tremendous,
      Heaven defend us!
  What a tale of cock and bull!

Both. In return for ⎰your⎱ own part
         ⎱my⎰
  ⎰You are⎱ making,
  ⎱ I am ⎰
  Undertaking, ⎰me⎱
  To instruct ⎱you⎰ in the art
    (Art amazing,
    Wonder raising)

Point. Of a jester, jesting free.
    Proud position—
    High ambition!

Wil. And a lively one I'll be,
  Wag-a-wagging,
  Never flagging!

Both. Tell a tale of cock and bull, &c.

[Exeunt together.

Enter Fairfax.

Fair. Two days gone, and no news of poor Fairfax. The dolts! They seek him everywhere save within a dozen yards of his dungeon. So I am free! Free, but for the cursed haste with which I hurried headlong into the bonds of matrimony with—Heaven knows whom! As far as I remember, she should have been young; but even had not her face been concealed by her kerchief, I doubt whether, in my then plight, I should have taken much note of her. Free? Bah! The Tower bonds were but a thread of silk compared with these conjugal fetters which I, fool that I was, placed upon mine own hands. From the one I broke readily enough—how to break the other!

Ballad.—*Fairfax.*

Free from his fetters grim—
　Free to depart;
Free both in life and limb—
　In all but heart!
Bound to an unknown bride
　For good and ill;
Ah, is not one so tied
　A prisoner still?

Free, yet in fetters held
　Till his last hour,
Gyves that no smith can weld,
　No rust devour!
Although a monarch's hand
　Had set him free,
Of all the captive band
　The saddest he!

Enter Meryll.

Fair. Well, Sergeant Meryll, and how fares thy pretty charge, Elsie Maynard?

Mer. Well enough, sir. She is quite strong again, and leaves us to-night.

Fair. Thanks to Dame Carruthers' kind nursing, eh?

Mer. Aye, deuce take the old witch! Ah, 'twas but a sorry trick you played me, sir, to bring the fainting girl to me. It gave the old lady an excuse for taking up her quarters in my house, and for the last two years I've shunned her like the plague. Another day of it and she would have married me! (*Enter Dame Carruthers and Kate.*) Good Lord, here she is again! I'll e'en go—(*going*).

Dame. Nay, Sergeant Meryll, don't go I have something of grave import to say to thee.

Mer. (*aside*). It's coming.

Fair. (*laughing*). I'faith, I think I'm not wanted here. (*Going.*)

Dame. Nay, Master Leonard, I've naught to say to thy father that his son may not hear.

Fair. (*aside*). True. I'm one of the family: I had forgotten!

Dame. 'Tis about this Elsie Maynard. A pretty girl, Master Leonard.

Fair. Aye, fair as a peach blossom—what then?

Dame. She hath a liking for thee, or I mistake not.

Fair. With all my heart. She's as dainty a little maid as you'll find in a midsummer day's march.

Dame. Then be warned in time, and give not thy heart to her. Oh, *I* know what it is to give my heart to one who will have none of it!

Mer. (*aside*). Aye, *she* knows all about that. (*Aloud.*) And why is my boy to take heed of her? She's a good girl, Dame Carruthers.

Dame. Good enough, for aught I know. But she's no girl. She's a married woman.

Mer. A married woman! Tush, old lady —she's promised to Jack Point, the Lieutenant's new jester.

Dame. Tush in thy teeth, old man! As my niece Kate sat by her bedside to-day, this Elsie slept, and as she slept she moaned and groaned, and turned this way and that way— and, "How shall I marry one I have never seen?" quoth she—then, "An hundred crowns!" quoth she—then, "Is it certain he will die in an hour?" quoth she—then, "I love him not, and yet I am his wife," quoth she! Is it not so, Kate?

Kate. Aye, aunt, 'tis even so.

Fair. Art thou sure of all this?

Kate. Aye, sir, for I wrote it all down on my tablets.

Dame. Now, mark my words: it was of this Fairfax she spake, and he is her husband, or I'll swallow my kirtle!

Meryll (*aside*). Is this true, sir?

Fair. (*aside to Meryll*). True? Why, the girl was raving! (*Aloud.*) Why should she marry a man who had but an hour to live?

Dame. Marry? There be those who would marry but for a minute, rather than die old maids.

Meryll (*aside*). Aye, I know one of them!

Quartet.—*Fairfax, Sergeant Meryll, Dame Carruthers, and Kate.*

Strange adventure! Maiden wedded
　To a groom she'd never seen—
　　Never, never, never seen!
Groom about to be beheaded,
　In an hour on Tower Green!
　　Tower, Tower, Tower Green!
Groom in dreary dungeon lying,
Groom as good as dead, or dying,
For a pretty maiden sighing—

Pretty maid of seventeen!
   Seven—seven—seventeen!

Strange adventure that we're trolling:
  Modest maid and gallant groom—
    Gallant, gallant, gallant groom!—
While the funeral bell is tolling,
  Tolling, tolling, Bim-a-boom!
    Bim-a, Bim-a, Bima-boom!
Modest maiden will not tarry;
Though but sixteen year she carry,
She must marry, she must marry,
  Though the altar be a tomb—
    Tower—Tower—Tower tomb!

[*Exeunt Dame Carruthers, Meryll, and Kate.*

Fair. So my mysterious bride is no other than this winsome Elsie! By my hand, 'tis no such ill-plunge in Fortune's lucky bag! I might have fared worse with my eyes open! But she comes. Now to test her principles. 'Tis not every husband who has a chance of wooing his own wife!

Enter Elsie.

Fair. Mistress Elsie!

Elsie. Master Leonard!

Fair. So thou leavest us to-night?

Elsie. Yes, Master Leonard. I have been kindly tended, and I almost fear I am loth to go.

Fair. And this Fairfax. Wast thou glad when he escaped?

Elsie. Why, truly, Master Leonard, it is a sad thing that a young and gallant gentleman should die in the very fullness of his life.

Fair. Then when thou didst faint in my arms, it was for joy at his safety?

Elsie. It may be so. I was highly wrought, Master Leonard, and I am but a girl, and so, when I am highly wrought, I faint.

Fair. Now, dost thou know, I am consumed with a parlous jealousy?

Elsie. Thou? And of whom?

Fair. Why, of this Fairfax, surely!

Elsie. Of Colonel Fairfax!

Fair. Aye. Shall I be frank with thee? Elsie—I love thee, ardently, passionately! (*Elsie alarmed and surprised.*) Elsie, I have loved thee these two days—which is a long time—and I would fain join my life to thine!

Elsie. Master Leonard! Thou art jesting!

Fair. Jesting? May I shrivel into raisins if I jest! I love thee with a love that is a fever—with a love that is a frenzy—with a love that eateth up my heart! What sayest thou? Thou wilt not let my heart be eaten up?

Elsie (*aside*). Oh, mercy! What am I to say?

Fair. Dost thou love me, or hast thou been insensible these two days?

Elsie. I love all brave men.

Fair. Nay, there is love in excess. I thank heaven, there are many brave men in England; but if thou lovest them all, I withdraw my thanks.

Elsie. I love the bravest best. But, sir, I may not listen—I am not free—I—I am a wife!

Fair. Thou a wife? Whose? His name? His hours are numbered—nay, his grave is dug and his epitaph set up! Come, his name?

Elsie. Oh, sir! keep my secret—it is the only barrier that Fate could set up between us. My husband is none other than Colonel Fairfax!

Fair. The greatest villain unhung! The most ill-favoured, ill-mannered, ill-natured, ill-omened, ill-tempered dog in Christendom!

Elsie. It is very like. He is naught to me —for I never saw him. I was blindfolded, and he was to have died within the hour; and he did not die—and I am wedded to him, and my heart is broken!

Fair. He was to have died, and he did *not* die? The scoundrel! The perjured, traitrous villain! Thou shouldst have insisted on his dying first, to make sure. 'Tis the only way with these Fairfaxes.

Elsie. I now wish I had!

Fair. (*aside*). Bloodthirsty little maiden! (*Aloud.*) A fig for this Fairfax! Be mine—he will never know—he dares not show himself; and if he dare, what art thou to him? Fly with me, Elsie—we will be married to-morrow, and thou shalt be the happiest wife in England!

Elsie. Master Leonard! I am amazed! Is it thus that brave soldiers speak to poor girls? Oh! for shame, for shame! I am wed—not the less because I love not my husband. I am a wife, sir, and I have a duty, and—oh, sir! thy words terrify me—they are not honest—they are wicked words and unworthy thy great and brave heart! Oh, shame upon thee! shame upon thee!

Fair. Nay, Elsie, I did but jest. I spake but to try thee—

(*Shot heard.*) *Enter Meryll, hastily.*

Mer. (*recit.*) Hark! What was that, sir?

Fair. Why, an arquebus—
Fired from the wharf, unless I much mistake.

Mer. Strange—and at such an hour! What can it mean?

Enter Chorus.

CHORUS.

Now what can that have been—
  A shot so late at night,
  Enough to cause affright!
What can the portent mean?

Are foemen in the land?
  Is London to be wrecked?
  What are we to expect?

What danger is at hand?
Let us understand
What danger is at hand!
Lieutenant enters, also Point and Wilfred.

RECITATIVE.

Lieut. Who fired that shot? At once the truth declare!

Wil. My lord, 'twas I—to rashly judge forbear!

Point. My lord, 'twas he—to rashly judge forbear!

DUET AND CHORUS.—*Wilfred and Point.*

Wil. Like a ghost his vigil keeping—
Point. Or a spectre all-appalling—
Wil. I beheld a figure creeping—
Point. I should rather call it crawling—
Wil. He was creeping—
Point.   He was crawling—
Wil. He was creeping, creeping—
Point.   Crawling!
Wil. He was creeping—
Point.   He was crawling—
Wil. He was creeping, creeping—
Point.   Crawling!
Wil. Not a moment's hesitation—
    I myself upon him flung,
    With a hurried exclamation
    To his draperies I hung;
    Then we closed with one another
    In a rough-and-tumble smother;
    Colonel Fairfax and no other
    Was the man to whom I clung!
All. Colonel Fairfax and no other
    Was the man to whom he clung!
Wil. After mighty tug and tussle—
Point. It resembled more a struggle—
Wil. He, by dint of stronger muscle—
Point. Or by some infernal juggle—
Wil. From my clutches quickly sliding—
Point. I should rather call it slipping—
Wil. With the view, no doubt, of hiding—
Point. Or escaping to the shipping—
Wil. With a gasp, and with a quiver—
Point. I'd describe it as a shiver—
Wil. Down he dived into the river
    And, alas, I cannot swim.
All. It's enough to make one shiver,
    With a gasp and with a quiver,
    Down he dived into the river,
    It was very brave of him!
Wil. Ingenuity is catching;
    With the view my king of pleasing,
    Arquebus from sentry snatching—
Point. I should rather call it seizing—
Wil.   With an ounce or two of lead
        I despatched him through the head!
All.   With an ounce or two of lead
        He despatched him through the head!

Wil. I discharged it without winking,
    Little time I lost in thinking,
    Like a stone I saw him sinking—
Point.   I should say a lump of lead.
All. He discharged it without winking,
    Little time he lost in thinking.
Wil. Like a stone I saw him sinking—
Point.   I should say a lump of lead.
Wil. Like a stone, my boy, I said—
Point. Like a heavy lump of lead.
Wil. Anyhow, the man is dead,
    Whether stone or lump of lead!
All.   Anyhow, the man is dead,
        And whether stone or lump of lead!
    Arquebus from sentry seizing,
    With the view his king of pleasing,
        Wilfred shot him through the head,
        And he's very, very dead.
And it matters very little whether stone or
        lump of lead;
It is very, very certain that he's very, very
        dead!

RECITATIVE.—*Lieutenant.*

The river must be dragged—no time be lost;
The body must be found, at any cost.
To this attend without undue delay;
So set to work with what despatch ye may!
    [*Exit.*

All.   Yes, yes,
    We'll set to work with what despatch we
        may!
Four men raise Wilfred, and carry him off on their shoulders.

CHORUS.

Hail the valiant fellow who
Did this deed of derring-do!
Honours wait on such an one;
By my head, 'twas bravely done!
Now, by my head, 'twas bravely done!
[*Exeunt all but Elsie, Point, Fairfax, and Phœbe.*

Point. (*to Elsie, who is weeping*). Nay, sweetheart, be comforted. This Fairfax was but a pestilent fellow, and, as he had to die, he might as well die thus as any other way. 'Twas a good death.

Elsie. Still, he was my husband, and had he not been, he was nevertheless a living man, and now he is dead; and so, by your leave, my tears may flow unchidden, Master Point.

Fair. And thou didst see all this?

Point. Aye, with both eyes at once—this and that. The testimony of one eye is naught—he may lie. But when it is corroborated by the other, it is good evidence that none may gainsay. Here are both present in court, ready to swear to him!

Phœ. But art thou sure it was Colonel Fairfax? Saw you his face?

Point. Aye, and a plaguey ill-favoured face,

o. A very hang-dog face—a felon face—a face to fright the headsman himself, and make him strike awry. Oh, a plaguey bad face, take my word for 't. (*Phœbe and Fairfax laugh.*) How they laugh? 'Tis ever thus with simple folk—an accepted wit has but to say "Pass the mustard," and they roar their ribs out!

Fair. (*aside*). If ever I come to life again thou shalt pay for this, Master Point.

Point. Now, Elsie, thou art free to choose again, so behold me: I am young and well-favoured. I have a pretty wit. I can jest you, gibe you, quip you, crank you, wrack you, riddle you—

Fair. Tush, man, thou knowest not how to woo. 'Tis not to be done with time-worn jests and thread-bare sophistries; with quips, conundrums, rhymes and paradoxes. 'Tis an art in itself, and must be studied gravely and concientiously.

TRIO.—*Elsie, Phœbe, and Fairfax.*

Fair. A man who would woo a fair maid,
    Should 'prentice himself to the trade;
      And study all day,
      In methodical way,
    How to flatter, cajole and persuade,
    He should 'prentice himself at fourteen,
    And practise from morning to e'en;
      And when he's of age,
      If he will, I'll engage,
    He may capture the heart of a queen!

All.   It is purely a matter of skill,
      Which all may attain if they will:
        But every Jack,
        He must study the knack
      If he wants to make sure of his Jill!

Elsie. If he's made the best use of his time,
    His twig he'll so carefully lime
      That every bird
      Will come down at his word,
    Whatever its plumage or clime.
    He must learn that the thrill of a touch
    May mean little, or nothing, or much:
      It's an instrument rare,
      To be handled with care,
    And ought to be treated as such.

All.   It is purely a matter of skill, &c.

Phœ. Then a glance may be timid or free,
    It will vary in mighty degree,
      From an impudent stare
      To a look of despair
    That no maid without pity can see!
    And a glance of despair is no guide—
    It may have its ridiculous side;
      It may draw you a tear
      Or a box on the ear;
    You can never be sure till you've tried!

All.   It is purely a matter of skill, &c.

Fair. (*aside to Point*). Now listen to me—'tis done thus. (*Aloud.*) Mistress Elsie,

there is one here who, as thou knowest, loves thee right well!

Point. (*aside*). That he does—right well!

Fair. He is but a man of poor estate, but he hath a loving, honest heart. He will be a true and trusty husband to thee, and if thou wilt be his wife, thou shalt lie curled up in his heart, like a little squirrel in its nest!

Point. (*aside*). 'Tis a pretty figure. A maggot in a nut lies closer, but a squirrel will do.

Fair. He knoweth that thou wast a wife—an unloved and unloving wife, and his poor heart was near to breaking. But now that thine unloving husband is dead, and thou art free, he would fain pray that thou wouldst hearken unto him, and give him hope that thou wouldst one day be his!

Phœ. (*alarmed*). He presses her hands—and he whispers in her ear! Odds boddikins, what does it mean?

Fair. Now, sweetheart, tell me—wilt thou be this poor good fellow's wife?

Elsie. If the good, brave man—*is* he a brave man?

Fair. So men say.

Point (*aside*). That's not true, but let it pass.

Elsie. If the brave man will be content with a poor, penniless, untaught maid—

Point (*aside*). Widow—but let *that* pass.

Elsie. I will be his true and loving wife, and that with my heart of hearts!

Fair. My own dear love! (*Embracing her.*)

Phœ. (*in great agitation*). Why, what's all this? Brother—brother—it is not seemly!

Point (*also alarmed, aside*). Oh, I can't let *that* pass! (*Aloud.*) Hold, enough, Master Leonard! An advocate should have his fee, but methinks thou art over-paying thyself!

Fair. Nay, that is for Elsie to say. I promised thee I would show thee how to woo, and herein lies the proof of the virtue of my teaching. Go thou, and apply it elsewhere! (*Phœbe busts into tears.*)

QUARTET.—*Elsie, Phœbe, Fairfax, and Point.*

Elsie and Fair. When a wooer
             Goes a-wooing,
             Naught is truer
             Than his joy.
             Maiden hushing
               All his suing—
             Boldly blushing—
               Bravely coy!

All. Oh, the happy days of doing!
    Oh, the sighing and the suing!
    When a wooer goes a-wooing,
      Oh, the sweets that never cloy!

Phœ. (*weeping*).   When a brother
        Leaves his sister
      For another,
        Sister weeps.
      Tears that trickle,
        Tears that blister—
      'Tis but mickle
        Sister reaps!

All.   Oh, the doing and undoing,
      Oh, the sighing and the suing,
      When a brother goes a-wooing,
      And a sobbing sister weeps!

Point.   When a jester
        Is outwitted,
      Feelings fester.
        Heart is lead!
      Food for fishes
        Only fitted,
      Jester wishes
        He was dead!

All.   Oh, the doing and undoing,
      Oh, the sighing and the suing,
      When a jester goes a-wooing,
      And he wishes he was dead!

[*Exeunt all but Phœbe, who remains weeping.*

Phœ.   And I helped that man to escape, and I've kept his secret, and pretended that I was his dearly loving sister, and done everything I could think of to make folk believe I *was* his loving sister, and this is his gratitude! Before I pretend to be sister to anybody again, I'll turn nun, and be sister to everybody—one as much as another!

Enter Wilfred.

Wil.   In tears, eh? What a plague art thou grizzling for now?

Phœ.   Why am I grizzling? Thou hast often wept for jealousy—well, 'tis for jealousy I weep now. Aye, yellow, bilious, jaundiced jealousy. So make the most of that, Master Wilfred.

Wil.   But I have never given thee cause for jealousy. The Lieutenant's cook-maid and I are but the merest gossips!

Phœ.   Jealous of thee! Bah! I'm jealous of no craven cock-on-a-hill, who crows about what he'd do an' he dared! I am jealous of another and a better man than thou—set that down, Master Wilfred. And he is to marry Elsie Maynard, the little pale fool—set that down, Master Wilfred—and my heart is well nigh broken! There, thou hast it all! Make the most of it!

Wil.   The man thou lovest is to marry Elsie Maynard? Why, that is no other than thy brother, Leonard Meryll!

Phœ. (*aside*).   Oh, mercy! what have I said?

Wil.   Why, what manner of brother is this, thou lying little jade? Speak! Who is this man whom thou hast called brother, and fon-

dled, and coddled, and kissed—with my conniv­ance, too! Oh! Lord, with my connivance! Ha! should it be this Fairfax! (*Phœbe starts.*) It is! It is this accursed Fairfax! It's Fair­fax! Fairfax, who—

Phœ.   Whom thou hast just shot through the head, and who lies at the bottom of the river!

Wil.   A—I—I may have been mistaken. We are but fallible mortals, the best of us. But I'll make sure—I'll make sure (*going*).

Phœ.   Stay—one word. I think it cannot be Fairfax—mind, I say I *think*—because thou hast just slain Fairfax. But whether he be Fairfax or no Fairfax, he is to marry Elsie—and—and—as thou hast shot him through the head, and he is dead, be content with that, and I will be thy wife!

Wil.   Is that sure?

Phœ.   Aye, sure enough, for there's no help for it! Thou art a very brute—but even brutes must marry, I suppose.

Wil.   My beloved! (*Embraces her.*)

Phœ. (*aside*).   Ugh!

Enter Leonard, hastily.

Leon.   Phœbe, rejoice, for I bring glad tid­ings. Colonel Fairfax's reprieve was signed two days since, but it was foully and maliciously kept back by Secretary Poltwhistle, who de­signed that it should arrive after the Colonel's death. It hath just come to hand, and it is now in the Lieutenant's possession!

Phœ.   Then the Colonel is free? Oh, kiss me, kiss me, my dear! Kiss me, again, and again!

Wil. (*dancing with fury*).   Ods bobs, death o' my life! Art thou mad? Am *I* mad? Are we *all* mad?

Phœ.   Oh, my dear—my dear, I'm well nigh crazed with joy! (*Kissing Leonard.*)

Wil.   Come away from him, thou hussy— thou jade—thou kissing, clinging, cockatrice! And as for thee, sir, devil take thee, I'll rip thee like a herring for this! I'll skin thee for it! I'll cleave thee to the chine! I'll—Oh! Phœbe! Phœbe! Who is this man?

Phœ.   Peace, fool. He is my brother!

Wil.   Another brother! Are there any more of them? Produce them all at once, and let me know the worst!

Phœ.   This is the real Leonard, dolt; the other was but his substitute. The *real* Leonard, I say—my father's own son.

Wil.   How do I know this? Has he "brother" writ large on his brow? I mistrust thy brothers! Thou art but a false jade!

[*Exit Leonard.*

Phœ.   Now, Wilfred, be just. Truly did I deceive thee before—but it was to save a pre­cious life—and to save it, not for me, but for another. They are to be wed this very day. Is not this enough for thee? Come—I am thy Phœbe—thy very own—and we will be wed in a year—or two—or three, at the most. Is not that enough for thee?

Enter Meryll, excitedly, followed by Dame Carruthers (who listens, unobserved).

Mer. Phœbe, hast thou heard the brave news?

Phœ. (still in Wilfred's arms). Aye, father.

Mer. I'm nigh mad with joy! *(Seeing Wilfred).* Why, what's all this?

Phœ. O, father, he discovered our secret through my folly, and the price of his silence is—

Wil. Phœbe's heart.

Phœ. O, dear, no—Phœbe's hand.

Wil. It's the same thing!

Phœ. Is it? *[Exeunt Wilfred and Phœbe.*

Mer. (looking after them). 'Tis a pity, but the Colonel had to be saved at any cost, and as thy folly revealed our secret, thy folly must e'en suffer for it! *(Dame Carruthers comes down.)* Dame Carruthers!

Dame. So this is a plot to shield this archfiend, and I have detected it. A word from me, and three heads besides his would roll from their shoulders!

Mer. Nay, Colonel Fairfax is reprieved. *(Aside.)* Yet if my complicity in his escape were known! Plague on the old meddler! There's nothing for it. *(Aloud.)* Hush, pretty one! Such blood-thirsty words ill become those cherry lips! *(Aside.)* Ugh!

Dame (bashfully). Sergeant Meryll!

Mer. Why, look ye, chuck—for many a month I've—I've thought to myself—"There's snug love saving up in that middle-aged bosom for someone, and why not for thee—that's me —so take heart and tell her—that's thee—that thou—that's me—lovest her—thee—and—and —well, I'm a miserable old man, and I've done it—and that's me!" But not a word about Fairfax! The price of thy silence is—

Dame. Meryll's heart?

Mer. No, Meryll's *hand.*

Dame. It's the same thing!

Mer. Is it!

DUET.—*Dame Carruthers and Sergeant Meryll.*

Dame. Rapture, rapture!
　　When love's votary,
　　Flushed with capture,
　　Seeks the notary,
　　Joy and jollity
　　Then is polity;
　　Reigns frivolity!
　　Rapture, rapture!

Mer. Doleful, doleful!
　　When humanity,
　　With its soul full

　　Of satanity,
　　Courting privity,
　　Down declivity
　　Seeks captivity!
　　Doleful, doleful!

Dame. Joyful, joyful!
　　When virginity
　　Seeks, all coyful,
　　Man's affinity;
　　Fate all flowery,
　　Bright and bowery,
　　Is her dowery!
　　Joyful, joyful!

Mer. Ghastly, ghastly!
　　When man, sorrowful,
　　Firstly, lastly,
　　Of to-morrow full,
　　After tarrying,
　　Yields to harrying—
　　Goes a-marrying.
　　Ghastly, ghastly!

Both. Rapture, &c.
　　　　[Exeunt Dame and Meryll.

FINALE.

Enter Yeomen and Women.

CHORUS OF WOMEN.

(Elegiacs.)

Comes the pretty young bride, a-blushing,
　　　　timidly shrinking—
Set all thy fears aside—cheerily, pretty
　　　　young bride!
Brave is the youth to whom thy lot thou art
　　　　willingly linking!
Flower of valour is he—loving as loving
　　　　can be!
　　Brightly thy summer is shining,
　　Fair as the dawn of the day;
　　Take him, be true to him—
　　Tender his due to him—
　　Honour him, love and obey!

Enter Dame, Phœbe, and Elsie as Bride.

TRIO.—*Phœbe, Elsie, and Dame Carruthers.*

'Tis said that joy in full perfection
　Comes only once to womankind—
That, other times, on close inspection,
　Some lurking bitter we shall find.
If this be so, and men say truly,
My day of joy has broken duly.

With happiness ⎰my⎱ soul is cloyed—
　　　　　⎱her⎰

This ⎰is my⎱ joy-day unalloyed!
　　⎱her⎰

All. Yes, yes, with happiness her soul is
　　　　cloyed!
　　This is her joy-day unalloyed!
　　Flourish. Enter Lieutenant.

Lieut. Hold, pretty one! I bring to thee
　　News—good or ill, it is for thee to
　　　　say.

Thy husband lives—and he is free,
And comes to claim his bride this very
day!

Elsie. No! no! recall those words—it cannot
be!

Ensemble.

Kate and Chorus.
Oh day of terror! Day of tears!
Who is the man who, in his pride,
Claims thee as his bride?
Dame Carruthers and Phœbe.
Oh day of terror! Day of tears!
The man to whom thou art allied
Appears to claim thee as his bride.
Lieut. Meryll and Wilfred.
Come, dry those unbecoming tears,
Most joyful tidings greet thine ears.
The man to who thou art allied
Appears to claim thee as his bride.
Elsie.
Oh, Leonard, come thou to my side,
And claim me as thy loving bride!
Oh day of terror! Day of tears!
*Flourish. Enter Colonel Fairfax, handsome-
ly dressed, and attended by other Gentlemen.*
Fair. (*sternly*).
All thought of Leonard Meryll set aside,
Thou art mine own! I claim thee as my bride.
All. Thou art his own! Alas! he claims thee
as his bride.
Elsie. A suppliant at thy feet I fall;
Thine heart will yield to pity's call!
Fair. Mine is a heart of massive rock,
Unmoved by sentimental shock!
All. Thy husband he!
Elsie (aside). Leonard, my loved one—come
to me.
They bear me hence away!
But though they take me far from thee,
My heart is thine for aye!
My bruised heart,
My broken heart,
Is thine, my own, for aye!
(*To Fairfax*) Sir, I obey,
I am thy bride;
But ere the fatal hour
I said the say
That placed me in thy power,

Would I had died!
Sir, I obey!
I am thy bride!
(*Looks up and recognises Fairfax.*) Leonard!
Fair. My own!
Elsie. Ah! (*Embrace.*)
Elsie and {With happiness my soul is cloyed,
Fair. {This is our joy-day unalloyed!
All. Yes, yes!
With happiness their souls are cloyed,
This is their joy-day unalloyed!
Enter Jack Point.
Point. Oh, thoughtless crew!
Ye know not what ye do!
Attend to me, and shed a tear or two—
For I have a song to sing, O!
All. Sing me your song, O!
Point. It is sung to the moon
By a love-lorn loon,
Who fled from the mocking throng, O!
It's the song of a merryman, moping mum,
Whose soul was sad and whose glance was
glum.
Who sipped no sup and who craved no
crumb,
As he sighed for the love of a ladye!
All. Heighdy! Heighdy!
Misery me, lackadaydee!
He sipped no sup and he craved no crumb,
As he sighed for the love of a ladye!
Elsie. I have a song to sing, O!
All. What is your song, O?
Elsie. It is sung with the ring
Of the songs maids sing
Who love with a love life-long, O!
It's the song of a merrymaid, nestling near,
Who loved her lord—but who dropped a tear
At the moan of the merryman, moping mum,
Whose soul was sad and whose glance was
glum,
Who sipped no sup and who craved no
crumb,
As he sighed for the love of a ladye!
All. Heighdy! Heighdy!
Misery me, lackadaydee!
He sipped no sup and he craved no crumb,
As he sighed for the love of a ladye!
*Fairfax embraces Elsie as Point falls in-
sensible at their feet.*

Curtain.

RUDDIGORE

OR,

THE WITCH'S CURSE

BY

Sir W. S. GILBERT

AND

Sir ARTHUR S. SULLIVAN

RUDDIGORE;

OR,

THE WITCH'S CURSE

ACT I.

SCENE.—*The fishing village of Rederring (in Cornwall.) Rose Maybud's cottage is seen* L.
Enter Chorus of Bridesmaids. They range themselves in front of Rose's cottage.
CHORUS OF BRIDESMAIDS.
Fair is Rose as bright May-day;
  Soft is Rose as warm west-wind;
Sweet is Rose as new-mown hay—
  Rose is queen of maiden-kind!
    Rose, all glowing
      With virgin blushes, say—
    Is anybody going
      To marry you to-day?
      SOLO.—*Zorah.*
Every day, as the days roll on,
Bridesmaids' garb we gaily don,
Sure that a maid so fairly famed
Can't long remain unclaimed.
Hour by hour and day by day
Several months have passed away,
Though she's the fairest flower that blows.
No one has married Rose!
      CHORUS.
    Rose, all glowing
      With virgin blushes, say—
    Is anybody going
      To marry you to-day?
Enter Hannah, from cottage.
Hannah. Nay, gentle maidens, you sing well but vainly, for Rose is still heart-free, and looks but coldly upon her many suitors.
Zorah. It's very disappointing. Every young man in the village is in love with her, but they are appalled by her beauty and modesty, and won't declare themselves; so, until she makes her own choice, there's no chance for anybody else.
Ruth. This is, perhaps, the only village in the world that possesses an endowed corps of professional bridesmaids who are bound to be on duty every day from ten to four—and it is at least six months since our services were required. The pious charity by which we exist is practically wasted!
Zor. We shall be disendowed—that will be the end of it! Dame Hannah—you're a nice old person—*you* could marry if you liked. There's old Adam—Robin's faithful servant—

he loves you with all the frenzy of a boy of fourteen.
Han. Nay—that may never be, for I am pledged!
All. To whom?
Han. To an eternal maidenhood! Many years ago I was betrothed to a god-like youth who woo'd me under an assumed name. But on the very day upon which our wedding was to have been celebrated, I discovered that he was no other than Sir Roderic Murgatroyd, one of the bad Baronets of Ruddigore, and the uncle of the man who now bears that title. As a son of that accursed race he was no husband for an honest girl, so, madly as I loved him, I left him then and there. He died but ten years since, but I never saw him again.
Zor. But why should you not marry a bad Baronet of Ruddigore?
Ruth. All baronets are bad; but was he worse than other baronets?
Han. My child, he was accursed!
Zor. But who cursed him? Not you, I trust!
Han. The curse is on all his line and has been, ever since the time of Sir Rupert, the first Baronet. Listen, and you shall hear the legend.

LEGEND.—*Hannah.*

Sir Rupert Murgatroyd
  His leisure and his riches
He ruthlessly employed
  In persecuting witches.
With fear he'd make them quake—
He'd duck them in his lake—
  He'd break their bones
  With sticks and stones,
And burn them at the stake!

      CHORUS.

This sport he much enjoyed,
Did Rupert Murgatroyd—
  No sense of shame
  Or pity came
To Rupert Murgatroyd!

Once, on the village green,
  A palsied hag he roasted,

And what took place, I ween,
  Shook his composure boasted,
For, as the torture grim
  Seized on each withered limb,
    The writhing dame
    'Mid fire and flame
Yelled forth this curse on him:—
"Each lord of Ruddigore,
  Despite his best endeavour,
Shall do one crime, or more,
  Once, every day, for ever!
This doom he can't defy
However he may try,
    For should he stay
    His hand, that day
In torture he shall die!"

The prophecy came true:
  Each heir who held the title
Had, every day, to do
  Some crime of import vital;
Until, with guilt o'erplied,
"I'll sin no more!" he cried,
    And on the day
    He said that say,
In agony he died!
                CHORUS.
And thus, with sinning cloyed,
Has died each Murgatroyd,
    And so shall fall,
    Both one and all,
Each coming Murgatroyd!
          [*Exeunt Chorus of Bridesmaids.*
*Enter Rose Maybud from cottage, with small
basket on her arm.*
Han. Whither away, dear Rose? On some
errand of charity, as is thy wont?
Rose. A few gifts, dear Aunt, for deserving
villagers. Lo, here is some peppermint rock for
old gaffer Gadderby, a set of false teeth for
pretty little Ruth Rowbottom, and a pound of
snuff for the poor orphan girl on the hill.
Han. Ah, Rose, pity that so much goodness
should not help to make some gallant youth
happy for life! Rose, why dost thou harden
that little heart of thine? Is there none here-
away whom thou could'st love?
Rose. And if there were such an one, verily
it would ill become me to tell him so.
Han. Nay, dear one, where true love is,
there is little need of prim formality.
Rose. Hush, dear aunt, for thy words pain
me sorely. Hung in a plated dish-cover to the
knocker of the workhouse door, with nought
that I could call mine own, save a change of
baby-linen and a book of etiquette, little wonder
if I have always regarded that work as a
voice from a parent's tomb. This hallowed
volume (*producing a book of etiquette*), composed, if I may believe the title-page, by no

less an authority than the wife of a Lord
Mayor, has been, through life, my guide and
monitor. By its solemn precepts I have learnt
to test the moral worth of all who approach
me. The man who bites his bread, or eats peas
with a knife, I look upon as a lost creature,
and he who has not acquired the proper way
of entering and leaving a room is the object
of my pitying horror. There are those in this
village who bite their nails, dear aunt, and
nearly all are wont to use their pocket combs
in public places. In truth I could pursue this
painful theme much further, but behold, I have
said enough.

Han. But is there not one among them who
is faultless, in thine eyes? For example—
young Robin. He combines the manners of a
Marquis with the morals of a Methodist.
Could'st thou not love *him?*
Rose. And even if I could, how should I
confess it unto him? For lo, he is shy, and
sayeth nought!

            BALLAD.—*Rose.*

If somebody there chanced to be
  Who loved me in a manner true,
My heart would point him out to me,
  And I would point him out to you.
(*Referring to book.*)
But here it says of those who point,
  Their manners must be out of joint—
      You *may* not point—
      You *must* not point—
  It's manners out of joint, to point!
Had I the love of such as he,
  Some quiet spot he'd take me to,
Then he could whisper it to me,
  And I could whisper it to you.
(*Referring to book.*)
But whispering, I've somewhere met,
  Is contrary to etiquette:
      Where can it be? (*Searching book.*)
      Now let me see— (*Finding reference.*)
      Yes, Yes!
It's contrary to etiquette!
(*Showing it to Hannah.*)
If any well-bred youth I knew,
  Polite and gentle, neat and trim,
Then I would hint as much to you,
  And you could hint as much to him.
(*Referring to book.*)
But here it says, in plainest print,
  "It's most unladylike to hint"—
      You *may* not hint,
      You *must* not hint—
  It says you mustn't hint, in print!
And if I loved him through and through—
  (True love and not a passing whim),
Then I could speak of it to you,
  And you could speak of it to him.

But here I find it doesn't do
To speak until you're spoken to.
(*Referring to book.*)

      Where can it be? (*Searching book.*)
      Now let me see— (*Finding reference.*)
      Yes, yes!
    "Don't speak until you're spoken to!"
                      [*Exit Hannah.*

Rose. Poor Aunt! Little did the good soul think, when she breathed the hallowed name of Robin, that he would do even as well as another. But he resembleth all the youths in this village, in that he is unduly bashful in my presence, and lo, it is hard to bring him to the point. But soft, he is here!

(*Rose is about to go when Robin enters and calls her.*)

Robin. Mistress Rose!
Rose. (*Surprised.*) Master Robin!
Rob. I wished to say that—it is fine.
Rose. It is passing fine.
Rob. But we do want rain.
Rose. Aye, sorely! Is that all?
Rob. (*Sighing.*) That is all.
Rose. Good day, Master Robin!
Rob. Good day, Mistress Rose! (*Both going—both stop.*)
Rose. } I crave pardon, I—
Rob. } I beg pardon, I—
Rose. You were about to say?—
Rob. I would fain consult you—
Rose. Truly?
Rob. It is about a friend.
Rose. In truth I have a friend myself.
Rob. Indeed? I mean, of course—
Rose. And I would fain consult you—
Rob. (*Anxiously.*) About him?
Rose. (*Prudishly.*) About *her.*
Rob. (*Relieved.*) Let us consult one another.

        DUET.—*Robin and Rose.*

Rob.
I know a youth who loves a little maid—
   (Hey, but his face is a sight for to see!)
Silent is he, for he's modest and afraid—
   (Hey, but he's timid as a youth can be!)
Rose.
I know a maid who loves a gallant youth,
   (Hey, but she sickens as the days go by!)
She cannot tell him all the sad, sad truth—
   (Hey, but I think that little maid will die!)
Rob. Poor little man!
Rose. Poor little maid!
Rob. Poor little man!
Rose. Poor little maid!
Both.
  Now tell me pray, and tell me true,

What in the world should the { young man } do?
                  { maiden }

Rob.
He cannot eat and he cannot sleep—
   (Hey, but his face is a sight for to see!)
Daily he goes for to wail—for to weep
   (Hey, but he's wretched as a youth can be!)
Rose.
She's very thin and she's very pale—
   (Hey, but she sickens as the days go by!)
Daily she goes for to weep—for to wail—
   (Hey, but I think that little maid will die!)
Rob. Poor little maid!
Rose. Poor little man!
Rob. Poor little maid!
Rose. Poor little man!
Both.
  Now tell me pray, and tell me true,

What in the world should the { young man } do?
                 { maiden }
Rose.
If I were the youth I should offer her my
                     name—
   (Hey, but her face is a sight for to see!)
Rob.
If I were the maid I should fan his honest
                     flame—
   (Hey, but he's bashful as a youth can be!)
Rose.
If I were the youth I should speak to her
                    to-day—
   (Hey, but she sickens as the days go by!)
Rob.
If I were the maid I should meet the lad
                  half way—
   (For I really do believe that timid youth
                  will die!)
Rose. Poor little man!
Rob. Poor little maid!
Rose. Poor little man!
Rob. Poor little maid!
Both.
I thank you, { miss, } for your counsel true;
         { sir, }

I'll tell that { youth } what { he } ought to do.
         { maid }   { she }
                      [*Exit Rose.*

Rob. Poor child! I sometimes think that if she wasn't quite so particular I might venture —but no, no—even then I should be unworthy of her!

(*He sits desponding. Enter Old Adam.*)

Adam. My kind master is sad! Dear Sir Ruthven Murgatroyd—

Rob. Hush! As you love me, breathe not that hated name. Twenty years ago, in horror at the prospect of inheriting that hideous title, and with it the ban that compels all who succeed to the baronetcy to commit at least one deadly crime per day, for life, I fled my home, and concealed myself in this innocent village under the name of Robin Oakapple. My younger brother, Despard, believing me to be dead, succeeded to the title and its attendant curse. For twenty years I have been dead and buried. Don't dig me up now.

Adam. Dear master, it shall be as you wish, for have I not sworn to obey you for ever in all things? Yet, as we are here alone, and as I belong to that particular description of good old man to whom the truth is a refreshing novelty, let me call you by your own right title once more! (*Robin assents.*) *Sir* Ruthven Murgatroyd! Baronet! Of Ruddigore! Whew! It's like eight hours at the sea-side!

Rob. My poor old friend! Would there were more like you!

Adam. Would there were indeed! But I bring you good tidings. Your foster-brother, Richard, has returned from sea—his ship the Tom-Tit rides yonder at anchor, and he himself is even now in this very village!

Rob. My beloved foster-brother? No, no—it cannot be!

Adam. It is even so—and see, he comes this way!   [*Exeunt together.*

Enters Chorus of Bridesmaids.

CHORUS.

From the briny sea
  Comes young Richard, all victorious!
Valorous is he—
  His achievements all are glorious!
Let the welkin ring
With the news we bring,
  Sing it—shout it—
  Tell about it—
Safe and sound returneth he,
All victorious from the sea!

Enter Richard. The girls welcome him as he greets old acquaintances.

BALLAD.—*Richard.*

I shipped, d'ye see, in a Revenue sloop,
  And, off Cape Finistere,
    A merchantman we see,
    A Frenchman, going free,
So we made for the bold Mounseer,
    D'ye see?
We made for the bold Mounseer.
But she proved to be a Frigate—and she up
                with her ports,
  And fires with a thirty-two!
    It come uncommon near,
    But we answered with a cheer,
  Which paralysed the Parly-voo!
    D'ye see?
  Which paralysed the Parly-voo,
Chorus.
  Which paralysed the Parly-voo, &c.

Then our Captain he up and he says, says he,
  "That chap we need not fear,—
    We can take her, if we like,

She is sartin for to strike,
  For she's only a darned Mounseer!
    D'ye see?
She's only a darned Mounseer!
But to fight a French fal-lal—it's like hittin'
                of a gal—
  It's a lubberly thing for to do;
    For we, with all our faults,
    Why we're sturdy British salts,
  While she's only a poor Parly-voo,
    D'ye see?
  While she's only a poor Parly-voo!"
Chorus.
  While she's only a poor Parly-voo, &c.

So we up with our helm, and we scuds before
                the breeze,
  As we gives a compassionating cheer;
    Froggee answers with a shout
    As he sees us go about,
  Which was grateful of the poor Mounseer,
    D'ye see?
  Which was grateful of the poor Mounseer!
And I'll wager in their joy they kissed each
                other's cheek
  (Which is what them furriners do),
    And they blessed their lucky stars
    We were hardy British tars
  Who had pity on a poor Parly-voo,
    D'ye see?
  Who had pity on a poor Parly-voo!
Chorus.
  Who had pity on a poor Parly-voo, &c.

HORNPIPE

[*Exeunt Chorus. Enter Robin.*

Rob. Richard!

Rich. Robin!

Rob. My beloved foster-brother, and very dearest friend, welcome home again after ten long years at sea! It is such deeds as yours that cause our flag to be loved and dreaded throughout the civilized world!

Rich. Why, lord love ye, Rob., that's but a trifle to what we *have* done in the way of sparing life! I believe I may say, without exaggeration, that the marciful little Tom-Tit has spared more French frigates than any craft afloat! But 'taint for a British seaman to brag, so I'll just stow my jawin' tackle and belay. (*Robin sighs.*) But 'vast heavin', messmate, what's brought *you* all a-cockbill?

Rob. Alas, Dick, I love Rose Maybud, and love in vain!

Rich. *You* love in vain? Come, that's too good! Why you're a fine strapping muscular young fellow—tall and strong as a to'-gall'n-m'st—taut as a fore-stay—aye, and a barrow-knight to boot, if all had their rights!

Rob. Hush, Richard—not a word about my true rank, which none here suspect. Yes, I

142

know well enough that few men are better calculated to win a woman's heart than I. I'm a fine fellow, Dick, and worthy any woman's love—happy the girl who gets me, say I. But I'm timid, Dick; shy—nervous—modest—retiring—diffident—and I cannot tell her, Dick, I cannot tell her! Ah. you've no idea what a poor opinion I have of myself, and how little I deserve it.

Rich. Robin, do you call to mind how, years ago, we swore that, come what might, we would always act upon our hearts' dictates?

Rob. Aye, Dick, and I've always kept that oath. In doubt, difficulty and danger, I've always asked my heart what I should do, and it has never failed me.

Rich. Right! Let your heart be your compass, with a clear conscience for your binnacle light, and you'll sail ten knots on a bowline, clear of shoals, rocks and quicksands! Well, now, what does my heart say in this here difficult situation? Why it says "Dick," it says—(it calls me "Dick" acos its known me from a babby)—"Dick," it says, "*you* ain't shy—*you* ain't modest—speak you up for him as is!" Robin, my lad, just you lay me alongside, and when she's becalmed under my lee, I'll spin her a yarn that shall sarve to fish you two together for life!

Rob. Will you do this thing for me? Can you, do you think? Yes (*feeling his pulse*). There's no false modesty about *you*. Your —what I would call bumptious self-assertiveness (I mean the expression in its complimentary sense), has already made you a bos'n's mate, and it will make an admiral of you in time, if you work it properly, you dear, incompetent old imposter! My dear fellow, I'd give my right arm for one tenth of your modest assurance!

SONG.—*Robin.*

My boy, you may take it from me,
  That of all the afflictions accurst
    With which a man's saddled
    And hampered and adled,
  A diffident nature's the worst.
Though clever as clever can be—
  A Crichton of early romance—
    You must stir it and stump it,
    And blow your own trumpet,
  Or, trust me, you haven't a chance.
    If you wish in the world to advance,
    Your merits you're bound to enhance,
    You must stir it and stump it,
    And blow your own trumpet,
  Or, trust me, you haven't a chance!
Now, take for example, *my* case:
  I've a bright intellectual brain—
    In all London city
    There's no one so witty—

I've thought so again and again.
I've a highly intelligent face—
  My features cannot be denied—
    But, whatever I try, sir,
    I fail in—and why, sir?
  I'm modesty personified!
    If you wish in the world to advance, &c.

As a poet, I'm tender and quaint—
  I've passion and fervour and grace—
    From Ovid and Horace
    To Swinburne and Morris,
  They all of them take a back place.
Then I sing and I play and I paint:
  Though none are accomplished as I,
    To say so were treason:
    You ask me the reason?
  I'm diffident, modest and shy!
    If you wish in the world to advance, &c.
                [*Exit Robin.*

Rich. (*looking after him*). Ah, it's a thousand pities he's such a poor opinion of himself, for a finer fellow don't walk! Well, I'll do my best for him. "Plead for him as though it was for your own father"—that's what my heart's a remarkin' to me just now. But here she comes! Steady! Steady it is! By the Port Admiral but she's a tight little craft! Come, come, she's not for you, Dick, and yet—she's fit to marry Lord Nelson! By the Flag of Old England, I can't look at her unmoved.

(*Enter Rose—he is much struck by her.*)

Rose. Sir, you are agitated—

Rich. Aye, aye, my lass, well said! I am agitated, true enough!—took flat aback, my girl, but 'tis naught—'twill pass. (*Aside*). This here heart of mine's a dictatin' to me like anything. Question is, have I a right to disregard its promptings?

Rose. Can I do aught to relieve thine anguish, for it seemeth to me that thou art in sore trouble? This apple—(*offering a damaged apple*).

Rich. (*looking at it and returning it*). No, my lass, 'taint that—I'm—I'm took flat aback —I never see anything like you in all my born days. Parbuckle me, if you ain't the loveliest gal I've ever set eyes on· There—I can't say fairer than that, can I?

Rose. No. (*Aside.*) The question is, is it meet that an utter stranger should thus express himself? (*Refers to book.*) Yes,—"Always speak the truth."

Rich. I'd no thoughts of sayin' this here to you on my own account, for, truth to tell, I was chartered by another; but when I see you my heart it up and it says, says it, "This is the very lass for *you*, Dick"—"speak up to her, Dick," it says—(it calls me Dick acos we was at school together)—"tell her all, Dick," it says, 'never sail under false colours—it's mean!" *That's* what my heart tells me to say, and in my rough, common-sailor fashion, I've said it, and I'm a-waiting for your reply. I'm a tremblin', miss. Lookye here—(*holding out his hand*). That's narvousness!

Rose (*aside*). Now, how should a maiden deal with such an one? (*Consults book.*) "Keep no one in unnecessary suspense." (*Aloud.*) Behold, I will not keep you in unnecessary suspense. (*Refers to book.*) "In accepting an offer of marriage, do so with apparent hesitation." (*Aloud.*) I take you, but with a certain show of reluctance. (*Refers to book.*) "Avoid any appearance of eagerness." (*Aloud.*) Though you will bear in mind that I am far from anxious to do so. (*Refers to book.*) "A little show of emotion will not be misplaced!" (*Aloud.*) Pardon this tear! (*Wipes her eye.*)

Rich. Rose, you've made me the happiest blue-jacket in England! I wouldn't change places with the Admiral of the Fleet, no matter who he's a-huggin' of at this present moment! But, axin' your pardon, miss (*wiping his lips with his hand*), might I be permitted to salute the flag I'm a-goin' to sail under?

Rose. (*Referring to book.*) "An engaged young lady should not permit too many familiarities." (*Aloud.*) Once! (*Richard kisses her.*)

DUET.—*Richard and Rose.*

Rich.
The battle's roar is over,
    O my love!
Embrace thy tender lover,
    O my love!
From tempests' welter,
From war's alarms,
O give me shelter
Within those arms!
Thy smile alluring,
All heart-ache curing,
Gives peace enduring,
    O my love!

Rose.
If heart both true and tender,
    O my love!
A life-love can engender,
    O my love!
A truce to sighing
And tears of brine,
For joy undying
Shall aye be mine,

Both.
And thou and I, love,
Shall live and die, love,
Without a sigh, love—
    My own, my love!

Enter Robin, with Chorus of Bridesmaids.

CHORUS.

If well his suit has sped,
Oh, may they soon be wed!

Oh, tell us, tell us, pray,
What doth the maiden say?
In singing are we justified
Hail the Bridegroom—hail the Bride!
Let the nuptial knot be tied:
    In fair phrases
    Hymn their praises,
Hail the Bridegroom—hail the Bride!"

Rob. Well—what news? Have you spoken to her?

Rich. Aye, my lad, I have—so to speak—spoke her.

Rob. And she refuses?

Rich. Why, no, I can't truly say she do.

Rob. Then she accepts! My darling! (*Embraces her.*)

BRIDESMAIDS.

Hail the Bridegroom—hail the Bride!
When the nuptial knot is tied, &c.

Rose (*aside, referring to her book*). Now, what should a maiden do when she is embraced by the wrong gentleman?

Rich. Belay, my lad, belay. You don't understand.

Rose. Oh, sir, belay, I beseech you!

Rich. You see, it's like this: she accepts—but it's *me!*

Rob. You! [*Richard embraces Rose.*

BRIDESMAIDS.

Hail the Bridegroom—hail the Bride!
When the nuptial knot is tied—

Rob. (*interrupting angrily*). Hold your tongues, will you! Now then, what does this mean?

Rich. My poor lad, my heart grieves for thee, but it's like this: the moment I see her, and just as I was a-goin' to mention your name, my heart it up and it says, says it—"Dick, you've fell in love with her yourself," it says; "be honest and sailor-like—don't skulk under false colours—speak up," it says, "take her, you dog, and with her my blessin'!"

Bridesmaids. "Hail the Bridegroom—hail the Bride!"—

Rob. Will you be quiet! Go away! (*Chorus make faces at him and exeunt.*) Vulgar girls!

Rich. What could I do? I'm bound to obey my heart's dictates.

Rob. Of course—no doubt. It's quite right —I don't mind—that is, not particularly—only it's—it *is* disappointing, you know.

Rose (*to Robin*). Oh, but, sir, I knew not that thou did'st seek me in wedlock, or in very truth I should not have hearkened unto this man, for behold, he is but a lowly mariner, and very poor withal, whereas thou art a tiller of the land, and thou hast fat oxen, and many sheep and swine, a considerable dairy farm and much corn and oil!

Rich. That's true, my lass, but it's done now, ain't it, Rob?

Rose. Still, it maybe that I should not be happy in thy love. I am passing young and little able to judge. Moreover, as to thy character I know naught!

Rob. Nay, Rose, I'll answer for that. Dick has won thy love fairly. Broken-hearted as I am, I'll stand up for Dick through thick and thin!

Dick (*with emotion*). Thankye, messmate! that's well said. That's spoken honest. Thankye, Rob! (*Grasps his hand.*)

Rose. Yet methinks I have heard that sailors are but worldly men, and little prone to lead serious and thoughtful lives!

Rob. And what then? Admit that Dick is *not* a steady character, and that when he's excited he uses language that would make your hair curl. Grant that—he does. It's the truth, and I'm not going to deny it. But look at his *good* qualities. He's as nimble as a pony, and his hornpipe is the talk of the fleet!

Rich. Thankye, Rob! That's well spoken. Thankye, Rob!

Rose. But it maybe that he drinketh strong waters which do bemuse a man, and make him even as the wild beasts of the desert!

Rob. Well, suppose he does, and I don't say he don't, for rum's his bane, and ever has been. He *does* drink—I won't deny it. But what of that? Look at his arms—tattooed to the shoulder! (*Dick rolls up his sleeves.*) No, no—I won't hear a word against Dick!

Rose. But they say that mariners are but rarely true to those whom they profess to love!

Rob. Granted—granted—and I don't say that Dick isn't as bad as any of 'em. (*Dick chuckles.*) You are, you know you are, you dog! a devil of a fellow—a regular out-and-out Lothario! But what then? You can't have everything, and a better hand at turning-in a dead-eye don't walk a deck! And what an accomplishment *that* is in a family man! No, no —not a word against Dick. I'll stick up for him through thick and thin!

Rich. Thankye, Rob, thankye. You're a true friend. I've acted accordin' to my heart's dictates, and such orders as them no man should disobey.

ENSEMBLE.—*Richard, Robin, Rose*
In sailing o'er life's ocean wide
Your heart should be your only guide;
With summer sea and favouring wind
Yourself in port you'll surely find.
SOLO.—*Richard.*
My heart says, "To this maiden strike—
  She's captured you.
She's just the sort of girl you like—
  You know you do.

If other man her heart should gain,
  I shall resign."
That's what it says to me quite plain,
  This heart of mine.
SOLO.—*Robin.*
My heart says, "You've a prosperous lot,
  With acres wide;
You mean to settle all you've got
  Upon your bride.
It don't pretend to shape my acts
  By word or sign;
It merely states these simple facts
  This heart of mine!
SOLO.—*Rose.*
Ten minutes since my heart said "white"—
  It now says "black."
It then said "left"—it now says "right"—
  Hearts often tack.
I must obey its latest strain—
  You tell me so.   (*To Richard.*)
But should it change its mind again,
  I'll let you know
(*Turning from Richard to Robin, who embraces her.*)

ENSEMBLE.
In sailing o'er life's ocean wide
No doubt the heart should be your guide,
But it is awkward when you find
A heart that does not know its mind!
[*Exeunt Robin with Rose* L. *and Richard* R.
Enter Mad Margaret. She is wildly dressed in picturesque tatters, and is an obvious caricature of theatrical madness.

SCENA.—*Margaret.*

Cheerily carols the lark
  Over the cot.
Merrily whistles the clerk
  Scratching a blot.
    But the lark
    And the clerk,
    I remark,
Comfort me not!

Over the ripening peach
  Buzzes the bee.
Splash on the billowy beach
  Tumbles the sea.
    But the peach
    And the beach
    They are each
Nothing to me!

    And why?
    Who am I?
Daft Madge! Crazy Meg!
Mad Margaret! Poor Peg!
  He! he! he! he! he! (*chuckling.*)

Mad, I?
Yes, very!

But why?
Mystery!
Don't call!
Whisht! whisht!
No crime—
'Tis only
That I'm
Love—lonely!
That's all!
Whisht! whisht!

BALLAD

To a garden full of posies
Cometh one to gather flowers,
And he wanders through its bowers
Toying with the wanton roses,
Who, uprising from their beds,
Hold on high their shameless heads
With their pretty lips a-pouting,
Never doubting—never doubting
That for Cytherean posies
He would gather aught but roses!

In a nest of weeds and nettles,
Lay a violet half-hidden,
Hoping that his glance unbidden
Yet might fall upon her petals.
Though she lived alone, apart,
Hope lay nestling at her heart,
But, alas, the cruel awaking
Set her little heart a-breaking,
For he gathered for his posies
Only roses—only roses!

    (Bursts into tears.)
    Enter Rose.

Rose. A maiden, and in tears? Can I do aught to soften thy sorrow? This apple—*(offering apple).*

Mar. *(Examines it and rejects it.)* No! *(mysteriously).* Tell me, are you mad?

Rose. I? No! That is, I think not.

Mar. That's well! Then you don't love Sir Despard Murgatroyd? All mad girls love him. *I* love him. I'm poor Mad Margaret—Crazy Meg—Poor Peg! He! he! he! he! *(chuckling.)*

Rose. Thou lovest the bad Baronet of Ruddigore? Oh, horrible—too horrible!

Mar. You pity me? Then be my mother! The squirrel had a mother, but she drank and the squirrel fled! Hush! They sing a brave song in our parts—it runs somewhat thus:—*(Sings.)*
"The cat and the dog and the little puppee
 Sat down in a—down in a—in a"
I forget what they sat down in, but so the song goes! Listen—I've come to pinch her!

Rose. Mercy, whom!

Mar. You mean "who."

Rose. Nay! it is the accusative after the verb.

Mar. True. *(Whispers melodramatically.)* I have come to pinch Rose Maybud!

Rose *(alarmed).* Rose Maybud!

Mar. Aye! I love him—he loved me once. But that's all gone, Fisht! He gave me an Italian glance—thus—*(business)*—and made me his. He will give *her* an Italian glance, and make *her* his. But it shall not be, for I'll stamp on her—stamp on her—stamp on her! Did you ever kill anybody! No? Why not? Listen—I killed a fly this morning! It buzzed, and I wouldn't have it. So it died—pop! So shall she!

Rose. But behold, *I* am Rose Maybud, and I would fain not die "pop."

Mar. You are Rose Maybud!

Rose. Yes, sweet Rose Maybud!

Mar. Strange! They told me she was beautiful! And *he* loves *you!* No, no! If I thought that, I would treat you as the auctioneer and land-agent treated the lady-bird—I would rend you asunder!

Rose. Nay, be pacified, for behold I am pledged to another, and lo, we are to be wedded this very day!

Mar. Swear me that! Come to a Commissioner and let me have it on affidavit! *I* once made an affidavit—but it died—it died—it died! But see, they come—Sir Despard and his evil crew! Hide, hide—they are all mad—quite mad!

Rose. What makes you think that?

Mar. Hush! They sing choruses in public. That's mad enough, I think! Go—hide away, or they will seize you. Hush! Quite softly—quite, quite softly!
    [*Exeunt together, on tiptoe.*
(Enter Chorus of Bucks and Blades, heralded by Chorus of Bridesmaids.)

CHORUS OF BRIDESMAIDS.

Welcome, gentry,
For your entry
Sets our tender hearts a-beating.
Men of station,
Admiration
Prompts this unaffected greeting.
 Hearty greeting offer we!

CHORUS OF BUCKS AND BLADES.

When thoroughly tired
Of being admired
By ladies of gentle degree—degree,
 With flattery sated,
 High-flown and inflated,
Away from the city we flee—we flee!

From charms intramural
To prettiness rural
The sudden transition
Is simply Elysian.
Come, Amaryllis,
Come, Chloe and Phyllis,
Your slaves, for the moment, are we!

CHORUS OF BRIDESMAIDS.

The sons of the tillage
Who dwell in this village
Are people of lowly degree—degree.
Though honest and active
They're most unattractive
And awkward as awkward can be—can be.
They're clumsy clodhoppers
With axes and choppers,
And shepherds and ploughmen
And drovers and cowmen
Hedgers and reapers
And carters and keepers,
But never a lover for me!

ENSEMBLE.—BUCKS AND BLADES.

When thoroughly tired, &c.

BRIDESMAIDS.

So welcome, gentry, &c.

Enter Sir Despard Murgatroyd.

SONG AND CHORUS—*Sir Despard.*

Sir D. Oh why am I moody and sad?
Ch. Can't guess!
Sir D. And why am I guiltily mad?
Ch. Confess!
Sir D. Because I am thoroughly bad!
Ch. Oh yes—
Sir D. You'll see it at once in my face.
  Oh why am I husky and hoarse?
Ch. Ah, why?
Sir D. It's the workings of conscience, of
  course.
Ch. Fie, fie!
Sir D. And huskiness stands for remorse,
Ch. Oh my!
Sir D. At least it does so in my case!

Sir D. When in crime one is fully em-
  ployed—
Ch. Like you—
Sir D. Your expression gets warped and
  destroyed
Ch. It do.
Sir D. It's a penalty none can avoid;
Ch. How true!
Sir D. I once was a nice-looking youth;
  But like stone from a strong cata-
  pult—
Ch. (*explaining to each other*). A trice—
Sir D. I rushed at my terrible cult—
Ch. (*explaining to each other*). That's vice—
Sir D. Observe the unpleasant result!
Ch. Not nice.
Sir D. Indeed I am telling the truth!

Sir D. Oh innocents, happy though poor!
Ch. That's we—
Sir D. If I had been virtuous, I'm sure—
Ch. Like me—
Sir D. I should be as nice-looking as you're!
Ch. May be.
Sir D. You are very nice-looking indeed!
  Oh innocents, listen in time—

Ch. We *doe,*
Sir D. Avoid an existence of crime—
Ch. Just so—
Sir D. Or you'll be as ugly as I'm—
Ch. (*loudly*) No! No!
Sir D. And now, if you please, we'll proceed.

(*All the girls express their horror of Sir
Despard. As he approaches them they fly
from him, terror-stricken, leaving him alone
on the stage.*)

Sir D. Poor children, how they loathe me
—me whose hands are certainly steeped in infamy, but whose heart is as the heart of a
little child! But what *is* a poor baronet to
do, when a whole picture-gallery of ancestors
step down from their frames and threaten him
with an excruciating death if he hesitate to
commit his daily crime? But ha! ha! I am
even with them! (*Mysteriously.*) I get my
crime over the first thing in the morning and
then, ha! ha! for the rest of the day I do
good—I do good—I do good! (*Melodramatically*). Two days since, I stole a child
and built an orphan asylum. Yesterday I
robbed a bank and endowed a bishopric. To-
day I carry off Rose Maybud, and atone with
a cathedral! This is what it is to be the sport
and toy of a Picture Gallery! But I will be
bitterly revenged upon them! I will give them
all to the Nation, and nobody shall ever look
upon their faces again!

Enter Richard.

Rich. Ax your honour's pardon, but—
Sir D. Ha! observed! And by a mariner!
What would you of me, fellow?
Rich. Your honour, I'm a poor man-o'-
war's man, becalmed in the doldrums—
Sir D. I don't know them.
Rich. And I make bold to ax your honour's advice. Does your honour know what
it is to have a heart?
Sir D. My honour knows what it is to have
a complete apparatus for conducting the cir-
culation of the blood through the veins and
arteries of the human body.
Rich. Aye, but has your honour a heart
that ups and looks you in the face, and gives
you quarter-deck orders that it's life and
death to disobey?
Sir D. I have not a heart of that descrip-
tion, but I have a Picture Gallery that pre-
sumes to take that liberty.
Rich. Well, your honour, it's like this—
Your honour had an elder brother—
Sir. D. It had.
Rich. Who should have inherited your title,
and with it its cuss.
Sir D. Aye, but he died. Oh, Ruthven!—
Rich. He didn't.
Sir D. He did *not?*
Rich. He didn't. On the contrary, he
lives in this here very village, under the name

147

of Robin Oakapple, and he's a-going to marry Rose Maybud this very day.

Sir D. Ruthven alive, and going to marry Rose Maybud! Can this be possible?

Rich. Now the question I was going to ask your honour is—ought I to tell your honour this?

Sir D. I don't know. It's a delicate point. I think you ought. Mind, I'm not sure, but I think so.

Rich. That's what my heart says. It says, "Dick," it says, (it calls me Dick acos it's entitled to take that liberty). "That there young gal would recoil from him if she knowed what he really were. Ought you to stand off and on, and let this young gal take this false step and never fire a shot across her bows to bring her to? No, it says, "you did *not* ought. And I won't ought, accordin'.

Sir D. Then you really feel yourself at liberty to tell me that my elder brother lives —that I may charge him with his cruel deceit, and transfer to his shoulders the hideous thraldom under which I have laboured for so many years! Free—free at last! Free to live a blameless life, and to die beloved and regretted by all who knew me!

DUET.—*Sir Despard and Richard.*

Rich. You understand?

Sir D.   I think I do,
      With vigour unshaken
      This step shall be taken.
    It's neatly planned.

Rich.   I think so too;
      I'll readily bet it
      You'll never regret it!

Both. For duty, duty must be done;
    The rule applies to every one,
    And painful though that duty be,
    To shirk the task were fiddle-de-dee!

Sir D. The bridegroom comes—

Rich.   Likewise the bride—
      The maidens are very
      Elated and merry;
    They are her chums.

Sir D.   To lash their pride
      Were almost a pity,
      The pretty committee!

Both But duty, duty must be done;
    The rule applies to every one,
    And painful though that duty be,
    To shirk the task were fiddle-de-dee!
    [*Exeunt Richard and Sir Despard.*

Enter Chorus of Bridesmaids and Bucks.

CHORUS OF BRIDESMAIDS.

Hail the bride of seventeen summers.
  In fair phrases
  Hymn her praises;
Lift your song on high, all comers,
  She rejoices
  In your voices.
Smiling summer beams upon her,

Shedding every blessing on her:
  Maidens, greet her—
  Kindly treat her—
We may all be brides some day!

CHORUS OF BUCKS.

Hail the bridegroom who advances,
  Agitated,
  Yet elated.
He's in easy circumstances,
  Young and lusty,
  True and trusty.

All. Smiling summer beams upon her, &c.

Enter Robin, attended by Richard and Old Adam, meeting Rose, attended by Zorah and Dame Hannah. Rose and Robin embrace.

MADRIGAL.

Rose. When the buds are blossoming,
    Smiling welcome to the spring,
    Lovers choose a wedding day—
    Life is love in merry May!

Girls. Spring is green—Fal lal la!
    Summer's rose—Fal lal la!

Quartet. It is sad when summer goes,
    Fal la!

Men. Autumn's gold—Fal lal la!
    Winter's grey—Fal lal la!

Quartet. Winter still is far away—
    Fal la!

All. Leaves in autumn fade and fall,
    Winter is the end of all.
    Spring and summer teem with glee:
    Spring and summer, then, for me!
    Fal la!

Hannah. In the spring-time seed is sown:
    In the summer grass is mown:
    In the autumn you may reap:
    Winter is the time for sleep.

Girls. Spring is hope—Fal lal la!
    Summer's joy—Fal lal la!

Quartet. Spring and summer never cloy,
    Fal la!

Men. Autumn, toil—Fal lal la!
    Winter, rest—Fal lal la!

Quartet. Winter, after all, is best—
    Fal la!

All. Spring and summer pleasure you,
    Autumn, aye, and winter too—
    Every season has its cheer
    Life is lovely all the year!
    Fal la!

GAVOTTE.

After Gavotte, enter Sir Despard.

Sir D. Hold, bride and bridegroom, ere you
      wed each other,
    I claim young Robin as my elder
      brother!
    His rightful title I have long en-
      joyed:
    I claim him as Sir Ruthven Murga-
      troyd!

All. O wonder!

Rose. (*Wildly.*)
> Deny the falsehood, Robin, as you
>> should
>> It is a plot!

Rob. I would, if conscientiously I could,
> But I cannot!

All. Ah, base one!

SOLO.—*Robin.*

As pure and blameless peasant,
> I cannot, I regret,
Deny a truth unpleasant,
> I am that Baronet!

All. He is that Baronet!

But when completely rated
> Bad baronet am I,
That I am what he's stated
> I'll recklessly deny!

All. He'll recklessly deny!
Rob. When I'm a bad Bart. I will tell tara-
> diddles!
All. He'll tell taradiddles when he's a bad
> Bart.   •
Rob. I'll play a bad part on the falsest of
> fiddles.
All. On very false fiddles he'll play a bad
> part!
Rob. But until that takes place I must be con-
> scientious—
All. He'll be conscientious until that takes
> place.
Rob. Then adieu with good grace .to my
> morals sententious!
All. To morals sententious adieu with
> good grace!
Zor. Who is the wretch who hath betrayed
> thee?
>> Let him stand forth!
Rich. (*coming forward.*) 'Twas I!
All. Die, traitor!
Rich. Hold, my conscience made me!
> Withhold your wrath!

SOLO.—*Richard.*

Within this breast there beats a heart
> Whose voice can't be gainsaid.
It bade me thy true rank impart,
> And I at once obeyed.
I knew 'twould blight thy budding
> fate—
I knew 'twould cause thee anguish
> great—
But did I therefore hesitate?
> No! I at once obeyed!

All. Acclaim him who, when his true heart
> Bade him young Robin's rank impart,
> Immediately obeyed!

SOLO.—*Rose* (*addressing Robin*).
> Farewell!

Thou had'st my heart—
> 'Twas quickly won!
But now we part—
> Thy face I shun!
> Farewell!
Go bend the knee
> At Vice's shrine,
Of life with me
> All hope resign.
> Farewell!

(*To Sir Despard.*) Take me—I am thy bride!
> *Bridesmaids.*

Hail the Bridegroom—hail the Bride!
When the nuptial knot is tied;
Every day will bring some joy
That can never, never cloy!

Enter Margaret, who listens.

Sir. D. Excuse me, I'm a virtuous person
> now—
Rose.   That's why I wed you!
Sir D. And I to Margaret must keep my
> vow!
Mar. Have I misread you?
> Oh joy! with newly kindled rapture
>> warmed,
>> I kneel before you!   (*Kneels.*)
Sir D. I once disliked you; now that I've
> reformed,
>> How I adore you! (*They embrace.*)
> *Bridesmaids*

Hail the Bridegroom—hail the Bride!
When the nuptial knot is tied;
Every day will bring some joy
That can never, never cloy!

Rose.

Richard, of him I love bereft,
> Through thy design,
Thou art the only one that's left,
> So I am thine!   (*They embrace.*)
> *Bridesmaids.*

Hail the Bridegroom—hail the Bride!
Let the nuptial knot be tied!
> DUET.—*Rose and Richard.*

Who, happy the lily
> When kissed by the bee;
And, sipping tranquilly,
> Quite happy is he!
And happy the filly
> That neighs in her pride;
But happier than any
> A pound to a penny,
A lover is, when he
> Embraces his bride!

DUET.—*Sir Despard and Margaret.*

Oh, happy the flowers
> That blossom in June,
And happy the bowers
> That gain by the boon,
But happier by hours
> The man of descent,
Who, folly regretting,

Is bent on forgetting
His bad baronetting,
    And means to repent!
TRIO.—*Hannah, Adam, and Zorah.*
Oh, happy the blossom
    That blooms on the lea,
Likewise the opossum
    That sits on a tree,
When you come across 'em,
    They cannot compare,
With those who are treading
The dance at a wedding,
While people are spreading
    The best of good fare!

SOLO.—*Robin.*
Oh, wretched the debtor
    Who's signing a deed!
And wretched the letter
    That no one can read!
But very much better
    Their lot it must be
Than that of the person
I'm making this verse on,
Whose head there's a curse on—
    Alluding to me!
Repeat ensemble with chorus.

DANCE.

END OF ACT I.

▼▼▼▼▼

ACT II.

SCENE.—*Picture Gallery in Ruddigore Castle. The walls are covered with full length portraits of the Baronets of Ruddigore from the time of James I.—the first being that of Sir Rupert, alluded to in the legend; the last, that of the last deceased Baronet, Sir Roderic.*

Enter Sir Ruthven and Adam melodramatically. They are greatly altered in appearance, Sir Ruthven wearing the haggard aspect of a guilty roué; Adam, that of the wicked steward to such a man.

DUET.—*Sir Ruthven and Adam.*

Sir Ruth. I once was as meek as a new-born
        lamb,
        I'm now Sir Murgatroyd—ha!
            ha!
            With greater precision,
            (Without the elision)
        Sir Ruthven Murgatroyd—ha!
            ha!
Adam.   And I, who was once his *valley-de-*
            sham,
        As steward I'm now employed—
            ha! ha!
        The dickens may take him—
        I'll never forsake him!
        As steward I'm now employed—
            ha! ha!
Both.   How dreadful when an innocent
            heart
        Becomes, perforce, a bad young
            Bart.,
        And still more hard on old Adam
        His former faithful *valley-de-sham!*
Sir Ruth. This is a painful state of things,
            Old Adam!

Adam. Painful, indeed! Ah, my poor master, when I swore that, come what would, I would serve you in all things for ever, I little thought to what a pass it would bring me! The confidential adviser to the greatest villain

unhung! Now, Sir, to business. What crime do you propose to commit to-day?

Sir Ruth. How should I know? As my confidential adviser, it's your duty to suggest something.

Adam. Sir, I loathe the life you are leading, but a good old man's oath is paramount, and I obey. Richard Dauntless is here with pretty Rose Maybud, to ask your consent to their marriage. Poison their beer.

Sir Ruth. No—not that—I know I'm a bad Bart, but I'm not as bad a Bart as all that.

Adam. Well, there you are, you see! It's no use my making suggestions if you don't adopt them.

Sir Ruth. (*melodramatically.*) How would it be, do you think, were I to lure him here with cunning wile—bind him with good stout rope to yonder post—and then, by making hideous faces at him, curdle the heart-blood in his arteries, and freeze the very marrow in his bones? How say you, Adam, is not the scheme well planned?

Adam. It would be simply rude—nothing more. But soft—they come!

Adam and Sir Ruthven retire, as Richard and Rose enter, preceded by Chorus of Bridesmaids.

DUET.—*Richard and Rose*

Rich.
Happily coupled are we,
    You see—
I am a jolly Jack Tar,
    My star,
And you are the fairest,
    The richest and rarest
Of innocent lasses you are,
    By far—
Of innocent lasses you are!

150

Fanned by a favouring gale,
    You'll sail
Over life's treacherous sea
    With me,
And as for bad weather
We'll brave it together,
And you shall creep under my lee,
    My wee!
And you shall creep under my lee!
For you are such a smart little craft—
Such a neat little, sweet little craft.
    Such a bright little, tight little,
    Slight little, light little,
Trim little, prim little craft!

Chorus.
      For she is such, &c.

Rose.
    My hopes will be blighted I fear,
      My dear;
In a month you'll be going to sea,
    Quite free,
    And all of my wishes
    You'll throw to the fishes
As though they were never to be;
    Poor me!
As though they were never to be.
And I shall be left all alone
    To moan,
And weep at your cruel deceit,
    Complete;
While you'll be asserting
Your freedom by flirting
With every woman you meet,
    You cheat,
With every woman you meet!

Though I am such a smart little craft—
Such a neat little, sweet little craft.
Such a bright little, tight little,
Slight little, light little,
Trim little, prim little craft!

Chorus.
      Though she is such, &c.

Enter Sir Ruthven.

Sir Ruth. Soho! pretty one—in my power at last, eh? Know ye not that I have those within my call who, at my lightest bidding, would immure ye in an uncomfortable dungeon? (*Calling.*) What ho! within there!

Rich. Hold—we are prepared for this (*producing a Union Jack*). Here is a flag that none dare defy (*all kneel*), and while this glorious rag floats over Rose Maybud's head, the man does not live who would dare to lay unlicensed hand upon her!

Sir Ruth. Foiled—and by a Union Jack! But a time will come and then—

Rose (*to Richard*). Nay, let me plead with him (*to Sir Ruth.*). Sir Ruthven, have pity In my book of etiquette the case of a maiden

about to be wedded to one who unexpectedly turns out to be a baronet with a curse on him is not considered. Time was when you loved me madly. Prove that this was no selfish love by according your consent to my marriage with one who, if he be not you yourself, is the next best thing—your dearest friend!

BALLAD.—*Rose.*
    In bygone days I had thy love—
      Thou hadst my heart.
    But Fate, all human vows above,
      Our lives did part!
    By the old love thou hadst for me
    By the fond heart that beat for thee—
    By joys that never now can be,
      Grant thou my prayer!

All (*kneeling*).
      Grant thou her prayer!

Sir Ruth. (*recit.*)
      Take her—I yield.

All.   Oh rapture!

Chorus.
    Away to the parson we go—
      Say we're solicitious very
    That he will turn two into one—
      Singing hey, derry down derry!

Rich.
    For she *is* such a smart little craft—

Rose.
    Such a neat little, sweet little craft—

Rich.   Such a bright little—
Rose.   Tight little—
Rich.   Slight little—
Rose.   Light little—
Both.   Trim little, prim little craft!

Chorus
    For she *is* such a smart little craft, &c.

[*Exeunt all but Sir Ruthven.*

Sir Ruth. For a week I have fulfilled my accursed doom! I have duly committed a crime a day! Not a great crime, I trust, but still in the eyes of one as strictly regulated as I used to be, a crime. But will my ghostly ancestors be satisfied with what I have done, or will they regard it as an unworthy subterfuge? (*Addressing Pictures.*) Oh, my forefathers, wallowers in blood, there came at last a day when, sick of crime, you each and every, vowed to sin no more, and so, in agony, called welcome Death to free you from your cloying guiltiness. Let the sweet psalm of that repentant hour soften your long-dead hearts, and tune your souls to mercy on your poor posterity! (*kneeling*).

(*The stage darkens for a moment. It becomes light again, and the Pictures are seen to have become animated.*)

CHORUS OF FAMILY PORTRAITS.
Painted emblems of a race,
    All accurst in days of yore

Each from his accustomed place
  Steps into the world once more.
(*The Pictures step from their frames and march round the stage.*)
Baronet of Ruddigore,
  Last of our accursed line,
Down upon the oaken floor—
  Down upon those knees of thine.

Coward, poltroon, shaker, squeamer,
Blockhead, sluggard, dullard, dreamer,
Shirker, shuffler, crawler, creeper,
Sniffler, snuffler, wailer, weeper,
Earthworm, maggot, tadpole, weevil!
Set upon thy course of evil
Lest the King of Spectre-Land
Set on thee his grisly hand!
(*The Spectre of Sir Roderic descends from his frame.*)
Sir Rod.
  Beware! beware! beware!
Sir Ruth.
    Gaunt vision, who art thou
    That thus, with icy glare
    And stern relentless brow,
    Appearest, who knows how?
Sir Rod.
    I am the spectre of the late
    Sir Roderic Murgatroyd.
  Who comes to warn thee that thy fate
    Thou cans't not now avoid.
Sir Ruth.
    Alas, poor ghost!
Sir Rod. The pity you
    Express, for nothing goes:
  We spectres are a jollier crew
    Than you, perhaps, suppose!
Chorus.
    We spectres are a jollier crew
    Than you, perhaps, suppose!
      SONG.—*Sir Roderic.*
When the night wind howls in the chimney
  cowls, and the bat in the moonlight flies,
And inky clouds, like funeral shrouds, sail over
  the midnight skies—
When the footpads quail at the night-bird's
  wail, and black dogs bay at the moon,
Then is the spectre's holiday—then is the
  ghosts' high-noon!
  Chorus.   Ha! ha!
    Then is the ghosts' high-noon!

As the sob of the breeze sweeps over the trees
  and the mist lie low on the fen,
From grey tomb-stones are gathered the bones
  that once were women and men,
And away they go, with a mop and a mow, to
  the revel that ends too soon,
For cockcrow limits our holiday—the dead of
  the night's high-noon!

  Chorus.   Ha! ha!
    The dead of the night's high-noon!

And then each ghost with his ladye-toast to
  their churchyard beds take flight.
With a kiss, perhaps, on her lantern chaps, and
  a grisly grim, "good-night";
Till the welcome knell of the midnight bell
  rings forth its jolliest tune,
And ushers in our next high holiday—the dead
  of the night's high-noon!

  Chorus.   Ha! ha!
    The dead of the night's high-noon!

Sir Ruth. I recognize you now—you are
the Picture that hangs at the end of the gallery.
Sir Rod. In a bad light. I am.
Sir Ruth. Are you considered a good likeness?
Sir Rod. Pretty well. Flattering.
Sir Ruth. Because as a work of art you are
poor.
Sir Rod. I am crude in colour, but I have
only been painted ten years. In a couple of
centuries I shall be an Old Master, and then
you will be sorry you spoke lightly of me.
Sir Ruth. And may I ask why you have
left your frames?
Sir Rod. It is our duty to see that our successors commit their daily crimes in a conscientious and workmanlike fashion. It is our duty
to remind you that you are evading the conditions under which you are permitted to exist.
Sir Ruth. Really I don't know what you'd
have. I've only been a bad baronet a week, and
I've committed a crime punctually every day.
Sir Ròd. Let us enquire into this. Monday?
Sir Ruth. Monday was a Bank Holiday.
Sir Rod. True. Tuesday?
Sir Ruth. On Tuesday I made a false income-tax return.
All. Ha! ha!
1st Ghost. That's nothing.
2nd Ghost. Nothing at all.
3rd Ghost. Everybody does that.
4th Ghost. It's expected of you.
Sir Rod. Wednesday?
Sir Ruth. (*melodramatically*). On Wednesday, I forged a will.
Sir Rod. Whose will?
Sir Ruth. My own.
Sir Rod. My good sir, you can't forge your
own will!
Sir Ruth. Can't I though! I like that! I
did! Besides, if a man can't forge his own
will, whose will can he forge?
1st Ghost. There's something in that.
2nd Ghost. Yes, it seems reasonable.
3rd Ghost. At first sight it does.

4th Ghost. Fallacy somewhere, I fancy!

Sir Ruth. A man can do what he likes with his own?

Sir Rod. I suppose he can.

Sir Ruth. Well then, he can forge his own will, stoopid! On Thursday I shot a fox.

1st Ghost. Hear, hear!

Sir Rod. That's better (addressing Ghosts). Pass, the fox, I think? (They assent.) Yes, pass the fox. Friday?

Sir Ruth. On Friday I forged a cheque.

Sir Rod. Whose cheque?

Sir Ruth. Old Adam's.

Sir Rod. But Old Adam hasn't a banker.

Sir Ruth. I didn't say I forged his banker —I said I forged his cheque. On Saturday I disinherited my only son.

Sir Rod. But you haven't got a son.

Sir Ruth. No—not yet. I disinherited him in advance, to save time. You see—by this arrangement—he'll be born ready disinherited.

Sir Rod. I see. But I don't think you can do that.

Sir Ruth. My good sir, if I can't disinherit my own unborn son, whose unborn son can I disinherit?

Sir Rod. Humph! These arguments sound very well, but I can't help thinking that, if they were reduced to syllogistic form, they wouldn't hold water. Now quite understand us. We are foggy, but we don't permit our fogginess to be presumed upon. Unless you undertake to—well, suppose we say, carry off a lady? (addressing Ghosts.) Those who are in favour of his carrying off a lady—(all hold up their hands except a Bishop). Those of the contrary opinion? (Bishop holds up his hands.) Oh, you're never satisfied! Yes, unless you undertake to carry off a lady at once—I don't care what lady—any lady—choose your lady—you perish in inconceivable agonies.

Sir Ruth. Carry off a lady? Certainly not, on any account. I've the greatest respect for ladies, and I wouldn't do anything of the kind for worlds! No, no. I'm not that kind of baronet, I assure you! If that's all you've got to say, you'd better go back to your frames.

Sir Rod. Very good—then let the agonies commence.

Ghosts make passes. Sir Ruthven begins to writhe in agony.

Sir Ruth. Oh! Oh! Don't do that! I can't stand it!

Sir Rod. Painful, isn't it? It gets worse by degrees.

Sir Ruth. Oh—oh! Stop a bit! Stop it, will you? I want to speak.

Sir Roderic makes signs to Ghosts, who resume their attitudes.

Sir Rod. Better?

Sir Ruth. Yes—better now! Whew!

Sir Rod. Well, do you consent?

Sir Ruth. But it's such an ungentlemanly thing to do!

Sir Rod. As you please. (To Ghosts.) Carry on!

Sir Ruth. Stop—I can't stand it! I agree! I promise! It shall be done.

Sir Rod. To-day?

Sir Ruth. To-day!

Sir Rod. At once?

Sir Ruth. At once! I retract! I apologize! I had no idea it was anything like that!

CHORUS.

He yields! He answers to our call!
    We do not ask for more.
A sturdy fellow, after all,
    This latest Ruddigore!
All perish in unheard of woe
    Who dare our wills defy;
We want your pardon, ere we go,
    For having agonized you so—
        So pardon us—
        So pardon us—
        So pardon us—
            Or die!

Sir Ruth.

    I pardon you!
    I pardon you!

All.   He pardons us—
        Hurrah!

(The Ghosts return to their frames.)
Chorus.

    Painted emblems of a race,
        All accurst in days of yore
    Each to his accustomed place
        Steps unwillingly, once more!

(By this time the Ghosts have changed to pictures again. Sir Ruthven is overcome by emotion.)

Enter Adam.

Adam. My poor master, you are not well—

Sir Ruth. Adam, it won't do—I've seen 'em —all my ancestors—they've just gone. They say that I must do something desperate at once, or perish in horrible agonies. Go—go to yonder village—carry off a maiden—bring her here at once—anyone—I don't care which—

Adam. But—

Sir Ruth. Not a word, but obey! Fly!

[Exeunt Sir Ruthven and Adam.

Enter Despard and Margaret. They are both dressed in sober black of formal cut, and present a strong contrast to their appearance in Act I.

DUET.

Des. I once was a very abandoned person—
Mar.   Making the most of evil chances.
Des. Nobody could conceive a worse 'un—
Mar.   Even in all the old romances.

Des.	I blush for my wild extravagances,
	But be so kind
	To bear in mind,
Mar.	We were the victims of circumstances! (*Dance.*)
	That is one of our blameless dances.

Mar.	I was once an exceedingly odd young lady—
Des.	Suffering much from spleen and vapours.
Mar.	Clergymen thought my conduct shady—
Des.	She didn't spend much upon linendrapers.
Mar.	It certainly entertained the gapers
	My ways were strange
	Beyond all range—
Des.	Paragraphs got into all the papers. (*Dance.*)

Des.	We only cut respectable capers.

Des.	I've given up all my wild proceedings.
Mar.	My taste for a wandering life is waning.
Des.	Now I'm a dab at penny readings.
Mar.	They are not remarkably entertaining.
Des.	A moderate livelihood we're gaining.
Mar.	In fact we rule
	A National School.
Des.	The duties are dull, but I'm not complaining. (*Dance.*)
	This sort of thing takes a deal of training!
Des.	We have been married a week.
Mar.	One happy, happy week!
Des.	Our new life—
Mar.	Is delightful indeed!
Des.	So calm!

Mar. So unimpassioned! (*wildly.*) Master, all this I owe to you! See, I am no longer wild and untidy. My hair is combed. My face is washed. My boots fit!

Des. Margaret, don't. Pray restrain yourself. Remember, you are now a district visitor.

Mar. A gentle district visitor!

Des. You are orderly, methodical, neat; you have your emotions well under control.

Mar. I have! (*wildly.*) Master, when I think of all you have done for me, I fall at your feet. I embrace your ankles. I hug your knees! (*Doing so.*)

Des. Hush. This is not well. This is calculated to provoke remark. Be composed, I beg!

Mar. Ah! you are angry with poor little Mad Margaret!

Des. No, not angry; but a district visitor should learn to eschew melodrama. Visit the poor, by all means, and give them tea and barley-water, but don't do it as if you were administering a bowl of deadly nightshade. It upsets them. Then when you nurse sick people, and find them not as well as could be expected, why go into hysterics?

Mar. Why not?

Des. Because it's too jumpy for a sick room.

Mar. How strange! Oh, Master! Master! —how shall I express the all-absorbing gratitude that—(*about to throw herself at his feet*).

Des. Now! (*warningly*).

Mar. Yes, I know, dear—it sha'n't occur again. (*He is seated—she sits on the ground by him.*) Shall I tell you one of poor Mad Margaret's odd thoughts? Well, then, when I am lying awake at night, and the pale moonlight streams through the latticed casement, strange fancies crowd upon my poor mad brain, and I sometimes think that if we could hit upon some word for you to use whenever I am about to relapse—some word that teems with hidden meaning—like "Basingstoke"—it might recall me to my saner self. For, after all, I am only Mad Margaret! Daft Meg! Poor Peg! He! he! he!

Des. Poor child, she wanders! But soft— someone comes—Margaret—pray recollect yourself—Basingstoke, I beg! Margaret, if you don't Basingstoke at once, I shall be seriously angry.

Mar. (*recovering herself*). Basingstoke it is!

Des. Then make it so.

Enter Sir Ruthven. He starts on seeing them.

Sir Ruth. (*aside*). Despard! And his young wife! (*Aloud.*) This visit is unexpected.

Mar. Shall I fly at him? Shall I tear him limb from limb? Shall I render him asunder? Say but the word and—

Des. Basingstoke!

Mar. (*suddenly demure*). Basingstoke it is!

Des. (*aside*). Then make it so. (*Aloud.*) My brother—I call you brother, still, despite your horrible profligacy—we have come to urge you to abandon the evil courses to which you have committed yourself, and at any cost to become a pure and blameless ratepayer.

Sir Ruth. But I've done no wrong yet.

Mar. (*wildly*). No wrong! He has done no wrong! Did you hear that!

Des. Basingstoke.

Mar. (*recovering herself*). Basingstoke it is.

Des. My brother—I still call you brother

you observe—you forget that you have been, in the eye of the law, a Bad Baronet of Ruddigore for ten years—and you are therefore responsible—in the eye of the law—for all the misdeeds committed by the unhappy gentleman who occupied your place.

Sir Ruth. I see! Bless my heart, I never thought of that! Was I very bad?

Des. Awful. Wasn't he? (*to Margaret*).

Sir Ruth. And I've been going on like this for how long?

Des. Ten years! Think of all the atrocities you have committed—by attorney as it were—during that period. Remember how you trifled with this poor child's affections—how you raised her hopes on high (don't cry, my love—Basingstoke, you know), only to trample them in the dust when they were at the very zenith of their fulness. Oh fie, sir fie—she trusted you!

Sir Ruth. Did she? What a scoundrel I must have been! There, there—don't cry, my dear (*to Margaret, who is sobbing on Sir Ruthven's breast*), it's all right now. Birmingham, you know—Birmingham—

Mar. (*sobbing*). It's Ba—Ba—Basingstoke!

Sir Ruth. Basingstoke! of course it is—Basingstoke.

Mar. Then make it so!

Sir Ruth. There, there—it's all right—he's married you now—that is, *I've* married you (*turning to Despard*)—I say, which of us has married her?

Des. Oh, *I've* married her.

Sir Ruth. (*aside*). Oh, I'm glad of that (*to Margaret*). Yes, he's married you now (*passing her over to Despard*), and anything more disreputable than my conduct seems to have been I've never even heard of. But my mind is made up—I *will* defy my ancestors. I *will* refuse to obey their behests, thus, by courting death, atone in some degree for the infamy of my career!

Mar. I knew it—I knew it—God bless you —(*hysterically*).

Des. Basingstoke!

Mar. Basingstoke it is! (*Recovers herself.*)

Patter-Trio.—*Sir Ruthven, Despard and Margaret.*

Sir Ruth.

My eyes are fully open to my awful situation—
I shall go at once to Roderic and make him an oration.
I shall tell him I've recovered my forgotten moral senses,
And I don't care two-pence halfpenny for any consequences.
Now I do not want to perish by the sword or by the dagger,

But a martyr may indulge a little pardonable swagger,
And a word or two of compliment my vanity would flatter,
But I've got to die to-morrow, so it really doesn't matter!

Des.   So it really doesn't matter—
Mar.   So it really doesn't matter—
All.

So it really doesn't matter, matter, matter, matter, matter!

Mar.

If I were not a little mad and generally silly
I should give you my advice upon the subject, willy nilly;
I should show you in a moment how to grapple with the question,
And you'd really be astonished at the force of my suggestion.
On the subject I shall write you a most valuable letter,
Full of excellent suggestions when I feel a little better,
But at present I'm afraid I am as mad as any hatter,
So I'll keep 'em to myself, for my opinion doesn't matter!

Des.   Her opinion doesn't matter—
Sir Ruth. Her opinion doesn't matter—
All.

Her opinion doesn't matter, matter, matter, matter, matter!

Des.

If I had been so lucky as to have a steady brother
Who could talk to me as we are talking now to one another—
Who could give me good advice when he discovered I was erring,
(Which is just the very favour which on you I am conferring),
My existence would have made a rather interesting idyll,
And I might have lived and died a very decent indiwiddle.
This particularly rapid, unintelligible patter
Isn't generally heard, and if it is it doesn't matter!

Sir Ruth. If it is it doesn't matter—
Mar.   If it ain't it doesn't matter—
All.

If it is it doesn't matter, matter, matter, matter, matter!

[*Exeunt Despard and Margaret.*
Enter Adam.

Adam (*guiltily.*) Master—the deed is done!
Sir Ruth. What deed?
Adam. She is here—alone, unprotected—
Sir Ruth. Who?
Adam. The maiden. I've carried her off—

I had a hard task, for she fought like a tiger-cat!

Sir Ruth. Great heaven, I had forgotten her! I had hoped to have died unspotted by Crime, but I am foiled again—and by a tiger-cat! Produce her—and leave us!

(*Adam introduces Old Hannah, very much excited, and exit.*)

Sir Ruth. Dame Hannah! This is—this is not what I expected.

Han. Well, sir, and what would you with me? Oh, you have begun bravely—bravely indeed! Unappalled by the calm dignity of blameless womanhood, your minion has torn me from my spotless home, and dragged me, blindfold and shrieking, through hedges, over stiles, and across a very difficult country, and left me, helpless, and trembling, at your mercy! Yet not helpless coward sir, for approach one step—nay, but the twentieth part of one poor inch—and this poniard (*produces a very small dagger*) shall teach ye what it is to lay unholy hands on old Stephen Trusty's daughter!

Sir Ruth. Madam, I am extremely sorry for this. It is not at all what I intended—anything more correct—more deeply respectful than my intentions towards you, it would be impossible for anyone—however particular—to desire.

Han. Bah, I am not to be tricked by smooth words, hypocrite! But be warned in time, for there are, without, a hundred gallant hearts whose trusty blades would hack him limb from limb who dared to lay unholy hands on old Stephen Trusty's daughter!

Sir Ruth. And this is what it is to embark upon a career of unlicensed pleasure!

(*Hannah, who has taken a formidable dagger from one of the armed figures, throws her small dagger to Sir Ruthven*).

Han. Harke, miscreant, you have secured me, and I am your poor prisoner; but if you think I cannot take care of myself you are very much mistaken. Now then, it's one to one, and let the best man win!

(*Making for him.*)

Sir Ruth. (*in an agony of terror*). Don't! don't look at me like that! I can't bear it! Roderic! Uncle! Save me!

Sir Roderic enters, from his picture. He comes down the stage.

Sir Rod. What is the matter? Have you carried her off?

Sir Ruth. I have—she is there—look at her —she terrifies me!

Sir Rod. (*looking at Hannah*). Little Nannikin!

Han. (*amazed*). Roddy-doddy!

Sir Rod. My own old love! Why, how came you here?

Han. This brute—he carried me off! Bodily! But I'll show him! (*about to rush at Sir Ruthven*).

Sir Rod. Stop! (*to Sir Ruthven*). What do you mean by carrying off this lady? Are you aware that, once upon a time, she was engaged to be married to me? I'm very angry—very angry indeed.

Sir Ruth. Now I hope this will be a lesson to you in future, not to—

Sir Rod. Hold your tongue, sir.

Sir Ruth. Yes, uncle.

Sir Rod. Have you given him any encouragement?

Han. (*to Sir Ruthven*). Have I given you any encouragement? Frankly now, have I?

Sir Ruth. No. Frankly, you have not. Anything more scrupulously correct than your conduct it would be impossible to desire.

Sir Rod. You go away.

Sir Ruth. Yes, uncle.   [*Exit Sir Ruthven.*

Sir Rod. This is a strange meeting after so many years!

Han. Very. I thought you were dead.

Sir Rod. I am. I died ten years ago.

Han. And are you pretty comfortable?

Sir Rod. Pretty well—that is—yes, pretty well.

Han. You don't deserve to be, for I loved you all the while, dear; and it made me dreadfully unhappy to hear of all your goings on, you bad, bad boy!

BALLAD.—*Hannah.*

There grew a little flower
　'Neath a great oak tree:
When the tempest 'gan to lower
　Little heeded she:
No need had she to cower,
For she dreaded not its power—
She was happy in the bower
　Of her great oak tree!
　　Sing hey,
　　Lackaday!
　Let the tears fall free
For the pretty little flower and the great
　　　　　　　　　　oak tree!

Both.　　　　Sing hey,
　　　　　　Lackaday! &c.

When she found that he was fickle,
　Was that great oak tree,
She was in a pretty pickle,
　As she well might be—
But his gallantries were mickle,
For Death followed with his sickle,
And her tears began to trickle
　For her great oak tree!

Both.　　　　Sing hey,
　　　　　　Lackaday! &c.

Said she, "He loved me never,
　Did that great oak tree,
But I'm neither rich nor clever,
　And so why should he?
But though fate our fortunes sever,
To be constant I'll endeavour,
Aye, for ever and for ever,
　To my great oak tree!"

Both.　　　　Sing hey,
　　　　　　Lackaday! &c.

Falls weeping on Sir Roderic's bosom.

*Enter Sir Ruthven, excitedly, followed by
all the characters and Chorus of Bridesmaids
and Bucks and Blades.*

Sir Ruth. Stop a bit—both of you.

Sir Rod. This intrusion is unmannerly.

Han. I'm surprised at you.

Sir Ruth. I can't stop to apologize—an idea
has just occurred to me. A Baronet of Ruddigore can only die through refusing to commit
his daily crime.

Sir Rod. No doubt.

Sir Ruth. Therefore, to refuse to commit
a daily crime is tantamount to suicide!

Sir Rod. It would seem so.

Sir Ruth. But suicide is, itself, a crime
—and so, by your own showing, you ought
never to have died at all!

Sir Rod. I see—I understand! Then I'm
practically alive!

Sir Ruth. Undoubtedly! (*Sir Roderic embraces Hannah.*) Rose, when you believed
that I was a simple farmer, I believe you loved
me?

Rose. Madly, passionately!

Sir Ruth. But when I became a bad baronet, you very properly loved Richard instead?

Rose. Passionately, madly!

Sir Ruth. But if I should turn out *not* to
be a bad baronet after all, how would you love
me then?

Rose. Madly, passionately!

Sir Ruth. As before?

Rose. Why, of course!

Sir Ruth. My darling!　　[*They embrace.*

Rich. Here, I say, belay!

Rose. Oh, sir, belay, if it's absolutely
necessary.

Sir Ruth. Belay? Certainly not!

FINALE.

All.　　Oh, happy the lily
　　　　When kissed by the bee;
　　　And, sipping tranquilly,
　　　　Quite happy is he;
　　　And happy the filly
　　　　That neighs in her pride;
　　　But happier than any,
　　　A pound to a penny,
　　　A lover is, when he
　　　　Embraces his bride!

CURTAIN.

RUDDIGORE

Authentic Libretto
of the new
GILBERT AND SULLIVAN LIBRARY

PRINCESS IDA

OR,

CASTLE ADAMANT.

BY

Sir W. S. GILBERT

AND

Sir ARTHUR S. SULLIVAN

—————

PRINCESS IDA;

OR,

CASTLE ADAMANT.

▼▼▼

ACT I.

SCENE.—*Pavilion attached to King Hilde-brand's Palace. Florian, Courtiers and Soldiers discovered.*

CHORUS.

Search throughout the panorama
For a sign of royal Gama,
  Who to-day should cross the water
  With his fascinating daughter—
    Ida is her name.

Some misfortune evidently
Has detained them—consequently
Search throughout the panorama
For the daughter of King Gama,
    Prince Hilarion's flame!

SOLO.

Flor. Will Prince Hilarion's hope be sadly
              blighted?
All.   Who can tell?
Flor. Will Ida break the vows that she has
              plighted?
All.   Who can tell?
Flor. Will she back out, and say she did not
              mean them?
All.   Who can tell?
Flor. If so, there'll be the deuce to pay be-
              tween them.
All.   No no—we'll not despair,
     For Gama would not dare
     To make a deadly foe
     Of Hildebrand, and so,
      Search througrout, &c.

Enter King Hildebrand, with Cyril.

Hild. See you no sign of Gama?
Flor.   None, my liege!
Hild. It's very odd indeed. If Gama fail
To put in an appearance at our Court
Before the sun has set in yonder west,
And fail to bring the Princess Ida here
To whom our son Hilarion was be-
    trothed
At the extremely early age of one,
There's war between King Gama and
    ourselves!
(*Aside to Cyril.*) Oh Cyril, how I
    dread this interview!
It's twenty years since he and I have
    met.
He was a twisted monster—all awry—

As though dame Nature, angry with her
    work,
Had crumpled it in fitful petulance!
Cyr. But, sir, a twisted and ungainly trunk
Often bears goodly fruit. Perhaps he
    was
A kind, well-spoken gentleman?
Hild.   Oh, no!
For, adder-like, his sting lay in his
    tongue.
(His "sting" is present, though his
    "stung" is past.)
Flor. (*looking through glass.*) But stay, my
     liege; o'er yonder mountain's brow
Comes a small body, bearing Gama's
    arms;
And now I look more closely at it, sir,
I see attached to it King Gama's legs;
From which I gather this corollary
That that small body must be Gama's
    own!
Hild. Ha! Is the Princess with him?
Flor.   Well, my liege,
Unless her highness is full six feet high,
And wears mustachios too—and smokes
    cigars—
And rides *en cavalier* in coat of steel—
I do not think she is.
Hild.   One never knows.
She's a strange girl. I've heard, and does
    odd things!
Come, bustle there!
For Gamma place the richest robes we
    own—
For Gama place the coarsest prison
    dress—
For Gama let our best spare bed be
    aired—
For Gama let our deepest dungeon
    yawn—
For Gama lay the costliest banquet
    out—
For Gama place cold water and dry
    bread!
For as King Gama brings the Princess
    here
Or brings her not, so shall King Gama
    have
Much more than everything—much less
    than nothing!

Song and Chorus.

Hild. Now hearken to my strict command
On every hand, on every hand—

Chorus.
To your command,
On every hand,
We dutifully bow!

Hild. If Gama bring the Princess here
Give him good cheer, give him good cheer.

Chorus.
If she come here
We'll give him a cheer,
And we will show you how.
Hip, hip, hurrah! hip, hip, hurrah!
Hip, hip, hurrah! hurrah! hurrah!
We'll shout and sing
Long live the King,
And his daughter, too, I trow!
Then shout ha! ha! hip, hip, hurrah!
Hip, hip, hip, hip, hurrah!
For the fair Princess and her good papa,
Hurrah! hurrah!

Hild. But if he fail to keep his troth,
Upon our oath, we'll trounce them both!
Chorus.
He'll trounce them both,
Upon his oath,
As sure as quarter day!

Hild. We'll shut him up in a dungeon cell
And toll his knell on a funeral bell.
Chorus.
From dungeon cell,
His funeral knell,
Shall strike him with dismay!
Hip, hip, hurrah! hip, hip, hurrah!
Hip, hip, hurrah! hurrah! hurrah!
As up we string
The faithless King,
In the old familiar way!
We'll shout ha! ha! hip, hip, hurrah!
Hip, hip, hip, hip, hurrah!
As we make an end of her false papa,
Hurrah! hurrah!

[*Exeunt all.*

Enter Hilarion.

Recit.—*Hilarion.*
To-day we meet, my baby bride and I—
But ah, my hopes are balanced by my fears!
What transmutations have been conjured by
The silent alchemy of twenty years!

Ballad—*Hilarion.*
Ida was a twelvemonth old,
Twenty years ago!
I was twice her age. I'm told,
Twenty years ago!
Husband twice as old as wife
Argues ill for married life.
Baleful prophecies were rife,
Twenty years ago!

Still, I was a tiny prince
Twenty years ago.
She has gained upon me, since
Twenty years ago.
Though she's twenty-one, it's true,
I am barely twenty-two—
False and foolish prophets you,
Twenty years ago!

Enter Hildebrand.

Hil. Well, father, is there news for me at last?

Hild. King Gama is in sight, but much I fear
With no Princess!

Hil. Alas, my liege, I've heard,
That's Princess Ida has forsworn the world,
And, with a band of women, shut herself
Within a lonely country house, and there
Devotes herself to stern philosophies!

Hild. Then I should say the loss of such a wife
Is one to which a reasonable man
Would easily be reconciled.

Hil. Oh, no!
Or I am not a reasonable man.
She *is* my wife—has been for twenty years!
I think I see her now.

Hild. Ha! let me look!

Hil. In my mind's eye, I mean—a blushing bride.
All bib and tucker, frill and furbelow!
How exquisite she looked, as she was borne,
Recumbent, in her foster-mother's arms!
How the bride wept—nor would be comforted
Until the hireling mother-for the-nonce
Administered refreshment in the vestry.
And I remember feeling much annoyed
That she should weep at marrying with me.
But then I thought, "These brides are all alike.
You cry at marrying me? How much more cause
You'd have to cry if it were broken off!"
These were my thoughts; I kept them to myself,
For at that age I had not learnt to speak.

[*Exeunt Hildebrand and Hilarion.*

Enter Courtiers.

Chorus. From the distant panorama
Come the sons of royal Gama.
They are heralds evidently,
And are sacred consequently,
Sons of Gama, hail! oh hail!

Enter Arac, Guron, and Scynthius.

SONG.—*Arac.*

We are warriors three,
  Sons of Gama, Rex,
Like most sons are we,
  Masculine in sex.

All Three.   Yes, yes, yes,
         Masculine in sex.

Arac.   Politics we bar,
      They are not our bent;
    On the whole we are
      Not ntelligent.

All Three.   No, no no,
         Not intelligent.

Arac.   But with doughty heart,
      And with trusty blade,
    We can play our part—
      Fighting is our trade.

All Three.   Yes, yes, yes,
         Fighting is our trade.

All Three. Bold, and fierce, and strong, ha!
           ha!
For a war we burn,
With its right or wrong, ha! ha!
  We have no concern.
Order comes to fight, ha! ha!
  Order is obeyed,
We are men of might, ha! ha!
  Fighting is our trade.
  Yes—yes, yes,
Fighting is our trade, ha! ha!
  Fighting is our trade.

Chorus. They are men of might, ha! ha!
  Fighting is their trade.
Order comes to fight, ha! ha!
Order is obeyed, ha! ha!
  Fighting is their trade!

Enter King Gama.

SONG.—*Gama.*

If you give me your attention, I will tell you
  what I am!
I'm a genuine philanthropist—all other kinds
  are sham.
Each little fault of temper and each social
  defect
In my erring fellow creatures, I endeavour
  to correct.
To all their little weaknesses I open people's
  eyes;
And little plans to snub the self-sufficient I
  devise;
I love my fellow creatures—I do all the good
  I can—
Yet everybody says I'm such a disagreeable
  man!
  And I can't think why!

To compliments inflated I've a withering
  reply;
And vanity I always do my best to mortify;
A charitable action I can skilfully dissect;
And interested motives I'm delighted to de-
  tect;

I know everybody's income and what everybody earns;
And I carefully compare it with the income-
  tax returns;
But to benefit humanity however much I
  plan,
Yet everybody says I'm such a disagreeable
  man!
  And I can't think why!

I'm sure I'm no ascetic; I'm as pleasant as
  can be;
You'll lways find me ready with a crushing
  repartee,
I've an irritating chuckle, I've a celebrated
  sneer,
I've an entertaining snigger, I've a fascinat-
  ing leer.
To everybody's prejudice I know a thing or
  two;
I can tell a woman's age in half a minute—
  and I do.
But although I try to make myself as
  pleasant as I can,
Yet everybody says I am a disagreeable man!
  And I can't think why!

Chorus. He can't think why!

Enter Hildebrand, Hilarion, Cyril and Florian.

Gama. So this is Castle Hildebrand? Well,
      well!
    Dame Rumour whispered that the
      place was grand:
    She told me that your taste was ex-
      quisite,
    Superb, unparalleled!

Hild. (*gratified.*)   Oh, really, king!

Gama. But she's a liar! Why, how old
      you've grown!
    Is this Hilarion? Why, you've changed
      too—
    You were a singularly handsome child!
(*To Florian.*) Are you a courtier? Come,
      then, ply your trade;
    Tell me some lies. How do you like
      your king?
    Vile rumour says he's all but imbecile.
    Now, that's not true?

Flor.   My lord, we love our king,
    His wise remarks are valued by his
      court
    As precious stones.

Gama.   And for the self same cause,
    Like precious stones, his sensible re-
      marks
    Derive their value from their scarcity!
    Come now, be honest, tell the truth for
      once!
    Tell it of me. Come, come, I'll harm
      you not.
    This leg is crooked—this foot is ill-
      designed—
    This shoulder wears a hump! Come,
      out with it!

Look, here's my face! Now, am I not the worst
    Of Nature's blunders?

Cyril.   Nature never errs.
To those who know the workings of your mind,
Your face and figure, sir, suggest a book
Appropriately bound.

Gama (*enraged*). Why, harkye, sir,
How dare you bandy words with me?

Cyril.   No need
To bandy aught that appertains to you.

Gama (*furiously*). Do you permit this, king?

Hild.   We are in doubt
Whether to treat you as an honoured guest,
Or a as traitor knave who plights his word
And breaks it.

Gama (*quickly*). If the casting vote's with me,
I give it for the former!

Hild.   We shall see.
By the terms of our contract, signed and sealed,
You're bound to bring the Princess here to-day!
Why is she not with you?

Gama.   Answer me this;
What think you of a wealthy purse-proud man,
Who, when he calls upon a starving friend,
Pulls out his gold and flourishes his notes,
And flashes diamonds in the pauper's eyes?
What name have you for such an one?

Hild.   A snob.

Gama. Just so. The girl has beauty, virtue, wit,
Grace, humour, wisdom, charity, and pluck.
Would it be kindly, think you, to parade
These brilliant qualities before *your* eyes?
Oh no, King Hildebrand, I am no snob!

Hild. (*furiously*). Stop that tongue,
Or you shall lose the monkey head that holds it!

Gama. Bravo! your king deprives me of my head,
That he and I may meet on equal terms!

Hild. Where is she now?

Gama.   In Castle Adamant,
One of my many country houses. There
She rules a woman's University,
With full a hundred girls, who learn of her.

Cyril. A hundred girls! A hundred ecstasies!

Gama. But no mere girls, my good young gentleman;
With all the college learning that you boast,
The youngest there will prove a match for *you*.

Cyril. With all my heart, if she's the prettiest!
(*To Flor.*) Fancy, a hundred matches—all alight!—
That's if I strike them as I hope to do!

Gama. Despair your hope; their hearts are dead to men.
He who desires to gain their favour must
Be qualified to strike their teeming brains,
And not their hearts. They're safety matches, sir,
And they light only on the knowledge box—
So *you've* no chance!

Flor. Are there no males whatever in those walls?

Gama. None, gentlemen, excepting letter mails—
And they are driven (as males often are
In other large communities) by women.
Why, bless my heart, she's so particular
She'll scarcely suffer Dr. Watts's hymns—
And all the animals she owns are "hers"!
The ladies rise at cockcrow every morn—

Cyril. Ah, then they have male poultry?

Gama.   Not at all,
(*Confidentially.*) The crowing's done by an accomplished hen!

DUET.—*Gama and Hildebrand.*

Gama. Perhaps if you address the lady
    Most politely, most politely—
Flatter and impress the lady,
    Most politely, most politely—
Humbly beg and humbly sue—
She may deign to look on you,
But your doing you must do
    Most politely, most politely!

All. Humbly beg and humbly sue, &c.

Hild. Go you, and inform the lady,
    Most politely, most politely,
If she don't, we'll storm the lady,
    Most politely, most politely!

(*To Gama.*)
    You'll remain as hostage here;
    Should Hilarion disappear,

We will hang you, never fear,
   Most politely, most politely!

All. {
He'll
I'll
You'll
} remain as hostage here, &c.

*Gama, Arac, Guron, and Scynthius are marched
off in custody; Hildebrand following.*

RECIT.—*Hilarion.*

Come, Cyril, Florian, our course is plain,
  To-morrow morn fair Ida we'll engage;
But we will use no force her love to gain,
  Nature has armed us for the war we
    wage!

TRIO.—*Hilarion, Cyril, and Florian.*

Hil. Expressive glances
    Shall be our lances,
      And pops of Sillery
      Our light artillery.
    We'll storm their bowers
    With scented showers
    Of fairest flowers
    That we can buy!
Chor. Oh dainty triolet!
    Oh fragrant violet!
    Oh gentle heigho-let!
      (Or little sigh)
    On sweet urbanity,
    Though mere inanity,
    To touch their vanity
    We will rely!
Cyr. When day is fading
    With serenading
      And such frivolity
      We'll prove our quality
    A sweet profusion
    Of soft allusion
    This bold intrusion
      Shall justify.
Chor. Oh dainty triolet, &c.
Flor. We'll charm their senses
    With verbal fences,
      With ballads amatory
      And declamatory.
    Little heeding
    Their pretty pleading
    Our love exceeding
      We'll justify!
Chor. Oh dainty triolet, &c.

*(Re-enter Gama, Arac, Guron, and Scynthius
heavily ironed, followed by Hildebrand.)*

RECIT.

Gama. Must we, till then, in prison cell be
    thrust?
Hild.   You must!
Gama. This seems unnecessarily severe!
Arac, Guron, and Scynthius. Hear, hear!

TRIO.—*Arac, Guron, and Scynthius.*

  For a month to dwell
  In a dungeon cell;
    Growing thin and wizen
    In a solitary prison,
  Is a poor look out
  For a soldier stout,
    Who is longing for the rattle
    Of a complicated battle—
  For the rum-tum-tum
  Of the military drum,
    And the guns that go boom! boom!

All. The rum-tum-tum
  Of the military drum, &c.

Hild. When Hilarion's bride
  Has at length complied
    With the just conditions
    Of our requisitions,
  You may go in haste
  And indulge your taste
    For the fascinating rattle
    Of a complicated battle.
  For the rum-tum-tum,
  Of the military drum,
  And the guns that go boom! boom!
All. For the rum-tum-tum
  Of the military drum, &c.

All. But till that time {
you'll
we'll
} here remain,

  And bail {
we
they
} will not entertain,

  Should she {
our
his
} mandate disobey,

{
Your
Our
} lives the penalty will pay!

*(Gama, Arac, Guron, and Scynthius are
marched off.)*

END OF ACT I.

ACT II.

*Gardens in Castle Adamant. A river runs
across the back of the stage, crossed by a rustic
bridge. Castle Adamant in the distance.*

*Girl graduates discovered seated at the feet
of Lady Psyche.*

CHORUS.

Towards the empyrean heights
  Of every kind of lore,
We've taken several easy flights,
  And mean to take some more.
In trying to achieve success

No envy racks our heart,
And all the knowledge we possess
  We mutually impart.

SOLO.—*Melissa.*

Pray what authors should she read
Who in Classics would succeed?

SOLO.—*Psyche,*

If you'd climb the Helicon,
You should read Anacreon,
Ovid's Metamorphoses,

Likewise Aristophanes,
And the works of Juvenal:
These are worth attention, all;
But, if you will be advised,
You will get them Bowdlerized!

CHORUS.
Ah! we will get them Bowdlerized!

SOLO.—*Sacharissa*.
Pray you tell us, if you can,
What's the thing that's known as Man?

SOLO.—*Psyche*.
Man will swear and Man will storm—
Man is not at all good form—
Man is of no kind of use—
Man's a donkey—Man's a goose—
Man is coarse and Man is plain—
Man is more or less insane—
Man's a ribald—Man's a rake,
Man is Nature's sole mistake!

CHORUS.
We'll a memorandum make—
Man is Nature's sole mistake!

And thus to empyrean height
Of every kind of lore,
In search of wisdom's pure delight,
Ambitiously we soar.
In trying to achieve success
No envy racks our heart,
For all we know and all we guess,
We mutually impart!

Enter Lady Blanche. All stand up demurely.
Bla. Attention, ladies, while I read to you
The Princess Ida's list of punishments.
The first is Sacharissa. She's expelled!
All. Expelled!
Bla. Expelled, because although she knew
No man of any kind may pass our walls,
She dared to bring a set of chessmen
here!
Sach. (*crying*). I meant no harm; they're only
men of wood!
Bla. They're men with whom you give each
other mate,
And that's enough! The next is Chloe.
Chloe. Ah!
Bla. Chloe will lose three terms, for yester-
day,
When looking through her drawing-
book, I found
A sketch of a perambulator!
All (*horrified*). Oh!
Bla. *Double* perambulator, shameless girl!
That's all at present. Now, attention,
pray!
Your Principal the Princess comes to
give
Her usual inaugural address
To those young ladies who joined yes-
terday.

CHORUS.
Mighty maiden with a mission,
Paragon of common sense,
Running fount of erudition,
Miracle of eloquence,
We are blind, and we would see;
We are bound, and would be free;
We are dumb, and we would talk;
We are lame, and we would walk.
Enter the Princess.
Mighty maiden with a mission—
Paragon of common sense;
Running fount of erudition—
Miracle of eloquence!
Prin. (*Recit.*) Minerva, oh hear me!

ARIA.
Oh, goddess wise
That lovest light,
Endow with sight
Their unillumined eyes.

At this my call,
A fervent few
Have come to woo
The rays that from thee fall.
Let fervent words and fervent thoughts be
mine,
That I may lead them to thy sacred shrine!

Women of Adamant, fair Neophytes—
Who thirst for such instruction as we give,
Attend, while I unfold a parable.
The elephant is mightier than Man,
Yet Man subdues him. Why? The elephant
Is elephantine everywhere but here (*tapping
her forehead*),
And Man, whose brain is to the elephant's,
As Woman's brain to Man's—(that's rule
of three)—
Conquers the foolish giant of the woods,
As Woman, in her turn, shall conquer Man.
In Mathematics, Woman leads the way:
The narrow-minded pedant still believes
That two and two make four! Why we can
prove,
We women—household drudges as we are—
That two and two make five—or three—or
seven;
Or five and twenty, if the case demands!
Diplomacy? The wiliest diplomate
Is absolutely helpless in our hands,
He wheedles monarchs—woman wheedles
him!
Logic? Why, tyrant Man himself admits
It's waste of time to argue with a woman!
Then we excel in social qualities:
Though Man professes that he holds our sex
In utter scorn, I venture to believe
He'd rather pass the day with one of you,
Than with five hundred of his fellow men!
In all things we excel. Believing this,

A hundred maidens here have sworn to
    place
Their feet upon his neck. If we succeed,
We'll treat him better than he treated us:
But if we fail, why then let hope fail too!
Le no one care a penny how she looks—
Let red be worn with yellow—blue with
    green—
Crimson with scarlet—violet with blue!
Let all your things misfit, and you your-
    selves,
At inconvenient moments come undone!
Let hair-pins lose their virtue: let the hook
Disdain the fascination of the eye—
The bashful button modestly evade
The soft embraces of the button-hole!
Let old associations all dissolve,
Let Swan secede from Edgar—Gask from
    Gask,
Sewell from Cross—Lewis from Allenby!
In other words—let Chaos come again!
(*Coming down.*) Who lectures in the Hall of
    Arts to-day!

Bla. I, madam, on Abstract Philosophy.
    There I propose considering, at length,
    Three points—The Is, the Might Be, and
        the Must:
    Whether the Is, from being actual fact,
    Is more important than the vague Might
        Be,
    Or the Migh Be, from taking wider scope,
    Is for that reason greater than the Is:
    And lastly, how the Is and Might Be
        stand
    Compared with the inevitable Must!
Prin. The subject's deep—how do you treat it,
    pray?
Bla. Madam, I take three possibilities,
    And strike a balance, then, between the
        three:
    As thus: The Princess Ida Is our head,
    The Lady Psyche Might Be—Lady
        Blanche,
    Neglected Blanche, inevitably Must.
    Given these three hypotheses—to find
    The actual betting against each of them!

Prin. Your theme's ambitious: pray you bear
    in mind
    Who highest soar fall farthest. Fare
        you well,
    You and your pupils! Maidens, follow
        me.
*Exeunt Princess and Maidens singing re-
frain of chorus, "And thus to empyrean
heights," &c. Manet Lady Blanche.*
Bla. I should command here—I was born to
    rule,
    But do I rule? I don't. Why? I don't
        know.
    I shall some day. Not yet. I bide my
        time.

I once was Some One—and the Wa
    Will Be
The Present as we speak becomes th
    Past,
The Past repeats itself, and so is Future
This sounds involved. It's not. It'
    right enough.

Song.—*Lady Blanche.*
Come mighty Must!
    Inevitable Shall!
In thee I trust.
    Time weaves my coronal!
Go mocking Is!
    Go disappointing Was!
That I am this
    Ye are the cursed cause!
Yet humble second shall be first,
    I ween;
And dead and buried be the curst
    Has Been!

Oh weak Might Be!
    Oh May, Might, Could, Would, Should
How powerless ye
    For evil or for good!
In every sense
    Your moods I cheerless call,
Whate'er your tense
    Ye are Imperfect, all!
Ye have deceived the trust I've shown
    In ye!
Away! The Mighty Must alone
    Shall be!   [*Exit Lady Blanche*
*Enter Hilarion, Cyril and Florian, climbin
over wall, and creeping cautiously among th
trees and rocks at the back of the stage.*

Trio.—*Hilarian, Cyril, Florian.*
        Gently, gently,
        Evidently
            We are safe so far,
        After scaling
        Fence and paling,
            Here, at last, we are!
Flor.   In this college
        Useful knowledge
            Everywhere one finds,
        And already
        Growing steady,
            We've enlarged our minds.
Cyr.   We've learnt that prickly cactus
        Has the power to attract us
            When we fall.
All.   When we fall!
Hil.   That nothing man unsettles
        Like a bed of stinging nettles,
            Short or tall.
All.   Short or tall!
Flor.   That bull-dogs feed on throttles—
        That we don't like broken bottles
            On a wall—
All.   On a wall.
Hil.   That sprin· ·uns breathe defiance!

And that burglary's a science
                    After all!

All.   After all.

FLORIAN.

A Woman's college! maddest folly going!
What can girls learn within its walls worth
    knowing?
I'll lay a crown (the Princess shall decide it)
I'll teach them twice as much in half-an-
    hour outside it.

HILARION.

Hush, scoffer; ere you sound your puny
    thunder,
List to their aims, and bow your head in
    wonder!
            They intend to send a wire
                To the moon—to the moon;
            And they'll set the Thames on fire
                Very soon—very soon!
            Then they learn to make silk purses
                With their rigs—with their rigs
            From the ears of Lady Circe's
                Piggy-wigs—piggy-wigs.
            And weazels at their slumbers
                They trepan—they trepan;
            To get sunbeams from cucumbers,
                They've a plan—they've a plan.
            They've a firmly rooted notion
            They can cross the Polar Ocean,
            And they'll find Perpetual Motion,
                If they can—if they can.

All.   These are the phenomena
                That every pretty domina
                    Is hoping at her
                    Universitee we shall see!

Cyr.   As for fashion, they forswear it,
                So they say—so they say—
            And the circle—they will square it
                Some fine day—some fine day—
            Then the little pigs they're teaching
                For to fly—for to fly;
            And the niggers they'll be bleaching,
                By and bye—by and bye!
            Each newly joined aspirant
                To the clan—to the clan—
            Must repudiate the tyrant
                Known as Man—known as Man—
            They mock at him and flout him,
            For they do not care about him,
            And they're "going to do without
                            him"
                If they can—if they can!
All.   These are the phenomena, &c.
Hil. So that's the Princess Ida's castle! Well,
        They must be lovely girls, indeed, if it
            requires   .
        Such walls as those to keep intruders off!
Cyr. To keep men off is only half their charge,
        And that the easier half. I much suspect
        The object of these walls is not so much
        To keep men off as keep the maidens in!
Flor. But what are these?

[*Examining some Collegiate robes.*

Hil. (*looking at them*). Why, Academic robes,
        Worn by the lady undergraduates,
        When they matriculate. Let's try them
            on. [*They do so.*
        Why, see,—we're covered to the very
            toes.
        Three lovely lady undergraduates
        Who, weary of the world and all its
            wooing—
Flor. And penitent for deeds there's no un-
            doing—
Cyr. Looked at askance by well-conducted
            maids—
All. Seek sanctuary in these classic shades!
        TRIO.—*Hilarion, Cyril, Florian.*
Hil. I am a maiden, cold and stately,
            Heartless I, with a face divine.
        What do I want with a heart, innately?
            Every heart I meet is mine!
All.   Haughty, humble, coy, or free,
                Little care I what maid may be.
            So that a maid is fair to see,
                Every maid is the maid for me!
                            (*Dance.*)
Cyr. I am a maiden frank and simple,
            Brimming with joyous roguery;
        Merriment lurks in every dimple,
            Nobody breaks more hearts than I!
All.   Haughty, humble, coy, or free,
                Little care I what maid may be.
            So that a maid is fair to see,
                Every maid is the maid for me!
                            (*Dance.*)
Flor. I am a maiden coyly blushing,
            Timid am I as a startled hind;
        Every suitor sets me flushing:
            I am the maid that wins mankind!
All.   Haughty, humble, coy, or free,
                Little care I what maid may be.
            So that a maid is fair to see,
                Every maid is the maid for me!
        (*Enter the Princess reading. She does not
        see them.*)
Flor. But who comes here? The Princess, as
            I live!
        What shall we do?
Hil. (*aside*). Why, we must brave it out!
    (*Aloud.*) Madam, accept our humblest rev-
            erence.
        (*They bow, then suddenly recollecting
                themselves, curtsey.*)
Prin. (*surprised*). We greet you, ladies. What
            would you with us?
Hil. (*aside*). What shall I say? (*Aloud.*)
            We are three students, ma'am,
            Three well-born maids of liberal estate,
            Who wish to join this University.
    (*Hilarion and Florian curtsey again. Cyril
    bows extravagantly, then, being recalled to
    himself by Florian, curtseys.*)
Prin. If, as you say, you wish to join our
            ranks

And will subscribe to all our rules, 'tis well.

Flor. To all your rules we cheerfully subscribe.

Prin. You say you're noblewomen. Well, you'll find
No sham degrees for noblewomen here.
You'll find no sizars here, or servitors,
Or other cruel distinctions, meant to draw
A line 'twixt rich and poor: you'll find no tufts
To mark nobility, except such tufts
As indicate nobility of brain.
As for your fellow-students, mark me well:
There are a hundred maids within these walls,
All good, all learned, and all beautiful:
They are prepared to love you: will you swear
To give the fulness of your love to them?

Hil. Upon our words and honours, ma'am, we will!

Prin. But we go further: will you undertake
That you will never marry any man?

Flor. Indeed we never will!

Prin.   Consider well,
You must prefer our maids to all mankind!

Hil. To all mankind we much prefer your maids!

Cyr. We should be dolts indeed, if we did not,
Seeing how fair—

Hil. (*aside to Cyril.*) Take care—that's rather strong!

Prin. But have you left no lovers at your home
Who may pursue you here?

Hil.   No, madam, none.
We're homely ladies, as no doubt you see,
And we have never fished for lover's love.
We smile at girls who deck themselves with gems,
False hair, and meretricious ornament,
To chain the fleeting fancy of a man,
But do not imitate them. What we have
Of hair, is all our own. Our colour, too,
Unladylike, but not unwomanly,
Is nature's handiwork, and man has learnt
To reckon Nature an impertinence.

Prin. Well, beauty counts for naught within these walls;
If all you say is true, you'll pass with us
A happy, happy time!

Cyr.   If, as you say,
A hundred lovely maidens wait within,
To welcome us with smiles and open arms,
I think there's very little doubt we shall!

QUARTETTE—*Princess, Hilarion, Cyril, Florian.*

Prin. The world is but a broken toy,
Its pleasures hollow—false its joy,
Unreal its loveliest hue,
Alas!
Its pains alone are true.
Alas!
Its pains alone are true.

Hil. The world is everything you say,
The world we think has had its day,
Its merriment is low,
Alas!
We've tried it, and we know,
Alas!
We've tried it, and we know.

TUTTI.

Prin. The world is but a broken toy,
Its pleasures hollow—false its joy,
Unreal its loveliest hue,
Alas!
Its pains alone are true,
Alas!
Its pains alone are true.

Hilarion, Cyril, Florian.
The world is but a broken toy,
Its pleasures hollow—false its joy,
Unreal its loveliest hue,
Alas!
Its pains alone are true.
Alas!
Its pains alone are true.

Exit Princess. The three gentlemen watch her off. Lady Psyche enters, and regards them with amazment.

Hil. I'faith, the plunge is taken, gentlemen!
For, willy-nilly, we are maidens now,
And maids against our will we must remain!

[*All laugh heartily*

Psy. (*aside*). These ladies are unseemly in their mirth.

(*The gentlemen see her, and, in confusion, resume their modest demeanour.*)

Flor. (*aside*). Here's a catastrophe, Hilarion!
This is my sister! She'll remember me,
Though years have passed since she and I have met!

Hil. (*aside to Florian*). Then make a virtue of necessity,
And trust our secret to her gentle care.

Flor. (*to Psyche, who has watched Cyril in amazement*). Psyche! Why, don't you know me? Florian!

Psy. (*amazed*). Why, Florian!

Flor.   My sister! (*embraces her*).

Psy.   Oh, my dear!
What are you doing here—and who are these?

Hil. I am that Prince Hilarion to whom
Your Princess is betrothed. I come to claim
Her plighted love. Your brother Florian

And Cyril, come to see me safely
    through.

Psy. The prince Hilarion? Cyril too? How
    strange!
    My earliest playfellows!

Hil.   Why, let me look!
Are you that learned little Psyche who
At school alarmed her mates because she
    called
A buttercup "ranunculus bulbosus?"

Cyr. Are you indeed that Lady Psyche, who
At children's parties drove the conjuror
    wild,
Explaining all his tricks before he did
    them?

Hil. Are you that learned little Psyche, who
At dinner parties, brought into dessert,
Would tackle visitors with "You don't
    know
Who first determined longitude—I do—
Hipparchus 'twas—B.C. one sixty three!"
Are you indeed that small phenomenon?

Psy. That small phenomenon indeed am I!
But gentlemen 'tis death to enter here:
We have all promised to renounce man-
    kind!

Flor. Renounce mankind? On what ground do
    you base
This senseless resolution?

Psy.   Senseless? No.
We are all taught, and, being taught,
    Believe
That Man, sprung from an Ape, is Ape
    at heart.

Cyr. That's rather strong.

Psy.   The Truth is always strong.

Song—*Lady Psyche.*

A Lady fair, of lineage high,
Was loved by an Ape, in the days gone by—
The Maid was radiant as the sun,
The Ape was a most unsightly one—
    So it would not do—
    His scheme fell through,
For the Maid, when his love took formal
    shape,
    Expressed such terror
    At his monstrous error,
That he stammered an apology and made his
    'scape,
The picture of a disconcerted Ape.

With a view to rise in the social scale,
He shaved his bristles, and he docked his
    tail,
    He grew moustachios, and he took his
    tub,
    And he paid a guinea to a toilet club—
    But it would not do,
    The scheme fell through—
    For the Maid was Beauty's fairest
    Queen,
    With golden tresses,

Like a **real princess's,**
While the Ape, despite his razor keen,
Was the apiest Ape that ever was seen!

He bought white ties, and he bought
    dress suits,
He crammed his feet into bright tight
    boots—
And to start in life on a bran new plan,
He christened himself Darwinian Man!
    But it would not do,
    The scheme fell through—
For the Maiden fair, whom the monkey
    craved,
    Was a radiant Being,
    With a brain far-seeing—
While Darwinian man, though well-behaved,
    At best is only a monkey shaved!

(*During this Melissa has entered unobserved; she looks on in amazement.*)

Mel. (*coming down*). Oh, Lady Psyche!

Psy. (*terrified*). What! you heard us then?
    Oh, all is lost!

Mel.   Not so! I'll breathe no word!
(*Advancing in astonishment to Florian.*)
How marvellously strange! and are you
    then
Indeed young men?

Flor.   Well, yes, just now we are—
But hope by dint of study to become,
In course of time, young women.

Mel. (*eagerly*).   No, no, no—
Oh don't do that! Is this indeed a man?
I've often heard of them, but, till to-day,
Never set eyes on one. They told me
    men
Were hideous, idiotic and deformed!
They're quite as beautiful as women are!
As beautiful, they're infinitely more so!
Their cheeks have not that pulpy soft-
    ness which
One gets so weary of in womankind:
Their features are more marked—and—
    oh their chins!
How curious!   (*Feeling his chin.*)

Flor.   I fear it's rather rough.

Mel. (*eagerly*). Oh don't apologise—I like it
    so!

Quintette.—*Psyche, Melissa, Hilarion, Cyril.
Florian.*

Psy. The woman of the wisest wit
    May sometimes be mistaken, O!
In Ida's views, I must admit,
    My faith is somewhat shaken, O!

Cyr. On every other point than this,
    Her learning is untainted, O!
But Man's a theme with which she is
    Entirely unacquainted, O!
     —acquainted, O!
     —acquainted, O!
    Entirely unacquainted, O!

All. Then jump for joy and gaily bound,
    The truth is found—the truth is found!
    Set bells a-ringing through the air—
    Ring here and there and everywhere—
    And echo forth the joyous sound,
    The truth is found—the truth is found!
                          [Dance.

Mel. My natural instinct teaches me
    (And instinct is important, O!)
    You're everything you ought to be,
    And nothing that you oughtn't, O!

Hil. That fact was seen at once by you
    In casual conversation, O!
    Which is most creditable to
    Your powers of observation, O!
      —servation, O!
      —servation, O!
    Your powers of observation, O!

All. Then jump for joy, &c.

Exeunt Psyche, Hilarion, Cyril and Florian.
Melissa going. Enter Lady Blanche.
Bla. Melissa!
Mel. (*returning.*) Mother!
Bla.   Here—a word with you.
    Those are the three new students?
Mel. (*confused*).   Yes they are.
    They're charming girls.
Bla.   Particularly so.
    So graceful, and so very womanly!
    So skilled in all a girl's accomplish-
      ments!
Mel. (*confused*). Yes—very skilled.
Bla.   They sing so nicely too!
Mel. They *do* sing nicely!
Bla.   Humph! It's very odd.
    Two are tenors, one is a baritone!
Mel. (*much agitated*). They've all got colds!
Bla.   Colds! Bah! D'ye think I'm blind!
    These "girls" are men disguised!
Mel.   Oh no—indeed!
    You wrong these gentlemen—I mean
      —why see,
    Here is an *étui* dropped by one of them
                (*picking up an étui*)
    Containing scissors, needles and—
Bla. (*opening it*). Cigars!
    Why these are men! And you knew
      this, you minx.
Mel. Oh spare them—they are gentlemen
      indeed,
    The Prince Hilarion (married years ago
    To Princess Ida) with two trusted
    friends!
    Consider, mother, he's her husband now,
    And has been, twenty years! Consider,
    too,
    You're only second here—you should be
    first.
    Assist the Prince's plan, and when he
    gains
    The Princess Ida, why, you *will* be first.

    You will design the fashions—think of
    that—
    And always serve out all the punish-
    ments!
    The scheme is harmless, mother—wink
    at it!
Bla. (*aside*). The prospect's tempting! Well,
    well, well, I'll try—
    Though I've not winked at anything for
    years!
    'Tis but one step towards my destiny—
    The mighty Must! the inevitable Shall!

    Duet.—*Melissa and Lady Blanche.*

Mel. Now wouldn't you like to rule the roast,
    And guide this University?
Bla.   I must agree
      'Twould pleasant be.
      (Sing hey a Proper Pride!)
Mel. And wouldn't you like to clear the coast
    Of malice and perversity?
Bla.   Without a doubt
      I'll bundle 'em out,
      Sing hey, when I preside!
Both. Sing, hoity, toity! Sorry for some!
Sing marry come up and { my / her } day will come!
    Sing Proper Pride
    Is the horse to ride,
    And Happy-go lucky, my Lady, O!
Bla. For years I've writhed beneath her
                 sneers,
    Although a born Plantagenet!
Mel.   Your'e much too meek,
      Or you would speak.
      (Sing hey, I'll say no more!)
Bla. Her elder I, by several years,
    Although you'd ne'er imagine it.
Mel.   Sing, so I've heard
      But never a word
      Have I e'er believed before!
Both. Sing, hoity toity! Sorry for some!
Sing marry come up and { my / her } day will come!
    Sing, she shall learn
    That a worm will turn.
    Sing Happy-go-lucky, my Lady, O!
                 [Exit Lady Blanche
Mel. Saved for a time, at least!
    Enter Florian, on tiptoe.
Flor. (*whispering*). Melissa—come!
Mel. Oh, sir! you must away from this at
    once—
    My mother guessed your sex! It was
    my fault—
    I blushed and stammered so that she ex-
    claimed,
    "Can these be men?" Then, seeing this,
    "Why these——
    "*Are men,*" she would have added, but "*are
    men*"
    Stuck in her throat! She keeps your
    secret, sir,

For reasons of her own—but fly from this
And take me with you—that is—no—not that!

Flor. I'll go, but not without you! (*bell*). Why, what's that?

Mel. The luncheon bell.

Flor. I'll wait for luncheon then!

Enter Hilarion with Princess, Cyril with Psyche, Lady Blanche and Ladies. Also "Daughters of the Plough" bearing luncheon.

CHORUS.

Merily ring the luncheon bell!
Here in meadow of asphodel,
Feast we body and mind as well,
So merrily ring the luncheon bell!

SOLO.—*Blanche.*

Hunger, I beg to state,
Is highly indelicate,
This is a fact profoundly true,
So learn your appetites to subdue.

All.　　Yes, yes,
We'll learn our appetites to subdue!

SOLO.—*Cyril* (*eating*).

Madam, your words so wise,
Nobody should despise,
Cursed with an appetite keen I am
And I'll subdue it—
And I'll subdue it—
And I'll subdue it with cold roast lamb!

All.　Yes—yes—
We'll subdue it with cold roast lamb!

Chorus. Merrily ring, &c.

Prin. You say you know the court of Hilde-brand?
There is a Prince there—I forget his name—

Hil. Hilarion?

Prin.　Exactly—is he well?

Hil. If it be well to droop and pine and mope,
To sigh "Oh, Ida! Ida!" all day long,
"Ida! my love! my life! Oh come to me!"
If it be well, I say, to do all this,
Then Prince Hilarion is very well.

Prin. He breathes our name? Well, it's a common one!
And is the booby comely?

Hil.　　Pretty well.
I've heard it said that if I dressed myself
In Prince Hilarion's clothes (supposing this
Consisted with my maiden modesty),
I might be taken for Hilarion's self.
But what is this to you or me, who think
Of all mankind with undisguised con-tempt?

Prin. Contempt? Why, damsel, when I think of man,
Contempt is not the word.

Cyr. (*Getting tipsy*). I'm sure of that,
Or if it is, it surely should not be!

Hil. (*aside to Cyril*). Be quiet, idiot, or they'll find us out.

Cyr. The Prince Hilarion's a goodly lad!

Prin. *You* know him then?

Cyr. (*tipsily*). I rather think I do!
We are inseparables!

Prin.　　Why, what's this?
You love him then?

Cyr.　　We do indeed—all three!

Hil. Madam, she jests (*Aside to Cyril*). Re-member where you are!

Cyr. *Jests?* Not at all! Why, bless my heart alive,
You and Hilarion, when at the Court,
Rode the same horse!

Prin. (*horrified*). Astride?

Cyr.　　Of course! Why not?
Wore the same clothes—and once or twice, I think,
Got tipsy in the same good company!

Prin. Well, these are nice young ladies, on my word!

Cyr. (*Tipsy*). Don't you remember that old kissing-song
He'd sing to blushing Mistress Lalage,
The ·hostess of the Pigeons? Thus it ran:

SONG.—*Cyril.*

(*During symphony Hilarion and Florian try to stop Cyril. He shakes them off angrily.*)

Would you know the kind of maid
Sets my heart a flame-a?
Eyes must be downcast and staid,
Cheeks must flush for shame-a!
She may neither dance nor sing,
But, demure in everything,
Hang her head in modest way,
With pouting lips that seem to say,
"Oh, kiss me, kiss me, kiss me, kiss me,
Though I die of shame-a"
Please you, that's the kind of maid
Sets my heart aflame-a!

When a maid is bold and gay
With a tongue goes clang-a,
Flaunting it in brave array,
Maiden may go hang-a!
Sunflower gay and hollyhock
Never shall my garden stock;
Mine the blushing rose of May,
With pouting lips that seem to say,
"Oh, kiss me, kiss me, kiss me, kiss me,
Though I die for shame-a!"
Please you that's the kind of maid
Sets my heart aflame-a!

Prin. Infamous creature, get you hence away!

Hilarion, who has been with difficulty re-strained by Florian during this song, breaks from him and strikes Cyril furiously on the breast.

Hil. Dog! there is something more to sing about!

Cyr. (*sobered*). Hilarion, are you mad?

Prin. (*horrified*).　　　　Hilarion?　Help!
　　Why these are men! Lost! lost! be-
　　trayed! undone!
　　　　　　　　　[*Running on to bridge*
　　Girls, get you hence!　Man-monsters,
　　　　if you dare
　　Approach one step, I——　Ah!
　　[*Loses her balance, and falls into the stream*
Psy.　　　　　　　　Oh, save her, sir!
Bla.　It's useless, sir,—you'll only catch your
　　death!
　　　　　　　　　　[*Hilarion springs in.*
Sach.　He catches her!
Mel.　　　　　And now he lets her go!
　　Again she's in his grasp—
Psy.　　　　　　　And now she's not,
　　He seizes her back hair!
Bla. (*not looking*).　　And it comes off!
Psy.　No, no!　She's saved!—she's saved!—
　　she's saved!—she's saved!

FINALE.
CHORUS OF LADIES.
Oh! joy, our chief is saved,
　　And by Hilarion's hand;
The torrent fierce he braved,
　　And brought her safe to land!
For his intrusion we must own
This doughty deed may well atone!
Prin.　　　　　Stand forth ye three,
　　　　　Whoe'er ye be,
And hearken to our stern decree!
Hil., Cyr., and Flor.　Have mercy, lady—dis-
　　　　　　regard your oaths!
Prin.　I know not mercy, men in women's
　　clothes!
　　The man whose sacrilegious eyes
　　Invade our strict seclusion, dies.
　　Arrest these coarse intruding spies!
(*They are arrested by the "Daughters of the
Plough."*)
Hil., Cyr., and Flor.　Have mercy, lady—dis-
　　　　　　regard your oaths!
Prin.　I know not mercy, men in women's
　　　　　　clothes!
(*Cyril and Florian are bound.*)
SONG.—*Hilarion.*
Whom thou hast chained must wear his chain,
　　Thou canst not set him free,
He wrestles with his bonds in vain
　　Who lives by loving thee!
If heart of stone for heart of fire,
　　Be all thou hast to give,
If dead to me my heart's desire,
　　Why should I wish to live?

Flo., Cyr., and Ladies.　Have mercy, O lady!

No word of thine—no stern command
　　Can teach my heart to rove,
Then rather perish by thy hand,
　　Than live without thy love!
A loveless life apart from thee

Were hopeless slavery,
If kindly death will set me free,
　　Why should I fear to die?
(*He is bound by an attendant, and the three
gentlemen are marched off.*)
　　　　　Enter Melissa.
Mel.　Madam, without the castle walls
　　　　An armed band
　　　Demand admittance to our halls
　　　　For Hildebrand!
All.　Oh horror!
Prin.　Deny them!
　　　We will defy them!
All.　Too late—too late!
　　　The castle gate
　　　Is battered by them!
(*The gate yields.　Soldiers rush in.　Arac,
Guron, and Scynthius are with them, but with
their hands handcuffed.*)
　　　　　ENSEMBLE.
　　　　　　GIRLS.
Rend the air with wailing,
　　Shed the shameful tear!
Walls are unavailing,
　　Man has entered here!
Shame and desecration
　　Are his staunch allies,
Let your lamentation
　　Echo to the skies!
　　　　　　MEN.
Walls and fences scaling,
　　Promptly we appear;
Walls are unavailing,
　　We have entered here.
Female execration
　　Stifle if you're wise,
Stop your lamentation,
　　Dry your pretty eyes!
　　　　Enter Hildebrand.
　　　　　RECIT.
Prin.　Audacious tyrant, do you dare
　　　To beard a maiden in her lair?
Hild.　Since you enquire,
　　　We've no desire
　　　To beard a maiden here, or anywhere!
Sol.　No no—we've no desire
　　　To beard a maiden here, or anywhere!
　　　　SOLO.—*Hildebrand.*
　　Some years ago
　　No doubt you know
　(And if you don't I'll tell you so)
　　You gave your troth
　　Upon your oath
　To Hilarion my son.
　　A vow you make
　　You must not break,
　(If you think you may, it's a great mistake),
　　For a bride's a bride
　Though the knot were tied
　　At the early age of one!
　　　And I'm a peppery kind of King,
　　　Who's indisposed for parleying
　　　To fit the wit of a bit of a chit,

And that's the long and the short of it.

Sol.

For he's a peppery kind of King, &c.
If you decide
To pocket your pride
And let Hilarion claim his bride,
Why, well and good,
It's understood.
We'll let bygones go by—
But if you choose
To sulk in the blues
I'll make the whole of you shake in your shoes.
I'll storm your walls,
And level your halls,
 In the twinkling of an eye!
  For I'm a peppery Potentate,
  Who's little inclined his claim to bate,
  To fit the wit of a bit of a chit,
  And that's the long and the short of it.

Sol. For he's a peppery Potentate, &c.

TRIO.—*Arac, Guron, and Scynthius.*

We may remark, though nothing can
 Dismay us,
That if you thwart this gentleman,
 He'll slay us.
We don't fear death, of course—we're taught
 To shame it;
But still upon the whole we thought
 We'd name it.
(*To each other*). Yes, yes, yes, better perhaps to name it.
Our interests we would not press
 With chatter,
Three hulkng brothers more or less
 Don't matter;
If you'd pooh-pooh this monarch's plan,
 Pooh-pooh it,
But when he says he'll hang a man,
 He'll do it.
(*To each other*). Yes, yes, yes, devil doubt he'll do it.

Prin. (*Recit.*). Be reassured, nor fear his anger blind,
His menaces are idle as the wind.
He dares not kill you—vengeance lurks behind!
Ar., Gur., Scyn. We rather think he dares, but never mind!
No, no—never, never mind!
Hild. I rather think I dare, but never, never mind!
Enough of parley—as a special boon,
We give you till to-morrow afternoon;
Release Hilarion, then, and be his bride,
Or you'll incur the guilt of fratricide!

ENSEMBLE.

Princess.
To yield at once to such a foe
 With shame were rife;
So quick! away with him, although
 He saved my life!
That he is fair, and strong, and tall,
Is very evident to all,
Yet I will die before I call
 Myself his wife!

The Others.
Oh! yield at once, 'twere better so,
 Than risk a strife!
And let the Prince Hilarion go—
 He saved thy life!
Hilarion's fair, and strong, and tall—
A worse misfortune might befall—
It's not so dreadful, after all,
 To be his wife!

SOLO.—*Princess.*
Though I am but a girl,
Defiance thus I hurl,
 Our banners all
 On outer wall
We fearlessly unfurl.
All. Though she is but a girl, &c.
Prin. That he is fair, &c.
The Others. Hilarion's fair, &c.
The Princess stands c., surrounded by girls kneeling. The King and soldiers stand on built rocks at back and sides of stage. Picture.

END OF ACT II.

ACT III.

SCENE.—*Outer Walls and Courtyard of Castle Adamant. Melissa, Sacharissa and ladies discovered, armed with battle axes.*

CHORUS.
Death to the invader!
 Strike a deadly blow,
As an old Crusader
 Struck his Paynim foe!
Let our martial thunder
Fill his soul with wonder,
Tear his ranks asunder,
 Lay the tyrant low!

SOLO.—*Melissa.*
Thus our courage, all untarnished,
 We're instructed to display:
But to tell the truth unvarnished,
 We are more inclined to say,
"Please you, do not hurt us."
All. "Do not hurt us, if it please you!"
Mel. "Please you let us be."
All. "Let us be—let us be!"
Mel. "Soldiers disconcert us."
All. "Disconcert us, if it please you!"
Mel. "Frightened maids are we."
All. "Maids are we—maids are we!"

Melissa.

But 'twould be an error
To confess our terror,
So, in Ida's name,
Boldly we exclaim:

CHORUS.

Death to the invader!
    Strike a deadly blow—
As an old Crusader
    Struck his Paynim foe!

Flourish. Enter Princess, armed, attended by Blanche and Psyche.

Prin. I like your spirit, girls! We have to meet
Stern bearded warriors in fight to-day;
Wear naught but what is necessary to
Preserve your dignity before their eyes,
And give your limbs full play.

Bla. One moment, ma'am
Here is a paradox we should not pass
Without enquiry. We are prone to say
"This thing is Needful—that, Superfluous"—
Yet they invariably co-exist!
We find the Needful comprehended in
The circle of the grand Superfluous.
Yet the Superfluous cannot be bought
Unless you're amply furnished with the Needful.
These singular considerations are—

Prin. Superfluous, yet not Needful—so you see
The terms may independently exist.
(*To Ladies.*) Women of Adamant, we have to show
That Woman, educated to the task,
Can meet Man, face to face, on his own ground,
And beat him there. Now let us set to work;
Where is our lady surgeon.

Sac. Madam, here!

Prin. We shall require your skill to heal the wounds
Of those that fall.

Sac. (*alarmed*). What, heal the wounded?

Prin. Yes!

Sac. And cut off real live legs and arms?

Prin. Of course!

Sac. I wouldn't do it for a thousand pounds!

Prin. Why how is this? Are you faint-hearted, girl!
You've often cut them off in theory!

Sac. In theory I'll cut them off again
With pleasure, and as often as you like,
But not in practice.

Prin. Coward! get you hence,
I've craft enough for that, and courage too,
I'll do your work! My fusiliers, advance,
Why, you are armed with axes! Gilded toys!

Where are your rifles, pray?

Chloe. Why, please you, ma'am,
We left them in the armoury, for fear
That in the heat and turmoil of the fight,
They might go off!

Prin. "They might!" Oh, craven souls!
Go off yourselves! Thank heaven, I have a heart
That quails not at the thought of meeting men;
I will discharge your rifles! Off with you! (*Exit Chloe.*)
Where's my bandmistress?

Ada. Please you, ma'am, the band
Do not feel well, and can't come out to-day!

Prin. Why this is flat rebellion! I've no time
To talk to them just now. But, happily,
I can play several instruments at once,
And I will drown the shrieks of those that fall
With trumpet music, such as soldiers love!
How stand we with respect to gunpowder?
My Lady Psyche—you who superintend
Our lab'ratory—are you well prepared
To blow these bearded rascals into shreds?

Psy. Why, madam—

Prin. Well?

Psy. Let us try gentler means.
We can dispense with fulminating grains
While we have eyes with which to flash our rage!
We can dispense with villainous saltpetre
While we have tongues with which to blow them up!
We can dispense, in short, with all the arts
That brutalize the practical polemist!

Prin. (*contemptuously*). I never knew a more dispensing chemist!
Away, away—I'll meet these men alone
Since all my women have deserted me!

(*Enter Chloe.*)

Chloe. Madam, your father and your brothers claim
An audience!

Prin. What do they do here?

Chloe. They come
To fight for you!

Prin. Admit them!

Bla. Infamous!
One's brothers, ma'am, are men!

Prin. So I have heard.
But all my women seem to fail me when
I need them most. In this emergency,

Even one's brothers may be turned to
use.
    [*Exeunt Blanche and Psyche.*
(*Enter Gama, quite pale and unnerved.*)
Gama. My daughter!
Prin. Father! thou art free!
Gama. Aye, free!
Free as a tethered ass! I come to thee
With words from Hildebrand. Those
  duly given
I must return to black captivity.
I'm free so far.
Prin. Your message.
Gama. Hildebrand
Is loth to war with women. Pit my
  sons,
My three brave sons, against these
  popinjays,
These tufted jack-a-dandy featherheads,
 And on the issue let thy hand depend!
Prin. Insult on insult's head! Are we a
  stake
For fighting men? What fiend pos-
  sesses thee,
That thou hast come with offers such
  as these
From such as he to such an one as I?
Gama. I am possessed
By the pale devil of a shaking heart!
My stubborn will is bent. I dare not
  face
That devilish monarch's black malig-
  nity!
He tortures me with torments worse
  than death,
I haven't anything to grumble at!
He finds out what particular meats I
  love,
And gives me them. The very choicest
  wines,
The costliest robes—the richest rooms
  are mine;
He suffers none to thwart my simplest
  plan,
And gives strict orders none should
  contradict me!
He's made my life a curse! (*Weeps.*)
Prin. My tortured father!
    SONG.—*Gama.*
Whene'er I spoke
Sarcastic joke
 Replete with malice spiteful,
This people mild
Politely smiled,
 And voted me delightful!
Now when a wight
Sits up all night
 Ill-natured jokes devising,
And all his wiles
Are met with smiles,
 It's hard, there's no disguising!
Oh, don't the days seem lank and long
When all goes right and nothing goes wrong.

And isn't your life extremely flat
With nothing whatever to grumble at!
Chorus. Oh, isn't your life, &c.

 When German bands
 From music stands
 Played Wagner imper*fect*ly—
 I bade them go—
 They didn't say no,
 But off they went directly!
 The organ boys
 They stopped their noise
With readiness surprising,
 And grinning herds
 Of hurdy-gurds
Retired apologising!

Oh, don't the days seem lank and long, &c.

Chorus. Oh, isn't your life, &c.

 I offered gold
 In sums untold
To all who'd contradict me—
 I said I'd pay
 A pound a day
To any one who kicked me—
 I bribed with toys
 Great vulgar boys
To utter something spiteful,
 But, bless you, no!
 They *would* be so
Confoundly politeful!
In short, these aggravating lads
They tickle my tastes, they feed my fads,
They give me this and they give me that,
And I've nothing whatever to grumble at!
Chorus. Oh, isn't your life, &c.
(*He bursts into tears, and falls sobbing on a
seat.*
Prin. My poor old father! How he must have
  suffered!
  Well, well, I yield!
Gama. (*hysterically*). She yields! I'm saved,
  I'm saved! (*Exit.*)
Prin. Open the gates—admit these warriors,
  Then get you all within the castle walls.
    [*Exeunt all but Princess.*
Prin. So fail my cherished plans—so fails my
  faith—
  And with it hope, and all that comes of
  hope!
    SONG.—*Princess.*
I built upon a rock,
 But ere Destruction's hand
  Dealt equal lot
  To Court and cot,
 My rock had turned to sand!
I leant upon an oak,
 But in the hour of need,
  Alack-a-day,
  My trusted stay
 Was but a bruised reed!

Ah, faithless rock,
My simple faith to mock!
Ah, trait'rous oak,
Thy worthlessness to cloke.

I drew a sword of steel,
But when to home and hearth
The battle's breath
Bore fire and death,
My sword was but a lath!
I lit a beacon fire,
But on a stormy day
Of frost and rime,
In wintertime,
My fire had died away!
Ah, coward steel
That fear can unanneal!
False fire indeed,
To fail me in my need!

[*Exit*

(*The gates are opened, and the girls mount the battlements as soldiers enter. Also Arac, Guron, and Scynthius.*)

CHORUS OF SOLDIERS.

When anger spreads his wing,
And all seems dark as night for it,
There nothing but to fight for it.
But ere you pitch your ring,
Select a pretty site for it,
(This spot is suited quite for it),
And then you gaily sing,
"Oh, I love the jolly rattle
Of an ordeal by battle,
There's an end of tittle, tattle,
When your enemy is dead
It's an arrant molley coddle
Fears a crack upon his noddle,
And he's only fit to swaddle
In a downy feather-bed!"

All. For a fight's a kind of thing
That I love to look upon,
So let us sing,
Long live the King,
And his son Hilarion!

SONG.—*Arac.*

This helmet, I suppose,
Was meant to ward off blows,
It's very hot,
And weighs a lot,
As many a guardsman knows,
So off that helmet goes!

All.   Yes, yes, yes,
So off that helmet goes!

(*Giving their helmets to attendants.*)

Arac. This tight-fitting cuirass
Is but a useless mass,
It's made of steel,
And weighs a deal,
A man is but an ass
Who fights in a cuirass,
So off goes that cuirass!

All.   Yes, yes, yes.

So off goes that cuirass!

(*Removing cuirasses.*)

Arac. These brassets, truth to tell,
May look uncommon well,
But in a fight
They're much too tight,
They're like a lobster shell!

All.   Yes, yes, yes.
They're like a lobster shell.

(*Removing their brassets.*)

Arac. These things I treat the same,
(*indicating leg pieces*)
(I quite forget their name)
They turn one's legs
To cribbage pegs—
Their aid I thus disclaim,
Though I forget their name—

All.   Yes, yes, yes.

Their aid {we}{they} thus disclaim!

(*They remove their leg pieces and wear close-fitting shape suits.*)

During this, Hilarion, Florian, and Cyril are brought out by the "Daughters of the Plough." They are still bound and wear the robes. Enter Gama.

Gama. Hilarion! Cyril! Florian! dressed as women!
Is this indeed Hilarion?

Hil.   Yes it is!

Gama. Why, you look handsome in your women's clothes!
Stick to 'em! men's attire becomes you not!

(*To Cyril and Florian*). And you, young ladies, will you please to pray
King Hildebrand to set me free again?
Hang on his neck and gaze into his eyes,
He never could resist a pretty face!

Hil.   You dog, you'll find though I wear woman's garb,
My sword is long and sharp!

Gama.   Hush pretty one!
Here's a virago! Here's a termagant!
If length and sharpness go for anything,
You'll want no sword while you can wag your tongue!

Cyr. What need to waste your words on such as he?
He's old and crippled.

Gama.   Aye, but I've three sons,
Fine fellows, young, and muscular, and brave,
They're well worth talking to! Come, what d'ye say?

Arac. Aye, pretty ones, engage yourselves with us,
If three rude warriors affright you not!

Hil. Old as you are I'd wring your shrivelled neck
If you were not the Princess Ida's father.

Gama. If I were not the Princess Ida's father,
And so had not her brothers for my sons,
No doubt you'd wring my neck—in safety too!
Come, come, Hilarion, begin, begin!
Give them no quarter—they will give you none.
You've this advantage over warriors
Who kill their country's enemies for pay,—
You know what you are fighting for—look there!

(*Pointing to Ladies on the battlements.*)

(*Desperate fight between the three Princes and the three Knights, during which the ladies on the battlements and the soldiers on the stage sing the following chorus*):

This is our duty plain towards
Our Princess all immaculate
We ought to bless her brothers' swords
And piously ejaculate:
Oh, Hungary!
Oh, Hungary!
Oh, doughty sons of Hungary!
May all success
Attend and bless
Your warlike ironmongery!
Hilarion! Hilarion! Hilarion!

(*By this time, Arac, Guron, and Scynthius are on the ground, wounded—Hilarion, Cyril and Florian stand over them.*)

Prin. (*entering through gate and followed by Ladies and Hildebrand*). Hold! stay your hands!—we yield ourselves to you!
Ladies, my brothers all lie bleeding there!
Bind up their wounds—but look the other way.
(*Coming down.*) Is this the end? (*Bitterly to Lady Blanche.*)
How say you, Lady Blanche—
Can I with dignity my post resign?
And if I do, will you then take my place?

Bla. To answer this, it's meet that we consult
The great Potential Mysteries; I mean
The five Subjunctive Possibilities—
The May, the Might, the Would, the Could, the Should.
Can you resign? The prince Might claim you; if
He Might, you Could—and if you Should, I Would!

Prin. I thought as much! Then, to my fate I yield—
So ends my cherished scheme! Oh, I had hoped
To band all women with my maiden throng,
And make them all abjure tyrannic Man!

Hild. A noble aim!
Prin. You ridicule it now;
But if I carried out this glorious scheme,
At my exalted name Posterity
Would bow in gratitude!
Hild. But pray reflect—
If you enlist all women in your cause,
And make them all abjure tyrannic Man,
The obvious question then arises, "How
Is this Posterity to be provided?"
Prin. I never thought of that! My Lady Blanche,
How do you solve the riddle?
Bla. Don't ask me—
Abstract Philosophy won't answer it.
Take him—he is your Shall. Give in to Fate!
Prin. And you desert me. I alone am staunch!
Hil. Madam, you placed your trust in Woman—well,
Woman has failed you utterly—try Man,
Give him one chance, it's only fair—besides,
Women are far too precious, too divine
To try unproven theories upon.
Experiments, the proverb says, are made
On humble subjects—try our grosser clay,
And mould it as you will!
Cyr. Remember, too,
Dear Madam, if at any time you feel,
A-weary of the Prince, you can return
To Castle Adamant, and rule your girls
As heretofore, you know.
Prin. And shall I find
The Lady Psyche here?
Psy. If Cyril, ma'am,
Does not behave himself, I think you will.
Prin. And you, Melissa, shall I find *you* here?
Mel. Madam, however Florian turns out,
Unhesitatingly I answer, No!
Gama. Consider this, my love, if your mama
Had looked on matters from your point of view
(I wish she had), why where would you have been?
Bla. There's an unbounded field of speculation,
On which I could discourse for hours!
Prin. No doubt!
We will not trouble you. Hilarion,
I have been wrong—I see my error now.
Take me, Hilarion—"We will walk this world
Yoked in all exercise of noble end!

And so through those dark gates across
    the wild
That no man knows! Indeed, I love
    thee—Come!"

FINALE.

Princess.   With joy abiding,
        Together gliding
          Through life's variety
          In sweet society,
        And thus enthroning
        The love I'm owning,
        On this atoning
         I will rely!

Chorus.   It were profanity
        For poor humanity

To treat as vanity
    The sway of Love.
In no locality
Or principality
Is our mortality
Its sway above!

Hilarion.   When day is fading,
        With serenading
          And such frivolity
          Of tender quality—
        With scented showers
        Of fairest flowers,
        The happy hours
         Will gaily fly!

Chorus.   It were profanity, &c.

CURTAIN.

Authentic Libretti
of the new
GILBERT AND SULLIVAN LIBRARY

PATIENCE;

OR,

BUNTHORNE'S BRIDE!

BY

Sir W. S. GILBERT

AND

Sir ARTHUR S. SULLIVAN

The Bass Publishers

PATIENCE;

OR,

BUNTHORNE'S BRIDE!

Dramatis Personae

COLONEL CALVERLEY
MAJOR MURGATROYD
LIEUT. THE DUKE OF
DUNSTABLE
} *(Officers of Dragoon Guards)*

REGINALD BUNTHORNE (*a Fleshly Poet*)

ARCHIBALD GROSVENOR (*an Idyllic Poet*)

MR. BUNTHORNE'S SOLICITOR

THE LADY ANGELA
THE LADY SAPHIR
THE LADY ELLA
THE LADY JANE
} *(Rapturous Maidens)*

PATIENCE (*a Dairy Maid*)

CHORUS OF RAPTUROUS MAIDENS AND OFFICERS OF
DRAGOON GUARDS.

ACT I.
Exterior of Castle Bunthorne.

ACT II.
A Glade.

PATIENCE;

OR,

BUNTHORNE'S BRIDE!

ACT I.

SCENE.—*Exterior of Castle Bunthorne. Entrance to Castle by draw-bridge over moat. Young ladies dressed in aesthetic draperies are grouped about the stage. They play on lutes, &c., as they sing, and all are in the last stage of despair. Angela, Ella, and Saphir lead them.*

CHORUS.

Twenty love-sick maidens we,
  Love-sick all against our will.
Twenty years hence we shall be
  Twenty love-sick maidens still.
Twenty love-sick maidens we,
And we die for love of thee.

SOLO.—Angela.

Love feeds on hope, they say, or love will die—

All.   Ah, miserie!
Yet my love lives, although no hope have I!

All.   Ah, miserie!
Alas, poor heart, go hide thyself away—
To weeping concords tune thy roundelay!
    Ah, miserie!

CHORUS.

All our love is all for one,
  Yet that love he heedeth not,
He is coy and cares for none,
  Sad and sorry is our lot!
    Ah, miserie

SOLO.—Ella.

Go, breaking heart,
  Go, dream of love requited;
Go, foolish heart,
  Go, dream of lovers plighted;
Go, madcap heart,
  Go, dream of never waking;
And in thy dream
  Forget that thou art breaking!

Chorus.   Ah, miserie!
Ella.   Forget that thou art breaking!
Chorus.   Twenty love-sick maidens, &c.

Ang. There is a strange magic in this love of ours! Rivals as we all are in the affections of our Reginald, the very hopelessness of our love is a bond that binds us to one another!

Saph. Jealousy is merged in misery. While he, the very cynosure of our eyes and hearts, remains icy insensible—what have we to strive for?

Ella. The love of maidens is, to him, as interesting as the taxes!

Saph. Would that it were! He pays his taxes.

Ang. And cherishes the receipts! (*Enter Lady Jane.*)

Saph. Happy receipts!

Jane (*suddenly*). Fools!

Ang. I beg your pardon?

Jane. Fools and blind! The man loves—wildly loves!

Ang. But whom? None of us!

Jane. No, none of us. His weird fancy has lighted, for the nonce, on Patience, the village milkmaid!

Saph. On Patience? Oh, it cannot be!

Jane. Bah! But yesterday I caught him in her dairy, eating fresh butter with a tablespoon. To-day he is not well!

Saph. But Patience boasts that she has never loved—that love is, to her, a sealed book! Oh, he cannot be serious!

Jane. 'Tis but a passing fancy—'twill quickly wear away. (*Aside.*) Oh, Reginald, if you but knew what a wealth of golden love is waiting for you, stored up in this rugged old bosom of mine, the milkmaid's triumph would be short indeed!

(*Patience appears on an eminence. She looks down with pity on the despondent ladies.*)

RECIT.

Pa. Still brooding on their mad infatuation!
    I think thee, Love, thou comest not to me!
    Far happier I, free from thy ministration,
    Than dukes or duchesses who love can be!

Saph. (*looking up*). 'Tis Patience—happy girl! Loved by a Poet!

Pa. Your pardon, ladies. I intrude upon you. (*Going.*)

Ang. Nay, pretty child, come hither. Is it true
    That you have never loved?

Pa.   Most true indeed.

Sopranos. Most marvellous!

Contraltos.   And most deplorable!

SONG.—Patience.

I cannot tell what this love may be
That cometh to all, but not to me,

It cannot be kind as they'd imply,
Or why do these ladies sigh?
It cannot be joy and rapture deep,
Or why do these gentle ladies weep?
It cannot be blissful as 'tis said,
Or why are their eyes so wondrous red?

Though everywhere true love I see
A-coming to all, but not to me,
I cannot tell what this love may be!
For I am blithe and I am gay,
While they sit sighing night and day
Think of the gulf 'twixt them and me,
"Fal la la la!"—and "Miserie!"

Chorus.
Yes, she is blithe, &c.
Pa.
If love is a thorn, they show no wit
Who foolishly hug and foster it.
If love is a weed, how simple they
Who gather it, day by day!
If love is a nettle that makes you smart,
Then why do you wear it next your heart?
And if it be none of these, say I,
Ah, why do you sit and sob and sigh?
Though everywhere, &c.

Chorus.
For she is blithe, &c.
Ang. Ah, Patience, if you have never loved, you have never known true happiness! (*All sigh.*)
Pa. But the truly happy always seem to have so much on their minds. The truly happy never seem quite well.
Jane. There is a transcendentality of delirium—an acute accentuation of supremest ecstasy—which the earthy might easily mistake for indigestion. But it is *not* indigestion—it is æsthetic transfiguration! (*To the others.*) Enough of babble. Come!
Pa. But stay, I have some news for you. The 35th Dragoon Guards have halted in the village, and are even now on their way to this very spot.
Ang. The 35th Dragoon Guards!
Saph. They are fleshly men, of full habit!
Ella. We care nothing for Dragoon Guards!
Pa. But, bless me, you were all engaged to them a year ago!
Saph. A year ago!
Ang. My poor child, you don't understand these things. A year ago they were very well in our eyes, but since then our tastes have been etherealized, our perceptions exalted. (*To others.*) Come, it is time to lift up our voices in morning carol to our Reginald. Let us to his door.
The ladies go off, two and two, into the Castle, singing refrain of "Twenty love-sick maidens we," and accompanying themselves on harps. Patience watches them in surprise, as she climbs the rock by which she entered.

March. Enter Officers of Dragoon Guards, led by Major.
CHORUS OF DRAGOONS
The soldiers of our Queen
  Are linked in friendly tether;
Upon the battle scene
  They fight the foe together.
There every mother's son
  Prepared to fight and fall is;
The enemy of one
  The enemy of all is!
Enter Colonel.

SONG.—*Colonel.*
If you want a receipt for that popular mystery,
  Known to the world as a Heavy Dragoon,
Take all the remarkable people in history,
  Rattle them off to a popular tune.
The pluck of Lord Nelson on board of the
      Victory—
Genius of Bismarck devising a plan—
The humour of Fielding (which sounds con-
      tradictory)—
  Coolness of Paget about to trepan—
The science of Jullien, the eminent musico—
  Wit of Macaulay, who wrote of Queen
      Anne—
The pathos of Paddy, as rendered by Bouci-
      cault—
  Style of the Bishop of Sodor and Man—
The dash of a D'Orsay, divested of quackery—
Narrative powers of Dickens and Thackeray—
Victor Emmanuel—peak-huntng Peveril—
Thomas Aquinas, and Doctor Sacheverell—
  Tupper and Tennyson—Daniel Defoe—
  Anthony Trollope and Mr. Guizot!
    Take of these elements all that is fusible,
    Melt them all down in a pipkin or crucible,
    Set them to simmer and take off the scum.
    And a Heavy Dragoon is the residuum!
Chorus. Yes! yes! yes! yes!
    A Heavy Dragoon is the residuum!
Col.
If you want a receipt for this soldier-like
      paragon,
  Get at the wealth of the Czar (if you can)—
The family pride of a Spaniard from Arra-
      gon—
  Force of Mephisto pronouncing a ban—
A smack of Lord Waterford, reckless and
      rollicky—
  Swagger of Roderick, heading his clan—
The keen penetration of Paddington Pollaky—
  Grace of an Odalisque on a divan—
The genius strategic of Cæsar or Hannibal—
Skill of Sir Garnet in thrashing a cannibal—
Flavour of Hamlet—the Stranger, a touch of
      him—
Little of Manfred (but not very much of
      him)—
  Beadle of Burlington—Richardson's show—
  Mr. Micawber and Madame Tussaud!
    Take of these elements all that is fusible,

Melt them all down in a pipkin or crucible,
Set them to simmer and take off the scum,
And a Heavy Dragoon is the residium!
All. Yes! yes! yes! yes!
And a Heavy Dragoon is the residuum!

Col. Well, here we are once more on the scene of our former triumphs. But where's the Duke?

Enter Duke listlessly, and in low spirits.

Duke. Here I am! (*Sighs.*)

Col. Come, cheer up, don't give way!

Duke. Oh, for that, I'm as cheerful as a poor devil can be expected to be who has the misfortune to be a duke, with a thousand a day!

Maj. Humph! Most men would envy you!

Duke. Envy *me?* Tell me, Major, are you fond of toffee?

Maj. Very!

Col. We are all fond of toffee.

All. We are!

Duke. Yes, and toffee in moderation is a capital thing. But to *live* on toffee—toffee for breakfast, toffee for dinner, toffee for tea—to have it supposed that you care for nothing *but* toffee, and that you would consider yourself insulted if anything but toffee were offered to you—how would you like *that?*

Col. I can quite believe that, under those circumstances, even toffee would become monotonous.

Duke. For "toffee" read flattery, adulation, and abject deference, carried to such a pitch that I began, at last, to think that man was born bent at an angle of forty-five degrees! Great heavens, what is there to adulate in me! Am I particularly intelligent, or remarkably studious, or excruciatingly witty, or unusually accomplished, or exceptionally virtuous?

Col. You're about as commonplace a young man as ever I saw.

All. You are!

Duke. Exactly! That's it exactly! That describes me to a T! Thank you all very much! Well, I couldn't stand it any longer, so I joined this second class cavalry regiment. In the army, thought I, I shall be occasionally snubbed, perhaps even bullied, who knows? The thought was rapture, and here I am.

Col. (*looking off*). Yes, and here are the ladies!

Duke. But who is the gentleman with the long hair?

Col. I don't know.

Duke. He seems popular!

Col. He *does* seem popular.

Bunthorne enters, followed by ladies, two and two, singing and playing on harps as before. He is composing a poem, and quite absorbed. He sees no one, but walks across the stage, followed by ladies.

They take no notice of Dragoons—to the surprise and indignation of those Officers.

CHORUS OF LADIES.
In a doleful train
    Two and two we walk all day—
For we love in vain!
    None so sorrowful as they
        Who can only sigh and say,
        Woe is me, alackaday!

CHORUS OF DRAGOONS.
Now is not this ridiculous—and is not this preposterous?
    A thorough-paced absurdity—explain it if you can.
Instead of rushing eagerly to cherish us and foster us,
    They all prefer this melancholy literary man.
    Instead of slyly peering at us,
    Casting looks endearing at us,
Blushing at us, flushing at us—flirting with a fan;
They're actually sneering at us, fleering at us, jeering at us!
    Pretty sort of treatment for a military man!

Ang. Mystic poet, hear our prayer,
    Twenty love-sick maidens we—
    Young and wealthy, dark and fair—
        All of county family.
        And we die for love of thee—
        Twenty love-sick maidens we!

Chorus of Ladies.
        Yes, we die for love of thee—
        Twenty love-sick maidens we!

Bun. (*aside—slyly*).
    Though my book I seem to scan
        In a rapt ecstatic way,
    Like a literary man
        Who despises female clay,
    I hear plainly all they say,
    Twenty love-sick maidens they.

Officers (*to each other*).
        He hears plainly, &c.

Saph. Though so excellently wise,
    For a moment mortal be,
    Deign to raise thy purple eyes
        From thy heart-drawn poesy.
    Twenty love-sick maidens see—
    Each is kneeling on her knee!
                    (*All kneel.*)

Chorus of Ladies.
        Twenty love-sick, &c.

Bun. (*aside*).
    Though, as I remarked before,
        Anyone convinced would be
    That some transcendental lore
        Is monopolizing me,
    Round the corner I can see
    Each is kneeling on her knee!

Officers (*to each other*).
        Round the corner, &c.

ENSEMBLE.
        Officers
Now is not this ridiculous, &c.

Ladies.

Mystic poet, hear our prayer, &c.

Col. Angela! what is the meaning of this?

Ang. Oh, sir, leave us; our minds are but ill-tuned to light love-talk.

Maj. But what in the world has come over you all?

Jane. Bunthorne! *He* has come over us. He has come among us, and he has idealized us.

Duke. Has he succeeded in idealizing *you?*

Jane. He has!

Duke. Good old Bunthorne!

Jane. My eyes are open; I drop despairingly; I am soulfully intense; I am limp and I cling!

(*During this Bunthorne is seen in all the agonies of composition. The ladies are watching him intently as he writhes. At last he hits on the word he wants and writes it down. A general sense of relief.*)

Bun. Finished! At last! Finished!

(*He staggers, overcome with the mental strain, into arms of Colonel.*)

Col. Are you better now?

Bun. Yes—Oh, it's you—I am better now. The poem is finished, and my soul has gone out into it. That was all. It was nothing worth mentioning, it occurs three times a day. (*Sees Patience, who has entered during this scene.*) Ah, Patience! Dear Patience! (*Holds her hand; she seems frightened.*)

Ang. Will it please you read it to us, sir?

Saph. This we supplicate. (*All kneel.*)

Bun. Shall I?

All the Dragoons. No!

Bun. (*annoyed—to Patience*). I will read it if *you* bid me!

Pa. (*much frightened*). You can if you like!

Bun. It is a wild, weird, fleshly thing; yet very tender, very yearning, very precious. It is called, "Oh, Hollow! Hollow! Hollow!"

Pa. Is it a hunting song?

Bun. A hunting song? No, it is *not* a hunting song. It is the wail of the poet's heart on discovering that everything is commonplace. To understand it, cling passionately to one another and think of faint lilies. (*They do so as he recites*)—

"OH, HOLLOW! HOLLOW! HOLLOW!"

What time the poet hath hymned
The writhing maid, lithe-limbed,
    Quivering on amarantine asphodel,
How can he paint her woes,
Knowing, as well he knows,
    That all can be set right with calomel?

When from the poet's plinth
The amorous colocynth
    Yearns for the aloe, faint with rapturous
        thrills,
How can he hymn their throes

Knowing, as well he knows,
    That they are only uncompounded pills?

Is it, and can it be,
Nature hath this decree,
    Nothing poetic in the world shall dwell?
Or that in all her works
Something poetic lurks,
    Even in colocynth and calomel?
        I cannot tell.   [*Exit Bunthorne.*

Ang. How purely fragrant!

Saph. How earnestly precious!

Pa. Well, it seems to me to be nonsense.

Saph. Nonsense, yes, perhaps—but oh, what precious nonsense!

Col. This is all very well, but you seem to forget that you are engaged to us.

Saph. It can never be. You are not Empyrean. You are not Della Cruscan. You are not even Early English. Oh, be Early English ere it is too late! (*Officers look at each other in astonishment.*)

Jane (*looking at uniform*). Red and yellow! Primary colours! Oh, South Kensington!

Duke. We didn't design our uniforms, but we don't see how they could be improved!

Jane. No, you wouldn't. Still, there *is* a cobwebby grey velvet, with a tender bloom like cold gravy, which, made Florentine fourteenth century, trimmed with Venetian leather and Spanish altar lace, and surmounted with something Japanese—it matters not what—would at least be Early English! Come, maidens. (*Exeunt Maidens, two and two, singing refrain of "Twenty love-sick maidens we." The Officers watch them off in astonishment.*)

Duke. Gentlemen, this is an insult to the British uniform—

Col. A uniform that has been as successful in the courts of Venus as on the field of Mars!

SONG.—*Colonel.*

When I first put this uniform on,
    I said, as I looked in the glass,
        "It's one to a million
        That any civilian
    My figure and form will surpass.
    Gold lace has a charm for the fair.
    And I've plenty of that, and to spare,
        While a lover's professions,
        When uttered in Hessians,
    Are eloquent everywhre!"
        A fact that I counted upon,
        When I first put this uniform on!
    CHORUS OF DRAGOONS.
        By a simple coincidence, few
        Could ever have counted upon,
        The same thing occurred to me,
        When I first put this uniform on!

Col. I said, when I first put it on,
    "It is plain to the veriest dunce

That every beauty
Will feel it her duty
To yield to its glamour at once.
They will see that I'm freely gold-
laced
In a uniform handsome and chaste"—
But the peripatetics
Of long-haired æsthetics
Are very much more to their taste—
Which I never counted upon,
When I first put this uniform on!

Chorus.
By a simple coincidence, few
Could ever have counted upon
I didn't anticipate that,
When I first put this uniform on!
                [*The Dragoons go off angrily.*
(*Enter Bunthorne, who changes his manner
and becomes intensely melodramatic.*)
    RECIT. AND SONG.—*Bunthorne.*
        Am I alone,
        And unobserved? I am!
    Then let me own
        I'm an æsthetic sham!
    This air severe
        Is but a mere
            Veneer!

    This cynic smile
        Is but a wile
            Of guile!
    This costume chaste
        Is but good taste
            Misplaced!
    Let me confess!

A languid love for lilies does *not* blight me!
Lank limbs and haggard cheeks do *not* de-
    light me!
    I do *not* care for dirty greens
        By any means.
    I do *not* long for all one sees
        That's Japanese.
    I am *not* fond of uttering platitudes
        In stained-glass attitudes.
    In short, my mediævalism's affection,
    Born of a morbid love of admiration!
        SONG.
If you're anxious for to shine in the high
    æsthetic line as a man of culture rare,
You must get up all the germs of the tran-
    scendental terms, and plant them every-
    where.
You must lie upon the daisies and discourse in
    novel phrases of your complicated state of
    mind,
The meaning doesn't matter if it's only idle
    chatter of a transcendental kind.
        And every one will say,
        As you walk your mystic way,
"If this young man expresses himself in terms
    too deep for *me*,

Why, what a very singularly deep young man
    this deep young man must be!"
Be eloquent in praise of the very dull old days
    which have long since passed away,
And convince 'em, if you can, that the reign
    of good Queen Anne was Culture's palmiest
    day.
Of course you will pooh-pooh whatever's fresh
    and new, and declare it's crude and mean,
For Art stopped short in the cultivated court
    of the Empress Josephine.
        And every one will say,
        As you walk your mystic way,
"If that's not good enough for him which is
    good enough for *me*,
Why, what a very cultivated kind of youth
    this kind of youth must be!"
Then a sentimental passion of a vegetable fash-
    ion must excite your languid spleen,
An attachment *à la* Plato for a bashful young
    potato, or a not-too-French French bean!
Though the Philistines may jostle, you will
    rank as an apostle in the high æsthetic band,
If you walk down Piccadilly with a poppy or
    a lily in your mediæval hand.
        And every one will say,
        As you walk your flowery way,
"If he's content with a vegetable love which
    would certainly not suit *me*,
Why, what a most particularly pure young man
    this pure young man must be."
[*At the end of his song Patience enters. He
sees her.*
    Bun. Ah! Patience, come hither. I am
pleased with thee. The bitter-hearted one,
who finds all else hollow, is pleased with thee.
For you are not hollow. *Are* you?
    Pa. No, thanks, I have dined; but—I beg
your pardon—I interrupt you.
    Bun. Life is made up of interruptions. The
tortured soul yearning for solitude, writhes
under them. Oh, but my heart is a-weary!
Oh, I am a cursed thing! Don't go.
    Pa. Really, I'm very sorry—
    Bun. Tell me, girl, do you ever yearn?
    Pa. (*misunderstanding him*). I earn my
living.
    Bun. (*impatiently*). No, no! Do you know
what it is to be heart-hungry? Do you know
what it is to yearn for the Indefinable, and
yet to be brought face to face, daily, with the
Multiplacation Table? Do you know what it
is to seek oceans and to find puddles?—to long
for whirlwinds and yet to have to do the best
you can with the bellows? That's my case.
Oh, I am a cursed thing! Don't go.
    Pa. If you please, I don't understand you
—you frighten me!
    Bun. Don't be frightened—it's only poetry.
    Pa. Well, if that's poetry, I don't like
poetry.
    Bun. (*eagerly*). Don't you? (*Aside.*) Can
I trust her? (*Aloud.*) Patience, you don't

like poetry—well, between you and me, *I* don't like poetry. It's hollow, unsubstantial—unsatisfactory. What's the use of yearning for Elysian Fields when you know you can't get 'em, and would only let 'em out on building leases if you had 'em?

Pa. Sir, I—

Bun. Patience, I have long loved you. Let me tell you a secret. I am not as bilious as I look. If you like, I will cut my hair. There is more innocent fun within me than a casual spectator would imagine. You have never seen me frolicsome. Be a good girl—a very good girl—and one day you shall. If you are fond of touch and go jocularity—this is the shop for it.

Pa. Sir, I will speak plainly. In the matter of love I am untaught. I have never loved but my great-aunt. But I am quite certain that, under any circumstances, I couldn't possibly love *you*.

Bun. Oh, you think not?

Pa. I'm quite sure of it. Quite sure. Quite.

Bun. Very good. Life is henceforth a blank. I don't care what becomes of me. I have only to ask that you will not abuse my confidence; though *you* despise me, I am extremely popular with the other young ladies.

Pa. I only ask that you will leave me and never renew the subject.

Bun. Certainly. Broken-hearted and desolate, I go. (*Recites.*)

"Oh, to be wafted away,
    From this black Aceldama of sorrow,
Where the dust of an earthy to-day
    Is the earth of a dusty to-morrow!"

It is a little thing of my own. I call it "Heart Foam." I shall not publish it. Farewell! Patience, Patience, farewell!

[*Exit Bunthorne.*

Pa. What on earth does it all mean? Why does he love me? Why does he expect me to love him? He's not a relation! It frightens me!

Enter Angela.

Ang. Why, Patience, what is the matter?

Pa. Lady Angela, tell me two things. Firstly, what on earth is this love that upsets everybody; and, secondly, how is it to be distinguished from insanity?

Ang. Poor blind child! Oh, forgive her, Eros! Why, love is of all passions the most essential! It is the embodiment of purity, the abstraction of refinement! It is the one unselfish emotion in this whirlpool of grasping greed!

Pa. Oh, dear, oh! (*Beginning to cry.*)

Ang. Why are you crying?

Pa. To think that I have lived all these years without having experienced this ennobling and unselfish passion! Why, what a wicked girl I must be! For it *is* unselfish, isn't it?

Ang. Absolutely! Love that is tainted with selfishness is no love. Oh, try, try, try to love! It really isn't difficult if you give your whole mind to it.

Pa. I'll set about it at once. I won't go to bed until I'm head over ears in love with somebody.

Ang. Noble girl! But is it possible that you have never loved anybody?

Pa. Yes, one.

Ang. Ah! Whom?

Pa. My great-aunt—

Ang. Great-aunts don't count.

Pa. Then there's nobody. At least—no, nobody. Not since I was a baby. But *that* doesn't count, I suppose.

Ang. I don't know. Tell me all about it.

DUET.—*Patience and Angela.*

Long years ago—fourteen, maybe—
    When but a tiny babe of four,
Another baby played with me,
    My elder by a year or more,
A little child of beauty rare,
With marvellous eyes and wondrous hair,
Who, in my child-eyes, seemed to me
All that a little child should be!
        Ah, how we loved, that child and I!
            How pure our baby joy!
        How true our love—and, by the bye,
            He was a little boy!

Ang. Ah, old, old tale of Cupid's touch!
            I though as much—I thought as much!
            He *was* a little boy!

Pa. (*shocked*).
            Pray don't misconstrue what I say—
            Remember, pray—remember, pray,
            He was a *little* boy!

And. No doubt! Yet, spite of all your pains,
            The interesting fact remains—
            He was a little *boy!*

Ensemble.
{Ah, yes, in } spite of all {my } pains, &c.
{No doubt! Yet,}   {your}
                        [*Exit Angela.*

Pa. It's perfectly dreadful to think of the appalling state I must be in! I had no idea that love was a duty. No wonder they all look so unhappy! Upon my word, I hardly like to associate with myself. I don't think I'm respectable. I'll go at once and fall in love with —(*Enter Grosvenor.*) A stranger!

DUET.—*Patience and Grosvenor.*

Gros. Prithee, pretty maiden—prithee, tell me true,
        (Hey, but I'm doleful, willow willow waly!)
        Have you e'er a lover a-dangling after you?

Hey willow waly O!
    I would fain discover
    If you have a lover?
Hey willow waly O!

Pa.   Gentle sir, my heart is frolicsome and
            free—
        (Hey but he's doleful, willow willow
            waly!)
    Nobody I care for comes a-courting me—
    Hey willow waly O!
        Nobody I care for
        Comes a-courting—therefore,
    Hey willow waly O!

Gros. Prithee, pretty maiden, will you marry
            me?
        (Hey but I'm hopeful, willow willow
            waly!)
    I may say, at once, I'm a man of prop-
            ertee—
    Hey willow waly O!
        Money, I despise it;
        Many people prize it,
    Hey willow waly O!

Pa.   Gentle sir, although to marry I design—
        (Hey but he's hopeful, willow willow
            waly!)
    As yet I do not know you, and so I must
            decline,
    Hey willow waly O!
        To other maidens go you—
        As yet I do not know you,
Both. Hey willow waly O!

Gros. Patience! Can't it be that you don't
recognise me?
Pa. Recognise you? No, indeed I don't!
Gros. Have fifteen years so greatly changed
me?
Pa. Fifteen years? What do you mean?
Gros. Have you forgotten the friend of
your youth, your Archibald?—your little play-
fellow? Oh, Chronos, Chronos, this is too bad
of you!
Pa. Archibald! Is it possible? Why, let me
look! It is! It is! It must be! Oh, how happy
I am! I thought we should never meet again!
And how you've grown!
Gros. Yes, Patience, I am much taller and
much stouter than I was.
Pa. And how you've improved!
Gros. Yes, Patience, I am very beautiful!
(*Sighs.*)
Pa. But surely *that* doesn't make you un-
happy?
Gros. Yes, Patience, gifted as I am with
a beauty which probably has not its rival on
earth, I am, nevertheless, utterly and complete-
ly miserable.
Pa. Oh—but why?
Gros. My child-love for you has never

faded. Conceive, then, the horror of my situation when I tell you that it is my hideous destiny to be madly loved at first sight by every
woman I come across!
Pa. But why do you make yourself so picturesque? Why not disguise yourself, disfigure
yourself, anything to escape this persecution?
Gros. No, Patience, that may not be. These
gifts—irksome as they are—were given to me
for the enjoyment and delectation of my fellow-
creatures. I am a trustee for Beauty, and it is
my duty to see that the conditions of my trust
are faithfully discharged.
Pa. And you, too, are a Poet?
Gros. Yes, I am the Apostle of Simplicity.
I am called "Archibald the All-Right"—for I
am infallible!
Pa. And is it possible that you condescend
to love such a girl as I?
Gros. Yes, Patience, is it not strange? I
have loved you with a Florentine fourteenth-
century frenzy for full fifteen years!
Pa. Oh, marvellous! I have hitherto been
deaf to the voice of love. I seem now to know
what love is! It has been revealed to me—it
is Archibald Grosvenor!
Gros. Yes, Patience, it is!
Pa. (*as in a trance*). We will never, never
part!
Gros. We will live and die together!
Pa. I swear it!
Gros. We both swear it!
Pa. (*recoiling from him*). But—oh, horror!
Gros. What's the matter?
Pa. Why, you are perfection! A source of
endless ecstasy to all who know you!
Gros. I know I am. Well?
Pa. Then, bless my heart, there can be noth-
ing unselfish in loving *you!*
Gros. Merciful powers! I never thought
of that!
Pa. To monopolize those features on which
all women love to linger! It would be unpar-
donable!
Gros. Why, so it would! Oh, fatal perfec-
tion, again you interpose between me and my
happiness!
Pa. Oh, if you were but a thought less
beautiful than you are!
Gros. Would that I were; but candour compels me to admit that I'm not!
Pa. Our duty is clear; we must part, and
for ever!
Gros. Oh, misery! And yet I cannot question the propriety of your decision. Farewell,
Patience!
Pa. Farewell, Archibald! But stay!
Gros. Yes, Patience?
Pa. Although I may not love *you*—for you
are perfection—there is nothing to prevent
your loving *me.* I am plain, homely, unat-
tractive!
Gros. Why, that's true!

Pa. The love of such a man as you for such a girl as I must be unselfish!

Gros. Unselfishness itself!

DUET.—*Patience and Grosvenor.*

Pa. Though to marry you would very selfish be—

Gros. Hey, but I'm doleful—willow willow waly!

Pa. You may, all the same, continue loving me—

Gros. Hey willow waly O!

Both. All the world ignoring,

{ You'll } { I'll } go on adoring—

Hey willow waly O!

[*At the end, exeunt despairingly, in opposite directions.*

FINALE.—ACT I.

Enter Bunthorne, crowned with roses and hung about with garlands and looking very miserable. He is led by Angela and Saphir (each of whom holds an end of the rose-garland by which he is bound), and accompanied by procession of maidens. They are dancing classically, and playing on cymbals, double pipes, and other archaic instruments.

CHORUS.

Let the merry cymbals sound,
  Gaily pipe Pandæan pleasure,
With a Daphnephoric bound
  Tread a gay but classic measure.
Every heart with hope is beating,
For at this exciting meeting
  Fickle Fortune will decide
  Who shall be our Bunthorne's bride!

Enter Dragoons, led by Colonel, Major and Duke. They are surprised at proceedings.

CHORUS OF DRAGOONS.

Now tell us, we pray you,
Why thus they array you—
Oh, poet, how say you—
  What is it you've done?

Duke. Of rite sacrificial,
By sentence judicial,
This seems the initial,
  Then why don't you run?

Col. They cannot have led you
To hang or behead you,
Nor may they *all* wed you,
  Unfortunate one!

CHORUS OF DRAGOONS.

Then tell us, we pray you,
Why thus they array you—
Oh, poet, how say you—
  What is it you've done?

RECIT.—*Bunthorne.*

Heart-broken at my Patience's barbarity,
  By the advice of my solicitor (*introducing his Solicitor*),
In aid—in aid of a deserving charity,

I've put **myself** up to be raffled for!

Maidens. By the advice of his solicitor
  He's put himself up to be raffled for!

Dragoons. Oh, horror! urged by his solicitor,
  He's put himself up to be raffled for!

Maidens. Oh, **heaven's** blessing on his solicitor!

Dragoons. A hideous **curse** on his solicitor!

(*The Solicitor, horrified at the Dragoons' curse, rushes off.*)

Col. Stay, we implore you,
  Before our hopes are blighted;
You see before you
  The men to whom you're plighted!

CHORUS OF DRAGOONS.

Stay, we implore you,
For we adore you;
To us you're plighted
To be united—

Stay, we implore you!

SOLO.—*Duke.*

Your maiden hearts, ah, do not steel
To pity's eloquent appeal,
Such conduct British soldiers feel.
(*Aside to Dragoons.*) Sigh, sigh, all sigh!
                [*They all sigh.*
To foeman's steel we rarely see
A British soldier bend the knee,
Yet, one and all, they kneel to ye—
(*Aside to Dragoons.*) Kneel, kneel, all kneel!
                [*They all kneel.*
Our soldiers very seldom cry,
And yet—I need not tell you why
A tear-drop dews each martial eye!
(*Aside to Dragoons.*) Weep, weep, all weep!
                [*They all weep.*

ENSEMBLE.

Our soldiers very seldom cry,
And yet { they } { we } need not tell you why—
A tear-drop dews each martial eye!
  Weep, weep, all weep!

Bunthorne (*who has been impatient during his appeal*).

Come, walk up, and purchase with avidity,
Overcome your diffidence and natural timidity,
Tickets for the raffle should be purchased with avidity.
  Put in half a guinea and a husband you may gain—
Such a judge of blue-and-white and other kinds of pottery—
From early Oriental down to modern terra-cotta-ry—
Put in half a guinea—you may draw him in a lottery—

Such an opportunity may not occur again.
Chorus. Such a judge of blue-and-white, &c.
(*Maidens crowd up to purchase tickets; during this Dragoons dance in single file round stage, to express their indifference.*)
Dragoons.
We've been thrown over, we're aware,
But we don't care—but we don't care!
There's fish in the sea, no doubt of it,
As good as ever came out of it,
And some day we shall get our share,
So we don't care—so we don't care!
(*During this the Girls have been buying tickets. At last Jane presents herself. Bunthorne looks at her with aversion.*)

RECIT.

Bun.
And are *you* going a ticket for to buy?
Jane (*surprised*).
Most certainly I am; why shouldn't I?
Bun. (*aside*).
Oh, Fortune, this is hard! (*Aloud.*) Blindfold your eyes;
Two minutes will decide who wins the prize!
(*Girls blindfold themselves.*)

CHORUS OF MAIDENS.

Oh, Fortune, to my aching heart be kind!
Like us, thou art blindfolded, but not blind!
Just raise your bandage, thus, that you may see, (*Each uncovers one eye.*)
And give the prize, and give the prize to me!
(*They cover their eyes again.*)
Bun. Come, Lady Jane, I pray you draw the first!
Jane (*joyfully*). He loves me best!
Bun. (*aside*). I want to know the worst!
(*Jane puts hand in bag to draw ticket. Patience enters and prevents her doing so.*)
Pa. Hold! Stay your hand!
All (*uncovering their eyes*). What means this interference?
Of this bold girl I pray you make a clearance!
Jane. Away with you, and to your milk-pails go!
Bun. (*suddenly*). She wants a ticket! Take a dozen!
Pa. No!

SOLO.—*Patience.*

If there be pardon in your breast
  For this poor penitent,
Who with remorseful thought opprest,
  Sincerely doth repent,
If you, with one so lowly, still
  Desire to be allied,
Then you may take me, if you will,
  For I will be your bride!
      (*Kneels to Bunthorne.*)
All.   Oh, shameless one!
      Oh, bold-faced thing!
    Away you run
      Go, take you wing,
    You shameless one!
      You bold-faced thing!

Bun. How strong is love! For many and
  many a week
  She's loved me fondly and has feared
    to speak,
  But Nature, for restraint too mighty
    far,
  Has burst the bonds of Art—and here
    we are!
Pa. No, Mr. Bunthorne, no—you're wrong
    again;
  Permit me—I'll endeavour to explain!
      SONG.—*Patience.*
Pa. True love must single-hearted be—
Bun.   Exactly so!
Pa. From every selfish fancy free—
Bun.   Exactly so!
Pa. No idle thought of gain or joy
  A maiden's fancy should employ—
  True love must be without alloy.
All.   Exactly so—
Pa. Imposture to contempt must lead—
Col.   Exactly so—
Pa. Blind vanity's dissension's seed—
Maj.   Exactly so—
Pa. It follows, then, a maiden who
  Devotes herself to loving *you* (*indicating
  Is prompted by no selfish view—
      [*Bunthorne*)
All.   Exactly so!
Saph. Are you resolved to wed this shameless one?
  Ang. Is there no chance for any other?
  Bun. (*decisively*). None! (*Embraces Patience.*)

      [*Exit Patience and Bunthorne.*
(*Angela, Saphir, and Ella take Colonel, Duke, and Major down, while Girls gaze fondly at other Officers.*)

SEXTETTE.

I hear the soft note of the echoing voice
  Of an old, old love, long dead—
It whispers my sorrowing heart "rejoice"—
  For the last sad tear is shed—
The pain that is all but a pleasure will change
  For the pleasure that's all but pain,
And never, oh never, this heart will range
  From that old, old love again!
      (*Girls embrace Officers.*)
Chorus. Yes, the pain that is all, &c.
      (*Embrace.*)
Enter Patience and Bunthorne.
As the Dragoons and Girls are embracing, enter Grosvenor, reading. He takes no notice of them, but comes slowly down, still reading. The Girls are all strangely fascinated by him, and gradually withdraw from Dragoons.
Ang. But who is this, whose god-like grace
  Proclaims he comes of noble race?
  And who is this whose manly face
  Bears sorrow's interesting trace?
      ENSEMBLE.—*Tutti.*
  Yes, who is this, &c.
Gros. I am a broken-hearted troubadour,

Whose mind's æsthetic and whose tastes
       are pure!

Ang. Æsthetic! He is æsthetic!

Gros. Yes, yes—I am æsthetic!
      And poetic!

All the Ladies. Then, we love you!

(*The Girls leave Dragoons and group, kneeling, around Grosvenor. Fury of Bunthorne, who recognizes a rival.*)

Dragoons.   They love him! Horror!

Bun. and Pa. They love him! Horror!

Gros.   They love me! Horror! Horror!
      Horror!

ENSEMBLE.—*Tutti.*

Girls.

Oh, list while we love confess
That words imperfectly express,
Those shell-like ears, ah, do not close
To blighted love's distracting woes!

Patience.

List, Reginald, while I confess
A love that's all unselfishness;
That it's unselfish, goodness knows,
You won't dispute it, I suppose?

Grosvenor.

Again my cursed comeliness
Spreads hopeless anguish and distress!
Thine ears, oh Fortune, do not close
To my intolerable woes.

Bunthorne.

My jealousy I can't express,
Their love they openly confess;
His shell-like ears he does not close
To their recital of their woes.

Dragoons.   Now is not this ridiculous, &c.

END OF ACT I.

▼▼▼▼▼▼▼

ACT II.

SCENE.—*A glade. Jane is discovered leaning on a violoncello, upon which she presently accompanies herself. Chorus of Maidens are heard singing in the distance.*

Jane. The fickle crew have deserted Reginald and sworn allegiance to his rival, and all, forsooth, because he has glanced with passing favour on a puling milkmaid! Fools! of that fancy he will soon weary—and then I, who alone am faithful to him, shall reap my reward. But do not dally too long, Reginald, for my charms are ripe, Reginald, and already they are decaying. Better secure me ere I have gone too far!

RECIT.—*Jane.*

Sad is that woman's lot who, year by year,
Sees, one by one, her beauties disappear,
When Time, grown weary of her heart-drawn
    sighs,
Impatiently begins to "dim her eyes"!
Compelled, at last, in life's uncertain gloamings,
To wreathe her wrinkled brow with well-saved
    "combings,"
Reduced, with rouge, lip-salve, and pearly
    grey,
To "make up" for lost time as best she may!

SONG.—*Jane.*

Silvered is the raven hair,
  Spreading is the parting straight,
Mottled the complexion fair,
  Halting is the youthful gait,
Hollow is the laughter free,
  Spectacled the limpid eye—
Little will be left of me
  In the coming by and bye!

Fading is the taper waist,
  Shapeless grows the shapely limb,
And although severely laced,
  Spreading is the figure trim!
Stouter than I used to be,
  Still more corpulent grow I—
There will be too much of me
  In the coming by and bye!

[*Exit Jane.*

Enter Grosvenor, followed by Maidens, two and two, each playing on an archaic instrument, as in Act I. He is reading abstractedly, as Bunthorne did in Act I, and pays no attention to them.

CHORUS OF MAIDENS.

Turn, oh turn in this direction,
  Shed, oh shed a gentle smile,
With a glance of sad perfection
  Our poor fainting hearts beguile!
On such eyes as maidens cherish
  Let thy fond adorers gaze,
Or incontinently perish
  In their all-consuming rays!

(*He sits—they group around him.*)

Gros. (*aside*). The old, old tale. How rapturously these maidens love me, and how hopelessly! Oh, Patience, Patience, with the love of thee in my heart, what have I for these poor mad maidens but an unvalued pity? Alas, they will die of hopeless love for me, as I shall die of hopeless love for thee!

Ang. Sir, will it please you read to us?

Gros. (*sighing*). Yes, child, if you will. What shall I read?

Ang. One of your own poems.

Gros. One of my own poems? Better not,

my child. *They* will not cure thee of thy love.
(*All sigh.*)

Ella. Mr. Bunthorne used to read us a poem of his own every day.

Saph. And, to do him justice, he read them extremely well.

Gros. Oh, did he so? Well, who am I that should take upon myself to withhold my gifts from you? What am I but a trustee? Here is a decalet—a pure and simple thing, a very daisy—a babe might understand it. To appreciate it, it is not necessary to think of anything at all.

Ang. Let us think of nothing at all.

GROSVENOR *recites.*

Gentle Jane was as good as gold,
She always did as she was told;
She never spoke when her mouth was full,
Or caught bluebottles their legs to pull,
Or spilt plum jam on her nice new frock,
Or put white mice in the eight-day clock,
Or vivisected her last new doll,
Or fostered a passion for alcohol.
And when she grew up she was given in marriage
To a first-class earl who keeps his carriage!

Gros. I believe I am right in saying that there is not one word in that decalet which is calculated to bring the blush of shame to the cheek of modesty.

Ang. Not one; it is purity itself.

Gros. Here's another.

Teasing Tom was a very bad boy,
A great big squirt was his favourite toy,
He put live shrimps in his father's boots,
And sewed up sleeves of his Sunday suits;
He punched his poor little sisters' heads,
And cayenne-peppered their four-post beds;
He plastered their hair with cobbler's wax,
And dropped hot halfpennies down their backs.
The consequence was he was lost totally,
And married a girl in the *corps de bally!*

Ang. Marked you how grandly—how relentlessly—the damning catalogue of crime strode on, till Retribution, like a poisèd hawk, came swooping down upon the Wrong-Doer? Oh, it was terrible!

Ella. Oh, sir, you are indeed a true poet, for you touch our hearts, and they go out to you!

Gros. (*aside*). This is simply cloying. (*Aloud.*) Ladies, I am sorry to appear ungallant, but this is Saturday, and you have been following me about ever since Monday. I should like the usual half-holiday. I shall take it as a personal favour if you will kindly allow me to close early to-day.

Saph. Oh, sir, do not send us from you!

Gros. Poor, poor girls! It is best to speak plainly. I know that I am loved by you, but I never can love you in return, for my heart is fixed elsewhere! Remember the fable of the Magnet and the Churn.

Ang. (*wildly*). But we don't know the fable of the Magnet and the Churn!

Gros. Don't you? Then I will sing it to you.

SONG.—*Grosvenor.*

A magnet hung in a hardware shop,
And all around was a loving crop
Of scissors and needles, nails and knives,
Offering love for all their lives;
But for iron the magnet felt no whim,
Though he charmed iron, it charmed not him,
From needles and nails and knives he'd turn,
For he'd set his love on a Silver Churn!

All. A Silver Churn?

Gros. A Silver Churn!
His most æsthetic,
Very magnetic
Fancy took this turn—
"If I can wheedle
A knife or a needle,
Why not a Silver Churn?"

Chorus. His most æsthetic, &c.

Gros. And Iron and Steel expressed surprise,
The needles opened their well-drilled eyes,
The penknives felt "shut up," no doubt,
The scissors declared themselves "cut out,"
The kettles they boiled with rage, 'tis said,
While every nail went off its head,
And hither and thither began to roam,
Till a hammer came up—and drove them home.

All. It drove them home?

Gros. It drove them home!

While this magnetic,
Peripatetic
Lover he lived to learn,
By no endeavour
Can magnet ever
Attract a Silver Churn!

All. While this magnetic, &c.

[*They go off in low spirits, gazing back at him from time to time.*

Gros. At last they are gone! What is this mysterious fascination that I seem to exercise over all I come across? A curse on my fatal beauty, for I am sick of conquests!

Patience appears.

Pa. Archibald!

Gros. (*turns and sees her*). Patience!

Pa. I have escaped with difficulty from my Reginald. I wanted to see you so much that

I might ask you if you still love me as fondly as ever?

Gros. Love you? If the devotion of a lifetime—(*Seizes her hand*).

Pa. (*indignantly*). Hold! Unhand me, or I scream! (*He releases her.*) If you are a gentleman, pray remember that I am another's! (*Very tenderly.*) But you *do* love me, don't you?

Gros. Madly, hopelessly, despairingly!

Pa. That's right! I never can be yours; but that's right!

Gros. And you love this Bunthorne?

Pa. With a heart-whole ecstasy that withers, and scorches, and burns, and stings! (*Sadly.*) It is my duty.

Gros. Admirable girl! But you are not happy with him?

Pa. Happy? I am miserable beyond description!

Gros. That's right! I never can be yours; but that's right!

Pa. But go now. I see dear Reginald approaching. Farewell, dear Archibald, I cannot tell you how happy it has made me to know that you still love me.

Gros. Ah, if I only dared—(*Advances towards her*).

Pa. Sir! this language to one who is promised to another! (*Tenderly.*) Oh, Archibald, think of me sometimes, for my heart is breaking! He is so unkind to me, and you would be so loving!

Gros. Loving! (*Advances towards her.*)

Pa. Advance one step, and as I am a good and pure woman, I scream! (*Tenderly.*) Farewell, Archibald! (*Sternly.*) Stop there! (*Tenderly.*) Think of me sometimes! (*Angrily.*) Advance at your peril! Once more, adieu!

[*Grosvenor sighs, gazes sorrowfully at her, sighs deeply, and exit. She bursts into tears. Enter Bunthorne, followed by Jane. He is moody and preoccupied.*

Jane sings

In a doleful train,
    One and one I walk all day;
For I love in vain—
    None so sorrowful as they,
    Who can only sigh and say,
        Woe is me, alackaday!

Bun. (*seeing Patience*). Crying, eh? What are you crying about?

Pa. I've only been thinking how dearly I love you!

Bun. Love me! Bah!

Jane. Love him! Bah!

Bun. (*to Jane*). Don't you interfere.

Jane. He always crushes me!

Pa. (*going to him*). What is the matter, dear Reginald? If you have any sorrow, tell it to me, that I may share it with you. (*Sighing*). It is my duty!

Bun. (*snappishly*). Whom were you talking with just now?

Pa. With dear Archibald.

Bun. (*furiously*). With dear Archibald! Upon my honour, this is too much!

Jane. A great deal too much!

Bun. (*angrily to Jane*). Do be quiet!

Jane. Crushed again!

Pa. I think he is the noblest, purest, and most perfect being I have ever met. But I don't love him. It is true that he is devotedly attached to me, but indeed I don't love *him*. Whenever he grows affectionate, I scream. It is my duty! (*Sighing.*)

Bun. I dare say.

Jane. So do I! *I* dare say!

Pa. Why, how could I love him and love you too? You can't love two people at once!

Bun. Oh, can't you though!

Pa. No, you can't; I only wish you could.

Bun. I don't believe you know what love is!

Pa. (*sighing*). Yes, I do. There was a happy time when I didn't, but a bitter experience has taught me.

[*Exeunt Bunthorne and Jane.*

BALLAD.—*Patience.*

Love is a plaintive song,
    Sung by a suffering maid,
Telling a tale of wrong,
    Telling of hope betrayed;
Tuned to each changing note,
    Sorry when *he* is sad,
Blind to his every mote,
    Merry when he is glad!
        Love that no wrong can cure,
            Love that is always new,
        That is the love that's pure,
            That is the love that's true!
Rendering good for ill,
    Smiling at every frown,
Yielding your own self-will,
    Laughing your tear-drops down,
Never a selfish whim,
    Trouble, or pain to stir;
Everything for him,
    Nothing at all for her!
        Love that will aye endure,
            Though the rewards be few,
        That is the love that's pure,
            That is the love that's true!

[*At the end of ballad exit Patience, weeping. Enter Bunthorne and Jane.*

Bun. Everything has gone wrong with me since that smug-faced idiot came here. Before that I was admired—I may say, loved.

Jane. Too mild—adored!

Bun. Do let a poet soliloquize! The damozels used to follow me wherever I went; now they all follow him!

Jane. Not all! *I* am still faithful to you.

Bun. Yes, and a pretty damozel *you* are!

Jane. No, not pretty. Massive. Cheer up! I will never leave you, I swear it!

Bun. Oh, thank you! I know what it is; it's his confounded mildness. They find me too highly spiced, if you please! And no doubt I *am* highly spiced.

Jane. Not for my taste!

Bun. (*savagely*). No, but I am for theirs. But I will show the world I can be as mild as he. If they want insipidity, they shall have it. I'll meet this fellow on his own ground and beat him on it.

Jane. You shall. And I will help you.

Bun. You will? Jane, there's a good deal of good in you, after all!

DUET.—*Bunthorne and Jane.*

Jane. So go to him and say to him, with compliment ironical—

Bun.　　Sing "Hey to you—
　　　　　Good day to you"—
　　And that's what I shall say!

Jane. "Your style is much too sanctified—
　　　　your cut is too canonical"—

Bun.　　Sing "Bah to you—
　　　　　Ha! ha! to you"—
　　And that's what I shall say!

Jane. "I was the beau ideal of the morbid
　　　　young æsthetical—
　　　　To doubt my inspiration was regarded as
　　　　heretical—
　　　　Until you cut me out with your placidity
　　　　emetical."—

Bun.　　Sing "Booh to you—
　　　　　Pooh, pooh to you"—
　　And that's what I shall say!

Both. Sing "Hey to you, good day to you"—
　　Sing "Bah to you, ha! ha! to you"—
　　Sing "Booh to you, pooh, pooh to
　　you"—

　　And that's what $\begin{Bmatrix} \text{you} \\ \text{I} \end{Bmatrix}$ shall say!

Bun. I'll tell him that unless he will consent to be more jocular—

Jane.　　Sing "Booh to you—
　　　　　Pooh, pooh to you"—
　　And that's what you should say!

Bun. To cut his curly hair and stick an eyeglass in his ocular—

Jane.　　Sing "Bah to you—
　　　　　Ha! ha! to you"—
　　And that's what you should say!

Bun. To stuff his conversation full of quibble and of quiddity—
　　　　To dine on chops and roly-poly pudding
　　　　with avidity—
　　　　He'd better clear away with all convenient rapidity.

Jane.　　Sing "Hey to you—
　　　　　Good day to you"—
　　And that's what you should say!

Both. Sing "Booh to you—pooh, pooh to
　　you"—
　　Sing "Bah to you—ha! ha! to you"—

Sing "Hey to you—good day to you"—
And that's what $\begin{Bmatrix} \text{I} \\ \text{you} \end{Bmatrix}$ shall say!

[*Exeunt Jane and Bunthorne together.*
Enter Duke, Colonel, and Major. They have abandoned their uniforms, and are dressed and made up in imitation of Æsthetics. They have long hair, and other outward signs of attachment to the brotherhood. As they sing they walk in stiff, constrained, and angular attitudes—a grotesque exaggeration of the attitudes adopted by Bunthorne and the young ladies in Act I.

TRIO.—*Duke, Colonel and Major.*

It's clear that mediæval art alone retains its
　　zest,
To charm and please its devotees we've done
　　our little best.
We're not quite sure if all we do has the Early
　　English ring;
But, as far as we can judge, it's something like
　　this sort of thing:
　　You hold yourself like this (*attitude*),
　　You hold yourself like that (*attitude*),
By hook and crook you try to look both angular and flat (*attitude*).
　　We venture to expect
　　That what we recollect,
Though but a part of true High Art, will have
　　its due effect.

If this is not exactly right, we hope you won't
　　upbraid;
You can't get high Æsthetic tastes, like trousers, ready made.
True views on Mediævalism Time alone will
　　bring,
But, as far as we can judge, it's something like
　　this sort of thing:
　　You hold yourself like this (*attitude*),
　　You hold yourself like that (*attitude*),
By hook and crook you try to look both angular and flat (*attitude*).
　　To cultivate the trim
　　Rigidity of limb,
You ought to get a Marionette, and form your
　　style on him (*attitude*).

Col. (*attitude*). Yes, it's quite clear that our only chance of making a lasting impression on these young ladies is to become as æsthetic as they are.

Maj. (*attitude*). No doubt. The only question is how far we've succeeded in doing so. I don't know why, but I've an idea that this is not quite right.

Duke (*attitude*). *I* don't like it. I never did. I don't see what it means. I do it, but I don't like it.

Col. My good friend, the question is not whether we like it, but whether they do. They understand these things—we don't. Now I shouldn't be surprised if this is effective enough —at a distance.

Maj. I can't help thinking we're a little stiff at it. It would be extremely awkward if we were to be "struck" so!

Col. I don't think we shall be struck so. Perhaps we're a little awkward at first—but everything must have a beginning. Oh, here they come! 'Tntion!

They strike fresh attitudes, as Angela and Saphir enter.

Ang. (*seeing them*). Oh, Saphir—see—see! The immortal fire has descended on them, and they are of the Inner Brotherhood—perceptively intense and consummately utter. (*The Officers have some difficulty in maintaining their constrained attitudes.*)

Saph. (*in admiration*). How Botticellian! How Fra Angelican! Oh, Art, we thank thee for this boon!

Col. (*apologetically*). I'm afraid we're not quite right.

Ang. Not supremely, perhaps, but oh, so all-but! (*To Saphir.*) Oh, Saphir, are they not quite too all-but?

Saphir. They are indeed jolly utter!

Maj. (*in agony*). I wonder what the Inner Brotherhood usually recommend for cramp?

Col. Ladies, we will not deceive you. We are doing this at some personal inconvenience with a view of expressing the extremity of our devotion to you. We trust that it is not without its effect.

Ang. We will not deny that we are much moved by this proof of your attachment.

Saph. Yes, your conversion to the principles of Æsthetic Art in its highest development has touched us deeply.

Ang. And if Mr. Grosvenor should remain obdurate—

Saph. Which we have every reason to believe he will—

Maj. (*aside, in agony*). I wish they'd make haste.

Ang. We are not prepared to say that our yearning hearts will not go out to you.

Col. (*as giving a word of command*). By sections of threes—Rapture! (*All strike a fresh attitude, expressive of æsthetic rapture.*)

Saph. Oh, its' extremely good—for beginners it's admirable.

Maj. The only question is, who will take who?

Col. Oh, the Duke chooses first, as a matter of course.

Duke. Oh, I couldn't think of it—you are really too good!

Col. Nothing of the kind. You are a great matrimonial fish, and it's only fair that each of these ladies should have a chance of hooking you. It's perfectly simple. Observe, suppose you choose Angela, I take Saphir, Major takes nobody. Suppose you choose Saphir, Major takes Angela, I take nobody. Suppose you choose neither, I take Angela, Major takes Saphir. Clear as day!

QUINTET.

Duke, Colonel, Major, Angela, and Saphir.

DUKE (*taking Saphir*).

If Saphir I choose to marry,
    I shall be fixed up for life;
Then the Colonel need not tarry,
    Angela can be his wife.

(*Duke dances with Saphir, Colonel with Angela, Major dances alone.*)

MAJOR (*dancing*).

In that case unprecedented,
    Single I shall live and die—
I shall have to be contented
    With their heartfelt sympathy!

ALL (*dancing as before*).

He will have to be contented
    With our heartfelt sympathy!

DUKE (*taking Angela.*)

If on Angy I determine,
    At my wedding she'll appear
Decked in diamond and ermine,
    Major then can take Saphir!

(*Duke dances with Angela, Major with Saphir, Colonel dances alone.*)

COLONEL (*dancing*).

In that case unprecedented,
    Single I shall live and die—
I shall have to be contented
    With their heartfelt sympathy!

ALL (*dancing as before*).

He will have to be contented
    With our heartfelt sympathy!

DUKE (*taking both Angela and Saphir*).

After some debate internal,
    If on neither I decide,
Saphir then can take the Colonel,
        (*Handing Saphir to Colonel.*)
Angy be the Major's bride!
        (*Handing Angela to Major.*)

(*Colonel dances with Saphir, Major with Angela, Duke dances alone.*)

DUKE (*dancing*).

In that case unprecedented,
    Single I must live and die—
I shall have to be contented
    With their heartfelt sympathy!

ALL (*dancing as before*).

He will have to be contented
    With our heartfelt sympathy.

[*At the end, Duke, Colonel, and Major, and two girls dance off arm in arm.*

Enter Grosvenor.

Gros. It is very pleasant to be alone. It is pleasant to be able to gaze at leisure upon those features which all others may gaze upon at their good will! (*Looking at his reflection in hand mirror*). Ah, I am a very Narcissus!

Enter Bunthorne, moodily.

Bun. It's no use; I can't live without admiration. Since Grosvenor came here, insipidity has been at a premium. Ah, he is there!

Gros. Ah, Bunthorne! come here—look! Very graceful, isn't it?

Bun. (*taking hand mirror.*) Allow me; I haven't seen it. Yes, it is graceful.

Gros. (*re-taking hand mirror*). Oh, good gracious! not that—this—

Bun. You don't mean that! Bah! I am in no mood for trifling.

Gros. And what is amiss?

Bun. Ever since you came here, you have entirely monopolised the attentions of the young ladies. I don't like it, sir!

Gros. My dear sir, how can I help it? They are the plague of my life. My dear Mr. Bunthorne, with your personal disadvantages, you can have no idea of the inconvenience of being madly loved, at first sight, by every woman you meet.

Bun. Sir, until you came here I was adored!

Gros. Exactly—until I came here. That's my grievance. I cut everybody out! I assure you, if you could only suggest some means whereby, consistently with my duty to society, I could escape these inconvenient attentions, you would earn my everlasing gratitude.

Bun. I will do so at once. However popular it may be with the world at large, your personal appearance is highly objectionable to *me*.

Gros. It is? (*Shaking his hand*). Oh, thank you! thank you! How can I express my gratitude?

Bun. By making a complete change at once. Your conversation must henceforth be perfectly matter-of-fact. You must cut your hair, and have a back parting. In appearance and costume you must be absolutely commonplace.

Gros. (*decidedly*). No. Pardon me, that's impossible.

Bun. Take care! When I am thwarted I am very terrible.

Gros. I can't help that. I am a man with a mission. And that mission must be fulfilled.

Bun. I don't think you quite appreciate the consequences of thwarting me.

Gros. I don't care what they are.

Bun. Suppose—I won't go so far as to say that I will do it—but suppose for one moment I were to curse you? (*Grosvenor quails.*) Ah! Very well. Take care.

Gros. But surely you would never do that? (*In great alarm.*)

Bun. I don't know. It would be an extreme measure, no doubt. Still—

Gros. (*wildly*). But you would not do it— I am sure you would not. (*Throwing himself at Bunthorne's knees, and clinging to him.*) Oh, reflect, reflect! You had a mother once.

Bun. Never!

Gros. Then you had an aunt! (*Bunthorne, affected.*) Ah! I see you had! By the memory of that aunt, I implore you to pause ere you resort to this last fearful expedient. Oh, Mr. Bunthorne, reflect, reflect! (*Weeping.*)

Bun. (*aside, after a struggle with himself.* I must not allow myself to be unmanned! (*Aloud.*) It is useless. Consent at once, or may a nephew's curse—

Gros. Hold! Are you absolutely resolved?

Bun. Absolutely.

Gros. Will nothing shake you?

Bun. Nothing. I am adamant.

Gros. Very good. (*Rising.*) Then I yield.

Bun. Ha! You swear it?

Gros. I do, cheerfully. I have long wished for a reasonable pretext for such a change as you suggest. It has come at last. I do it on compulsion!

Bun. Victory! I triumph!

DUET.—*Bunthorne and Grosvenor.*

Bun.   When I go out of door
    Of damozels a score
      (All sighing and burning,
      And clinging and yearning)
  Will follow me as before.
  I shall, with cultured taste,
  Distinguish gems from paste,
    And "High diddle diddle"
    Will rank as an idyll,
  If I pronounce it chaste!

Both.   A most intense young man,
      A soulful-eyed young man,
    An ultra-poetical, super-æsthetical,
    Out-of-the-way young man!

Gros. Conceive me, if you can,
  An every-day young man:
    A commonplace type,
    With a stick and a pipe,
  And a half-bred black-and-tan;
    Who thinks suburban "hops"
    More fun than "Monday Pops,"
  Who's fond of his dinner,
  And doesn't get thinner
    On bottled beer and chops.

Both.   A commonplace young man,
    A matter-of-fact young man,
    A steady and stolid-y, jolly Bank-holiday
    Every-day young man!

Bun.   A Japanese young man,
    A blue-and-white young man,
  Francesca di Rimini, miminy, piminy,
    Je-ne-sais quoi young man!

Gros.   A Chancery Lane young man,
    A Somerset House young man,
  A very delectable, highly respectable,
    Threepenny bus young man!

Bun.   A pallid and thin young man,
    A haggard and lank young man,

A greenery-yallery, Grosvenor Gallery,
    Foot-in-the-grave young man!

Gros.   A Sewell & Cross young man,
    A Howell & James young man,
    A pushing young particle—what's the
        next article—
    Waterloo House young man!

Ensemble.

Bun.   Conceive me, if you can,
    A crotchety, cracked young man,
    An ultra-poetical, super-æsthetical,
    Out-of-the-way young man!

Gros.   Conceive me, if you can,
    A matter-of-fact young man,
    An alphabetical, arithmetical,
    Every-day young man!

[*At the end, Grosvenor dances off. Bunthorne remains.*

Bun. It is all right. I have committed my last act of ill-nature, and henceforth I'm a changed character. (*Dances about stage humming refrain of last air.*)

Enter Patience. She gazes in astonishment at him.

Pa. Reginald! Dancing! And—what in the world is the matter with you?

Bun. Patience, I'm a changed man. Hitherto I've been gloomy, moody, fitful—uncertain in temper and selfish in disposition—

Pa. You have, indeed! (*Sighing.*)

Bun. All that is changed. I have reformed. I have modelled myself upon Mr. Grosvenor. Henceforth I am mildly cheerful. My conversation will blend amusement with instruction. I shall still be æsthetic; but my æstheticism will be the most pastoral kind.

Pa. Oh, Reginald! Is all this true?

Bun. Quite true. Observe how amiable I am. (*Assuming a fixed smile.*)

Pa. But, Reginald, how long will this last?

Bun. With occasional intervals for rest and refreshment, as long as I do.

Pa. Oh, Reginald, I'm so happy! Oh, dear, dear Reginald, I cannot express the joy I feel at this change. It will no longer be a duty to love you, but a pleasure—a rapture—an ecstasy!

Bun. My darling! (*Embracing her.*)

Pa. But—oh, horror! (*Recoiling from him.*)

Bun. What's the matter?

Pa. Is it quite certain that you have absolutely reformed—that you are henceforth a perfect being—utterly free from defect of any kind?

Bun. It is quite certain. I have sworn it.

Pa. Then I never can be yours!

Bun. Why not?

Pa. Love, to be pure, must be absolutely unselfish, and there can be nothing unselfish in loving so perfect a being as you have now become!

Bun. But stop a bit! I don't want to change—I'll relapse—I'll be as I was—interrupted!

Enter Grosvenor, followed by all the young ladies, who are followed by chorus of Dragoons. He has had his hair cut, and is dressed in an ordinary suit of dittos and a pot hat. They all dance cheerfully round the stage in marked contrast to their former languor.

Chorus.—*Grosvenor and Girls.*

Gros.
    I'm a Waterloo House young man,
    A Sewell & Cross young man,
    A steady and stolid-y, jolly Bank-holiday,
    Every-day young man!

Girls.
    We're Swears & Wells young girls,
    We're Madame Louise young girls,
    We're prettily pattering, cheerily chattering,
    Every-day young girls!

Bun. Angela—Ella—Saphir—what—what does this mean?

Ang. It means that Archibald the All-Right cannot be all-wrong; and if the All-Right chooses to discard æstheticism, it proves that æstheticism ought to be discarded.

Pa. Oh, Archibald! Archibald! I'm shocked—surprised—horrified!

Gros. I can't help it. I'm not a free agent. I do it on compulsion.

Pa. This is terrible. Go! I shall never set eyes on you again. But—oh, joy!

Gros. What is the matter?

Pa. Is it quite, quite certain that you will always be a commonplace young man?

Gros. Always—I've sworn it.

Pa. Why, then, there's nothing to prevent my loving you with all the fervour at my command!

Gros. Why, that's true.

Pa. My Archibald!

Gros. My Patience! (*They embrace.*)

Bun. Crushed again!

Enter Jane.

Jane (*who is still æsthetic*). Cheer up! I am still here. I have never left you, and I never will!

Bun. Thank you, Jane. After all, there is no denying it, you're a fine figure of a woman!

Jane. My Reginald!

Bun. My Jane!

Flourish. Enter Colonel, Major, and Duke.

Col. Ladies, the Duke has at length determined to select a bride! (*General excitement.*)

Duke. I have a great gift to bestow. Approach, such of you as are truly lovely. (*All come forward, bashfully, except Jane and Patience.*) In personal appearance you have all that is necessary to make a woman happy. In common fairness, I think I ought to choose the only one among you who has the misfortune to be distinctly plain. (*Girls retire disappointed.*) Jane!

Jane (leaving Bunthorne's arms.) Duke!
(*Jane and Duke embrace. Bunthorne is utterly disgusted.*)

Bun. Crushed again!

FINALE.

Duke.   After much debate internal,
    I on Lady Jane decide,
  Saphir now may take the Colonel,
    Angy be the Major's bride!

(*Saphir pairs off with Colonel, Angela with Major, Ella with Solicitor.*)

Bun.   In that case unprecedented,
    Single I must live and die—
  I shall have to be contented
    With a tulip or li*l*y!

(*Takes a lily from button-hole and gazes affectionately at it.*)

All.   He will have to be contented
    With a tulip or li*l*y!

Greatly pleased with one another,
    To get married we decide,
Each of us will wed the other,
    Nobody be Bunthorne's Bride!

DANCE.

CURTAIN.

Authentic Libretto
of the new
GILBERT AND SULLIVAN LIBRARY

TRIAL BY JURY

BY

Sir W. S. GILBERT

AND

Sir ARTHUR S. SULLIVAN

_____

The Bass Publishers

TRIAL BY JURY

𝕯𝖗𝖆𝖒𝖆𝖙𝖎𝖘 𝕻𝖊𝖗𝖘𝖔𝖓𝖆𝖊

THE LEARNED JUDGE

THE PLAINTIFF

THE DEFENDANT

COUNSEL FOR THE
PLAINTIFF

USHER

FOREMAN OF THE
JURY

ASSOCIATE

FIRST BRIDESMAID

SCENE.—*A Court of Justice.*

*Barristers, Attorneys, Jurymen and Public
discovered.*

TRIAL BY JURY

▼▼▼▼

SCENE.—*A Court of Justice.*
Barristers, Attorneys, Jurymen and Public discovered.

CHORUS.
Hark, the hour of ten is sounding;
Hearts with anxious fears are bounding,
Hall of Justice crowds surrounding,
 Breathing hope and fear—
For to-day in this arena,
Summoned by a stern subpœna,
Edwin, sued by Angelina,
 Shortly will appear.

Enter Usher.
SOLO.—*Usher.*
Now, Jurymen, hear my advice—
All kinds of vulgar prejudice
 I pray you set aside:
With stern judicial frame of mind,
From bias free of every kind,
 This trial must be tried.

CHORUS.
From bias free of every kind,
 This trial must be tried.
(*During Chorus, Usher sings fortissimo,
 "Silence in Court!"*)
Usher.
Oh, listen to the plaintiff's case:
Observe the features of her face—
 The broken-hearted bride.
Condole with her distress of mind:
From bias free of every kind,
 This trial must be tried!

CHORUS.
 From bias free, &c.
Usher.
And when amid the plaintiff's shrieks,
The ruffianly defendant speaks—
 Upon the other side;
What *he* may say you needn't mind—
From bias free of every kind,
 This trial must be tried!

CHORUS.
From bias free, &c.
Enter Defendant.
RECIT.—*Defendant.*
Is this the Court of the Exchequer?
All.
 It is!
Defendant (*aside*).
 Be firm, be firm my pecker,
Your evil star's in the ascendant!

All.
 Who are you?
Defendant.
 I'm the Defendant!
Chorus of Jurymen (*shaking their fists*).
 Monster, dread our damages.
 We're the jury,
 Dread our fury.
Defendant.
Hear me, hear me, if you please,
 These are very strange proceedings—
For permit me to remark
 On the merits of my pleadings
You're at present in the dark.
(*Defendant beckons to Jurymen—they leave
the box and gather round him as they sing
 the following*):—
That's a very true remark—
On the merits of his pleadings
We're entirely in the dark!
Ha! ha!—ho! ho!

SONG—*Defendant.*
When first my old, old love I knew,
 My bosom welled with joy;
My riches at her feet I threw—
 I was a love-sick boy!
No terms seemed too extravagant
 Upon her to employ—
I used to mope, and sigh, and pant,
 Just like a love-sick boy!
 Tink-a-Tank—Tink-a-Tank.
But joy incessant palls the sense;
 And love, unchanged will cloy,
And she became a bore intense
 Unto her love-sick boy!
With fitful glimmer burnt my flame,
 And I grew cold an coy,
At last, one morning, I became
 Another's love-sick boy.
 Tink-a-Tank—Tink-a-Tank.
Chorus of Jurymen (*advancing stealthily*).
 Oh, I was like that when a lad!
 A shocking young scamp of a rover,
I behaved like a regular cad;
 But that sort of thing is all over.
I am now a respectable chap
 And shine with a virtue resplendent,
And, therefore, I haven't a rap
 Of sympathy with the defendant!
 He shall treat us with awe,
 If there isn't a flaw,
Singing so merrily—Trial-la-law!
Trial-la-law—Trial-la-law!

205

Singing so merrily—Trial-la-law!
(They enter the jury-box.)

RECIT.—*Usher (on Bench).*
Silence in Court, and all attention lend.
Behold your Judge! In due submission bend!
Enter Judge on Bench.

CHORUS.
All hail great Judge!
　　To your bright rays,
　　We never grudge
　　Ecstatic praise.
　　　　　All hail!
May each decree
　　As statute rank,
　　And never be
　　Reversed in Banc
　　　　　All hail!

RECIT.—*Judge.*
For these kind words accept my thanks, I pray.
A Breach of Promise we've to try to-day.
But firstly, if the time you'll not begrudge,
I'll tell you how I came to be a Judge.
All.
He'll tell us how he came to be a Judge!
Judge.
　　Let me speak!
All.
　　Let him speak, &c.

SONG—*Judge.*
When I, good friends, was called to the bar,
　　I'd an appetite fresh and hearty,
But I was, as many young barrister are,
　　An impecunious party.
I'd a swallow-tail coat of a beautiful blue—
　　A brief which I bought of a booby—
A couple of shirts and a collar or two,
　　And a ring that looked like a ruby!

CHORUS.
　　A couple of shirts, &c.
Judge.
In Westminster Hall I danced a dance,
　　Like a semi-despondent fury:
For I thought I never should hit on a chance
　　Of addressing a British Jury—
But I soon got tired of third class journeys,
　　And dinners of bread and water;
So I fell in love with a rich attorney's
　　Elderly, ugly daughter.

CHORUS.
　　So he fell in love, &c.
Judge.
The rich attorney, he jumped with joy,
　　And replied to my fond professions:
"You shall reap the reward of your pluck,
　　my boy,
At the Bailey and Middlesex Sessions.
You'll soon get used to her looks," said he,
　　"And a very nice girl you'll find her!
She may very well pass for forty-three
　　In the dusk, with a light behind her!"

CHORUS.
　　She may very well, &c.
Judge.
The rich attorney was good as his word;
　　The briefs came trooping gaily,
And every day my voice was heard
　　At the Sessions or Ancient Bailey.
All thieves who could my fees afford
　　Relied on my orations,
And many a burglar I've restored
　　To his friends and his relations.

CHORUS.
　　And many a burglar, &c.
Judge.
At length I became as rich as the Gurneys—
　　An incubus then I thought her,
So I threw over that rich attorney's
　　Elderly, ugly daughter.
The rich attorney my character high
　　Tried vainly to disparage—
And now, if you please, I'm ready to try
　　This Breach of Promise of Marriage!

CHORUS.
　　And now, if you please, &c.
Judge.
For now I'm a Judge!
All.
　　And a good Judge too!
Judge.
Yes, now I'm a Judge!
All.
　　And a good Judge too!
Judge.
Though all my law be fudge,
Yet I'll never, never budge,
But I'll live and die a Judge!
All.
　　And a good Judge too!
Judge (pianissimo).
It was managed by a job—
All.
　　And a good job too!
Judge.
It was managed by a job!
All.
　　And a good job too!
Judge.
It is patent to the mob,
That my being made a nob,
Was effected by a job.
All.
　　And a good job too!
*Enter Counsel for Plaintiff. He takes his
place in front row of Counsels' seats.*
RECIT.—*Counsel.*
Swear thou the Jury!
Usher.
Kneel, Jurymen, oh, kneel!
*(All the Jury kneel in the Jury-box, and so
are hidden from audience.)*
Usher.
Oh, will you swear by yonder skies,

Whatever question may arise,
'Twixt rich and poor—'twixt low and high,
That you will well and truly try.
*Jury (raising their hands, which alone are
visible).*

To all of this we make reply,
By the dull slate of yonder sky:
That we will well and truly try.
(All rise with the last note.)

RECIT.—*Counsel.*
Where is the Plaintiff?
Let her now be brought.

RECIT.—*Usher.*
Oh Angelina! Come thou into Court!
Angelina! Angelina!
Enter the Bridesmaids.
Chorus of Bridesmaids.
Comes the broken flower—
Comes the cheated maid—
Though the tempest lower, ·
Rain and cloud will fade!
Take, oh maid, these posies:
Though thy beauty rare
Shame the blushing roses—
They are passing fair!
Wear the flowers till they fade;
Happy by thy life, oh maid!
*(The Judge, having taken a great fancy to
1st Bridesmaid, sends her a note by Usher,
which she reads, kisses repturously, and
places in her bosom.)*
Enter Plaintiff.

SOLO—*Plaintiff.*
O'er the season vernal,
Time may cast a shade;
Sunshine, if eternal,
Makes the roses fade;
Time may do his duty;
Let the thief alone—
Winter hath a beauty,
That is all his own.
Fairest days are sun and shade.
I am no unhappy maid!
*(The Judge, having by this time trans-
ferred his admiration to Plaintiff, directs
the Usher to take the note from 1st
Bridesmaid and hand it to Plaintiff, who
reads it, kisses it rapturously, and places
it in her bosom.)*
Chorus of Bridesmaids.
Wear the flowers, &c.
Judge.
Oh never, never, never, since I joined the
human race,
Saw I so exquisitely fair a face.
The Jury (shaking their forefingers at him).
Ah, sly dog! Ah, sly dog!
Judge (to Jury).
How say you is she not designed for capture?
Foreman (after consulting with the Jury).
We've but one word, my lord, and that is—
Rapture!

Plaintiff (curtseying).
Your kindness, gentlemen, quite overpowers!
The Jury.
We love you fondly, and would make you ours!
*The Bridesmaids (shaking their forefingers
at Jury).*
Ah, sly dogs! Ah, sly dogs!
The Jury (shaking their fists at Defendant).
Monster! Monster! Dread our fury!
There's the Judge and we're the Jury!
Come, substantial damages!
Substantial damages!
Damages! dam——
Usher.
Silence in Court!
RECIT.—*Counsel for Plaintiff.*
May it please you, my lud!
Gentlemen of the jury!
Aria.
With a sense of deep emotion,
I approach this painful case; .
For I never had a notion
That a man could be so base,
Or deceive a girl confiding,
Vows, *etcetera*, deriding.
All.
He deceived a girl confiding,
Vows, *etcetera*, deriding.
Counsel.
See my interesting client,
Victim of a heartless wile!
See the traitor all defiant
Wear a supercilious smile!
Sweetly smiled my client on him,
Coyly woo'd and gently won him.
All.
Sweetly smiled, &c.
Counsel.
Swiftly fled each honeyed hour
Spent with this unmanly male!
Camberwell became a bower,
Peckham an Arcadian Vale,
Breathing concentrated otto!—
An existence à *la* Watteau.
All.
Breathing concentrated otto! &c.
Counsel.
Picture, then, my client naming,
And insisting on the day;
Picture him excuses framing—
Going from her far away;
Doubly criminal to do so,
For the maid had bought her *trousseau!*
All.
Doubly criminal, &c.
(Plaintiff falls sobbing on Counsel's breast.)
Counsel (to Plaintiff).
Cheer up, my pretty—oh cheer up!
Jury.
Cheer up, cheer up, we love you!
*(Counsel leads Plaintiff fondly into Wit-
ness-box, he takes a tender leave of her,
and resumes his place in Court.)*

(Plaintiff reels as if about to faint.)

Judge.

That she is reeling
Is plain to me!

Foreman.

If faint you're feeling
Recline on me!

(She falls sobbing on to the Foreman's breast.)

Plaintiff (feebly).

I shall recover
If left alone.

All (shaking their fists at Defendant.)

Oh, perjured lover,
Atone! atone!

Foreman.

Just like a father
I wish to be.

> *(Kissing her.)*

Judge (approaching her.)

Or, if you'd rather
Recline on me!

(She jumps on to Bench, sits down by the Judge, and falls sobbing on his breast.)

Counsel.

Oh! fetch some water
From far Cologne!

All.

For this sad slaughter
Atone! atone!

Jury (shaking fists at Defendant).

Monster, monster, dread our fury,
There's the Judge, and we're the Jury!

Song.—*Defendant.*

Oh, gentlemen, listen, I pray
 Though I own that my heart has been ranging,
Of nature the laws I obey,
 For nature is constantly changing.
The moon in her phases is found,
 The time and the wind and the weather,
The months in succession come round,
 And you don't find two Mondays together.
 Ah! Consider the moral, I pray,
  Nor bring a young fellow to sorrow,
 Who loves this young lady to-day,
  And loves that young lady to-morrow.

Bridesmaids (rushing forward, and kneeling to Jury).

 Consider the moral, &c.

You cannot eat breakfast all day,
 Nor is it the act of a sinner,
When breakfast is taken away,
 To turn his attention to dinner;
And it's not in the range of belief,
 To look upon him as a glutton.
Who, when he is tired of beef,
 Determines to tackle the mutton.
 Ah But this I am willing to say,
 If it will appease her sorrow,
 I'll marry this lady to-day,
 And I'll marry the other to-morrow!

Bridesmaids.

But this he is willing to say, &c.

Recit.—*Judge.*

That seems a reasonable proposition,
To which, I think, your client may agree.

Counsel.

But, I submit, m'lud, with all submission,
To marry two at once is Burglaree!

> *(Referring to law-book.)*

In the reign of James the Second,
It was generally reckoned
As a rather serious crime
To marry two wives at a time.

(Hands book up to Judge, who reads it.)

All.

Oh, man of learning!

Quartette.

Judge.

A nice dilemma we have here,
That calls for all our wit:

Counsel.

And at this stage, it don't appear
That we can settle it.

Defendant.

If I to wed the girl am loth
A breach 'twill surely be—

Plaintiff.

And if he goes and marries both,
It counts as Burglaree!

All.

A nice dilemma, &c.

Duet.—*Plaintiff and Defendant.*

Plaintiff (embracing him rapturously).

I love him—I love him—with fervour un-
  ceasing.
 I worship and madly adore;
My blind adoration is ever increasing,
 My loss I shall ever deplore.
Oh, see what a blessing, what love and ca-
  ressing
 I've lost, and remember it, pray,
When you I'm addressing, are busy assessing
 The damages Edwin must pay!

Defendant (repelling her furiously).

I smoke like a furnace—I'm always in liquor—
 A ruffian—a bully—a sot;
I'm sure I should thrash her, perhaps I should
  kick her,
 I am such a very bad lot!
I'm not prepossessing, as you may be guessing,
 She couldn't endure me a day;
Recall my professing, when you are assessing
 The damages Edwin must pay!

(She clings to him passionately; after a struggle, he throws her off into arms of Counsel.)

Jury.

We would be fairly acting,
 But this is most distracting!
If, when in liquor, he would kick her,
 That is an abatement.

Public.

She loves him, and madly adores, &c.

RECIT.—*Judge.*

The question, gentlemen—is one of liquor;
  You ask for guidance—this is my reply:
He says, when tipsy, he would thrash and kick
    her,
  Let's make him tipsy, gentlemen, and try!

Counsel.

    With all respect
    I do object!

Plaintiff.

    I do object!

Defendant.

    I don't object!

All.

    With all respect
    We do object!

Judge (tossing his books and papers about).

  All the legal furies seize you!
  No proposal seems to please you,
  I can't sit up here all day,
  I must shortly get away.
  Barristers, and you, attorneys,
  Set out on your homeward journeys;
  Gentle, simple-minded usher,
  Get you, if you like, to Russ*her!*
  Put your briefs upon the shelf,
  I will marry her myself!

(*He comes down from Bench to floor of
Court. He embraces Angelina.*)

FINALE

Plaintiff.

  Oh, joy unbounded,
  With wealth surrounded,
  The knell is sounded
    Of grief and woe.

Counsel.

  With love devoted

  On you he's doated,
  To castle moated
    Away they go.

Defendant.

  I wonder whether
  They'll live together
  In marriage tether
    In manner true!

Usher.

  It seems to me, sir,
  Of such as she, sir,
  A judge is he, sir,
    And a good judge too!

CHORUS.

  Oh, joy unbounded, &c.

Judge.

  Yes, I am a Judge.

All.

  And a good Judge too!

Judge.

  Yes, I am a Judge.

All.

  And a good Judge too!

Judge.

Though homeward as you trudge,
You declare my law is fudge,
Yet of beauty I'm a judge.

All.

  And a good Judge too!

Judge.

  Though defendant is a snob.

All.

  And a great snob too!

Judge.

  Though defendant is a snob,
  I'll reward him from my fob.

All.

  So we've settled with the job.
  And a good job too!

CURTAIN.